To Michelle

SIX
IN GREEN

You so "Zane"!

SIX
IN GREEN

VON BLACK

Library of Congress Control Number:		2010906807
ISBN:	Hardcover	978-1-4500-9228-9
	Softcover	978-1-4500-9227-2
	Ebook	978-1-4500-9229-6

To order additional copies of this book, contact:
Xlibris Corporation
1-888-795-4274
www.Xlibris.com
Orders@Xlibris.com
78734

Dedicated To
William "Ba'y Boy" Smallwood
A man who never gave up!
He Died Trying

"I love you, Pops. Hope to see you in the resurrection."

Death, I believe, has no answers. A man named Job asked God to conceal him there until his (God's) anger turned back (Job 14:12-15). He thought that living during his lowest point was worse than being dead. I think that if you prepare for death by making a good name for yourself, then you will be remembered by the only one that can give you life again. *-Ecclesiastes 7:1*

Prologue

A frail little white boy stands opposite a gate next to the CO's desk positioned front and center at the north side of a vast rectangular expanse. The area is filled with metal-framed beds bolted to the floor, with portable TV's at the side of most and a myriad of not-so-merry men. Men have been in this very room for fifteen years or more, holding on to more like paragraphs than sentences.

His blue eyes are wide and unblinking as they dart from left to right and straight again, probing the room like a trained appraiser from a bank. Cradling his sheets, blanket, second set of blues, and the temporary hygiene kit under his forearms, he flinches when the gate clicks and buzzes. Released from its locked state, the gate slowly swings partially ajar with a loud creepy squeal straight out of an Alfred Hitchcock flick. That only instigates the terror that is bubbling just beneath this poor kid's skin. His entire body is stiff as a totem pole except his eyeballs. His head is fidgeting ever so slightly, reminiscent of a bobblehead doll.

"Step in," says the guard sitting at the desk to the young man's left. "John Faulkner?" he asks.

John is jolted at the sound of his name but can't break the trance that he's in.

What was that? Did I hear my name? Am I dreaming about being here? I can't believe I'm in the joint with all these maniacs who ain't doin' nothing but waiting for the Lord's Day. Christ!

"Step in the gate!" snaps the guard.

That was enough to make John snap out of it. He yanks his head toward the officer, still unable to control any other muscle below his neck. Then he turns back and looks slowly up and down at the iron bars towering thirteen feet to the ceiling. John gazes through, and his attention falls on a couple of guys staring at him like a sirloin steak. Reluctantly, he steps toward the gate, pushing it open with a kick from his boots.

The weight of the swinging gate carries it back to a locked position, slamming shut behind John, who is now easy prey for the lions, who will surely devour him as soon as they get the chance.

"Number?" blurts the corrections officer.

John looks down at the number printed on his shirt. "9527523."

"Bed D22," he tells John as he points him down the far right isle. John leans sideways to peer down the perilous wing marked D on the floor. The depth of the aisle gives him tunnel vision. Sounds around him begin to bounce about in his head without an echo. He can't make out anything, yet he can hear a big black brute of a man heave out a laugh from a long distance down the elongated passageway.

The man is looking in John's direction as if the joke was on him and as if he was destined to become the source of this laughing man's ecstatic pleasures for years to come. John finally blinks when his eye and the brute's eyes lock with one another, and the man's laughing face melts to an expression of query. This is not a good place for a scrawny white boy or a black one, for that matter, to be staring at someone. Especially when you're in a place where most people have nothing to lose, nothing to gain, and virtually no one to answer to.

I'm not going to be able to do this, John thinks to himself. *I knew I shouldn't have killed him. I should have just run away, or better, took out the trash. Anything but grabbing that damn shotgun. Why Dad? Why'd you dare me?*

John's still a mere boy, not even old enough to buy liquor, as if that ever stopped him from drinking. And he had been drinking that night he was arrested—the night his father set a booby trap for him to stumble over.

Mr. and Mrs. Faulkner were middle-aged parents in their late forties to early fifties. Mrs. Faulkner, a round lady with a hairdo like Wilma from the *Flintstones,* had an apron on and a knitted shirt to match with her navy blue skirt. She was not at all pretty, just a regular old white lady who just took care of the family. Mr. Faulkner was a red-faced redneck with a potbelly. He didn't appear to be into the latest fashions, sporting a pair of brown polyester trousers and a cream-colored, open-collared shirt. He was clean-cut but hardly what you'd call tall, dark, and handsome. He was just a blue-collar, who wore a white shirt, and just wanted to come home to a meal, a beer, his easy chair, and an empty garbage can.

"John," he yelled from the kitchen, "Where's that rebellious little prick? He never does a fricking thing I tell him to do."

It was late, and the Faulkners were just about to turn in for the night when Mr. Faulkner decided to set the trash in the middle of the kitchen floor for John to walk right into, coming through the side door. He placed the filled garbage can six feet from the door; just far enough into the darkness of the room, out of sight. John was out and more than likely wouldn't come in until late, and he'd have to walk through the path in which his chore was awaiting him.

Before going upstairs to bed, his father took one more triumphant gander back at the little jape he had set up to inform him of John's arrival, and with a devilish grin, he reached for the light switch to click off the light, leaving the kitchen pitch-black. Hours passed by.

Caboogaloogaboombamboom!

"What the hell . . . ," slurred John. "What the . . . ? Who?"

It is completely dark beyond the area where John's semicasual B-boots are visible near the open door.

"John?" Katie, his girlfriend, called from the doorway. "Are you . . . John, are you OK? Get up off the floor, silly. Turn the light on for peace sake."

They both were wasted off Yegamister Elixir, and they had planned on sneaking down to the basement and finishing their night off with some wild, kinky teenage sex. He was nineteen and she seventeen, and both were horny as hell. As John wrestled to get his hand beneath him to push himself up off the kitchen floor, there was a thunderous roll of drumming on the stairs from the hallway. In seconds, the stinging rays from the 100-watt bulb in the ceiling light was blazing into the pupils of the two drunken horny toads, forcing them to cover their eyes with both hands.

"Agghh," John complained, "Shit, Dad. Turn the damn light out. Why the hell is the can in the middle of the floor?"

"Look at yourself," shouted his father. "You're a disgrace. And who do you think you're talking to in that tone, young man?" Then turning his attention to Katie, "And what the hell are you doing here, you little whore?" he shouted as he stepped over John toward Katie who was still standing at the threshold of the door.

She was a pretty girl, with long blonde hair down to her shoulders. She was wearing a Futura halter top and a thigh-revealing black skirt with matching toenail polish. Her green eyes were open wide as she took her hands down from her eyes after hearing Mr. Faulkner call her a whore. She turned red with resentment as he reached for her shoulder, swirling her about face, and thrust her out the door with a subtle shove in her back before slamming the door behind her all in one motion.

John had rolled over on his buttocks by then and was leaning back on his palms. He was in dismay beyond belief at his father's disdain. He didn't have time to reflect on the fact that his father had never acted this indignant in his life. "You, son of a bitch!" John bawled with pure venom. "Who the hell do you think you are?"

Mr. Faulkner turned and faced him with a rage that only appeared on his face once before, and that was when he walked in his bedroom and found his Goody Two-shoes wife looking at a black porno film while she ravaged her pubic canal with a rather exaggerated black shaft of a dildo.

"I told you to take the gotdamn trash out before you left. You think you can just waltz around here, eat up all the food, drive the car, dump in my toilet, and don't do anything I tell you to do?"

John grabbed the table to pull himself up on his feet to face his father and said, "You got . . . damn right. *Hiccup.*"

Prrtch went the skin-clapping lash of Mr. Faulkner's right hand across the face of his son.

"You son of a . . . ," John murmured as he slowly stumbled back with his eyes frozen in shock at the hostility that his sheepish father was displaying. "Why, you . . . I'll show you," John said, darting off to the coat closet to grab the Mossberg shotgun that was leaning against the corner of the closet's interior doorframe.

Storming back through the swinging Wild Wild West doors to the kitchen, with the gun aimed toward the ceiling, *Krtchkish*—he pumped the gun, forcing the round that was already in the chamber to fly across the room; his father just stood there shocked and awed at the sight of his young boy, brandishing his own hunting rifle that hadn't seen any action in over five years.

"*You* take out the trash, old man," John taunted, aiming the long barrel at the center of his father's chest. His father's face became stoned, but it wasn't long before the expression of trauma slid to appall, then to grim audacity.

You little prick. Mr. Faulkner thought to himself. "I double dare ya."

Chapter 1

Benjamin Powell is a smooth dude who has enough money to support his lavish habits of tuna fish, chicken, and turkey along with vegetables from out of the kitchen in every single hookup he's eaten on every day of the week for the last four and a half years. He has a color TV with remote, a fresh pair of "butter" Timberland boots, two pairs of Jordan, and New Balance sneakers lined under his bunk. He's wearing a Wes Unsel throwback jersey and blue jeans as he lies back across his bed.

In his locker, he has a CD collection that people on the street don't even have. He's not at all supposed to have all the CDs he has, but he's quite popular with the guards. He's paid off enough for them to keep him informed of shakedowns, but most of the time, his collection is loaned out to other inmates in the joint. He's like the jailhouse Blockbuster rental. For a couple of cigarettes you had a CD for a night or two. That was before they outlawed smoking in Maryland Institutions. Now, you can't find a cigarette anywhere in the whole system on commissary. Of course, inmates still smoke cigarettes, weed, crack, and everything else they want, but it's become way too expensive to use cigarettes for money, so now the currency is U.S. stamps. Benji has more stamps than the post office, which he uses to buy everything else he wants. He doesn't smoke, so his locker stays packed with all kinds of goodies.

It's 6:17 p.m. and Benji is laid back, watching *Sanford and Son*. He doesn't watch television unless sports are on, but Fred is hilarious, and he looks forward to watching him every day to get his daily laugh.

Grady has moved in with Fred and Lamont, because he can't stand it at the Fletcher's house, where they fight every day. Fred truly regrets letting

Grady move in because Grady snores like a bear with sinus congestion, and Lamont won't let up, "I told you, Pop, not to let him move in." Fed up, Fred decides to collaborate with Lamont to stage a fight, seconds before Grady walks through the door. The maylay of uppercuts and haymakers from Fred propagates an escalating guffaw from Benji and Mark, who is standing at the foot of Benji's bunk. They're howling laughter and coughing makes it appear as if they've just gotten shot with pepper spray.

As the scene winds down and Grady walks out with his suitcase and coat, their laughter subsides, and that's when Mark notices a white boy at the top of the isle through all the bodies crisscrossing and clouding the width of the aisle. The boy's face is pale as a Jason mask, and he seems to be staring right at Mark.

What the hell is he looking at?

Mark's defenses rise, and his vexation condescends his former feelings of elation. He reacts much like a playful pitbull would if it turned to see another dog approaching his master. Mark's defense are put on high alert.

The head disappears, and a scrawny little drip slowly moseys into sight and painfully paces down the center of the aisle. Bodies move to the side and activity stalls as a brand-new face trots through the crowded tier. Fear is prominent in every movement of John's limbs, and his head is swiveling back and forth with watchful eyes as he absorbs the scene and the faces like a photo journalist, scouring the expressions and praying to see a pleasant face that shows some sense of welcome, someone who appears to recognize him. Fat chance! John is a suburban, son-of-a-pecker who's never got his ass kicked by a gangster, let alone shook hands with one.

He doesn't know any niggas, white or black, and he sure doesn't have any money to pay anybody for protection. He's done for. He'll probably get raped tonight, probably not, but his thoughts have him trembling so hard that he can barely walk or breathe.

Should I try to fight or just let him have it? My god, what if there're two of them or three? What if there's a line? A whole frickin' line. He thinks to himself.

There're close to one hundred beds in this dormitory, but it seems more like five hundred to John. There's an aisle intersecting with the aisle that John is walking down. He stops there to allow a guy to cross his path, and then he continues toward his bunk just beyond Mark, the big laughing brute who's not any longer laughing. John's sanctuary is quite far from the only person who might be able to help him, making it all the more terrifying for the poor kid. The C.O.'s desk is at least forty yards away from John's sleeping quarters and not even in sight. There is a hundred thousand sounds flying in every direction, so the CO wouldn't be able to distinguish a scream for help from a holler for a loony dune. That's a Little Debbie Swiss Roll or Dunkin' Stick. Who knows why they call them loony dunes! But whatever the case, our little parent killer is in deep do-do, and now he regrets the day he was earthed. He'd rather beat his dick with a handful of glass than get all the crap beat out of him and be raped shitless by a bunch of black nigger heathens or white Aryan bigots. He'd rather have taken his chances on the plane that went down in Pittsburgh on 9/11 than be walking to his doom down this jailhouse aisle.

Why is that big cocksucker looking at me like that?

John sees Mark about fifteen feet ahead, and he's looking at John with a smirk on his face that doesn't at all look like a grin. Rather it looks devilishly maniacal, as if Mark has a plan for little John. His eyes are probing John, and his upper lip is cocked, revealing his Dracula fang tooth. Mark looks away from John for a moment to say something to the guy whose feet are visible to John.

Watch this Benji, John reads from Mark's lips as he nods toward John. The dude on the bed, Benji, pokes his head out into the aisle from behind the TV. The sounds around John seem to have been muted slightly. Or has everyone just stopped talking to stare at him? Certainly it's the latter, and his throat is swelling in his neck, making it hard for him to breathe or swallow his own saliva.

He starts to hear whistles and chants from remote places all around him.

"We got some fresh meat y'all," yells someone.

"Ain't nothing like some virgin butt," chants another.

Mark starts to smile and lick his lips as John approaches him. "Come on over here to papa," he says gently, sporting a pair of massive biceps bulging out of a too small white T-shirt. Mark's an older guy in his late thirties and carries a rock-solid frame. His chest is broad, with a matching neck. He can barely manage to fit into his T-shirt that is stretched to the point that his nipples and the hair on his chest pimple the surface of his shirt. The shirt would surely burst into shreds if he takes a deep breath and flexes his muscles. He stands about six foot three and his legs hardly go with his upper body. He seems to have gotten lazy after doing his reps. His state-issued blue Dickey trousers are rolled up just below his knees, and his brown shower shoes showcase the ugliest set of toes that John has ever seen. John grimaces and stops only three feet from Mark, waiting for the big brute to make way as the other hecklers did before him. Mark winks instead, and John manages to gulp down a tiny glob of spit that seemed to be the size of a mothball. It even left a nasty taste in his mouth like one.

Benji snickers under his breath and lowers his head to hide his smile from John. "Go ahead with that bullshit, Mark," he murmured only loud enough for Mark to hear. Mark shushes him and takes a step toward the quivering little white boy.

"Ain't you gonna give me a kiss?" Mark asks John like he just came home from a long trip.

John looks to the side for help, but there is none. *Are you guys just gonna let this happen to me? What kind of freaks are you? Somebody do something; kick his ass. Call him a faggot. Something.* John thinks, as he looks at all the blank black and very few white faces witnessing the spectacle.

"Hey, you big bully. Won't you come over here and pick on somebody your own size?" calls out a voice from the midst of the onlookers behind John.

Suddenly, John's heart began to sing; his tears that had welled up in his eyes flows down his candy-apple red face like a mountain stream, and he feels like he has just been pardoned by the governor seconds before he was to be strapped down to the chair. Relief never ever, ever, felt so liberating in all his natural-born life. But who, what, where was this knight in shining armor? His roving eyes couldn't find his deliverer, his gangster chronicle, for this is certainly a historical event of monumental proportions in this feeble little drip's existence.

My god! Will this guy turn me into his sex slave in exchange for him saving my life? Christ! Will I have to suck his cock and his cock only? Uhg! Maybe not. But why would anybody in his right mind stand up to this Goliath. Where is he?

John tries to relive the voice and remember where exactly he may have heard it before. Nothing. Never heard it. Doesn't recognize it, so who?

There is a harmonious shuffle of feet and turning of bodies and heads toward the direction where the voice came from. It's evident that the person is directly behind John. John can hear the sound of several feet stopping to his rear. He looks at the Goliath before him, and Mark's face is bolstering instant venom and death. Suddenly, John feels that his savior didn't scare this monster one bit. In fact, it seems John is right in the middle of a riot forming just as a storm does over the warm waters of the Atlantic Ocean—a storm growing in power and velocity—a storm that will eventually become a hurricane that will certainly kill.

Mark makes a call through his hands that he places in front of his mouth like a bullhorn. "Aeyo, Aeyo, Aeyo!" He yells, "Aeyo, Aeyo, Aeyo!"

Within seconds, black guys are scrambling and jumping over beds, all coming toward the call in distress. John sees three, maybe four guys standing on a bed and one of them moves a piece of the ceiling and down comes a white bucket. All of the men take objects out of the bucket and then run in different directions, also toward the call made by Mark, handing objects to men waiting in the wings of the forming battlefield. People who don't wish to get caught up in the riot began to move far away from the place where John is standing.

Now, John's face is terrified all over again. He's not sure if he would rather have a "train" run on him and lived to regret it or die right here, right now as he surely will, once the murders commence. His legs become weak beneath him, and he can feel himself woozing. He's going out.

"I know you ain't talkin' to me!" grunts Mark, with a movement similar to that of a ferocious gorilla swatting vines, as he makes his way past John, flinging him out the way like a rag doll.

The voice from behind John is again speaking, and now John can see him. The face—it's not familiar to him. He's never seen this man nor has he ever seen any of the other ghost faces behind this impressive warrior.

With a step forward, he meets Mark face-to-face, and their convexed heaps beneath their T-shirts mesh; both men are of the same height, only the white man is a mite taller. Neither is suffering from any fruitless obesity. Two stone hedges squared off amidst a legion of willing and able butchers and barbarians.

"I don't see any other bullies around here besides me, and I ain't talkin' to myself," says the knight.

Once again, John feels reassured that he just might live after all, because the behemoth that he sees standing in his defense shows no sign of fear even though he and his band of militants are severely outnumbered. But like trained soldiers, they waver not. Flinch is not in their vocabulary and certainly not a notion that any of them are willing to entertain, even in the face of unavoidable slaughter.

All this over me, thinks John.

Mark is breathing heavy like a bull. Particles of mucus from his nostrils spatter onto his mustache with every exhaling puff of his lungs. His nose is scrunched up between his demonic eyes, his snarling lips are like a crushed soda can, and his ire is just the contrary to that of the man who stands before him.

That man is Tom. Thomas Foreman and he's the head of the Aryan sect here at the Cut in Jessup, Maryland. His family is here. His brothers—they stand behind him ready to kill—ready to die. Tom's an apt killer, trained as a Navy Seal and will kill at least ten of his attackers before he falls limp in death. He's taught all of his brothers most of his tactics, and they're itching to make use of them. So even though they're greatly outnumbered, this is nowhere near an unfair advantage, and Benji knows it.

"Wait!" Benji commands as he wriggles his body through the men assembled in the aisle. "Mark, chill, man. Tom, what's this all about? Why you all in that? You know ain't nobody gonna do nothin' to the lil nigga. Nigga's just messin' with 'em."

That's what guys do to little pip-squeaks that come in the jail, petrified, thinking everybody new gets beaten up and raped. The fact is that there are so many fags, queens, and bisexuals in the joint nowadays, that there's no need to go through all that just to get your rocks off. A dude really has to be trying to get himself a piece of virgin ass to make him go through the motions of forced rape. So basically, there must be more to it for Tom to come down the aisle to take up for a defenseless white boy that wasn't going to be bothered in the first place. That's what has made Mark so angry. That's why mayhem is about to unleash, the war call is made, and the bucket is dropped.

Just anybody can't make that call. It takes a very significant member of the black guerilla family to give the "Aeyo" call. Somebody that the brothers would die for in an instant—somebody that everybody loves, fears, or both. When that call is made, blacks scramble in a nervous frenzy to see who is making the call and if that person is already being hit. Hit in the joint means stabbed; then all hell breaks loose.

You're not told if you're allowed to make the call; you just can, and if you do and you're not supposed to, that will result in a vicious ass kicking for you. No matter how big you are. You'd have been better off being stabbed to death.

The sound of the call opens everybody's pores, and even the cool, calm, and collected Benjamin Powell can feel the crack of his butt sweating. Tom doesn't show it, but he too is afraid to die, and he can't control the trepidation that secretes a deluge of perspiration out of every single pore on his body. It's a lot like the way an armed bank robber feels just before he springs out of the car to run up in the bank. No matter how many times you've done it, you can never get used to the uncertainty of who might be in the bank and who might be waiting for you once you come out. Tom's men have never seen him show any sign of fear. To them, Tom is invincible, but they can't help but notice the beads of sweat on his shiny baldhead. No matter. If it's going down, some niggas are gonna die today as far as they're concerned.

John can't believe what he is seeing; a brigade of white, short-haired, no-haired, swastika-tattoo bearing, black-boot wearing, no-holds-bar rebel white boys behind a pillar of death, calm as can be, surrounded by a tribe of go-hard, gangster-to-the-bone, masked-up, bare-faced, kill-somebody-quick, going for nothing-ass-niggas with attitudes. Both groups have members with wrapped hands and long sharp objects protruding from the wrapping.

Tribulation is about to fall upon us all, and I'm to blame. Everybody's gonna die, and if I can just slip under this bed before anybody notices, that'll be a good thing. Let 'em kill each other; then I can have the whole jail to myself.

Chapter 2

Iblis roves around in the lower realm. So much darkness. So much nothingness is surrounding him. Even the mighty cherubim of the upper realm dare not come too close to the indomitable one. His radiance is transparent, and his size makes a leviathan puny in comparison. His appearance is that of a Minotaur, except he has wings of a reptile and claws of an eagle at his feet. He doesn't walk, for there is not a surface on which to do so; rather his roving is more like a hover seeking to devour someone or something—in his case, the entire inhabited earth.

He hates the inhabitants of the earth because of their sole existence. He despises the earth itself because of her material matter. How disgusting it all is to him! He loathes the whole universe just because. He'd give his own doomed existence just to be able to annihilate it all with one clap of his mighty palms. And he could too, except he is forbidden to do so. The Omega would read his thoughts and paralyze his spirit with an instantaneous wrath that would make him smolder like doused hot coals.

Iblis doesn't take pleasure in being summoned by the Omega, which hasn't happened in over three hundred and sixty-two earthly years; so feeling the Omega's dominance incinerate his faculties and make them burn, as if he himself was made of material that can actually do so, strikes such a fear in him that human words can only tickle the surface of the truth, no matter how melodramatic of an attempt is made. The feeling of his dread is simply incomprehensible. Just believe the mere thought of him rendering physical harm to even a minute speck of dust wouldn't dare fathom into his mind.

Instead, Iblis uses the power of influence to bring about destruction. There is nothing in the material realm that carries greater weight in the outcome of events that affect mankind than the power of influence. It is the single thing that caused all the newborn sons of Bethlehem, under the age of two, to be killed by King Herod, the force behind the execution of Jesus. It was also responsible for the plot behind the World Trade Center attacks and even the reason why all mankind is a slave to Death and Hades. What else but the power of influence made Adam and Eve eat that damn fruit? It probably didn't even taste that good.

And Iblis has called a wager with the Almighty himself to prove that all of mankind is unworthy of the blessings of life and that he will destroy us all by turning us away from the path of the true purpose. That is why he is roving like a mad beast. That's why he'll lash out at any spirit who'd dare violate his domain. Even his loyal servants do not beckon his call at close range, rather they use telepathy to respond to his commands, but for now, he's musing.

He is contemplating whom he must focus on—who on earth is to be the aim of his deception. There is something tingling in his senses, telling him that there is someone, or will be someone soon, that will bring his world that much closer to its end. The Great War is coming, and he knows it because there is much activity in the spirit of the enlightened ones, his brethren, who have access to the sacred decrees, privileged only to the inhabitants of the upper realms of which he and his own were ousted when Apollyon became king and cleaned his father's house. The day is drawing near, though no one, not even Apollyon knows, but it is very near. However, it won't take place until certain things have transpired on the earth. One of those things requires the working of a man—a single man on earth. This Iblis knows. This man will not trigger the war but will produce the fruits that will fuel the occurrences that will make the prophecies complete. The prophecy must not occur, or Iblis will be no longer. He must find this man and destroy him, but lurking in the outskirts of heaven will do him no good, so Iblis swarms over to an opening that is a gateway, so it seems. The warped ripple in the open space of darkness before him appears to be a portal of some sort to another dimension. The ripple has no front or back. It's just there like the hoop of a ringmaster at the Barmen and Bailey Circus, only there are no flames.

The large circular channel is a door between the spirit realm and the material realm. In the spirit realm, there is no such thing as objects of substance, such as water and rocks or even gas. Here, there is nothing but purity and energy. Energy is everywhere; only it's invisible and more powerful than any gas mass bubble floating around in the countless galaxies of our universe. How small our universe is compared to the spirit realm, which amounts to our universe times infinity! It's so immense that not even a brain like Albert Einstein's can imagine its size, let alone theorize it.

Iblis is in the lower level of this realm where it is dark and no light shines except the illumination of the beings that pass through this layer of blackness. But now, there is only Iblis—alone. He prefers it that way ever since he was cast out of the light and into Tartarus where, very soon, he'll be bound with chains by Apollyon for a thousand years with his legion of spirit brethren of which Iblis is the ring leader. O! How beautifully he was created! But he lusted over his own magnificence, wanting to be glorified and praised, even worshiped. Sad, how he envied his grand creator and the one who sits at the right hand of that One!

O, how he misses the light even though the light is from the one who sanctioned his demise! Nevertheless, Iblis yearns for the light, but he'll remain in dense darkness and be forever pitiful for abandoning his original plight. He will never ever be able to find the Omega's favor again, so now he only wishes hate and destruction to all that has the favor of the Omega and is set on doing all that he can to bring about the destruction to all that he can.

Anger swells within him every time he contemplates what he'd do to Apollyon if only he was strong enough. Those thoughts are weighing down on him now, and his radiance is blazing brighter and brighter, causing him to become less and less transparent, and in an instant, he disappears into the gateway before him, leaving only a short trail of fading light at the portal he just vanished through. On the other side, Iblis left still another trail of fading light that streams from the center of the vortex. Strangely though, this light is being sucked into the hole from which it came. It's obviously a black hole.

Chapter 3

"I think you've got a chip on your shoulder, and I'm about to knock it off for you," warns Mark.

Tom gives a wincing smile but doesn't reveal any of his tartar-stained teeth. He looks squarely into the pupils of Mark's eyes nearly able to see his optic nerve. "Go ahead. Make my day," he encourages, practically begging Mark to set it off.

Benji knows too well that today will be his last day on earth if war breaks out while he's still standing this close to Tom when he starts to unleash his own brand of wrath. He wishes he wasn't standing where he is right now, maybe then he'd have a fighting chance, but as it is, if there's a clash this very moment, he'll bear the brunt of Tom's initial onslaught, and Benji's quite aware of just how lethal Tom is. He has thought of the pros and cons, and his hypothesis of the outcome is catastrophic for both sides. As far as the pros are concerned, there are none.

"Tom," Benji asks, "do you wanna die? I mean, look around. Is the kid worth all this commotion?"

"Nope," says Tom.

"Just what I thought." Mark snarls through his teeth. "He don't want it . . . Do you, white boy?"

The answer Tom gives will determine if he lives or dies, or worst, whether he's respected or not. Tom comes from a background where death is an honor and from places where it's indubitably probable, so why would he falter now in the face of death? He thinks about his compadres.

What about them? Hell, I can kill this nigger in two quick blows to his neck. But then they'll savage us. They don't even know that rotten kid.

"I'll tell you what I want. I want you to leave the boy alone and get the hell out of my face with your bad breath. Somebody got a mint for this dude?"

"Cut the bull, Tom," Benji interjects before Mark can respond to Tom's comment. "If the kid's your peeps, why didn't you just say so instead of bringing in the army brigade? You act like you want beef."

"Beef? . . . No beef. Mr. Yuck here, is the one who wants beef."

"Mark," Benji pleads turning to Mark, "let it ride. It's nuffin'."

And for real, if I were you, I'd back up off that crazy ass white boy 'cause he's about to gut you like a fish with that blade he has cuffed in his hand. I told you about the cat, but you still think you can handle him, Benji thinks to himself.

Mark eases the tension in his muscles and settles the frown on his face into a mean mug. He can sense that Benji doesn't want him to make the truce any more difficult to call than necessary. Apprehension is so high in the air that one ill-fated word from Mark could spark a response from Tom that would ignite an apocalypse consuming most of the dormitory. Heads will be bashed and lungs will be punctured relentlessly with rusty nails cleaved out of the bed frames bolted to the floor. Television sets and any other heavy object that can be used to inflict mortal damage will surely fly with detrimental results. There will be men slumped, with their throats smiling and pouring blood, like altar lambs. Death will be everywhere and often, leaving a horrendous scene for the investigators to clean up. Thomas Foreman is prepared for whatever comes. It's Mark's call.

"So you want the little white boy all to yourself?" Mark teases. "Is that what it is? I always knew you were humping your little butt-boys."

Tom's blood boils, and he wants to lash out, but instead, he stares Mark straight into his eye without a response to the wisecrack. The two of them have a staring match to prove to each other whose eyelids are stronger. Tom can see that Mark is by no means about to blink his eyes, and his own eyes are burning like hell. Here's one battle he's sure to lose because he doesn't want to give Mark any more ammunition to launch more wisecracks. If he doesn't blink now, he'll shed a tear, and that's a no-no.

"The kid is my niece's boyfriend," Tom says as he rolls his eyes over to Benji. "Her mom wrote me and told me to look out for him. I don't give a rat's ass what happens to the little dude, but my folks do. I'd die for my sister," Tom says bluntly, looking around for John.

Benji follows Tom's eyes and darts his own around the area for John as well. John has managed to vanish. No one can seem to find the source of all the commotion. The defiance that gripped the demeanors of the two rival forces has transformed in an instant to momentary solidarity. A moment ago, these men were watching each other like hawks, waiting for the other to twitch before the bashing was to begin. Now, everyone h. taken down their guards, at the least bit concerned whether the enemy will take a cheap shot, and is looking around for the petrified face that was walking down the aisle only a few minutes ago.

"Where'd that little nigga disappear to?" Benji mumbles to himself.

The casual glances gradually progress into a slight rummage, with bodies moving and ducking to look behind and under things.

"Here's the little punk," utters a scratchy-voiced black man as he grabs John by the crown of his dusty brown-haired head and the back of his collar and then snatches him to his feet from under the bed he had hidden after being tossed aside by Mark.

John looks like a lost puppy; he's flush red well past his collarbone. He looks pitiful, and everybody is looking in his direction. All of the sudden, there's a violent eruption of howling laughter and the "once soldiers at war turned search party" have now become a Def Comedy crowd of cackling mercenaries at the mere thought that they were all about to shred each other limb from limb over this little dweeb. And just like that, the dorm is back to normal as the men start to disperse in a rush to hide their weapons before the goon squad bombards through the gate to lock the tier down and search for weapons and contraband. Everybody runs for their living quarters to press their bunk because anyone caught standing when the goon squad comes through will be clobbered.

Click . . . Boom . . . The sound of stampeding army boots can be heard beating the concrete floor. Benji lies on his bed and watches everyone else try to scramble to get to their own beds before they're caught standing. John's bed is the next bed after Benji's, and he's figured out that he'd better copy what he sees Benji doing. Here they come.

Chapter 4

The sunlight that usually shines through the window onto Jessica Glockner's desk is absent today. The sky is filled with dark clouds, making it a gloomy "hump day" Wednesday. It's 4:17 p.m., and Jessica has already filled her black Coach bag with her *Washington Post,* sunglasses, *Terry McMillan* novel, and her portfolio-keeper, ready to jet out the door before anybody can ask her to do something before she leaves for the day. On her desk sits her key chain, which looks more like a gladiator's weapon than a woman's set of keys, complete with pepper spray, a nail clipper, over fifteen keys, a picture holder, a Jesus fish symbol, and several small key rings that help keep the various keys easily distinguishable from one another. A nylon rope dangles off the side of the desk, extending from the keys sitting next to her hat.

These keys are not assembled this way by coincidence either. She's thirty years old with no children, no man, at least, not one she can call her own, and she lives in a high-rise apartment building in a community that's not known for its tranquility. She lives in District Heights, Maryland, in the Oakcrest Towers. Most people from the inner city streets of Washington DC come to this community, thinking that everything is sweet and serene but soon find out that the high-rises on Good Hope Road in Southeast are more peaceful.

Her car was stolen the first week after moving in, and two months later, a serial rapist was reported to be loose in Suitland, which is the neighboring community to hers. To her relief, the suspect was beaten to death by a man that was said to have caught the rapist stalking his girlfriend right outside their apartment window.

Ever since, she's been committed to preparing for battle in case she must defend herself.

Also, on her desk are several pictures, work papers, a stack of religious books, and brochures. *The Final Call,* a Nation of Islam newspaper, sits on her desk where she had been reading it before she went to the bathroom. She likes reading this newspaper because it tells her things about stories in the black community that, in her opinion, should make national headlines. She also likes Minister Louis Farrakhan; although she's not a Muslim, she thinks he's the only man since Malcolm X who says things in public that expose the secret societies that oppress the black man in America. He's her hero even though he hasn't done a damn thing for black empowerment since the Million Man March. The speech alone did enough for the moral of blacks in this country for the rest of his life and theirs.

She also likes to have long conversations with the handsome Muslim brother who makes it a point to be at the McDonalds next to her office building every single morning. She stops there at least three times a week before 7:45 a.m. to get her a cup of coffee and an egg McMuffin before waltzing her elegance into the all-glass, gold office building built by Bob Johnson for his once owned Black Entertainment Television empire. She thinks he's the biggest wimp in the world after he sold out the company to Viacom, but who can blame him? A dollar value with the word *billion* in it would make anybody dance. A whole, half, or quarter sounds good at any rate when it comes to that word.

Jessica's discussions with the brother could range from religion to boxing but never sex and relationships. He once brought the subject up, but she quickly dropped her head and lost eye contact with him. He politely changed the subject without a single mention of anything remotely close to the topic again. She's in love with a Muslim brother who is a member of the Sunni community. There's a stark difference from the Nation of Islam, whom the Sunnis believe is an inappropriate sect of Islam. She wouldn't dare speak to this brother on any topic that belongs to her man, herself included. That would be disrespectful to her man, and she'd never go that far.

But how can she feel so loyal to a man that she can't fully claim? The fact is she doesn't want to believe that she'll never have him. His name is Benjamin Powell; he's incarcerated in Jessup, Maryland. He's been there long enough for her to miss him but not long enough for her to want somebody else. She's been his secret concubine since her sophomore year at Howard University, where she majored in journalism. She was the sexy conservative college girl with the phat ass and pretty face that drove men wild. He was the fly ass hustler with the Coupé Benz, handsome face, and the five-carat diamond tennis bracelet in the black velvet case with a red satin bow, just a friendly gift.

He had a girlfriend when they met. He didn't lie about her, and since she accepted the arrangement, there was never a dispute about who came first. She's been with him through two childbirths by this other woman, one short incarceration and one long one. She's been there through hundreds of thousands, even millions of dollars that have passed over her dining room table and stacks of bricks piled in the closets of every apartment she's lived in since she gave him the first set of keys. He's actually been the one who decided when and where she moved. She's never paid a single bill or purchased any clothes with her own money during their thirteen-year relationship. Nor has she missed Frankie Beverly and Maze when they've come to town over the years, but during Benji's long hiatus from the scene, Jessica hasn't had much interest in anything outside of work other than spending weekends with her niece Shaquita, the child on her key-chain, and returning love letters in response to the weekly letter she receives from Benji.

Besides those things and occasional Bible studies she's been having with some Bible students, who catch her at home from time to time, her daily activities are stultifyingly mundane. She doesn't particularly take joy in the Bible students coming unannounced, but once the Bible opens and the conversation begins, erudition takes hold of her. However, nothing compares to the love she feels from Benji while she reads his letters. It brings gratifying feelings that she can't explain.

She hopes his love won't change for her once he finds out that she's becoming more acquainted and comfortable with the Christian faith. The meetings with the Bible students are really strengthening her faith in God through Jesus and that will certainly be a complication for them when he comes home and realizes it. She knows he always imposes his will upon her, but now that she understands more about her own beliefs, she won't allow him to do that where her salvation is concerned, if there's such a thing. Whatever the case, she won't allow him to convert her.

Jessica folds the *Final Call* newspaper and drops it into the wastebasket sitting under her red raincoat hanging on a hook at the top of her cubical wall. Reaching to turn off her radio, Jessica tips over a white Styrofoam cup of water.

"Shut!" she quirks as she quickly picks up the cup and grabs a tissue to clean up the water. Jessica hasn't been cursing much lately. She doesn't even hang around many people who do that. She's cut back all her school girlfriends mainly because Benji insisted that they all were scandalous whores. Whenever he'd come to her house and finds she had company over there, he'd get irritated because he could not do anything that looked out of the ordinary, raising suspicion that he was conducting any type of drug business at Jessica's house, or else, as far as he was concerned, one of her treacherous friends would make known to the larcenous underworld where they might be able to find a mother lode of drugs and a bundle of money. Jessica could see that he didn't like her having company, and sometimes he would just leave and say he'd be right back, but she knew he didn't have anywhere to go. That was just punishment for her having company, so she made it a habit not to have any. It was bad enough she didn't have him the time that she wanted, and she wasn't about to let some girltalk deprive her of the time she got. Not one minute of it. Her friends, of course, none of them liked Benji. They thought he was controlling her and had her on a string.

"He's not going to leave that girl," they'd say. "Girl, he got you trippin'. You need to leave his ass alone."

But nothing they said ever sank into her heart. She just started to believe more and more of what Benji was saying about them. Eventually, she stopped calling them altogether. The only one she didn't stop hanging out with was Lou-Lou, her hairdresser. Lou never said a word negative about Benji, and she always had her own money, so Jessica didn't have to always be the one taking the bill. In addition, Lou never required much of Jessica's time in order to be considered a real friend. They've been friends for over ten years, and Jessie wouldn't dream of having someone else doing her hair. She's convinced that no one could satisfy her needs like Lou-Lou. Nowadays, they still hang out, meeting at the old BET Soundstage in Landover. It's now called Jaspers, but it's still the same old joint with the same old people.

She's thinking of stopping there before she goes home, to have a couple of Apple Martinis. "Man, I need a drink," she says aloud to herself, "and to get the hell out of here."

After cleaning up the mess, she rolls her chair beneath the desk, sits down on top of the corner of the desk, and picks up the phone to make a call. She dials a number and then faces the window, looking out into the gloomy skyline menacing over the ghetto side of the city. In the distance, she can see the Love Nightclub, a club she's never been to, but they're going to have Jill Scott there in two weeks. That will likely be the first time she'll go there. Her coworkers are regulars there, and they all come to work, telling her all about the man or woman they picked up over the weekend. She gets a kick out of all the sex stories that both the men and women tell her almost every day.

"Hello," asks the person on the other end of the phone.

"Hey girl. What you doin'?"

"Jessie?"

"Yeah girl. What's up?"

"Um . . . I ain't heard from you in a while. What do I owe this privilege?" says the woman, who is actually being sarcastic. "Is the sky falling or something?"

"Look, girl, I ain't call you for all that."

"So what you call me for? You finally coming' around and gonna let me come over there and lap on that pussy?"

"Man, bye." Jessie grieves.

"All man, I'm just playin' with your sad ass. How's my baby?"

The woman is Jessica's first cousin, Denise Glockner. Denise is a lesbian who has three children by one of their cousins. The Glockner family is one of the few black families in Washington, DC, area that have practiced incest as a ritual rather than a sick fantasy ride. Their great-great-grandparents were white and black and didn't want their family to go through what all the other dark-skinned people in America were going through because of the darkness of their skin, so they taught their children to keep it in the family.

These days the young Glockners have deviated from their forefather's customs and have taken more and more sips of the sweet dark berry. And more of the females have drifted from the opposite sex altogether, but on the other hand, are rampant in their gay prowess, starting their adventures at a tender age and continuing into the teenage years and beyond.

"I'm fine," Jessica says calmly in a playful voice. "I didn't want anything. I just wanted to see if you felt like meeting me at the Soundstage." BETians are stuck on the old name. "Girl, I need a drink."

"Whaaat? 'Miss I'm trying to change my life' wants to drink?" taunts Denise.

"Shut your hatin' ass up and meet me. I'll be there in forty minutes or less. I'm about to leave work now."

"All righty. I'll be there."

"OK."

They exchange good-byes, and Jessica hangs up the phone, flings her coat over her shoulders like the caped crusader, grabs her things, and strolls out her nook toward the elevators.

Her walk is so graceful that men get whiplash every time she passes by. Her bounce is ever so rhythmic to each step that an onlooker can hardly distinguish whether she is floating or bouncing. If not for the up and down swaying of her long, stringy, black hair, one would think she's on skates.

She doesn't often wear very revealing clothes, but today she has put on an earth-tone skirt that hugs her hips from the top of her waist to the bottom of her reverberating gluteus muscles. Her thighs are like "plattow," and you can certainly see where they meet her torso. Jessica's calf muscles are out of the Kersey family, and she stands five foot eleven. Rather tall for a woman. A true racehorse in every sense of the word—a stallion.

Charlie Hinton, one of BETs many vice presidents, jumps up from his desk, cradled in his private office as Jessica ambles past his door.

"Jessica," he calls.

With a poignant step and pivot to respond to his sexually harassing halt of her advancement toward the seventh floor elevators, "Yes, Mr. Hinton. How can I help you on my way out the door?" she asks, rolling her eyes in his direction.

His eyes are probing her curvy extremities and then slowly up her midsection to the limited cleavage shot that broadcast enough for his nomadic eyes to gander.

"There you go with that 'Mr.' bull."

"Well, you are my superior. I'd better show some respect."

"Oh no," he sang. "I'm not your superior, I'm your friend . . . Would love to be, anyway."

"That's nice . . . but ahh . . . , why did you call me?"

Charles contemplates for a moment, trying to make up something because he hadn't had time to think of anything to justify stopping her before she bent the corner. "The memo," he blurts. "Did you see it?"

Now, why don't you just cut the crap? I know goodness well you don't care if I saw a memo about a damn computer virus going around. Why don't you just ask me out, so I can politely turn you down and stop waiting for me to feed into your phony pleasantries?

"Yes, I saw it . . . And?"

"Which one did you see?" he probes because he hadn't even seen it himself. He was hoping that she would mention it in her response.

Jessica nudges her neck back as she blinks and makes a face as if she just sniffed a bad smell. Puzzled, she asks, "How many memos went out? I only got the one about the virus."

The melody of a xylophone ascends in Charles' head. How wonderful for her to walk right into his little trap, telling him just what he needs to know!

"Yes . . . ," he drags, "the virus memo. Do you think that may be the cause of why my computer has blinked out at home? My daughter called me and told me that the computer was out. Damn it."

You know what Jessie, she thinks to herself. *Just flatter him. Your job is on the line here. If you tell this imbecile to go fly a kite, he might have the outs for you and start making things harder around here than things have to be. That;s all you need is to have a boss at your job who loves to become a splinter under your fingernail.*

"Ouch," she whispers at the thought of it.

"Yeah, that hurts when your computer goes on the blink, doesn't it?" he agrees with himself and then laughs out loud with his corny self, "Ha-ha-ha . . . hswhooo."

He just cracks himself up.

Jessica nods her head forward and puts her hand over her forehead as she giggles incredulously hard under her breath at how ridiculous he just made himself look. She can't believe this man is such an asinine person. He almost made her lungs burst from trying to suppress the guffaw that is dammed at the door of her trachea. If Jessica had not been able to hold it back, she'd have laughed a little bit too hard, making it obvious that she was laughing at him instead of with him.

"You're so crazy, Charles."

His eyes light up with glee at the sound of his first name rolling off her tongue. Charles takes another glance at the bulge of slight cleavage, then he takes a deep breath, exhaling slowly through his puffed out cheeks, visualizing her bucket naked. His manhood pulsates and then relaxes back into its flaccid posture in the sack of his Fruit of the Loom—the old-fashioned white ones with the blue and yellow stripes around the waistband—a true geek.

"Well, I won't hold you," he says.

Thank goodness, she thinks.

"But maybe one day we can go out to dinner after work?"

In your dreams, please. "I told you. I have a boyfriend."

"Well, why doesn't . . ."

"Mr. Hinton," she interjects.

He closes his eyes and realizes he's messing up. She's back to that Mr. Hinton junk.

"OK . . . OK. I'm sorry . . . I was just . . ."

"I know. I understand. Maybe one day, but right now . . . no," she says softly as she gives him a fake smile and turns for the elevator.

He accepts that with a hint of optimism. She said *"one day."* And that is enough for him to sleep at night. Charles Hinton will have sweet dreams tonight. He can't wait to get in bed and make love to his wife so he can fantasize about Jessie.

"Bye, Jessie."

"Bye."

Chapter 5

A woman exits Jaspers, and a man follows close behind her. They both double take in Jessica's direction as she approaches them with that runway walk. The couple is in their mid-forties and appears to be married since the two of them have on similar wedding bands. The woman looks Jessica up and down, taking one last look back into her pretty face. Jessica looks at the woman in her observant eyes and shuns away because she often feels embarrassed about her beauty. The feeling is twofold when it's an older woman and worse when the woman is with her man and she catches him staring. It's not that she's ashamed of her beauty. It's just she feels sorry for the women who look at her so enviously.

He better not be looking either, thinks the woman about her man.

He knows he shouldn't take the chance in getting caught, but he can't help himself. *Good god a'mighty! I'd better not look too hard. I know she's watching me.*

His wife walks past Jessica, who enters into the open door that the man is holding for her. With his wife's back to him, he takes the opportunity to get a good look at Jessica's legs. His wife stops and looks back at him with laser-piercing eyes as if she could feel that he was not right behind her and that he was still looking at Jessica. He looks up at his wife and scrunches the expression on his face.

"What! I'm just holding the door."

There are two young ladies coming out the door as Jessica disappears into the building. They both saw how the man was looking at Jessica, and they snicker because they find it funny that he got caught by his wife and then lies to make it seem like he wasn't doing anything.

Inside the restaurant, there's a cozy waiting area with multicolored carpet, and there's a reception station where there are two hostesses. One of them is very young and short with her hair in a ponytail revealing her smooth yellow complexion. The other woman standing to her right is almost as tall as Jessica and apparently around the same age. Both of the women have been working here for a while and are used to seeing beautiful women come through the door but still can't help being paralyzed momentarily before smiling to show hospitality and asking Jessica how many people are in her party.

There are several televisions encased in a glass wall cabinet behind the two hostesses. To the left of Jessie there are about eight people sitting on plush Arabian-style leather benches up against the wall. The ceiling to the floor is covered with carpet in this area where the people are waiting to be called for seating. This made-for-celebrities atmosphere is elegant, warm, and upscale; very attractive to Jessica, and that's what draws her here more so than anywhere else.

"I'm meeting someone at the bar," Jessica tells the two ladies.

The women nod, and the older one waves Jessica through. She has a choice of which side of the reception desk she may enter the main room of the restaurant to reach the bar. Jessica chooses to go to the left so she can use the ladies room before filling her system with fluids that she knows her body will reject and send straight to her bladder, overflowing it and forcing her to go running to the restroom later. She just wants to make room so she won't need to go as soon as she has had one drink.

Meanwhile, Denise is sitting near the bar in one of the three booths off to the side. There is a dwarf standing at the table talking to her. He's about five foot two with a full beard and a streak of gray on his crown, which becomes him, but he's way too short for her.

"See, I told you, shorty. You gonna get me in trouble. I tried to tell you I was gay. There goes my girlfriend right there."

Mr. Shorty stands up straight and gives her a no-teeth smile and then shakes his head indignantly because he doesn't recall telling her that his name was Shorty. *Dyke bitch.*

"Yeah, you did say you were gay," he comments as he turns in the direction that Denise has gestured.

There is a tall, redbone, thoroughbred of a woman walking directly toward him. Her hair is floating in the flow of the air that surges around her face like an aerodynamic jet stream. Her eyes are affixed to his, and a bad case of drop-jaw befalls him. The mere thought of this Venus actually putting those voluptuous lips on another woman angers and delights him all at the same time, generating a feeling in his testosterone that he'd never experienced. His strength fades, and he feels his legs give a bit to the weight of his body. He'd forgotten that he was standing on them. Love at first sight has just occurred, and there's nothing he can do about it. She's gay, so he thinks.

His mouth gets dry when he becomes nervous, which causes his breath to become rancid. He reaches in his pocket for the pack of Big Red that he bought earlier. Nothing. He's left it in the car on the console.

What difference does it make anyway? This lady is gay. She won't give me the time of day anyway. Just like this dyke right here. Man, I'd give her every dime in my pocket if I thought it would help. Damn.

Jessica can see that Denise has a little friend, keeping her company, and she takes no time getting acquainted with him. "Hello, I'm Jessie," she says politely to Mr. Shorty. She knows he's a guy that's only trying to see how far he can get with Denise, even though it's obvious by the way she's dressed that she's probably gay. "Niecey, I didn't know you were bringing a friend along."

"I love . . . I mean," Mr. Shorty fumbles, "No, we just met. I'm sorry, ma'am. I didn't mean to intrude. I was just making small talk."

"No, no, it's OK. You don't have to go," Jessie says. "What's your name?"

"Marvin."

"Oh well, nice to meet you, Marvin. Would you like to join us for a little while?"

The gates of heaven have just opened up above Marvin, and he thinks the whole room has become a bit brighter all of the sudden. *Down boy. Down. She's just being nice. Don't get your hopes up. Go with the flow, buy both of them a drink, don't talk about sex or anything stupid like that and please, please stop staring.*

"If it's alrightwith Niecey," Marvin says.

"Hey, she invited me here. If it's alrightwith her, it's *all righty then* with me."

"What will you two be drinking?"

"Two apple martinis please," Jessie says.

"Girl, you must be trippin'." Niecey says. "Speak for yourself. I want a White Russian. Double shot."

"Well, excuse me. But I wasn't talking about you anyway."

Niecey is astonished at Jessie and starting to wonder if something is really wrong because she has never known Jessie to drink a double of anything. She looks at her, trying to detect a sign of distress, but there appears to be none.

"Are you OK, Jessie?"

"Oh, I'm fine. I just want a drink. I feel like getting a little twisted, that's all. Is something wrong with that?"

Marvin steps over to the bar and asks a bartender named Jason for their drinks and waits at the bar for them. He wants to give the ladies a little privacy before he interrupts their love talk.

"So what's the deal? I know you ain't called me just to have a drink. You know I'm a freak, and that's why you've been avoiding me. The only time you ever call me is when there's some drama. Whose ass do I have to kick?"

Jessie puffs out a breath of air and then contemplates for a moment before turning to Niecey, who has a short Halle Berry-style hair cut. She's pretty as Jessie, but her teeth aren't the straight set of pearls that Jessie has, and her body is nice but is a bit bony beside the beast underneath Jessie's skin. She is Jessie's age but looks a generation younger because of the hip-hop manner in which she carries herself. Instead of a skirt, she wears Bebe jeans. Instead of a raincoat, she has on a leather bomber jacket with patches all over it. She also has on a tight T-shirt with "Mchunu" across the breast. That's certainly one thing about Niecey that outshines Jessie. Her breast. Who cares that they're perfectly rounded and plumped with the assistance of silicone implants? All the world cares about is that they are live—in the flesh.

"Take your coat off. Stay awhile," Jessie tells Niecey.

"Shh . . . girl, it's cold in here. They still got the air conditioner on . . . Ain't even that hot outside."

"Un . . . but, umm, anyway girl, are you ready for this?" Jessie prompts.

Niecey's eyes nearly pop out their sockets as she leans forward on the table, resting her weight on her crossed forearms and elbows that glide to a stop once her breasts land on the table to help support her. She strives off gossip.

"She called my job."

There is a cold silence between the two of them while Niecey wonders if she should know who *she* is supposed to be. She doesn't like it when she isn't on point. She should know whom Jessie is talking about, otherwise Jessie would not have just said "she."

She . . . ? Think, girl. Think. Who called her job? Jessie's voice is echoing in Niecey's mind.

The silence is stretching a tad bit too long. Niecey holds her breath as if doing so will make things quieter so she can think deeper. Refusing to be defeated, she scans the table for clues. There are none. Slowly, her pupils waver down to her hand. Then, finally submitting to defeat, Niecey takes a deep breath.

"She? Who is *she*?"

"Salina."

Niecey is stumped again. She makes the stinky smell face, for once again, the words from her dear cousin are wrapped in a shroud of mystery, forcing Niecey to dig deep on this one. No way will she fail again, so with brazen determination, she looks up to the cathedral ceiling adorned with charcoal black painted beams and pipes, and with her fist balled tight, she repeats the name aloud so that it might strike a bell awakening her memory. "Salina, Salina, Salina," her eyes gaping wider and wider with each mention of the name as an alarm is sounding in her head and her memory is jarred. "Salina . . . Salina?" she says getting louder and louder, feeling that she's on the verge of figuring this thing out. "Salina!" she screeches, jolting Jessie, nearly inducing a heart attack. "Benji's girl? How'd she find out about you and where you work?"

"She not only called my job, but she called my house too."

"Your house too? All hell naw! Now, who could have told her all that?"

"I have no idea. Benji's been gone for almost five years, so it ain't like she could have followed him there. And if somebody was gonna tell her about me, why would they wait all these years to do it with him in jail." Jessie wonders. "I can't see his sisters telling her. They can't stand her."

"I thought they were close with her," Niecey recalls.

They used to be close, but Salina started some stuff between Benji's sisters and their cousins, so ever since, they've put distance between Salina and themselves. Besides, they love Benji to death and would never betray the loyalty that they share.

Benji is the family jewel, and no one would want to bring turmoil to his life by telling his 'main girl' that he has a chick on the side. It had to be someone at the jail that knows somebody who knows somebody, or it could be a close friend or even one of Jessie's friends.

Who would want to do something like this? Jessie asks herself for the hundredth time.

Jessie lowers her eyelids to a peep and observes Niecey's body language and facial expression. She appears to be as bewildered as Jessie does, but Niecey is convincing; she'll sell her body, soul, and farm to get done what she wants done. She's never liked that Jessie wasn't into the family heritage, depriving her of a taste of her most attractive cousin. Niecey's a relentless liar and a master of deceit. No one in the family trusts her with their mate, male or female, yet she's loyal to those she really cares about. Still, no one knows just whom she really cares about. She's just not to be trusted. Sad, but it's true, and Jessie realizes it but feels in her heart that she's just being paranoid, so she turns away to avoid appearing obvious that she's testing Niecey's reaction to detect any guilt. She doesn't want to hurt her feeling, after all, out of all the people her naughty cousin has crossed, she's never thrown any shade at Jessie, and that Jessie also knows.

They sit there at the table in silence, gazing off into the faces of the happy-hour guest of the dimly lit luxury bar and grill. Niecey looks more concerned than upset, because she just wishes her older cousin could just be happy. To her, Jessie is the nicest person in the world and doesn't deserve this type of aggravation. She wants to say, "Just leave his ass alone," but she knows that's not what Jessie needs to hear right now. This situation is far more complicated than that at this point; she has no idea what to say that could help Jessie. She looks at the sorrow written all over Jessie's face as Mr. Shorty puts their drinks down on the table.

"Did somebody die?" Marvin asks.

No one answers him. No one even acknowledges his presence. They both just sit there mesmerized by the thoughts whirling around in their heads. How bad can things get from this point? Salina is a known crazy person when it comes to Benji and women who chase him.

Chapter 6

Five men, dressed in all black, sit in a family room, two walls adorned with every sort of electronic component known to man. Plasma, surround sound, DVD, multidisk CD player, DAT player, a stereo system, a sixty-inch Trinitron sitting cattier corner, and a couple of Pentium fives have the screensaver bouncing large 3D words across the screen—*Die Trying.*

There are other pieces of furniture in the room as well, two black leather sofas, a recliner, a glass table, and matching end tables. The carpeted room is semidark even though there are two lamps shining in opposite corners of the room. The bulbs in these lamps are certainly in need of changing because they can't cut the darkness in the room far enough to shed light on the objects, sitting on the coffee table located in the center of the room. The room is in the basement of a rambler and takes up most of the space beneath the house except for a bedroom, a storage room, and a full bathroom—perfect for a bachelor who lives with his mother not burdened with any dependents.

This is Fatts' domain, and he and his band of stone cold killers are sitting around the table and preparing for a caper they've been coveting for the past few weeks. That's all they do. Plot and pilfer. Killing isn't part of the plan, especially not when innocent people are involved, but his men have been known to body many men. These type of men are needed in this line of work because one never knows when he'll encounter a hero.

Today, the plot is on a civilian who happens to be a drug dealer with lots of cash in his house. These are the most dangerous type of robberies because on these moves anything can happen. Dudes who sell drugs, especially caked-up dealers, carry guns and generally have a plan of action thought out in the event of an ambush. They know it's coming. The question is when and where.

For these men, those questions are already answered, and they've set their target. There's no doubt about whether or not it's going down. They've made it their baby, and everyone has a part to play.

There's no talking at the table right now, just sounds of clicking guns, slapping clips, dropping bullets to the glass surface of the coffee table and fifty cent's debut album.

"'Cause when that window rolls down and that AK comes out, you can squeeze your little handgun till you run out, then you can run for your backup, but them machine-gun shell gonna tear your back up . . . God's on your side? Shid, I'm alrightwith that, 'cause we gone reload them clips and come right back. It's a fact, homie," the lyrics spit as the men pass a blunt around, getting high as a helicopter.

Fatts is a short, stout dude with a clean face. He looks like a miniature Fat Albert from the hit comic show from Bill Cosby. He's twenty-six and the leader of the pack and the one with all the brains. The other guys are smart enough, but Fatts is a criminal genius. He doesn't leave a rock unturned in the DC area. He's robbed so many drug dealers that people call him "Robin the Hood." They'd rob their mothers if they heard that she had enough to make the breakdown worth the while.

Daryl, Fatts' right-hand man is sitting beside him. They've been hanging together for so long that they're starting to look more and more alike. He's not much taller than Fatts and not that much thinner either, but he's a lot dumber. Daryl is the type of dude that'll buy a full-grown Rottweiler for two hundred dollars from a crackhead, leave it in the yard, then come home, and wonder who the hell stole his dog. After six months, he'll turn around, buy another dog that looked just like the one that got stolen from him, get this from the same dude, and then name the dog the same name that he named the first one. He'll leave the dog in the yard again and guess what? Gone again. Idiot.

Without Fatts, Daryl would have been locked up a long time ago. He's not self-sustaining like Luther, another man sitting across from them.

Luther is a seasoned vet. He's done more crimes and capers than Daryl has had one-night stands. In a word, Luther is *vicious*. He usually is the one who finds the targets and brings the idea to Fatts so he can go look at it and devise the various options that they discuss in preparation for the move. Luther is a suave-buttermilk, chocolate-skinned gangster who knows his stuff. Women are suckers for this guy, and the player-haters hate him but are too afraid to show it.

Luther is famous for using broads to do his scouting work. He charms them into giving him information and keeping their mouth shut about his obvious plans. Sometimes, he has girls who are all for it and even willing to seduce men in order to lure them into a trap as was the case with their last victim. "Lisa of the World" was her name, and she was phat as a country mule. One day he took her for a ride and let her out the car to walk past some guys that he was preying on. She walked down the street on the opposite side of the street, and sure enough, the big fish out of the bunch walked over to her, said a few words, and before long, they were walking back across the street to get into his car. Luther followed them, and once they got to the Marriott in Greenbelt, Luther sprung out, flashed the heat on him, and then walked the guy to the navy blue Ford Windstar that he was driving. They took the man to his house and made off with ninety thousand dollars. The guy saw Luther's face, but he doesn't care. If he thought that he was a real threat, he would have left him with a hole in his head. If he runs across him again, he'll probably extort him for more cash. Luther doesn't hang anywhere in particular and surely doesn't trust anybody but Fatts, so he feels like he's untouchable.

There are two other men in the room, one of which is sitting in the recliner with bloodshot red eyes. His complexion is matching the crimson-stained whites of his eyes. His hair is twisted in long pigtails that drape down the side of his face like a little white girl in a horror flick. His chin is long with a patch of hair at its end. He looks like a Mexican Snoop Dogg possessed by demons. He's methodically taking his time to load very long bullets into a black banana clip and filling it until the bullets can no longer breathe. He slaps it into an old AK-47 and snatches back on the side, releasing it with a clacking thud, and then he holds the gun in the air, pointing it to the ceiling, marveling at its majesty with the adoration of a beauty queen.

The other guy is pacing back and forth with an anxious rout over the carpet in his path. All the while, he's skinning the thin membrane, protecting the scar tissue of his bottom lip with nibbles from his front teeth. His skin is black as soot, and the light that reflects off his skin casts a bluish luminescence, which explains his nickname Blue. Blue is driving the rest of them crazy with his silent rage, but they're used to it. He's always a nervous wreck just before the move, but the most stealth of all at launch time, beating everybody to the point and always making the situation a quiet, incident-free apprehension.

They all are ready and have been waiting for this day because money is low and none of them have jobs or sell drugs although Fatts has decided that it's time that they do. It's time for them to have regular income before somebody dies or goes to jail. He certainly doesn't want anybody to die on either side of the performance. Turning a robbery into a homicide must be avoided at all costs, even if that means walking away empty-handed. If it was up to any of the others that wouldn't be the case, but it's not up to them, so nobody has any intention on killing unless, of course, somebody makes the wrong move.

Boyyy, let this punta even think about it, thinks Lil Papi, the Hispanic Snoop Dog. *I'll kill that punta dead,* he continues in Spanish.

Blue is concentrating and walking himself through the motions of what he needs to do. *All right, first thing you do is take your gun off safely, get out the car, aim your gun at him, tell him to show his hands, and then make him lie down . . . No . . . that'll cause too much of a scene. Run to him and make him turn around and take his hands out his pockets and walk with his back to you. Tell Luther to put the shades on him.*

The sunshades that they have are straight out of the punk rocker's disco tech and are painted over the lenses with black paint rendering the person wearing them blind. They call them the Plank Walkers.

I need to call Tina and see if she's gonna get the Dro from Diesel before he goes out of town, Luther reminds himself. *I ain't tryin' to be smokin' no bush all weekend.*

I'm horny as hell, Daryl realizes as he sits there doing nothing but watching everybody else go through their own ritual in preparation for the job. All he ever thinks about is girls, like he's some kind of Mac daddy or something. He's more like a trick because all he ever does is spend his money on the girls he meets. He's making plans to pick up one of his hood-rats later on to take her shopping, and then to the motel. Daryl isn't ugly, but he has absolutely no rap for the chicks, instead, he just spends money on them, but after a while, he figured out that the real fly girls don't come cheap and taking them shopping only got him a big hug and a kiss, then they'd rant and rave about how he's their new brother, so he's regressed to the happy-meal-hoes a long time ago.

Fatts raises his hands up in the air while he stands up from the sofa and stretches his body, rising up on his tippy toes. "Y'all ready for the low down?" he asks, lowering his arms to an outstretched position like an aerobics instructor.

"What's the deal?" asks Luther.

Fatts runs down everything that he's observed about the target, and everyone is listening. Blue is asking a million and one questions as he always does, and Fatts answers them as best as he can. Blue's questions are actually the questions that help make the whole scene clearer to everybody, even to Fatts, who has analyzed the scene at least three times for hours at a time.

Blue is like the child in school that asks the questions in class that everybody has but doesn't have the gall to interrupt the teacher's flow to ask. Blue doesn't care if some of his questions seem obvious and stupid. He wants to know exactly what he's getting himself into because if it doesn't sound foolproof, he's not going. He isn't a gangster, and besides that, he has a family that expects him to come home every night. He's an entrepreneur and only rolls on these missions because he can always use the extra money to fuel his projects, but more than that, Fatts has never gone on any type of robbery mission without Blue and has vowed not to ever do so; therefore, Luther and Daryl, who depend on these moves to survive, practically make Blue come along. He really doesn't have a choice in the matter.

After everybody becomes comfortable with the logistics of the plan, especially Blue, they all look at Lil Papi. Lil Papi is trigger-happy and is a known killer. He's killed at least two people that the police know of and more than five others that his crew knows about. Lil Papi used to be a hit man for Rayfus back in the late 1980s when he was still in high school and hasn't much changed about his state of mind or his arsenal. He's had that AK since 1992, and it has more than his own share of bodies on it. If he's caught with it, he'll be brought up on murder charges that haven't been solved in over a decade.

"Don't forget, Papi," Fatts commands. "No killing."

Lil Papi pokes out his bottom lip and slowly nods his head nonchalantly. Maybe he was answering yes to Fatts' command, or maybe he was bobbing his head to the beat of the 50 Cent song that is playing out of the nearby speaker, but whatever the case, Fatts isn't satisfied with his response.

Fatts stares at him until Papi looks him in his eyes. Fatts pierces his eyes and tips his head forward and makes an impatient expression.

"Dog . . . I'm not going to kill nobody. Stop playing with me, Homes," Papi drags in his Spanish accent.

"Don't homes me, nigga. Chill. That's all you do," returns Fatts.

Lil Papi cocks his head back resentfully and smirks his lips. "Come on. Let's go, man."

Everybody springs to their feet and follows Fatts up the stairs, tucking their guns away under their jackets, looking like a task force of bounty hunters. Scary sight.

Chapter 7

Benji heads to the phones up against the wall in the day area of the dorm. There aren't any phones available, but Benji never sits too long before a particular brown nose shortens his conversation or decides not to make an additional call just so Benji can get his phone.

"Here you go, dog. I'll just use the joint later," says the ass kisser who Benji has never given the time of day.

"Thanks, slim," says Benji.

Benji always shows sincere gratitude to people when they do something for him even though he knows that they're doing it for something in return. That's just his nature, but he doesn't trust many people as far as he can throw them. If you're not family, he has his eye on you, but family to Benji isn't measured in blood content. Family to Benji are people who show true love and have proven their trustworthiness. That simple. But even family can betray you, but that's life.

"B," Benji says in the phone to identify himself to the person on the other end of the collect call, and then he leans back on the wall while he waits for the call to be accepted. After no one answers the phone, he stands up, hangs up the phone, and then dials another number.

"B," he repeats and then assumes his previous position. "Dog, what's up, baby?!"

It's Richter, Benji's lieutenant, over the gang of drug dealers that works for him on the streets to move all the coke he fronts out. He's been waiting to hear from Benji so he can hear the details about what's going on with him and Salina. "What's up on it, dog?"

"Not too much. What's really goin' on?"

"I don't know. You tell me, playa," Richter says inquisitively, giggling as he talks. "Give me the low down, champ."

Benji can sense that there's information about something that he should already know about, but he hasn't been informed of anything. He talked to Salina yesterday, and she didn't mention anything, although she did sound a little short. He's been trying to call Jessie, but she hasn't been home during the times he's called. He'd also talked to Bink, his best friend, but he didn't mention anything either, so what could Richter be probing about? What has been heard?

"Man, what the hell are you talking about?"

"Oh, so you don't know what Salina is up to? *Mannn.*" Richter drags. He's caught wind of some news about Benji's main squeeze. "A'ight. This is what's happening," he slurs jokingly, not used to being the source of gossip concerning some females. "Your girl called my girl and asked about Jessie. And she's trippin' hard."

Benji's scrotums tighten up and a churning nausea brews up in his stomach. All of the sudden, Benji doesn't feel so well. His bowels purge out his intestines and press hard against his anal sphincter.

"What'd she say?" Benji asks, anxious and feeling the sting of perspiration spouting out of his pores.

"Man, she said she knows you've been screwin' Jessie for years. She knows she works at BET, that you've been paying her bills, and you paid her way through grad school. Everything."

"Man, who the . . . !" Benji hollers at the top of his lungs. Half of the dorm looks in his direction.

"Yeah, joe. Somebody's running their mouth. You think one of your sisters or cousins told her?"

"Naw, man. They wouldn't do that."

"Unn . . . un," Richter wonders.

"All man."

Benji blows a blast of air out of his puckered lips and closes his conversation with his friend, hangs up the phone, and makes another call. He calls Jessie again but receives her answering machine and then he tries Bink, but he's seldom home in the daytime, so that's a waste of time trying. Both Bink and Jessie have jobs, but he can't call them collect there. He tries the house because there has been times that he's caught them playing hooky from work.

He wants to call his house but for what? So he can just listen to Salina huff and puff like she did last night when he talked to her? Now he understands why he was getting the cold shoulder. She knows something, and she's trying to get every nook and cranny before she drops the bombshell. She's such a bitch, but Benji puts up with her because he loves her, and they have a family together with a house and two kids. Not to mention, she's a real freak in the bed, and he likes it.

Their sex is the wildest and nastiest sex he's ever had with any woman, plus she's game to help him fulfill some of his own sexual desires such as a *Ménage* à trios. At least she says she's game. Besides the sex, he doesn't like her very much, but which man does like his woman very much? Even though they're not married, he treats her as if they are. They've been together for so long, common law presides over their arrangement, and any judge would give her much of her just due in the event of a major separation along with the fact that everything's in both of their names except the house. That's in her name.

I know this girl is really gonna get on my nerves now. I hope Poah didn't say nothing about Jessie . . . but why would she do something like that? But who then? I can't even imagine. This is crazy.

Benji is frustrated out of his mind and has the same feeling that he felt when the jury came back into the courtroom before they handed down his guilty verdict. The judge sentenced him to twenty years in prison, suspended ten with five years of supervised probation. The sentence frizzled the hairs on the back of his neck and made him dizzy enough to try to sit down before the judge finished talking. He stood back up, but that was only because two deputy sheriffs stepped close behind him and told him to.

Benji walks over to the bathroom door and disappears from the sight of the concerned convicts who have been watching him since his outburst. Inside the bathroom, he walks over to the Cadillac and wipes the seat off, clearing it of any and all wet droplets. The Cadillac is what they call the handicap toilet. It has a longer partition, which gives an individual the needed privacy for taking a dump. None of the stalls have doors on them, so unless you're in the Cadillac, you're in the open. He sits down and mulls over the explanations he'd better have for Salina when she finally decides to interrogate him like the FBI. He knows she won't say anything until she comes to visit him in person. By then, she'll have enough evidence to make him break down and just tell the truth, the whole truth, and nothing but the truth.

Chapter 8

Jessie is feeling dismal. She thought that going to the bar would make her feel better, allowing her mind to be freed of all the concerns surrounding this daunting revolution in her relationship with her beloved Don Juan. Her spiraling mood is causing a migraine to pulsate in her temples, driving her to the couch still wearing her red raincoat. She drops her Coach bag in the middle of the floor and peels her rain hat off her head as she collapses to her brown leather sofa.

The living room light was already on when she came through the door because it's usually dark outside when she comes home, especially after Labor Day, and it's almost time for the grocery stores to start selling pumpkins, so she has made a habit over the years of just leaving a light on near the front door.

Her apartment is furnished with luxurious Scandinavian pieces. There are several tall lamps around the house, but most of them are turned off. The art on the walls are phallic Picasso paintings and some African head sculptures. There is wall-to-wall carpet under a large oriental throw rug in the center of the living room floor. There is also a giant-size wall unit filled with all types of electronics, photos, crystal animal sculptures, and brass images.

She lies down on her side with her head propped up on a sofa pillow. Her eyes are open, but she isn't seeing what her eyes are looking at. She's seeing vivid pictures of wishful thinking.

Benji is walking through the door. He smiles a big smile, and Jessie walks over to him and hugs him tight, laying her head on his shoulder. He kisses her on her lips and holds her ever so tenderly.

Jessie blinks and comes back to reality wishing she could sink back into the daydream she was having. She tries, but the vision isn't as intense as it was when she first drifted off into her thoughts.

Ring . . . Ring . . . Ring.

Jessie jumps up after the third ring, deciding to answer the phone after all. She snatches the cordless off the base furiously, expecting to answer the phone and hear the woman's voice that she doesn't want to speak to—Salina. She kind of hopes it is her, so she can tell her a thing or two. She'd like to tell her to grow up and get a life. If Jessie were the foul-mouth type, she'd curse her out like a sailor and let her know what she was going to do to her when she sees her, but she's not a gangster chick and doesn't think of cursing even though she uses an occasional "ass" or "damn," which she feels is appropriate for a lady. She'd never allow herself to let this woman get her out of her character.

"Hello," answered Jessie in her polite working voice.

"Boo!"

It's Denise playing on the phone. She knows Jessie is on edge every time the phone rings, so she's decided to call and keep her mind preoccupied.

"Girl, you simple," Jessica replies.

"Did she call you?"

"No, in fact, I just got in here ten minutes ago. I haven't even checked to see if she left me any nasty messages yet."

"Hold on."

Jessica clicks over and calls her answering service to check her messages. After listening to her messages and deleting all the irrelevant messages as she sifts through the voices, listening for Salina's infamous tone and finds she has left many messages. She clicks Niecey back on the line.

"Denise?"

"I'm still here."

"All right, listen. She left a bunch of messages. Here we go." Jessie plays Salina's first message.

"Yeah, um . . . Jessica . . . This is Benji's *woman,* and I would like to talk to you. You can call me on my cell phone. The number, 202-555-0557. I'll be waiting for your call," Salina says in a very slow nasty tone.

"Un . . ." Denise smirks as Jessie pushes the phone to go to the next message.

"I called you on your job, but I guess you didn't work today. Humph. I suppose you didn't have to. Must be nice. Well, if you're half a woman, you would call me. I know you got the number, but just in case you didn't, write it down the first time. Here it is again."

"That broad got problems," heckles Denise.

"202-555-0557. Just feel free to call me. I'll be up. I don't have anything else to do, so make the call. Holla."

"Look," Salina starts in the next message sounding rather annoyed, "I don't think you understand. You *need* to call me and stop avoiding me. I hope you ain't acting like a coward 'cause I'm a grown woman. I don't have time for playing phone tag with you. This can be resolved like civilized people, or it can get ugly. One thing's for sure. If you don't respond to me, there *will* be a problem."

"Un . . . I know this trick ain't . . . oh, naw. See, Jessie, she's trippin'. You know you shouldn't have let me hear that. I'ma crush her!" Niecey exclaims.

Niecey is no longer interested in what Salina is saying. All she knows is that this woman has just violated, and she is going to pay for it. Niecey is not a peacemaker; she has no intentions on having her cousin consider calling Salina. All Niecey wants to know right now is where she can find her because her anger is escalating her blood pressure to heart-aching levels. She can feel her blood boiling and sweat popping to her skin's surface.

"I have not even the slightest idea what she wants to talk to me about so badly. If somebody has told her something about me and Benji, then she needs to take that up with them."

"I don't care what she has to say or what she wants to talk about. She just threatened you, and I'm not having that. Where is her beauty salon?"

"Well, maybe I should just call her," Jessie wonders out loud. "If she's going through all this to talk to me, I should, at least, confront her woman-to-woman. I would probably be acting the same way if I was in her shoes."

Niecey is quiet for a moment, remembering her feminine side and understanding why Jessie would consider talking to the woman, but she shows no sympathy.

"Go ahead, call her . . . Call her while I'm on the phone, but I'ma tell you like this. If she says one thing out the way, I'ma kick her ass. Simple as that."

"Naw. I'm not gonna call her with you on the phone."

Knock, knock, and knock.

It's 9:17 p.m. on a Wednesday, and Jessie has never had an unannounced visit, especially not after dark. If she does get one, it's maintenance, but they're never unannounced, and never *this* late, so who could be at the door at a time like this in the midst of so much drama? Jessie is high-strung, and the pounding in her heart thumps so hard that she can feel it bang against her sternum like an African drum. The sound can be heard in her ears, and a mini-ulcer ignites in her stomach giving her pangs all over her insides. She can feel a sudden numbness proliferate in the nerves of her left arm, and she can hardly take a deep breath. All the symptoms of a heart attack.

"Shh," Jessica whispers.

"What," Niecey whispers back, not knowing why she's whispering.

"Somebody's knocking at my door."

"Go, see who it is."

"I am. Shh . . ."

They both are whispering, for what, nobody knows; regardless, Jessica does not want to be heard while she's tiptoeing to the door. Down the hallway from the bathroom past the closet, Jessie reaches the tiled foyer at the front door, not saying a word while she holds the phone to her ear, expecting to reach the door to see it bursts open with a swat team coming through it.

That has always been a phobia of hers ever since she saw the stacks and stacks of money that Benji shuffled through the money machine that sits dormant in a plastic trash bag in her bedroom closet. She has never imagined that she'd see Benji, whom she saw as a mild-mannered person, conduct himself like a kingpin drug lord, but after seeing her entire dining room table turn into a Treasury Department workstation, she became thoroughly convinced that he certainly wasn't Mr. Nice Guy and nowhere near being a two-bit hustler either. She's in love, deeply in love, with a man that a couple of DEA, FBI, or IRS agents could retire off.

Could she have called the police to try to get me locked up? Maybe she thinks Benji has money and drugs stashed here. Is she at the door with some friends to kill me?

Jessie has several outlandish thoughts circulating in her mind; her steps gets lighter and her movement slower as she moves her squinted eye into position at the peephole.

Knock, knock, knock, knock, and knock.

"Jessie," a man's voice calls from the other side of the door.

"Who is . . . ?" Jessie whispers as she breathes a sigh of relief from the sound of the man's familiar voice. "Bink?" She continues with delight. She peeks through the hole with a smile and reaches for the lock on the door.

"Niecey, it's Bink. I wonder what . . ."

"He probably got some news for you. She probably called him too."

Jessie opens the door and greets Bink with a friendly hug and a few pats on the back. The kind of pats that says that this is nothing more than a sisterly hug. He's an inch shorter than she is but about the same in skin complexion only slightly darker. He's still in his work clothes, suit, and tie. He works for a software firm located in Rockville, where he troubleshoots the company's proprietary file-tracking software for end-users like Merrill Lynch, First Union, and many other blue-chip corporate conglomerates.

They release one another, and then she steps aside for him to come in and have a seat. "Niecey, let me call you back." She hangs up the phone and sits down on the sofa. The television is on, but they're not paying any attention. She's too preoccupied with anticipation of what he has to say, and he's too preoccupied with her cleavage and legs. Their eyes meet, and Bink can see the anxiousness in Jessie's expression, so he won't keep her in suspense.

"Sorry, I came over unannounced, but I tried to call you several times, so I decided to come see if your car was out there. Maybe you just weren't answering your phone. Benji was starting to think something was wrong because he hasn't been able to catch you for the past couple of days either."

"He has?" she says surprisingly. She's been hoping to hear from him and is glad to know that he's trying hard to get in contact with her. Hard enough to send his friend to check on her. The thought makes her feel all-warm inside. She wants to tell him all about Salina calling her, but she doesn't want to jump the gun. "So you came over here to make sure nobody's come over here and left me for dead," she said jokingly.

Bink, being Benji's best friend in the whole world, should already know what's going on. They're like brothers ever since they met in high school when Benji saw Bink fighting a dude named Mantac. They both went to high school with Mantac, who was the king of all bullies to walk their school's hallways. He was a boxer but wouldn't hesitate to show off his boxing skills on the street. Mantac was sharp, and you couldn't tell him that he wasn't a slugging version of Sugar Ray Leonard. No one dared say anything out of the way to this cat because not only did he have superb boxing skills that have left a lineage of fallen contenders, but he also had a gang of flunkies who thought they were 'the shit' just because they were hanging with him. These guys would die for him if he asked them to, especially, Elroy, his number one flunky and gun busser. If there was a situation that Mantac thought was a chance he might lose, he'd send Elroy for the gun.

Elroy is carrying out a life sentence right now for a murder he committed for Mantac. Mantac was about to fight a dude that was also known for knocking people clean out, and he wasn't about to take any chances on being embarrassed by that dude in front of all the people that were out there who would love to run around and tell the world how he got the fur tore off his ass.

"Handle that, youngin," Mantac told Elroy, who reached his hand under his shirt, walked out into the middle of the street in front of the

Ebony Inn, whipped out a big black .357 Magnum, and aimed it at the guy, who was just standing there shocked, looking down the barrel of the gun.

Pow!

The clap bounced off the brick walls of the building like a super ball in every direction, leaving the guy with a bloody tarantula in the center of his white T-shirt, stretched out with all his limbs extended to the four corners of the earth. Of course, somebody snitched, and Elroy was arrested.

Mantac had avoided that embarrassment but had no idea what he was getting himself into when he picked on Bink. Bink was into the books, a smart kid and wasn't much of a crowd follower, but he had big brothers who he had to fight when he was coming up in Barry Farms, not to mention all the bad kids he grew up with in the notorious neighborhood in South East Washington DC. He had lots of practice in fighting.

And fight is what he did. Bladensburg High would never see another rumble like the fight between Mantac and Bink. Mantac smacked the taste out of Bink's mouth with a mighty pimp slap. Benji was sitting close by and saw the whole thing. He wanted to jump up and fight Mantac himself because though he didn't know Bink at that time, he did recognize that Bink minded his own business and didn't do anything to provoke such a vicious assault. But before Benji could get his thoughts together to say something to Mantac, the little brown-skinned curly head boy was all over Mantac, kicking, biting, swinging, scratching, and wrestling. Mantac was overwhelmed for a moment but reversed the brutality with a series of kidney shots, hooks, and uppercuts. Bink went down but quickly got right back up swinging and snarling like a distempered dog.

Benji was so impressed with the way the little guy handled himself against Mantac, even though he got knocked out, that he took him under his wing and eventually came to love him like a brother—a brother he always wished he had. They've been inseparable ever since.

So since Bink is Benji's most trusted friend, Jessie thinks, why not confide this revolution in him? After all, none of Benji's other friends even knows where Jessica lives. She wants to tell him so bad, but then again, she doesn't want to tell him something that she hasn't already told Benji. That just seems so inappropriate to her. She contemplates for a moment, sinking into the patterns in the rug on the floor. She blinks, then rivets her eyes on Bink, and then hesitates. Bink can see that she has something important to say. "What Jess? What's going on?"

She doesn't know where to start or what to say. Saying Salina's name out of her mouth churns her stomach and dries her mouth like saltine crackers.

What am I supposed to tell him? Benji's babies' mama is mad 'cause she found out that I was screwing her man? . . . He's not her man, anyway. She thinks to herself.

"Nothing. I was about to tell you something, but I can't think of what it was." She was lying, and Bink knows it.

"Now, Jessie, why are you sitting over there, lying through your pretty white teeth?" he asks.

Jessie shucks at the compliment with a reflective smile, and then she widens her eyelids and takes a deep breath. "All right, Bink. Let me tell you what's going on. Your man Benji has a blabber mouth in his clique or family, one or the other, but all I know is Salina has been calling me here at my house and at my job."

"At your job?" Bink is flabbergasted at hearing that Salina has been calling Jessie, and even more astonished that she's been calling her job. "How the hell did she get your number at your job?"

"I have no idea. I was hoping you might have heard something and had some news for me."

"Naw, I haven't talked to her for a minute."

A minute in Bink's vernacular means a long period of time. But of course, he's lying through his teeth. He's just got off the phone with Salina less than an hour ago. He talks to Salina almost every day, and that's what he'd be telling Jessie if he were up to any good. The fact is, he's been waxing Salina's ass like Raindance car polish, digging deep into her nappy dugout for two years now. He goes to Benji's house, keeps the grass cut for him, then skeets in his sheets, and doesn't even put a sock on the pickle. Salina's had three abortions since Benji's been in jail. So much for Bink, making sure the ole girl stays in line until his friend comes home.

"Well, I don't know what I should do. She's left her number for me to call, but I haven't."

"What did she say?"

"Nothing much but *did* act like she was trying to be civilized even though I could hear the hurt in her voice. But I feel, as though, she needs to take all this up with Benji. I ain't trying to talk to her. I don't know what Benji might say about that . . . you know? He might think I told her more than she was supposed to know. I'd better talk to him first, right?"

"Yeah, you're right," Bink agrees. "You shouldn't call her. Let Benji handle it."

Typical man, Jessie mulls. *Let the man tell his girl the lies she needs to hear to cover his own ass. Don't you go verifying the truth? Let him smooth out his own mess. Niggas.*

"I suppose you're right. I'm not going to call her. I'll wait to talk to him."

Bink stares off into the fading light down the dark hallway, leading back to Jessie's sleeping quarters as he tries to come up with a line that he can say that'll make Jessie rethink the situation that she's in with Benji, being the second lady. He's been sleeping with Salina, but he would leave the country if he could be the husband of Mrs. Jessica Williams. He's joked with Jessie and Benji a hundred times about how he was the one who pointed Jessie out at the Howard Homecoming, but Benji ended up getting her because Bink was too speechless to go at her himself.

Jessie has confided many times in Bink that he was actually more her type than Benji, but then she was in love with him, so there's no use in crying over spilt milk; however, now that their big secret is certain to turn into a big drama, there just might be a glimmer of hope. No. Jessie loves Benji to death and the thought of not loving him is not humanly possible for her. Furthermore, even if she was to ever fall out of love with him, she'd never end up with a man who even remotely knows Benjamin Powell. She'd be too afraid that her undercover drug lord, ex-boyfriend would find her and her husband and hang them both from a lamppost.

"Jessie," Bink says softly, "when will you go ahead with your life? You're too wonderful a woman to waste your life away being a chic on the side."

Jessie knows he's right, but she doesn't want to believe that all the love Benji has shown her is just for convenience. "I won't," she replies with a proclaimed assurance in her tone. "One day, Benji will come to his senses and make me his wife."

Wishful thinking for Jessie that sounds like a symphony orchestra to her own ears as the words melodiously flow from her mouth. For an instant, Jessie enjoys a stirring summer breeze of morning freshening delight emanate across her heart.

His wife. I like the way that sounds . . . I love you, Jessie. Will you marry me? Yes. She smiles at her intimate thoughts.

Hic.

Jessie prays that that was just a lung contraction and not a full-fledged hiccup. She rests her hand on her collarbone and sits still for a moment waiting . . . waiting . . . waiting.

Hic! . . . Hic.

"Oh god," she says.

"What? What's wrong?"

"I got the damn hicc . . ."

Hic. Her lungs interject.

"Hiccups. Now where'd that come from?" she continues.

Bink gets up to walk to the kitchen, while Jessie kicks her shoes off and lounges back on the cushion of her soft sofa. Lying back, she calls to Bink, whom she can hear rummaging in the refrigerator.

"Get me a glass of water, please."

"Umm . . . um . . . You got smothered turkey, string beans, and some more stuff. Who you be cookin' all this for?"

"For you. You about to eat it, ain't you?"

Bink comes back in the room and hands Jessie a tall glass of water and walks back into the kitchen and makes him a plate of food. After heating it up in the microwave, he comes back into the living room to find Jessie sound asleep, balled up in the corner of the sofa.

He sits beside her and eats his plate of food. There is a movie on the television, but he eats his food, never looking up. Once he finishes, he sits the plate down on the floor, lies back to rest his eyes, and falls fast asleep too.

When Bink opens his eyes again, Jessica is now coming out of her room down the end of the hall. She walks into the bathroom and closes the door. Bink raises his head and stands up. Jessica opens the door and steps out of the bathroom with a long nightgown, one that is transparent enough to see the silhouette of her robust physic. She turns and sees him standing at the end of the hallway. He's standing there, staring and lusting at her. Her gown is open and shows the roundness of her inner breast, revealing the brown outer skin of her nipples. His eyes slowly travel down to her midsection at the gap between her thighs. Bink can see a black patch of stringy pubic hairs. He begins to walk toward her, and Jessie continues to stand there, looking at him with desire in her eyes. Her long hair draping down her shoulders remind him of Apollonia. She is so beautiful! So sensual! He can't wait to reach her and press his lips on hers.

Every step he takes, he removes an article of clothing. Off comes the shirt. Off come the watch and his wife-beater T-shirt. He unbuckles his belt and snatches it out of his charcoal gray Dockers. He drops his pants and lifts his foot to yank his Hugo Boss loafers off. He nearly loses his balance but is able to get his foot back to the floor before he falls up against the wall.

Jessie puts her hands on her hip, spreading the bottom of her gown, fully revealing the bottom half of her body, then slides the gown off her shoulders, and drops her arms, allowing the gown to drop to her heels. Jessie appears as an angel of light in Bink's eyes. Her body is a perfect sculpture, but Bink can't understand why he can't seem to get any closer to her even though he's been walking toward her for what seems like a mile. Still she stands there, emitting a radiance that makes her skin glow. Her eyes are like ice, and he can feel himself starting to fall.

A shotgun barrel comes out of the bedroom door followed by a man with a firm grip on it. The man is Benji, and he's also naked.

"What are you doing here?" Benji's voice roars.

"Nothing man. Nothing."

"Well, nothing this?"

And Benji points the long barrel down at Bink's dangling sack and then a blast sounds, and Bink can see a big ball of fire shoot from the front of the gun, but he doesn't feel anything.

Bink opens his eyes, and he's sweating all over. His shirt is wet, and he's still lying on the couch. He reaches for his balls and the meager bulge is still there. Jessie is nowhere in sight, but his plate is still on the floor where he set it before he dozed off into dreamland. He swallows to put his heart back down where it belongs, then he sits up, and looks around, relieved that it was only a nightmare; however, he's still shaken up. He calls out to Jessie just to double check, because things looked so real, too vivid for him to have been in La-La land, but there's no answer. She's sound asleep in her Posturepedic king-size bed and has been since she was driven out of the living room by Bink's deafening snore.

He gets up and yawns as he stumbles to the door to leave, locking the doorknob behind him.

Chapter 9

Fatts and Daryl ride the front seat of a royal blue 1972 "deuce and a quarter" (Buick Electra) with smoked tinted windows. The interior is white with royal blue piping around the seats. The speakers are vibrating the loose metal on the car, making the car rattle every time the bass kicks in. They're on their way to the block where Lil Papi hangs out when they're all not together. From there, they'll leave to go back to their stake out location where they sat for hours the other night waiting for their next victim to show up. He never did, so today they're meeting up to try again.

The duffel bag with all their tools in it is sitting on the backseat, and it has something poking out the side of it. It's likely the AK that Lil Papi has orgasms over just staring at it. Inside, also are the vests, masks, and gloves. The Plank Walkers are on the front floor of the car along with a pair of handcuffs. Neither of them is saying anything. They're just listening to the loud music and thinking about whatever it is they're thinking about.

The sun is starting to set, and the weather is perfect for a cracked window. Daryl puts a brown cigar filled with some Arizona green to his lips and takes a heavy pull. The light at the tip blazes a fiery hot orange, and then it fades once he can't inhale anymore. He holds the smoke in his lungs as long as he can, and then exhales it slowly out of his mouth and nose. The weed is crucially strong and has Fatts and Daryl twisted like Billy Blisted. Daryl tries hard to hold back from choking but can't help it. He starts coughing and gagging violently until he's all teary eyed, and his throat makes a gross phlegm gagging sound. He heaves a glob from his throat and rolls the window down to spit it out. He hawk-spits a ball of mucus and saliva as hard as he can, hoping that the wind won't carry it against the side of the glistening paint job of the car.

He tried but not hard enough. The wind broke the glob up into a thousand particles, splattering it all over the side of the car like a modern painting. Fatts glares over at Daryl, daring him to have fouled up the torpedo launch. He doesn't say anything as he snatches the "bob" from his seemingly dying friend, and then he takes an apprehensive pull, testing the waters before taking an elephant-size whiff of the joint. He doesn't want to make the same mistake that Daryl made.

They turn down East Capitol Street, and then after a few blocks down they turn up Fifty-eighth Street. Blue and Lil Papi are standing under a streetlight attached to a lamppost that is the memorial of one of their fallen soldiers. Porky was murdered in the very spot where they're standing. There're at least fifty empty bottles of top-shelf liquor standing on the curb, grass, and sidewalk. Old deflated balloons sway to and fro as they're attached to green and red metallic balloon strings that are wrapped around the pole and some of the bottles. There's a Porky Pig stuffed animal hanging from the lamppost, and R.I.P. is spray painted on the wood in orange paint.

Blue has a Bob Marley joint of his own, and he passes it to Luther, who passes the bob that he already has in his other hand to Lil Papi. Fatts and Daryl walk over to the row house and sit on the step at the front door. They didn't know that Luther and Blue would already be there when they got there. This is perfect, no waiting around for anybody, and as soon as they're ready to leave, they can, with no delay.

"What's that joint hittin' on Lu," calls Daryl from the step.

"You don't need to know, you damn emphysema patient. Go suck on a respirator." Luther laughs at Daryl because he's always gagging on strong weed.

"Man, go suck a fat baby's . . . ," Daryl tries to respond but is interrupted.

"Why don't both of y'all suck my dick and pass the bob," Fatts interjects. "Can't neither one of y'all jone? Corny ass niggas."

"Blue. Where's the van?" asks Luther.

"In the lot over there."

"Let's roll then. We need to be in that parking spot before somebody takes it," Luther explains. "We missed him last time because he came home and left earlier than we thought he would. It's been three whole days."

It has been three days since they all set out from Fatts' mother's house on a mission to get their man. The dude they're trying to rob is a guy who's serving coke to half of uptown. His name is Toby, and he's had a nine-year run at it. He's never affected by the so-called cocaine droughts that fall upon the Washington-Baltimore area every two months when there's news of a major drug bust somewhere else in the world.

It can be a bust somewhere in Nova Scotia, and people will still be talking about there's a drought in DC. That's true for many, but that's only because their connect is full of crap. They say the prices are up, so they raise their prices without much argument. There's actually never an increase on the price they pay, but just in case there actually is a drought, they wouldn't want to have sold everything at a lesser price, missing out on a chance to make extra profit. That extra profit pays the bills when a real drought comes along. The word that there's a drought, fake or real, spreads as fast as the heat from the center of an atomic bomb explosion. Before anybody knows it, everybody with drugs are holding them or charging an outrageous price.

Toby, however, is never affected by the drought plagues. He never holds his product, and he never raises his prices. Well, if he does raise them, the price is still always under the going rate, so he has a loyal clientele base that controls mostly all of the highly profitable drug strips in his area. That means they're pumpin' out drugs like a fuel station. Also, Toby has never been busted or robbed according to the girl who has put Luther on his trail. She claims to know all about him and so far, she's been right on point. The problem isn't her information; it's their timing.

Luther is getting edgy because he knows all they have to do is get their dude in their hands, and he'll be counting over a hundred Gs, maybe two, for himself. Everybody's gonna be caked up off this one.

"Get the bag, Daryl. Time to go. Let's go," Luther says as he pats his hip checking for his Desert Eagle.

Daryl goes to the Buick and reaches in the backseat for the tool bag. The others cross the street and walk into an alley that leads into a small parking lot behind a row of project townhouses. They walk to a teal green Nissan Quest that has tinted windows on the rear and side glass but none on the two front windows. They all put their gloves on before reaching for the door handles to get in. Daryl comes straggling around the corner, hops in the back and then slides the door shut.

The radio stays off once they are in motion, and by the time Fatts turns onto Southern Avenue, headed southbound toward the old HOBO Shop, the van is filled with smoke and chatter about how the move has to go down, and how important it is that it goes down tonight.

The sun is almost submerged beneath the distant horizon's ridgeline, yet the sky is still illuminated by the burnt-orange reflection that volcanic ash creates when the sun's rays shine upon the earth's atmosphere at a forty-five-degree angle. Visibility is reduced just below daylight clarity, and children are still riding their bikes up and down the streets or playing on the sidewalks. However, the further they drive away from the inner city, the darker it gets and the less you see children playing outside.

As the Quest pulls into the community that the target lives in, the movement of the van slows to a crawl as they survey the area, checking for police cruisers that may be lying in the cut, waiting for a call to come over the radio for whatever crime that a person might commit is this quaint suburban community.

The van's lights are off as it is not yet imperative that they be on. The occupants relish in the anonymity, knowing that no one is taking a second look at them.

The van comes to an abrupt stop in the middle of the street. Everybody is startled, and they all look to see what has rattled Fatts, making him slam on brakes like that. Just then a pink plastic ball bounces out into the street right in front of the hood of the van, followed by a young girl holding onto a purple and pink jump rope. She's dragging it clean out into the street. No look. No stop. Nothing. She just balls out of the driveway into the street, right in front of the already stopped van.

Bonnnnnnk! Bomp. Bonnnnnnk!

The child freezes, stopping right in front of the van, facing it with her brown eyes bulging and her braids dangling. She is about eight years old with a butter-pecan complexion. Her mouth is hanging wide, and she's missing at least two of her teeth.

"Dumb ass little . . . ," a voice shouts from the van.

"Look before you go running out into the street," says another.

"I should get out, spank you, and take you to your mother," says the first voice.

The van remains motionless while the petrified little girl, wearing a red and white Powerpuff Girls shirt, makes a horridly squeamish face, appearing as if she's just been slimed. She slowly leans over to pick up the jump rope that she was dragging before she had the daylights scared out of her, and then she continues toward her ball that has rolled under a car that is parked across the street from the driveway she came out of.

"Get the ball for her somebody," sparks Fatts.

Luther gets out of the van and pulls his gloves off and lays them in his seat. He and the little girl meet each other at the ball. She shyly looks up at him with tears in her eyes. He grins pleasantly and shakes his head, then bends over, and yanks the ball from between the under carriage of the car and the asphalt. He rips the ball from the clutches of the car's grip and then gently hands the ball to the little girl. He seems like a tower to her as he stands up above her.

"Thank you," she says in a soft monotone and then starts to walk back to her yard, once again, without looking to see if the coast is clear to venture out into the thoroughfare of the street. She has her eyes glued on Luther as she walks away.

"Wait," he says looking both ways up and down the street, "you have to stop walking out into the street like that. Make sure you look both ways. You're too pretty to be run over by a big bad car. OK?"

"OK," she says, turning to look up the street gingerly, sticking her head beyond the van to see if a car is coming up the street. She sees her next-door neighbor's white Mercedes Benz coming up the street in the distance.

"Luther! Get in the damn car! Here he comes," shouts Fatts.

Luther looks to his left and then back down at the little girl in front of him. "Wait for the car to pass, then run in the house, and be careful," he pleads.

Luther gets in the van, careful not to touch anything, and they all put their masks on. There's no time to put on the rest of the gear they have in the duffel bag, so Daryl just pulls out the AK and slides it into Lil Papi's lap. Luther puts his gloves on and slams the door. The Benz passes by, and the little girl runs across the street and stops at the curb to turn around and looks back at the van. Fatts pulls off slowly, trying to time his approach toward the 600 Coupé Benz that is pulling in the driveway of the single-family home next door to the one in front of which they are sitting.

The little girl waves, but her vigor fades wearily. Her eyes squint, and her face is a guise of confusion because the faces she saw a moment ago that reminded her of her uncles and older cousins have now changed. The man in the driver's seat looks more like someone out of a movie that she's seen her mommy and daddy watching.

My daddy has a DVD movie like them. Heat?

She watches the van pull into the driveway of her next-door neighbor, but it stops short of fully entering the yard. Feet drop out of the opposite side of the van and scampers toward the house. She can't see the driver's door of the van because of the hedge that divides the neighbor's yard from her family's. She can, however, hear deliberate voices but can't quite make out exactly what they're saying.

" . . . . uck down . . . see your . . . !"

"Alright . . . got it . . ."

Then suddenly, she hears nothing. She feels that there is something very wrong and thinks she should go tell her mother.

"Mommy, Mommy," the little girl calls urgently, running into the open garage toward a door leading into the house. Pounding the door as she enters the house, she turns for the kitchen where she finds her mother sitting at the kitchen nook, reading her horoscope out of the *Washington*

Post. "Mommy! Some men with 'head' masks on their faces went in that man's yard next door."

Her mother looks at her nonchalantly. "What?" she murmurs, waiting for a response to her question. She looks back at the newspaper, wrinkling her eyebrow to pinpoint the spot on the page she had been reading before she was so rudely interrupted.

"The men next door, Mommy . . . ," not wanting to tell her mother too much about how she came to take notice of them in the first place, she says "they . . . looked scary, and the man next door just . . ."

"Shanique, what did I tell you about that man next door? He is up to no good and that you are to stay away . . ."

"I know, Mommy, but the men in the van . . ."

"Look! The men in the van, if they came to see him, they're certainly up to no good too. Mind your business and stay away from that house . . . Do I have to make you play in the backyard?"

Defeated, Shanique lowers her head, looks down at the mahogany and white no-wax tile floor, and mutters, "No, ma'am."

"Did you bring our toys in the house? It's getting dark outside. Time to come in, anyway."

"Yes, ma'am. I'll go get them."

She slowly mopes back outside and out to the sidewalk. She looks down the sidewalk and can still see the van sitting there. Now it is virtually dark outside, and no one is outside on the whole street of her quiet block. She lives in the Marlboro Meadows Community Development in Upper Marlboro, Maryland. The community has long had a reputation of housing drug lords who move here from the city, calling themselves moving way out into the boondocks, but that notion couldn't be farther from the truth. Marlboro Meadows is like uptown Landover. Cats from inner city DC are so green when it comes to the Maryland suburbs, and Toby is finding out right now that he didn't hide good enough from DC's most shady.

Chapter 10

Inside the house, Toby is lying on the kitchen floor. There is a Nike gym bag open on the wooden countertop, resting between the sink and a tall black refrigerator. The ceiling fan is spiraling in high propulsion, and the lights are on in every room as well as the flame on the stove. The flame is heating a knife blade while Luther twirls it round and round, looking down with a sinister glare at the bound and gagged Toby, who is mumbling over and over through a scarf that is tied in such a way as to expose his lips and teeth, "That's all I got. I swear. That's all I got."

In the bag on the counter are five kilos of coke wrapped individually in complex conglomerations of plastic, rubber, bounce fabric softener sheets, and packed with petroleum gel. Accompanying the bricks is seventy-eight thousand dollars in cash, bundled up in stacks of five thousands. This money, he had planned on dropping off at the house before going to meet his next customer, who was going to be waiting for him at the Popeye's Chicken in the Eastover Shopping Center parking lot in Oxon Hill, Maryland, just across the district line.

"Yeah. Sure you're right," Luther heckles. "Nigga, we know you got some real scrilla around here somewhere. Way more than that lunch money over there in that bag. We got all night, joe. If you wanna play games . . . we can play," he says looking at the knife that is starting to turn red hot from the glow of searing metal.

Toby blinks, his thoughts cast him off into a comatose state, seeing visions of the men standing around him, ambushing his girlfriend coming in the front door. Snapping back to reality, he looks at the Spanish marksman that is aiming the big machine gun at him as if there was a possibility that he could break free from the handcuffs, get up, and disarm all five men before Luther can jab that scorching hot blade into his flesh. No way, but still Lil Papi hasn't even blinked. He has every intention of ripping this dude to shreds if he tries anything.

Why is this guy so pressed to keep aiming that damn gun at me? These niggas gonna probably kill me if I don't give them that money soon. But naw, forget that. How much money do they expect a nigga to have at his house at one time? They got bricks in the bag. A key a piece and then some. Plus about ten thousand a piece. That's enough. How much money do they think they're supposed to get on a move? These niggas are greedy. I ain't givin' them my stash. They just gonna have to kill me, Toby thinks in subtle defiance. He surveys his captors before closing his eyes to play possum. He sees them all just standing there—five big black cookie monsters that have just gobbled him up and are about to devour him. No one is searching the house for more money, no ransacking or plundering of his expensive diamonds in his bedroom, and no larceny of expensive electronics. Nothing of the sort. They all are just looking at him, eyes calm and nonthreatening. Cool as can be, except for, of course, the irreverent Luther, with eyes of malevolent antagonism. Besides him, everyone is just plainly staring down at him. A diabolic ambience consumes the room.

These niggas are crazy. They're gonna torture me. "Look, man, I'm telling you. That's all I got." *Look at 'em. Just standin' there. Do they even hear me? Do they understand the words coming out of my mouth?* Toby wonders while at the same time trying to talk the men into believing that what he has in the bag is all that he has in the house. "I'll take you to where my stash is in the city . . . Come on, man, I got over a hundred thousand more dollars and about another ten keys there."

He's not lying either, but Luther has been informed by his girl that Toby has more money than she's ever seen in her life right there at his house. Luther lifts the knife from the flame and holds it up like a test tube. Smoke ascends from the glowing metal, and then he looks at Blue and nods his head. Blue sits Toby up and holds his arms straight out in front of him. Fatts doesn't like when Luther tortures people, but he knows that's the only way to make most niggas tell the truth.

Fatts walks out the kitchen and goes into the other room to turn on the radio. He turns the volume up loud enough to make the dishes in the sink vibrate and fall to a more stable position. Toby's eyes are golf balls on his face, and his breathing is bordering hyperventilation. Luther kneels down beside Toby and looks him in his eyes, dangling the piping hot knife less than an inch from Toby's bare forearm. He inches the knife closer, and the blazing heat literally disintegrates the hairs sprouting from his skin.

"Hslhoo, hslhoo, hslhoo." Toby breathes frantically, almost as if he's trying to blow out the metal torch that's singing the hairs on his arm. "OK! OK! OK!" Toby blabbers through the scarf, "I'll give it po you!" His words are garbled because of the scarf and his fear.

Still holding the knife calmly in place, Luther spreads a sinister grin under his mask. The smile is evident by the way his eyes are squinted so tightly. "Where is it?"

Toby fumbles with his words, while Blue tightened the grip on his hands. Daryl walks behind Toby and unties the gag.

"In the deep freezer. Look in the bottom of the deep freezer under the pork chops. Please, man, just take it. Don't kill me, please. I'll get it back, then maybe y'all will be able to rob me again, but if you kill me, what good would that do? There's more under the baseboard, under the cabinet, right there. Altogether it's over eight hundred. Maybe more," Toby blurts out all in one breath.

"Well, why'd you make our job so hard? Why'd you have to go and lie?" asks Luther.

"Man, I had to try my hand. Wouldn't you have done the same thing? It's all good. Y'all come off today. I ain't mad at you . . . Just don't kill me, man. Y'all ain't got to kill me."

Luther raises the knife away while Daryl goes over to the cabinet to check for the money. He opens the cabinet, snatches all the cleaning products, trash bags, and miscellaneous kitchen oddities and slews them across the floor.

"How do you open this thing," Daryl asks. "Fatts?!" he yells.

Benji turns the volume down on the radio and yells from the other room. "Y'all call me?"

"Yeah," Daryl and Blue call out simultaneously.

"Come help me with this," he grumbles as he tries to fumble with the cabinet floor. "How do you open this thing, slim?"

"Just find the hole against the sidewall panel and pull it up, and the freezer is in the room he just came out of," Toby says, directing his attention to Benji as he comes through the door.

"Freezer? Something's in the deep freezer," Benji asks, stopping in his tracks and turning to revisit the family room he just came out of.

"All righty then," exclaims Daryl with extreme delight. He pulls on a clear plastic bag filled with Franklin faces, big and small.

Lil Papi turns away from Toby for the first time since they entered the man's yard. He lowers his gun and marvels at the incredulous laundry in the bag.

"Today is a very good day," he says in Spanish. Papi puts his gun on the floor and reaches inside of his jacket. Blue releases Toby's hands when he sees the duct tape emerge from Lil Papi's pocket. Papi steps over to Toby, removes the cuffs, and then hog-ties his hands and feet with the tape. This part of the process brings a feeling of relief to Toby, to see all of the men moving in frantic preparation for departure. Getting tied up with the tape is a reassuring prospect that his prayers may be answered, and he just might survive.

Thank you, Lord. Thank you so much. Please just let these niggas leave. I don't care nothing about that money. I just wanna live. Please.

Chapter 11

A valley of monumental proportions cascades as far as the eyes can see. There are episodes of clustered hills of seemingly pure white snow, but there's no snow at all covering the enchanting terrain located at the base of the valley walls. Soft, shimmering water flows down the steep walls of this imposing valley from a source that is nowhere to be found. There's no river, no ocean, no spring, or geyser. There's not even a melting glacier from which the water could be flowing. How could it be? There's no sun even to melt such a glacier, yet light permeates the entire surface of everything in visibility.

How can this water overwhelm every single inch of this vast valley's walls and have no apparent water supply to facilitate the continued gushing of googillions of gallons of sparkling clear, smooth flowing water that make no sound as it rushes around large crystal-clear boulders that pimple the wall of the valley like a teenage valedictorian? The stones are flawless diamonds, glistering bright as a lighthouse beacon shining in the darkness of night. But there is no darkness here. There are no clouds or moon. There's not even a shadow to be found on either side of the tallest object.

The sky doesn't exist. What's up is sideways. What's down is up. Gravity is an assumption, for relativity is merely a pleasurable requirement for the fantasies of the inhabitants that exist in this pacific, enthralling place. The laws that govern our universe, such as gravity and inertia have no jurisdiction here; there is no star to glorify in this enchantment because the light in this world is its essence. The light is all that will ever consume the open spaces of this place, and *beautiful* is the world that insults the sublimity of its magnificence.

From a proximity perpendicular to the base of the valley floor, above in the far distance, maybe thousands of miles, there is another land mass, only its seems suspended in midair. The mass is too far away for the human eye to appreciate the details of its surface, but it's obviously a mountainous region. There are specimens in sight, and they appear to be doves—white doves, flying in a great multitude, approaching the valley at a velocity that would penetrate the sound barrier, causing a rapid succession of sonic booms if sound was a reality here.

But here, no sound is to be heard. Sound is an action rather than a reaction, which means sound doesn't occur as a result of movement and collision, rather it is produced by the beings that have the power to conjure up its usefulness, if it had any, but it doesn't. Sound is nothing but noise that is totally unnecessary in this splendid peacefulness, where communication is done via telepathy.

The winged creatures approach the valley in a swooping glance of the fluid-drenched walls, splashing a tidal wave of water that is carried away in a convection that trails the enormous swarm. The mighty creatures are not doves at all, too big to be such. They have the likeness of man, but their bodies glow and are abnormally huge. Each of the creatures is over eleven feet tall, and the proportions of their robust extremities are the envy of any Schwarzenegger-wanna-be. They have wings of eagles, protruding from their backs and have feet of pure gold. Their wings are soft as marshmallows, yet tough as silk fence, and the faces of these creatures resemble that of every wild beast of the field, including man. Their eyelids remain shut, giving them the appearance that they are fast asleep, only they aren't. They're fully aware of everything around them as they browse the sanctuary of the white terrain like flamingos in a riverbed basking in the freshness of a cool breeze. These peaceful beings have blissful expression on their faces and sporting smiles of the Mona Lisa engraved across their faces. The upper realm devolves extreme delight to all its inhabitants that are privileged to its domain.

These creatures are cherubim, servants to the Omega, and the brothers of Apollyon, who is the Lord of them all, answering only to the Almighty himself. The Omega, is the Ancient of Days. The one whom no one else is greater.

And as for the cherubim, they are basking in peace for the time, for they well know that the Great Day of the Omega's fury is fast approaching. That day will be a period of war, both in the heavens and upon the earth, when the sovereignty of their father will be vindicated and brought to its completion. Iblis and his lesser brethren will battle the likes of these cherubim for the last time but will by no means prevail, and the powerful Iblis will be no match for Apollyon and his myriad, and they will certainly vanquish Iblis and his follower, throwing them into a state of unconsciousness for a thousand years, unable to bring calamity upon a soul.

Millions of light aeons away from this valley, the Omega communicates with Apollyon. They are not alone. There are even mightier creatures than the cherubim in their midst. These are seraphim, and they stand around the Omega's throne with their faces covered by their wings. Here, there is no valley, no water, or giant boulders. There is nothing remotely similar to anything in nature—just these beings are in the presence of majesty and indescribable, unapproachable light broadcasting from the Omega. There is no way of being able to tell how big or small he is. No way of deciphering a shape or contour. One can only see light laced with every color of the rainbow. Light that is blinding to even the cherubim who were created to keep perfect order in the Omega's magnificent kingdom, which may explain why their eyelids remain sealed shut all the time. When the Omega summons them, they beckon his call at a speed faster that they can close their eyes, causing unbearable pain and suffering; therefore, they keep them shut in anticipation of his call.

Apollyon, on the other hand, is unaffected by the sight of his father and is able to look at him at great length before needing to turn aside in submission to his greatness. Now, he submissively stares into the lower area of the light, seldom setting his focus on the upper area of his father's magnificence for much longer than a thought as the Omega confides a troubling revelation.

My most highly regarded, truly I say to you, members of your lesser fold have brought to mind questions defiant of my grand purpose. My son, only because of the love that I have is why their existence has found refuge to this very moment. Now go. Seek those who have brought my glee to a low that I do not recall since your equal fell in love with his own bestowed beauty and strength and questioned my authority. Do not take leisure, for I can still hear the thoughts that they dare not communicate to one another but keep to themselves, and my wrath is being held back with long-suffering and undeserved kindness that is only reserved for weak flesh. Now, go before I annihilate them.

The spirits of the upper realm all pray for the day to come about when their kingdom will be rid of Ibis and his army of evil cherubim, jinn, and analim, making way for a sin-free existence, but some of the more powerful spirit creatures, namely the cherub, feel that the kingdom should not have to wait until an event occurs on the earth before the Great War to banish all badness is waged. Many fathom that the spirit realm should be cleansed immediately; then the true servants of the Most High may be able to enjoy a peaceful existence and receive all the blessings that the Creator has to offer.

So Apollyon takes off to a desolate place in the upper realm where there's nothing but infinite light. Pure unadulterated whiteness surrounds Apollyon in every direction. He stands in an upright position, yet his feet rest upon nothing. He is founded sternly on the empty space below him—the whiteness.

Apollyon raises his hands above his head like a graceful ballerina, and then slams them back down to his side with a thunderous clap followed by a verbal command that emits a shower of sparks out of his mouth.

"Faquatwo lu elim akize im fatwal," he shouts in a language not known in the material realm.

In an instant, myriad upon myriad of Apollyon's likeness appears in his midst all with expressions of terror that consumed them the very moment their bliss was disturbed by the thunderous sound of the voice of the mighty Lord. The stun has pilfered all courage that was embedded in their souls and grips their demeanor with the greatest severity, causing them all to open their eyes to see firsthand the rage that has conquered their beloved prince of peace. Why has he summoned them to such a distant reach of their realm, to the ends of nothingness where even the one seated upon the throne has not ventured since times indefinite, even times before Apollyon, the firstborn, was installed at the hands of the Alpha and the Omega?

A multitude that no number can explain stands frozen in fear before their Lord, waiting for him to communicate his thoughts, hopefully not verbally. Apollyon scans the faces of his brethren, and the compassion he has for them subsides the rage within him. He calms himself so that he can communicate with them so as not to strike fear in them anymore than he already has. He closes his eyes and muses over what he must say to reassert their father's plans for the coming new kingdom.

Chapter 12

It's a bright sunny day. Not an intruding cloud in the whole expanse that stretches above the industrial horizon in the clearing. It reminds one of a deep blue sea. A hawk of some sort circles around a wooded area, appearing to have found its prey or possibly the carcass of a road-kill victim on a nearby street.

There's a chain-linked fence, topped with razor wire, encompassing the yard where Lil Chucky, dressed in his blues, is sitting on a bench next to a dude named Koca Moe. Lil Chucky is actually John. It's been nearly eight months since John first came to this jail, and Benji has grown quite fond of him.

Anyway, John, who's now called Lil Chucky by all the guys on the compound, has been hanging with Koca Moe all day in Benji's absence. Benji has gone back up. His appeal is being heard on his case back at the court in Prince George's County, so he won't be back until maybe next week. Hopefully, he'll be going home. Meanwhile, Koca Moe, who looks like a black Mr. Clean with his bald head, white T-shirt, and friendly smile has become somewhat of a refuge for Lil Chucky while Benji's away.

The two of them are watching Mark as he bench-presses 220 pounds in repetitions of ten. Mark is pumping the iron with constant, steady power, pushing away from his chest, inhaling as he brings the bar back down to touch his diaphragm, and bouncing it slightly to start its unfaltering incline to his arm's length locked position. Ten muscle busting rep; up, then down; up, then down, expelling sweat and saliva into the air above his face through determined lips until he reaches ten, and then looks over his head to find the bar's nesting place.

"Wooooo," Mark calls out in a satisfied way as he stands up and swings his arms backward and forward stretching his massive pythons. "Man . . . that felt good. What you gonna do, Coke? You ain't gonna ever get like this babysitting."

"Aw, nigga. I might not be as bulky as you are, but your physique has a ways to go to measure up to the standards of something I'm trying to reach for . . . Believe that," Koca Moe recants.

"Oh, yeah?" replies Mark. "Well, don't talk me to death. Show me what you can do with them dumbbells. Mr., I want a body like Tony Atlas." Mark continues sarcastically, "I don't see you breakin' your neck to lie down on that bench." Koca Moe isn't a little guy, but he could use some buffing up to go along with his good looks and smooth, dark, brown skin. He's not enthused about joining Mark,s gym, but Mark won't let up, always insisting that he should workout with him. "You need to work out, read a book or something, and stop running around here messing with these punks and fags. They gonna give you the bug if they already haven't. Come on and join my gym so you can build those muscles up, so when you get out next year and hit the beach, you can flex on them bammas and drive the girls wild."

Mark nags him every day, so Koca Moe submits sometimes, but he refuses to get into full swing, neither does he intend to. He only works out from time to time to shut Mark up for a change. Pumping iron is how Mark gets through his time, and he's done it every single day for the past six years. Koca Moe and Mark were friends on the street, so Koca Moe feels obligated to work out with him sometimes.

"I'll be right back, shorty," Koca Moe says to Lil Chucky. "Let me go over here and show this fool that he ain't the only he-man around here."

"Yeah, right . . . We'll see if you got some He-man in you. Two twenty. Think you can handle that partner? Ten reps straight. No arm standing or else I'ma push them jonts down on you and break your ribs," Mark warns as Koca Moe lays his back down on the bench and places his hands in a comfortable position on the bar.

"Nigga . . . I can do two twenty with your mama's arms. What you talkin' about Willis? . . . Man, I got this. Come on," Koca Moe commands sharply, motioning Mark to lift the weights so he can reserve his strength for the ten agonizing reps his arms and chest are about to endure.

Koca Moe does the first five with flowing ease, but the sixth rep comes up a little slower than the former, and number seven brings an arch to his back to begin the next heave. Mark can see he is struggling and steps to Koca Moe's head as if he's daring him to hold the weights in an arm-locked position for more than a second.

The eighth rep has Koca Moe breathing like a track star running a fifty-yard dash in second place and giving it all he has to just tie the race, and he's starting to think he'll never make it through nine without bursting a blood vessel.

"Come on, Coke, you can do it," cheers on Lil Chucky getting up from the bench to get closer to the strong-man contest. "Push Coke. Just two more to go!"

Damn! Two? Koca Moe thinks to himself.

This eighth one he's pushing is taking everything he can muster as the iron barbells reach another hilt before descending back down to his chest.

"Heut!" Koca Moe grunts as he power-drives rep number nine toward an arm-locked position. His body is trembling, and the barbells are moving in slow motion as if the air above him somehow has turned into sand making it impossible to move this object that only moments ago moved fast and freely through the same two-foot area on its way down to his chest.

"Aghhh!" screams Koca Moe within the final inch of reaching the top of the rep, but he knows there is one more left, and that scream was really an acknowledgement of that fact.

A small audience is forming to see what the commotion is all about. The faces of the men are poised for an eruption of laughter in the event that Koca Moe bonks, or worse, gets crushed by the weights doing its utmost to resist his constant effort to force them to go in the opposite direction of Moe's chest. It's evident that the only one rooting for Koca Moe's success is Lil Chucky. Everybody else is dying to get a good laugh for the day, and Koca Moe knows it, and he refuses to be an object of ridicule for the next five days, so in order to complete this last rep, he awakens a willingness from deep inside himself that he's never before called upon. The arch in his back is convex enough to go in a McDonald's magazine ad as Koca Moe begins the final push.

"You can do it, champ. You can do it, push . . . push," Lil Chucky urges.

"He ain't gonna make it," says a shirtless lanky black guy resting a basketball under his arm.

The antagonism that Mark was displaying toward Koca Moe has now changed its tone. Mark is shouting at the top of his lungs, pressing him on like Apollo Creed, clutching his fist and motivating Moe to win the fight against his own agonizing body. "Push that thang boy, Push it! You big chump! Push it! . . . Don't think . . . Push!"

"That nigga 'bout to die," someone remarks aloud.

Phueeeet goes the sound of a rupturing gas bubble as it blasts out of Koca Moe's butt.

"Uuuah," someone shouts in disgust, followed by an outbreak of laughter.

"Grab it, grab it," pleads Koca Moe only four inches away from victory, farting again while he strains to keep the weights from crashing down on him.

Mark grabs the middle of the bar and two other laughing black men grab both sides of the bar's ends. Lil Chucky had even made a move to help but stopped short once he saw the big boys come to the rescue. The men raise the weights to the bar's resting place on the stand, and the limp Koca Moe lies on the bench with both arms flailed to the side hanging lifelessly from their sockets.

He's exhausted beyond his comprehension. The world around him is spinning so he closes his eyes to make it stop, but he still feels as if he's floating in a time warp. Destination, Jablip.

He lies there until he starts to breathe normal and all the hecklers have teed off on him for five minutes straight. Preparing to get up from his folly, Koca Moe opens his eyes and sees his little buddy standing there quietly, not saying a word, waiting to make sure Koca Moe is all right.

"You almost made it," Lil Chucky says warmly like a little brother.

Koca Moe slowly rises to an upright position on the bench and extends his hand to give Lil Chucky a grateful brother-man handshake for his inspirational exertions that got him through rep eight and nine. "Thanks, dog. I appreciate that. I got something for you in my box too, if you're hungry."

"All right. Cool."

The workout crushed Koca Moe, and the effect it has left on his energy-robbed body reminds him of the first time he had an ejaculation when he was quite young. He thinks back to that time he experimented with the girl that was staying the weekend with his family while her parents were gone to Jamaica, and the thoughts conjure up lustful thoughts in his heart as he looks at Lil Chucky. He doesn't really care about the poor kid, and now with Benji away from the jail unable to guard his vulnerable friend, Chucky is unknowingly becoming prey.

Hate to do it to you youngin, but I need to feel some virgin ass.

The thought has Koca Moe's johnson bone hard. He can't wait to carry out his rape. Contriving joy has rejuvenated him and as he and Lil Chucky go into the building, he playfully holds Chucky's head under his armpit. Little does Lil Chucky know that he's taking part in foreplay.

Chucky goes straight to the bathroom, and Koca Moe goes to his bunk, where he reaches into his locker and grabs a couple of cakes, and then he walks over to the far wall to the counseling room. This puts him in the path that Lil Chucky has to walk to get to his sleeping quarters from the bathroom. There he waits patiently for his prey.

"Coke! What the hell you up to?" yells Mark an aisle away.

He doesn't answer. He just looks at Mark and nods up and down. Mark pierces his eyes at him as a disgusting thought comes to mind from the sight of those Looney Dune cakes in Moe's hand. He turns to his right and looks up the aisle at the hapless poor boy that is about to be traumatized by a man that Mark can't go against in a situation like this. He pitifully looks back at his friend and then drops his head in reproach. He raises his head again and then says, "You're on your own, dog."

Koca Moe knows that that means if the little guy tells anyone what happens to him and the Aryans come for him, he won't be able to count on his main man for assistance, but his lust cripples his better judgment, and with Benji gone to court for his modification hearing, there's no one to stop him from receiving his prize. His heart starts to pound from anticipation, and his mouth is watering like a big bad wolf. He doesn't swallow the fluids in his mouth because he plans to use it for lubrication.

"Hey, Lil Chucky," he calls out holding up the cakes, "here you go, buddy."

Chapter 13

Benji sits in the bullpen waiting to be transferred back to his dormitory in the building next door. He will be released today after almost five years of incarceration. He'll miss his friends here but not the daily routine of doing the same thing every single day. He can't wait to get back to his plush lifestyle of Persian rugs, luxury sports cars, high-class restaurants, and excursions with the two women in his life, especially Jessie. They have so much fun together.

"Hey, man, y'all can let me go back and pack up while y'all do all that paperwork. I'm trying to get the hell out of here. My ride is outside."

For twelve minutes or so, no one responds to Benji's pleas until a female guard he's been sweet on comes by and hangs her hands through the bars.

"So you're leaving me without getting a taste of the berry, huh?" she asks in a low seductive voice.

The woman is pretty for a jail corrections officer, and she's been planning on giving Benji a shot the first chance she got, but she thought she had plenty of time to make that happen. Benji always gives her compliments on how beautiful her lips are. He never really was thinking that he would ever have a chance to be with her in any way, but charm is a part of his constant efforts to get what he wants, even in jail.

"Ms. Jackson, how are you?"

"Fine as you look," she answers.

"Um, better not say that too loud, or my jealous girlfriend might hear you. She's right outside, and she has good ears."

"Oh, is that her in the white Lexus?"

"Yeah. I'm sure."

"Humph. Well, I guess I can't walk you back and step in a room on the way. You might not have any left for her by the time you get home."

"I guess not," he smiles as he responds.

"Well, I guess I'll walk you back anyway, but you can at least get one of those kisses you always said you needed."

Benji grabs his bag lunch he brought from the courthouse and walks to the bars where Ms. Jackson is unlocking the bar door. "You'd better be careful, Ms. Jackson. You could lose your job for messing around with the inmates."

"Yeah, I guess you're right. You sure are lucky. You're getting away before I got my hands on you. I had big plans for that thing in your pants. Maybe you'll be back one day."

"Not in your dreams!"

They walk down a long corridor to a door that is locked, and she has to call control to open it. Once through the door, she escorts him to the F dorm where the fellas are doing what they're always doing—talking on the telephone, watching TV, listening to the radio, playing cards or chess, and working out, but there is something not so normal about his friend Lil Chucky. If Benji goes to the infirmary for an hour, Lil Chucky acts as if Benji left the country to serve in a war, but Benji's been off to face something worse than a needle. He went to face a judge in Upper Marlboro, Maryland. And Lil Chucky shows no sign of concern or glee toward Benji. The high-spirited glow that embellishes his facial expression whenever he sees Benji after a long period of time is absent, and it tells Benji that something really bad has happened to his little buddy. Benji sees John, not Lil Chucky in the face of the kid lying on the bed next to his.

The distinctly depressing look on John's face tells Benji immediately that someone has tricked the boy and has obviously threatened to kill him if he says a word to anyone. That would explain why the dorm is still in one piece, unless Tom is to blame for John's dismay, but that is most unlikely. Benji knows he can't leave without getting to the bottom of this, but that may take all night, and Salina is outside already, waiting for him to walk out the door. Benji's eyes dart around the room looking for a face that shows guilt or even acknowledgment of willingness to drop a kite for him to pick up.

Benji turns to Lil Chucky and says, "What's up, dog? I'm going home, thanks to you."

John knew he would be coming back with news like that, and he's happy for him inside, but his depression won't allow him to show it on the outside. He can only muster a half smile and a glance at Benji, knowing that unless he killed himself or checked into protective custody, there would be many more days like this once Benji hits the high road.

Benji takes a moment to reflect, then he says, "Don't worry. It'll never happen again."

John looks at Benji, sure that he will find out who put him through his pain and humiliation without him having to say a word. As Benji walks toward Mark's bunk, a smile creeps across John's face, and for a moment he feels like living again.

"Mark! Don't play no games with me, man," Benji commands. His face is delirious and his eyes are filled with tears of anger. "What the hell happened to my youngin?"

Mark is lying on his bunk taking a nap. He raises his head and frowns in confusion, "What the hell are you talking about? What happened to who?"

Of course, he knows exactly who he's talking about and what happened to him, but he sure plays it off well. Benji can see that Mark has been asleep for a while because of the welt on the side of his face from the impression the pillow left in his skin. He doesn't want to put his friend under the gun and besides, he might not have any idea of the foul play that has unfolded anyway.

"Man, one of these faggy . . . ass . . . niggas did something to lil' shorty. I swear, I'ma kill somebody!" Benji is irate, and he knows that one of the onlookers knows what has happened, and he's scanning their faces for a clue, something.

Bingo.

Benji gets a nod from a known fag who has been victimized by Koca Moe and others around the Cut's compound. The guy gets up off his bunk and walks over toward the phones. On the way, he drops a piece of paper so that the trailing Benji can pick it up.

Benji stops at the kite, and then looks around to see if anybody is paying any attention to him and the move the fag made. Of course, everyone is staring because he's Benji, he's just come back from court and no one has heard the news of whether or not he's going home.

Damn, he says in his mind as he grills the nosey dudes in their eyes until they all look away. He looks down then bends over to pick up the kite and takes it to the bathroom so he can read and react to the tip in private. He opens the folded piece of paper but isn't that surprised at the name written therein.

Koca Moe.

"Oh yeah?"

Calmly, Benji drops the kite into the toilet, flushes, and leaves the restroom. He walks over to a man at the phone. This is the same guy who always gives Benji the phone whenever he's on it, cutting many of his calls short on a regular basis. The man, once again, cuts his call short, but Benji doesn't even want the phone; he only wants to ask a favor of the guy. Benji whispers something into the man's ear, and he responds positively. Almost as if this is the moment he's been waiting for all his life, or maybe he's been looking for a reason to get at Koca Moe for a long time. This man's name is Quack; he's a cold-blooded killer, and Benji has just put him on a murder mission.

Across the large room, Benji can see Koca Moe by Lil Chucky's bed saying something to him. That only reconfirms what Benji already knows. Now there's no question in his mind about what has happened, and it'll all be taken care of for the little fella. He won't have to worry about Koca Moe or anybody else after Benji's gone.

Benji walks toward his bunk to pack his belongings, and Koca Moe walks away before Benji can get anywhere near them. Little does he know, he'll be called by a new name soon—Done Deal.

John doesn't feel like the confident Lil Chucky that Benji had labeled him by. Now that Benji has bid him his final farewell, hugged him, and left him with a shipload of commissary snacks, he feels that he won't be able to survive his stay here at the Cut. Being raped by someone he thought was a friend has made him feel that he can trust no one, and with Benji out of the picture, it's open season on him now. He has no one to lean on for protection, not even the Aryans, who have labeled him a wigger since he's always around the blacks. Wiggers are hated by supremacist more so than non-whites are because they're looked down upon as traitors, earning names like Benedict Arnold and Zebra. John has heard Arnold a few times, but he's ignored it and moved on. Now, he wishes he'd have joined their clique. Too late now. He's on his own and will have to settle for being Koca Moe's sex slave unless he kills himself or better kills Koca Moe. John, however, doesn't know where to start in the matter of premeditated murder. Sure, he killed his father all right, but that was a big accident. It doesn't take a coldhearted killer to pull a trigger, but stabbing a man to death sure does. That requires a different kind of animal. An animal that doesn't live in John, so he may as well get used to lollipops and corks.

But wait. What is this that John is seeing? A black guy is reaching up to the ceiling and pulling down the white bucket. He's passing around objects to three other men. John feels perspiration dripping from his underarms.

I didn't say anything. Why are they going to kill me? Please, I don't wanna die. Where's Koca Moe? I gotta tell him that I didn't say anything.

John hops to his feet and races down the aisle as quickly as he can. He turns left down the cross path that connects the aisles together. He can see the four men spreading out coming in his direction. John's heart is racing faster than his feet are moving, and the pounding is hurting his chest.

Koca Moe. Gotta tell him I didn't say anything. I don't wanna die.

John turns left up the B wing, reaches Koca Moe's bed, and finds him lain back, taking a nap. John is about to reach for Koca Moe's foot and call out his name when he's grabbed from behind by a man that is standing nearby. The man has his hair in dreadlocks and is wearing a sky blue T-shirt and a pair of navy blue shorts. He's a stocky shorty guy, and he has a firm hold on John.

"Ko . . ." John tries, but the man covers his mouth. Just then the four stalkers are coming and are very near. John nearly faints from the thought of death and closes his eyes, because he doesn't want to witness his own mutilation. Nothing happens. Suddenly . . . *Puka, puka, puka, puka . . ,.* "Aggh, Aggh! Aggh . . . Y'all mother . . . aggh!"

The sound of the massacre fills the air, and John opens his eyes and is appalled at what he sees. The four henchmen are jabbing the sharp objects into the chest, neck, head, stomach and back of Koca Moe. Repeatedly and unremorsefully, they pummel the screaming slab. They seem possessed in the appearance of their glaring eyes and gnashing teeth. The overlapping of their pounding upon the body of Koca Moe sounds a lot like a bunch of kids beating the dust out of an area rug hanging across a clothesline. The horrific sound is accompanied by a fading squeal until the body of their victim becomes a bloody heap, and all movements and signs of life disappears. Oh, he's dead.

Thanks Benji, thinks Lil chucky as a boyish grin spreads slowly across his face. And just like that, John is back to feeling like Lil Chucky again.

Chapter 14

On the stove, a large gray pot of Maryland crabs are steaming next to a forty-ounce bottle of Miller Genuine Draft, Old Bay Seasoning, garlic powder, vinegar, and an open bottle of Imperial Nectar Champagne, Benji's favorite drink. He doesn't drink hard liquor very much. He's a health-conscious individual, who tries to stay as close to nature as he can, even when he's indulging in stimulants.

The kitchen is a rather large one adorned with hanging pots lined on one wall and glass pasta container lining the counter below. There's enough room to add another stove, refrigerator, breakfast table, and a dual sink with room to spare. The addition to the kitchen was made to the house for the purpose of accommodating family gatherings and fight night parties. Otherwise, the space is useless, but today there are tables linked along the wall and three stacks of folded chairs by the patio door. Today is a very special day. Benji's home and the family haven't joined together like this since he has been gone. How they've all missed the cookouts at Benji's!

No one knew for certain if Benji would be coming home today or not, but people in his family always told him to count his blessings because it seems he always receives them in the nick of time, so it's not unusual for them to have planned for the best and went out to purchase food, Moet, beer, crabs, and charcoal all in preparations for good news so that the women could start cooking right away.

Benji has a traditional family where the women get married, the men head the house, the kids do the chores, and dinner is served on four days plus Sunday. Everybody in the family doesn't adhere to that same lifestyle, but most of them do.

Salina hasn't returned with the man-of-the-hour yet, but they know she's on the way. There are containers and pots covered with Reynolds Wrap on the dining room table, and more pots and pans filled with meats and casseroles in the oven. All the cooking was done by Benji's mother and Salina's mother, who don't like each other one bit but are phony enough toward one another to dwell in the same space long enough to get through a special occasion. And since they both love Benji dearly, today couldn't be more special for the both of them as their faces glow with joy at the thought of their Benji on his way home from that nasty old jail.

Salina's mother is short and thin with a small mustache at the corners of her upper lip. Her hair is cut in a short curl, speckled with maroon hair coloring, and she is wearing a slew of gold bracelets and rings. She's about fifty with the legs of a twenty-five-year-old. You can't tell her that she's any older than forty. She even lies about her age if someone should dare ask. She plays the motherly role toward Benji, but she's shown him several times that she'd hop in the bed with him in a heartbeat. Salina isn't aware of her mother's seductive advance toward Benji, but she doesn't trust her around him anyway. She knows her mother thinks she's Ms. Thang, and she likes young men, so to leave her around Benji unattended for too long would be asking for it. Benji's mom has noticed the way she looks at him, and she doesn't like it. She tells him to watch out for her because she's a slut. She knows her type.

Salina's mom, Beverly Jones has been divorced three times, mother of six. She still looks fairly young but she's put on a few pounds with age and has never been able to get rid of her stomach since she gave birth to her last child thirteen years ago. Her weight has frustrated her, but it sure hasn't hindered her promiscuity. Not one bit. In fact, she's more promiscuous than she was when she was in her twenties. She often changes boyfriends, makes him fall in love only to invite him to a swing party where she meets up with her friends and swap mates, often ending up in the same bed with their swingers. She's told Benji about the parties but has never suggested that he and Salina come to one. It could be because she figures Benji might one day feed into her advances and join her himself. She made it perfectly clear that she's attracted to him, but Benji has never considered responding to her, nor would he do such a thing. As much as he can't stand Salina at times, he'd never cross the line like that. However, Ms. Jones is in no hurry. Salina is right not to trust her, and Benji's mother is right to tell her baby to watch out for this heifer. She's a *humdinger.*

Marsha, Benji's mother, on the other hand is a conservative woman. She is the elder of the two women with streaks of gray in her hair. She wears her hair in a mushroom style and has none of the jewelry that Beverly has on. She's a bit taller and her skin is a hazelnut brown, if that's even a skin complexion. Her build is normal for a woman in her mid- to late fifties, and her clothing covers her figure, but she certainly isn't fat. She's actually quite fit, and that's evident from the way she's hustling around the kitchen, trying to get everything ready for the hoards of people they are expecting.

The kitchen has four entrances into it. The main entrance is next to the refrigerator. It leads out to a hallway that joins the dining room, a bathroom, a closet, and the foyer at the front door. The other entrance to the end of the counter beside the other side of the refrigerator, leads to a landing that connects the garage, the laundry room, and a spacious pantry that's big enough to store food that'll last a year. Then there is the sliding glass patio door adjacent to an extraordinary wooden deck equipped with a rollout canopy that covers the entire deck in case of a washout rainstorm. The fourth entrance is over by the extended part of the kitchen, leading to the family room, where there are young members of Benji's family playing PlayStation including his nine-year-old son Benji Jr.

Jr. is a spitting image of his father brandishing the same head, nose, and mouth. Salina hates that he looks so much like his father because all she ever hears is, *"He's so cute. He looks just like his father."* That really burns her up, and the bad part about it, she can only show her teeth and say, *"He sure does, doesn't he? Thank you."*

Their elder daughter Nakeisha is outside, with her twin cousins, waiting for her parents to come strolling down the street. She misses her daddy more than her cheating mother does. She knows her mother has been in the sack with Bink, but she's old enough to understand that it's up to her father to catch her in the act. Telling him would put her in the blame for wrecking the family, and that's the last thing she wants to happen. She loves both of her parents even though her mother gets on her last nerve. Maybe now, with Benji back home, she'll be able to go out and do big girl stuff. He always says that she's Daddy's big girl. He knows she's responsible.

Nakeisha is already starting to develop into a young lady, and boys have started calling the house more frequently giving her mother the notion that she's doing something she has no business doing. Her so-called boyfriend, Gino, is sitting on the curb in front of the house while she stands facing the hill that her parents' car will come down to get to their house. Her cousins Keisha and Teisha are singing a teasing cheer that makes Nakeisha blush and is annoying the hell out of Gino.

"La La and Gino, sittin' in the tree, *k-i-s-s-i-n-g.*"

Besides that, there is not much being said. Just silence between the two young lovebirds, wishing they were alone so they could talk to each other without the Boppsie twins having something to say.

The tires of a truck beat down the pavement, and the thump of its booming system can be felt on the street. It's a white Cherokee Laredo, and it has all the windows tinted dark with shiny chrome wheels.

"Here comes Bink," Nakeisha says drearily. She likes Bink, but doesn't think too highly of him since she knows how her father trusts him, yet he's still going behind his back and boinking her mother. But the fonder she grows of Gino, the less she likes Bink because she's starting to relate her father's situation to herself, wondering if one of her good friends would end up doing the same thing to her.

Look at him. Over here just like nothing's going on. Is this how it really is? Is that what's going to happen to me with Gino? Just like Jerry Springer.

Bink smiles and waves to her as he gets out of the truck. He knows what types of things are probably going through her mind at the age of thirteen. He only hopes Salina knows what she's talking about when she assured him that the kids wouldn't say anything because they don't know what's going on. She's right about Jr. but dead wrong about what her daughter knows, yet she is right about her not saying anything.

She waves back but can't bring herself to fake a smile. She just watches him until he disappears behind the door, sending a probing glance back at her. The sound of two cars attracts her attention away from Bink and the closing door. In anticipation, she darts her eyes up the hill, with a yank of her head, filled with individual plats only to be disappointed. No Lexus. More friends and family. Nakeisha is starting to wonder what's keeping them. It's almost six thirty; the judge had made her father a free man seven hours ago. She knows he had to go back to jail to get his things, but *do they know he's supposed to be let out* she wonders. *How long can that take?* She's getting tempted to go in the house and call her mother's cell phone but wouldn't dare leave Gino out here with Keisha and Teisha. Both of them think they're God's gift to the world, and the taunting song they keep singing is beginning to make Nakeisha suspect that they're just singing it to get attention from Gino. It could be her paranoia, but she thinks the kiss they smack with their lips at the end of the chant has been added as a sly tactic to blow a kiss at Gino. She notices they look at him and then giggle after they smack.

"Do y'all mind!" exclaims Nakeisha.

The both of them make a playfully bewildered gesture, then snap their fingers simultaneously as if they've practiced the move a million times together, and sing the chant again like they didn't even hear Nakeisha say a word.

"Oh, boy," says Nakeisha, shaking her head and crossing her arms across her chest. "Come on, Daddy."

Just then a white car, with its light on, prowls over the hill and glides down toward Nakeisha. Nakeisha's smile spreads from ear to ear, and she steps out into the middle of the street with her hands spread apart like a crossing guard. The approaching car slows to a slither and the occupants are grinning delightfully as the car comes within striking distance of the child who lies on her belly and faces down on the hood, giving the car a great big hug and a kiss. Then, she scampers to the driver's door and yanks at the handle. The door is locked, so her hand slips off the handle; she stumbles back and is tripped up by the curb. She lands in the grass and hurts nothing but her pride.

Kak, kak, kak, laugh her cousins Keisha and Teisha.

Benji turns to Salina, and they squeeze out a quick giggle themselves; then he turns back around while he rolls the window down, wipes the smile off his face, and then says, "Baby, are you all right?"

Gino has jumped to his feet by now and has come within a foot of reaching for Nakeisha's hand, but she shows him that she doesn't want any help getting up.

"Ha-ha. Real funny!" she sparks at her cousins. She looks up at Gino and says softly, "I'm OK. I can get up. I only fell in the grass."

She doesn't allow the spill to spoil the moment as she gets up and turns back into the excited little muskrat she was before her debacle. She spreads the smile back across her face, turning her attention back to her father. Benji puts the car in park, leaps out of the car, walks over to his baby, and sweeps her up off the ground, and bear-hugs her as he twirls around.

"Daddy," she sings.

They embrace for a moment, then suddenly, the roar of four motorcycles drowns all other sounds. The bikes are in two distinct assortment of colors: red, black, and green, and white, blue, and green. Two of them are chromed from the frame to the rims, all equipped with loud pipes that scare all the birds and squirrels away. Even caterpillars hobble into tree barks, and a roving feline peeks from under a parked car. But while the beasts of the earth run, duck, and hide from the deafening sound of the motorcycle pipes, the humans do just the opposite. Within seconds, Jr, his cousins, friends, the kids down the street, the teens up the hill, and some kids they've never even seen before are ooing and ahhing at the motorcycles and the wheelies that the riders are popping up and down the street.

Benji is just as excited as the kids are while he looks at the daredevil stunt riders.

Man. Who taught these cats to ride like this? I remember, before I went in, Richter wouldn't even go over ninety miles per hour. Now he's holding wheelies? I gotta get one of these joints. Which one is Richter?

A red and black bike rolling on its front wheel is headed straight at Benji. The rear end of the bikes is four feet off the ground and the rider is pointing at him with his left hand. Benji's not sure if the bike will be able to stop without running him over, so he steps to the side, but the bike stops on a dime and pauses with the rear wheel suspended in the air for a second or more then down the back tire crashes to the asphalt, and the rider takes off his helmet. It's Richter, and they exchange hugs and pounds before the dude even turns off the bike. The others get off their bikes and walk over to Benji and do the same. They haven't seen him since he went to jail, so they're just as excited as his family is about him being released. They're his crew, and they've missed him dearly. Funny, how your main man never comes to see you in jail, but that doesn't mean that they don't love you. The other three guys are Amp, Bootemup, and Tony. Richter has some age on them all including Benji, who is older than the other three.

Benji's only twenty-nine, but he looks more mature than that. He's been in the money since he was fifteen, running a rather large drug ring for someone that age. He had runners uptown, downtown, and in the suburbs by age seventeen and was dealing in keys before he hit twenty. He's light years ahead of the pack: he only needs to settle down and start a business, then he'll be set for life. Salina knows that, and she can't stand the sight of these four men. They mean nothing but trouble for Benji as far as she's concerned and wishes they'd never come. *How'd they find out that he was out so quick anyway?* Salina thinks.

"What's up wit' chall? Y'all been ridin' a lot, haven't you?" Benji inquires.

"Yeah man. We couldn't wait until you came home so we could burn you up," Richter tells him. "We saw y'all come in the neighborhood. We were waiting on you."

"Yeah, we timed you perfectly, only we didn't think you'd have the car parked in the middle of the street," Amp adds. "It's a good thing I didn't jump the hill like I started to. I'da kilt my damn self."

"I know it's some food in that joint. Let me at it," says Tony, the dark stocky one out of the crew. He's just the opposite of Richter, who is as skinny as a broomstick, as tall as a doorframe, and as light as toilet paper. His nappy hair is blond, and his eyes are gold. He's an albino with lots of style—handsome but scary looking.

Bootemup, on the other hand, is a short wavy-haired fellow about the same brown complexion as Benji, except he has a few pox marks on his face and arms. He has a little goatee on his chin that doesn't connect with his mustache. Amp also has a brown complexion, but his skin is smooth with no blemishes. He's about five foot nine and weighs about 170 pounds. Quite normal.

Benji invites them all around to the back of the house where they can put their helmets on the deck and enter into the house right where the food is. Tony's the first one to attack the food, forsaking the washing of his hands, the blessing of his food, and the whole nine yards. He just loads his plate with chicken, greens, macaroni and cheese, sweet potatoes, corn on the cob, and as much of anything else that will fit on his plate.

There are empty bottles of Moet all over the family room. The children can be heard through the open side window, and the two grandmothers are in the kitchen cleaning up, still maintaining their friendly exchanges to put up with one another. There are card games going on, and people everywhere having a good time together. Benji and his men have taken over the PS3, betting fifty dollars a game on Madden Football and NBA Live. Amp is the best in Madden, Live, riding bikes, basketball on the real court, swimming, saving money, and anything else you dare to compete against him in. You name it, Amp can do it, and if he can't, he'll be right back after he takes a couple of weeks to practice. Guaranteed, the next time he sees you, he'll challenge you and then beat the hell out of you. Sickening!

Once, he spent five months in the Round One Boxing Gym learning how to box just so he could beat up a bully named Quick, who was known as the best fighter in the neighborhood. He challenged Quick to go in the ring with him, referee, and all. By the end of the third round, Amp had knocked Quick clean out. A ten count. After that, Quick didn't bully anybody else in the neighborhood because he knew that there was somebody who could handle him. He saved his trash talking for people in school and for newcomers but never any of Amp's buddies.

Amp is "Mr. Do Everything the Best," and he's probably the best PlayStation player in the world, so no one dares to play him for any money. That's why he's on the side betting on anything and everything. First downs, field goals, red zone scoring, point spreads, anything that someone will say bet to. Up to five hundred dollars. He's up a couple of thousand.

Benji doesn't play the games and neither does Bink, who is sitting on the couch, watching and laughing. Benji is twisted and out for the count after drinking two bottles of Moet to himself. He's out cold with his head reared back in his recliner with his trap wide open. He's not snoring, but his tongue is arid dry from sleeping with his mouth open like that. He'll need a lemon when he wakes up to bring it back to normal.

The fellas are too drunk to ride their bikes, so they'll crash out here tonight, of course, to Salina's dismay, but what can she say? She was hoping to make love to her man tonight, but that is a far-gone conclusion. No whoopee for her tonight, unless, of course, she sneaks in a quickie with Bink, but he'd never risk getting caught like that. He'd get beaten up, stoned, beat with helmets, shot, and torched for violating so flagrantly, so she just mopes upstairs, leaving the children with her mother and Mrs. Powell.

"You going to bed, honey?" asks Marsha.

"Yes, ma'am. Y'all got the kids?"

"Naw, Benji got 'em," Beverly, her mother, says sarcastically. "You just go to bed. Don't worry about the kids. You need to be taking your man up there with you before something happens to him."

Salina looks back at her mother with contempt but doesn't feed into her remark. She knows exactly what she's referring to, but she doesn't want to get into it with her in front of Benji's mother. Besides, she just can't bring herself to believe that her mother would seriously ever stoop so low. Marsha, on the other hand, puts nothing past the old "floozies" and has made up her mind after hearing that statement not to leave the house anytime soon. Marsha knows that she's no good, and that's why she despises her so. In fact, if she saw Beverly's car broke down on the side of the interstate highway with her waving a white rag and a flare, standing on the roof of her broken down car, she'd act like she didn't see her and pass right on by. She wishes she could leave now, but after hearing that remark, she's not going anywhere until Beverly does. It could be a long night.

Chapter 15

Domingo is a fitting name for a three-hundred-pound Mexican sitting at a table that has a smaller diameter than his waistline. The metal chair is nonexistent under the Jabba the Hutt who is suffocating it under his weight. He leans forward and grabs his twelve-ounce bottle of Corona beer. He takes a swig and then a gulp that drains most of the beer out of the bottle, then he takes a look around the empty bar with exception to a couple of loyal beer drinkers that come here every day after they've finished working in the hot sun.

It's Tuesday evening, and this Latino bar is the place that Domingo comes to from time to time to meet people to talk business. He knows it's safe here because the people who own the joint are on his payroll. The man sitting behind the counter is a foot away from a sawed-off shotgun, and there's a door to the rear of Domingo that he has the liberty to fall back into and shut in the event of the police coming in to get him. He's not wanted or anything like that, but he's responsible for a lot of the narcotics floating around the Adams Morgan section of NW Washington DC, so he never knows when the Feds might try to make a move on him.

There's a man sitting across the room, who is more than likely Domingo's stickman undoubtedly holding the heat in case of some drama. At a table next to where he is sitting, there is an amigo sitting at a table filled with empty Corona bottles that he has downed since early this afternoon. He surely doesn't need any more seeing as how he's already slumped with his forehead rested on the table, shrouded by his arms. "Uno mas," he slurs holding his index finger up until his arm grows weary and crashes back down to the table.

No mas, Domingo says to himself with a smirk on his face. He finds this guy hilarious and looks forward to getting a laugh at him every time he comes in this joint.

Domingo looks at his watch and then back at the door. He's waiting for his cousin, Lil Papi, who hangs with the Negros. Papi has called and told him that he has *muchos dineros*, and he wants to get down. Domingo has kilos of cocaine coming in weekly from New Mexico, and Papi is ready to take part in the family business. There is a lot of love between the two of them, but Domingo has heard horror stories about the things Lil Papi does with the homies, and he's not sure if he can still trust that his little primo hasn't been brainwashed by his little crew to get him to bring the family some trouble. How do you defend yourself against your own family?

Domingo never sits and waits for anybody, but Lil Papi isn't just anybody, so he'll sit until his tardiness gets to be ridiculous. Domingo's a drug lord, but looking at him, you would never come to that conclusion. He does not wear jewelry, no fancy clothes, nor does he walk around with wads of money. He just seems like a big fat Mexican.

"Que pasa, mi primo."

Domingo looks up and sees Lil Papi walking through the door wearing his hair in Snoop Dogg style pigtails and a green and yellow Seattle Supersonics basketball jersey. Number ten.

"Ernesto," Domingo shouts as he struggles to get up from the chair to greet his cousin with a hug.

Even though they live in the same city, they haven't seen each other in over a year. Domingo does his thing, and Lil Papi does his, but there's no love loss. Fatts is behind Lil Papi, but Domingo doesn't pay him much attention. Lil Papi had already told him that he would be with someone that he wanted Domingo to meet, but right now, Fatts is invisible while Domingo deals with family issues.

After they exchange hugs and pounds, Domingo pauses, acting as if he's wondering who Fatts is supposed to be, but it's all an act. He must do things like that to keep people off balance. He never wants anybody to get to the point of thinking it's cool to bring just anybody around him. "Quien es?"

"O si," Lil Papi begins in Spanish and continues that way because he knows Domingo will speak more freely as long as he thinks the stranger doesn't understand what he's saying. "He's my good friend, and he's very smart. Most of the money we have is his and he wants us to stop acting crazy and start making our own money. You know I'm very crazy, but he's not that way. He won't mess things up, and that's why I brought him with me. You know I've never brought nobody around the family, so that should tell you that this is good."

"You mean to tell me that you want me to trust him to handle my business over you?"

"No, I'm not saying that, but I'm just saying that, I trust him with my life primo, so you can surely trust him to do good business. Besides, primo, he has his own money with mine." Papi replies in Spanish. Fatts is completely in the dark about what they're talking about, but he doesn't seem to be anxious to know either. He knows that Lil Papi is going to make it happen.

Domingo turns and waddles back over to the table where he was sitting and takes a seat. Both Lil Papi and Fatts follow suit as they watch and wait for Domingo to speak. There is a long silence between Domingo burping and taking consecutive swigs of his third beer. Domingo is thinking about whether or not he'll go through with it. He looks at the two young men sitting across from him, and they both look like two sick puppies. Domingo is reluctant to go through with it, but how can he turn his cousin away without at least giving him a chance to burn his own bridge?

"I wanna see your crew and your block," Domingo says in English.

They don't show it, but in their minds they are screaming and jumping up and down like kindergarten kids who were waiting for the ice cream truck to finally come around the corner.

"OK. When?" Papi asks with a subdued smile.

"Now, right now. Take me to your hood. His hood. If I like what I see, I'll give you more coca than your crackhead friends can smoke."

There's always a hidden agenda in a smart man's motives, whether it's for safety or for greed. The real reason for Domingo's demands to see their hoods is not to see whether or not they have blocks that can move the product, rather he wants to see Fatts in his own element. He wants to see how the hood reacts toward him. If he's a snitch, then the hood won't be open arms toward him, but if on the other hand, he's respected, it'll show. As far as Domingo is concerned, Fatts is an undercover federal agent, who has been slick enough to fool his little cousin, but he can't fool the whole hood, so while they ride he'll be looking to see if people are looking at them sideways. It's important that they do this now because he needs to know before he goes on to make any decisions.

If Fatts is a true blue All-American nigga, the marriage is officially bound with respect, love, but never trust. Trust is reserved for blood. No gringos. He knows one day Papi will learn that the hard way. Hopefully he won't die before he realizes it.

They ride in Fatts' car because, again, Domingo will be hawking the facial expressions when they hit the blocks. He knows a man's car is his ID in the hood. They can see you coming from a mile away, so this is the subtle tactic that he is going to use to take notice of the things he wants to know about Fatts. While they ride, Domingo keeps insisting that the radio be turned up loud so he can hear his favorite songs. Really, he could care less about hearing the music, he actually wants to avoid talking until he is comfortable around the man in the driver's seat.

Fatts has an idea that he's not in Domingo's favor yet, so he doesn't try to press the issue. After the second time he asked for the radio to be turned back up, he knew that he wasn't trying to talk to him about any business. Fatts just blast the radio, and if it were not for Lil Papi turning it down to chat with Domingo between songs, it would have been blasting all the way to southeast from Columbia Road NW where they had met up with the Mexican walrus.

Since Fatts also knows that Domingo doesn't trust him one bit, he stays off the phone. He doesn't want to give an impression that he's staging anything that Domingo is about to see once they get in the hood. He knows exactly what Domingo is doing and why he's doing so.

So he wants to see if they respect me? I'll show him. Humph. They more than respect me. They worship me.

As foul as that may sound, he's right. There is a mixture of emotions that surrounds the people in Fatts' acquaintance. Some of them love him. Many of them wish he were dead, but all of them fear him. The fear can be mistaken as respect, but only a small handful of his associates actually respect him without the fear factor, and they're the ones who are close enough to him to know the real Fatts. The genius trapped inside of a maniacal demon capable of *anything* against *anybody* at *any* time. As far as Fatts is concerned, *anybody* can get it!

As they drive down Georgia Avenue, Fatts ponders all the places he's going to take Domingo, and his first stop is going to be Park Road, which is only a few blocks down the street. They turn left onto Park Road where Skiba and a whole mob of dudes are standing around doing what they do, day in and day out. He rolls the darkly tinted window down and at least four of the eleven guys standing on the strip approach both sides of the car.

"What's up, fat boy? I see you got the Terminator with you," Skiba jokes concerning Lil Papi. "What's up, killer?"

"Same ole," Lil Papi responds with an up nod, changing from the friendly mood he was just in before they rolled the windows down. Just like that, Domingo sees his little cousin Ernesto transform into Lil Papi. The whole scene impresses him.

"Who's the big Mexican in the back? A hostage?" says a bucktooth dude leaning in the passenger window. There's a subdued chuckle. Domingo didn't find it amusing but doesn't feed into it. He knows what his cousin's been doing to get by, so the wisecrack rolls off. Besides, Lil Papi is loyal to his family, and his men know it. They wouldn't even consider speaking of bringing a move to Domingo for fear that Papi would zap out on them. If there's anybody that they fear, it's Lil Papi. He's a firecracker with a short fuse.

After leaving there, Fatts takes Domingo on a citywide tour of the most treacherous boroughs in the city: The Terrace, The Lane, The Quarters, The Farms, The Avenue, The Circle, The Worth, even The Land out Maryland—everywhere he knows thugs that are going to show some hood love. Domingo is thoroughly sold on the idea that Fatts is the man, and he is capable of moving any amount of drugs that he will give him. He wishes now that Ernesto would have brought this guy around a long time ago. Everybody would be rich by now. He would have been able to move back home and be sending hundreds of bricks back to Washington instead of having to babysit them like he's been doing for the past few years.

Domingo has seen enough and tells Fatts to head back uptown to Columbia Road. They jet through Fifty-eighth Street where the rest of their crew is waiting for them to return with good news. They've heard for a long time how stacked up Lil Papi's cousin is, and they expect that once the connect is established, they'll be able to take over the streets by flooding the strips with coke. They can't imagine that Lil Papi has been 'welling' about how big his cousin is in the coke game, so their expectations are high, and the anticipation is making them over-anxious, so when they see Fatts' car cut through the block without stopping, Daryl calls Fatts on his cell phone.

Inside the car, Fatts looks at his cell phone then answers it. "Daryl. We'll be back later. Stop calling." Then he hangs up and heads uptown.

Once they get back in front of the bar where they met with Domingo, he asks, "Do you have anything in this car that you need, primo?"

"Nothing, but that bag in the trunk with the money we brought for you," says Lil Papi.

"OK, homes. Here, take these key to my car. I'll take this one. How much is in the bag?"

Fatts doesn't like the sound of that. He looks at Lil Papi as he takes the keys from Domingo and pushes the button for the alarm. Up the street a set of headlights flash on and off. Fatts takes a squinting look at the car and can see that the car is a big body Benz sitting on at least twenty-inch chrome rims. He looks back at Domingo who is waiting for an answer to his question.

"A hundred Gs," Fatts says.

"All right, Papi. You owe me three hundred. Call me next Friday."

"Si."

And just like that, Fatts and his band of mercenaries are on. Twenty bricks at twenty grand a piece, and they don't even have to leave the district. It's hard enough to get a key for less than twenty-two in New York, so to get it at that price without having to drive or fly a single mile is incredible to them. Fatts is flabbergasted after he does the math in his head.

Twenty thousand? Man, we can sell 'em at twenty-three and they'll fly. This has got to be too good to be true. I know that price is gonna to get better. I feel noid already. Damn.

Chapter 16

Jessica sits at a table with Denise and other members of her family. There is a man sitting beside her wearing a black suit jacket and an oversized necktie. He's smiling and savoring the attention he and Jessica are receiving from everybody in the room. There is champagne glass filled with sparkling white bubbly champagne. Everyone is dressed to impress, and many are wearing identical colors. It seems everyone is dressed for a wedding. A tall cake sits on a table across the room. There's an article standing graciously atop the cake, and it appears to be a bride and groom trinket. The onlooker moves toward the cake to get a closer look. With each daunting step, the object becomes more and more certain to be a bride and a groom. It is a bride and groom.

"No! No! No!"

Benji opens his eyes wide to find Salina standing before him. She's staring at him with a blank face, not at all happy, not about to wish him a good morning. Benji raises his head to take a look around the room, and sees that everyone is gone. The television is showing a demo of Madden Football, and daylight is shining through slight cracks in the blinds on the windows. All of the trash and bottles have been cleaned up and the furniture is all in its respective places. Everything is in order except Salina's attitude and the look on her face.

Salina resembles her mother without the stomach. She has a similar short curly hairdo, and she flaunts about the same amount of bangles and rings. Her jewelry *blings* a lot more than her mom's though, courtesy of Benjamin Powell.

"What? You were dreaming about your girlfriend? Dreamin' 'bout what you gonna do to her while I'm at work? You sure ain't make love to me your first day home," she says all in one breath.

"Oh my god," Benji says, flopping his head back down on the cushion of his fluffy easy chair. He shakes his head and brings his left hand to his forehead with a frustrated slap and massage. "Do you have something you have to get off your chest?"

Benji has talked to Jessica several times about Salina stalking her. He pleaded with her to ignore Salina, promising to do something about it when he came home, but the stalking got so bad that the police had to respond to BET just missing Salina after she had destroyed Jessica's paint job on her Toyota Avalon. That's when Jessica had a friend from the Prince George's County Police Department pay Salina a visit at her salon and threaten to walk her out in handcuffs if any further complaints of harassment were made. After that all the calls stopped, and Salina never made mention of any knowledge of the affair to Benji. She just persists in a lot of doubletalk and smart-aleck remarks. Benji has never fed into any of it, but he's as fed up with Salina's mouth as he's ever been, so decides to challenge her to speak her mind.

"You damn right I do!" she outbursts. "For starters, I hope you plan on getting a job. Just 'cause the judge took back your little bit of time don't mean you can come home doin' the same stuff that put you there in the first place . . . I'm tellin' you, Benji. I ain't sittin' through another one of your vacations 'cause the next one makes you a three-time loser. They gonna knock your boots off, and next time you ain't gonna be so lucky. You need to grow up."

"What the hell are you talkin' about?" Benji interrupts. "First of all, I'm not your child. Second, if I wanna get a job, I'll get a job. In fact, I ain't never gonna get a job. I'm caked up! I'll start a business and work for myself, but until then, if I wanna hustle, then I'ma hustle."

"Well, if that's what you're gonna do, you need to do it somewhere else. I don't want that stuff around me, nor anybody who has anything to do with it, and that means Richter, Amp, Bootsy, and Poopsie or whatever their damn names are. I'm getting too old for that. I need a real man, not a boy."

"Well, then you need to find him!" Benji hollers at the top of his voice, angry enough to haul off and pimp smack her.

"Maybe I already have," she taunts.

"Well, I hope he's laying the pipe real good, 'cause I'ma save this one for a woman who deserves it."

"As a matter of fact, the dick is real good, and I'm gonna make sure I bounce on it tonight. You ain't gotta worry about that . . . so you can take your little peter on over there to that slut Jessie!" Benji is shocked that she actually came out of her mouth with Jessie's name. "Yeah, I know all about cha," she continues, "been screwin' her since when? . . . '92,

'93? Somewhere around there. Um . . . huh . . . go ahead with your little Jessie, and I'ma keep right on swallowing that nigga's dick, cum, and all. You faggot!"

Prtch! Benji smacks her.

Benji has never hit a woman, so the feeling is new to him. It doesn't feel good, but it doesn't make him feel sorry either. He actually wants to hit her again and again until her lips swell, and she can't run her mouth anymore. He's up out of his chair now and ready to pounce on her, but he resists. She's always viewed Benji as a softy, showing him little to no respect and just because he just smacked the taste out her mouth doesn't make her anymore fretful.

She holds her face on the side he just smacked and slowly turns her face back toward him to its pre-slap position.

I know this punk ass nigga didn't just smack me in my face. I'ma kill this nigga.

The pits of her eyes have darkened, and a lone tear trickles down her red face. One side is redder than the other. Her eyelids have all but disappeared, and her mouth is open causing her cheek muscles to ripple. She appears to have awaken from the dead and to have seen a ghost all at the same time. Pure malice is screaming from her eyes as she slowly moves to walk past Benji to enter into the kitchen.

"Oh . . . no . . . you didn't just . . . smack me in my face. This is gonna be the last bitch you ever smack," she murmurs in a stale murky voice.

Once past him, she peps up her step to a near run and flashes around the corner into the kitchen. Benji shakes his head and throws his hands in the air. He asks himself, "Why did you just do that?"

Clink. Shurret. The sound of a knife being pulled out of the knife holder from inside the kitchen awakens Benji's peripheral vision looking for the first object he can find that might obstruct her ability to stab him. He picks up a stack of magazines and throws them at her as she comes darting around the corner carrying the biggest knife in the set.

The magazines catch her square in the face but have no effect on her forward charge. Benji sees nothing else that he can pick up to hit her with that won't put her in a coma, so he does the only thing he can do to protect himself. Run. With the agility of Barry Sanders and the swiftness of a church mouse, Benji makes his way around, over and past the furniture in the family room, then the living room, and out the front door. He is in the Lexus, backing out the driveway and taking off up the street before Salina can make it to the front door after falling and stumbling over a trail of chairs, coat racks, and lamps that Benji hurled in the trail behind him to hinder the chasing mad lady.

In the rearview mirror, he can see her in the front yard pumping the Jason knife in the air. Certainly, she's telling the world the things she's gonna do to him when she catches him.

✧   ✧   ✧

Rinnng. Rinnng.

"Detective Miles," answers a man with blue eyes and a crew cut appearing to be an ex-army soldier. Lindsey Miles of the Federal Bureau of Investigation is sitting at his desk eating a club sandwich and skipping through the folder of a gun dealer who has been going back and forth to North Carolina bringing back as many guns as his Chevy Tahoe can stock.

The suspect's name is Trevor Roach, and he's a thirty-six-year-old ex-drug offender figuring that hustling guns is safer than making drug deals as far as the cops go. He's probably right seeing as how he's been going strong for ten years or more and hasn't so much as been pulled over by the police. He was locked up once for a year since he left junior high school for selling all types of drugs. Now, his hustle is sweet since he's quit selling drugs and started selling guns.

He rides through various hoods unannounced. Somebody on the block, one of the many blocks that he frequents, sees his truck and before the truck can get close enough for Trevor to see anyone, one of the prospective buyers is already in the street waving him down like a kid does an ice-cream truck. There are not too many things that would make a thug act that way, but guns are one of them. He sells them everything from Glocks, to Machs, to Techs, to Desert Eagles and doesn't have to go any further than his first stop because before he can move anywhere more guys come after being notified that guns are in the hood. He's never had a problem with the police, and even when they rode through while he was making transactions, he passes around bootleg CDs and urges everyone to keep cool as if they're only buying some music from a CD hustler. It's worked every time.

"You don't say," Detective Miles says to the person on the phone as he smiles from ear to ear, but it abruptly disappears because of something the caller says, "Well, you make sure that warrant gets lost, I mean eighty-sixed. He's probably on parole, and I don't wanna see him sit for another five years just for smacking his girlfriend who is later gonna be sorry that she even called the police. We've been waiting a long time for him to get back. Now you tell your boys to lay off. In fact, red flag him in your database as off limits . . . right . . . you bet . . . all right, talk to you soon."

Miles hangs up the phone and looks at his partner who is sitting at the desk facing his, "Guess which one of our guys is back in town."

"No. I'd rather you just tell me," replies Jeffery Faraday in a calm, sarcastic voice.

"Benjamin Powell."

Faraday's eyes light up like the Fourth of July, and he rears back in his seat, putting his pen in his mouth like a Garcia Vega. He takes a moment, then he looks back at Miles, and says, "So who was that on the phone?"

Miles favors Lou Forigno minus the muscles and the green skin—scary sight with or without the FBI jacket. "That was a lieutenant at District 3 in Prince George's. Says one of his officers just told him that a woman put a warrant out for Benjamin Powell's arrest sometime this morning, and they're looking for him now. He's driving that same white Lexus he had when he was out five years ago."

"Well . . . Let's get the file. We've got some *real* work to do." Faraday says as he stands up and reaches for the Trevor Roach folder. "You just caught a break, Roach."

Chapter 17

There's not much that Benji would need to do in order to jump right back into the swing of what he left behind before he was stopped on a traffic violation and arrested for having a few of ounces of powder cocaine in his car. He also had a handgun, but they didn't find that. Salina took it out of the car after she picked the car up from the police impound. Since the car was in her name, the police couldn't legally confiscate the car. That's the only reason it didn't become the property of Prince George's County.

Lindsey Miles and Jeffery Faraday were highly upset about the arrest because they knew Benji was a much bigger dealer than that, and the bust really hampered their investigation. They were very close to getting an informant to make a buy directly from Benji but saw it all go down the drain with the trial.

Benji didn't get much time for the charge, only six years, but he had been violated by his probation officer for catching a new charge while being on parole. Therefore, he had to do time for the new charge and three years on the violation. Now that he's out, he doesn't intend on doing anything that will land him back in jail because another charge will make him a career criminal, and that'll get him fifteen years before the judge can even consider what he's going to give him for a conviction on the actual crime.

Even though Benji has no plans of jumping back into the drug game, he does, however, intend on carrying out some other risky plans, which may prove to be very lucrative for him. He left quite a bit of money behind with various loved ones. He has a hundred thousand at his parents' house, a hundred and sixty at his house with Salina, fifty thousand at his sister's house, and another hundred or so at Jessie's. Jessie lives in a high-rise apartment building, and fortunately, maintenance hasn't stumbled upon the bag full of money that sits unhidden on the floor of her walk-in bedroom closet.

Altogether, Benji should have close to four hundred thousand dollars, but of course, his expectations are low where Salina and his sister are concerned. Salina has a beauty salon that she opened up since he went to jail, and Benji knows she went overboard trying to make it the most lavish salon in the DC metropolitan area. On top of that, she has no regard for finances and budgeting. She thinks just because the money is there, she can spend it. That's why she can never keep any money in the bank. Benji hopes he has some money there, but he has no true hopes of retrieving what he left there, especially now that the cat is out the bag concerning his relationship with Jessie. Not that that would have made a difference.

Benji's headed to his sister's house but needs to get some cash from somewhere before he even gets there or else he'll be sitting on the side of the Southeast Expressway out of gas. Little does he know that the car he's driving has been called in stolen to the police, and if he gets pulled over right now, he'll be locked right back up less than twenty-four hours after being released. Benji has always said that women are contriving, but that didn't go for the women that are close to him, just all the other women, so he'd never think that his children's mother would have him in the predicament that she has him in now—on parole and driving a stolen car with no gas in it. He hopes he has enough in it to make it to Landover.

There are red brake lights filling every lane up ahead, and the traffic appears to be at a standstill from Benji's vantage point, at the peak of a slope on the long shoulderless highway. Hating to sit in rubbernecking traffic, he bogarts his way to the far right lane and veers off the thoroughfare with a glancing swoosh past a metal pole that divides the roadway and the exit ramp, leading to Nallie Hellen Borroughs Avenue. He's a very aggressive driver who could very easily be the lead driver to "Stagecoach." If you've never seen "Stagecoach" in action, just go to Washington DC and sit at Freedom Square next to 1600 Pennsylvania Avenue and wait for the presidential motorcade to storm through. Pay close attention to the car at the very front, which spearheads through the already stopped traffic. That's Benji. Driving the way Benji does, it isn't long before he is on Martin Luther King Highway in Landover, Maryland. Whipping the corner at Flagstaff in the town of Kentland, where he grew up, he's almost at his sister's house. His parents don't live far from where his sister lives, but no one's home there right now, and he doesn't have a key to their house since he lost it years ago. He's about to find out just how much money his sister has gaffled from him, and hopefully it's not much, because he doesn't like when his sister lets him down. He puts so much faith in her and she in him. They're each other's biggest fans.

Benji still has the key to her house on the same key chain he got locked up with, and he assumes that she's not home now because he doesn't see her car, but he still rings the doorbell. He doesn't know if she has a friend that lives there like so many girls do. You never know what is going on in people's lives nowadays because everyone is so secretive. After a few seconds, no one responds to the doorbell, so Benji uses his key and enters the house.

Inside the house, Benji walks into the kitchen, passing through the living room, with a disbelieving double take at the furniture inside the house. There's an exotic sofa made of blue leather and shaped like a shoehorn. The buttons that decorate the design give the piece a rich look, making it seem like something you should only look at and not sit on. There is no other furniture in the room that appears to match it as a set, but there is definitely furniture that equals its oddity, such as the high-back medieval chair nestled in the corner by an end table made of marble and glass. The African statues and paintings style the room giving it a surreal, auspicious feel.

I hope like hell you ain't use my money to pay for all this. I'ma confiscate everything in here, Benji thinks to himself as he marvels at a bust of a Pharaoh.

He darts up the steps to climb up into the attic where he remembers tucking his money under a layer of fiberglass insulation. Halfway up the stairs, he abruptly stops and goes back down the stairs to get something to drink out of the refrigerator. He finds a few of his favorite beer, Heineken, grabs one and turns it up until half of it is swallowed. The freeze from the beer hits his brain and forces him to slam the bottle down on the counter and grab hold of his forehead. The excruciating pain envelopes his cranium and by now he's almost ready to scream.

"Aggh, aggh!" he agonizes. "Damn it!"

Releasing the tight squint of his eyes, Benji stands back on his feet and shakes his head after the pain subsides, and his brain returns back to normal. Then he gets the beer and takes another swig of it as if he hasn't had enough. After finishing it, he takes off again up the stairs to his sister's bedroom. There is nothing for him to climb on in order to get himself up into the attic, so he has to go all the way back downstairs to get a chair out of the dining room, then return and climb up into the attic. After pushing the thin layer of plywood up and over the framed opening of the attic's entrance, he, with both hands, pulls himself up into the hole and disappears beyond the blackness in the attic.

Ahh, nobody has even touched the money. It's still just like I left it. Baby sis must be doin' a'ight for herself then. Either that or she has a nigga with some bread.

Benji drops the money down through the hole in the ceiling and drops himself down through the same, then he calls Richter on his cell phone. There is no answer, but he leaves a message telling him to pick him up a cell phone from his friend who owns Beaconn Communications over on Good Hope Road in SE Washington. Beaconn Communications is the only place in the whole area that you can get a Sprint under an alias name. An indication that he's not completely reformed. What does a legit-minded person need with an alias cell phone?

I'll just get enough money stacked to get my business off the ground then I'll quit for good. A few moves here and there should do it, he rationalizes. *Three dump trucks, some off-shore investments, and two college funds for La La and Ben are all I'll shoot for.*

Benji really had all the intentions in the world of not coming out of jail and touching one gram of coke, but the minute he got a whiff of the sweet aroma of those greenbacks with the small faces on them and the smell of crack mixed with old dirty lenin paper, he couldn't fight the compulsion his spirit voiced in his heart. False reasoning has him thinking that he'll be able to start bringing in thousands of dollars again and just be able to give it up once he's stacked enough money to satisfy his goals. That's usually how it starts out for newly released kingpins, but the constant flow of revenue isn't something very easy for a human being to cut off. Benji believes he's mentally stronger than the average feeble-minded dude and won't allow himself to get into any rhythm. He figures he'll make a few large purchases from the connect that he has in California, and he'll quit dealing as soon as he reaches his projected goals. Sounds easy enough.

Since the judge took back all the time remaining on his sentence, he doesn't have any parole officer to answer to on his last case, but he's still on parole for the old case, so he's not free to leave the state of Maryland. However, he plans a trip to the west coast anyway, but before he goes, he must make contact with his people out there so he doesn't waste a trip for nothing. People have a tendency of falling off the face of the earth nowadays. A person used to be able to just pop up in town and call their people to let them know that they're in town. Not anymore. He'll be sure to contact his people before he makes any plans to fly out, and since he's just getting out of jail, he doesn't have to worry about the Feds trailing him. He's like a baby sparrow just learning to fly, free to spread his wings. At least that's what he thinks. He carries the chair back downstairs with the bag of money atop the seat of the chair. He finishes another beer while making a few calls before he leaves the house.

One of the people he calls is Jessie, but he knows she's not home. He only wanted to leave a message on her answering service letting her know that he'd be released from jail tomorrow. He wants to surprise her tonight, so he can see the big smile on her face when he shows up at her door. But just before he began to leave his message after the beep, he changes his mind and hangs up the phone. He has a better idea. He'll leave his release as a total surprise and just show up completely unannounced.

That'll really be a surprise.

Benji has, for a long time, wanted to leave Salina for several reasons, but the biggest reason is because the woman that he loves the most is Jessie. Besides that, Salina has no respect for his manhood. They've been together for so long that she views him more as the child that he was when they first met than the strong, authoritative, and kind man he's developed into; she's never really been the cooking type. Not to mention that he just doesn't like the person that Salina is. She's mouthy, arrogant, conceited, rude, and again, she can't cook. It's really not her fault that she can't cook though. Benji has himself to blame for that because he had always taken her out to eat before the children were born.

However, Jessie is all the woman that Benji ever wanted, but the children he has with Salina have kept him put. That's no longer going to be a factor. He loves his children deeply, but he can't stand to deprive himself of what he feels is best for his sanity, future, and destiny.

He will not go back to his home. She can have it and everything in it, including what's left of the hundred and sixty thousand dollars. He's through.

Chapter 18

After a long day's work, Jessica is tired and famished. Her stomach is growling, and all she can think of is heating up the salmon, rice, and gravy that she fixed last night for dinner. Her lunch was knocked over by the flirtatious Charles Hinton, who is always trying to be her friend, and today was no different from any other day for old Charles. He made it a point to go down to the cafeteria after he saw Jessie leave the seventh floor to go down to for lunch. He watched the elevator floor indicator move down to one and waited a few minutes to allow Jessie to commit to eating in the building by not going out into the parking lot to her car; once he saw that she was staying, he grabbed his sports jacket and headed for the elevators.

Down in the cafeteria, Jessie bought a salad, cocktail shrimp, and water. At BET, everyone is concerned with their appearance, so salads and seafood is a hot commodity, but for Jessie, it's a requirement. Her figure is so intact that diverting from the diet she's lived on since her second year in college would be a sin. She has no idea what results would follow if she were to change her eating habits. *"If it ain't broke, don't fix it,"* her grandmother always used to say before she died, and Jessie has always followed that advice during the course of her life.

"If I could just take a picture of the way you look now," Charles said as he watched Jessie from behind, adjusting her well-dressed body. "My, my. Don't you look nice today?"

Jessie didn't turn from the cashier. She just continued as if she wasn't hearing anyone speak. How sickening this man is with his redundant lines and juvenile attempts at flattering her! The cashier handed Jessica her change, and she put it in her red purse hanging under her arm. The red skirt she is wearing is extra tight and above her knees by two inches, which is unusual for Jessie, but she was feeling somewhat sexy this morning when she got dressed for the day.

Jessie is really sick of this guy, but, what can she do? He's her boss and capable of making things really good for her or worse than she could ever imagine. She took a deep breath, and then turned to face her predator with her food in her hands on an orange tray.

"Oops," she said, swinging the tray right into the chest of Charles, who was standing entirely too close to her to begin with. "Charles!" she exclaimed with a disheartened expression on her face as he tried to catch the falling tray only making matters worse.

Caclump!

"Oh, shoot," mumbled Charles with salad dressing spattered all over his pants leg and shoes. "I'm terribly sorry, Jessie. I'll buy you another one."

"No . . . no, thank you. I'm not hungry anyway. I'll just go back to work."

"You'll do nothing of the sort," he demanded. "I said I'll buy you another salad. Don't make me suffer! If you don't eat because of me, I'll have a very bad day."

Jessie inhaled and looked up at the ceiling wanting not to be rude, but she really didn't want him to buy her anything; she just wanted to pick up her water and go back upstairs far away from Mr. Charles, and that's exactly what she did.

"No, really Charles, I'm not hungry. Thanks anyway. Bye."

She walked off, leaving him standing there, holding the orange tray in his hand, looking dumb.

It's been a long day for Jessie, and she's glad to be pulling into the parking lot of her complex. She longs to be in the comfort of her own home. Jessie parks her new Aurora and walks into the high-rise apartment at Oakcrest Towers.

In the lobby, there is a couple talking in a foreign language, they appear to be African because they both are very dark-skinned and wearing colorful gownlike garments that go down to their ankles. The woman has African braids and the man has a small bush that needs combing. Their comments are brief and sharp toward each other, and Jessie can tell that they are having a dispute even though they're not shouting or showing any signs of anger.

They walk out the glass double doors as Jessie's high heels clip-clop on the large white ceramic tiles in the foyer of the lobby. She walks up the four-carpeted steps as she takes a look at herself in the bronze mirrors that cover the entire wall to the right of the steps. Once she reaches the top of the steps, Jessie walks straight to the mailboxes in a room across the floor from the mirrored wall. She's walking with a renewed urgency in great anticipation of receiving a letter from Benji. It's been two whole weeks since she's got a letter from her love, and now every day she expects to receive one. His letters make her day, and she looks forward to reading them more than she looks forward to hearing his voice on the phone. There's something that makes her insides tingle when she reads the handwritten words of the man she wishes was her husband.

Come on, baby, please have written me today.

Her family used to think that she was crazy to wait on a man that wasn't even hers to begin with, but Jessie never showed any signs of giving her love to any other man, so they know that she's really in love with this guy. They've never met him with the exception of her mother and cousin Niecey because Jessie is not very close with the rest of her family, but that's not because they don't love her; it's just she chooses to keep her distanced. Benji is all the family that Jessie needs. She loves him dearly, and as gorgeous as she is, it's amazing that she hasn't been involved with another man since she's been Benji's mistress. That kind of thing is unheard-of in America, but Jessie's an example of a woman who has exclusive devotion. She refuses to think that she is wasting her beauty on a man she'll never have. Jessie will grow old knowing that she lived her life just as she was intended to live it as long as she dies with the love of Benjamin Powell.

She loves to see the envelope marked Jessie Powell. It makes her heart melt, and to her dismay, there is nothing but an *Essence* magazine, a Verizon phone bill, a Macy's bill, and junk mail on top of junk mail. She grills the inside of the empty mailbox to see if a letter might miraculously pop into it. Nothing happens.

"Damn it," she says to the mailbox, which has let her down once again.

Jessie slams the mailbox door and just as she walked in the mailroom, she walks out; only the strut has turn into a meander toward the elevator. It doesn't matter how she walks though, she's built like a brick house and her movement is as graceful as any Miss America. As she approaches the elevator, she notices that another one of her admirers is standing there. He had seen her coming in behind him; he should have already been gone up by now, but he didn't push the call button for the elevator because he wanted to ride up with her, so he decided to wait until she finished getting her mail, and then he would push the button. As Jessie walks up, she notices that the light on the call button isn't lit, then she looks at him, and he's just staring at her. She stands there to see how long he's going to stand there before he realizes that he hasn't pushed the button yet for the elevator to come. After about thirty seconds, she giggles. He wonders what's so funny and starts to think that maybe he has a booga hanging out of his nose, or maybe she's laughing at the way he shaped up his mustache. He wipes his nose.

"How long do you think the elevator is going to be before it decides to come down to the first floor?" Jessie comments with a smirk on her face.

"Oh, snap. I'm lunchin'. I've been just standing here, waiting on the elevator and never pushed the button." He's quite embarrassed, but realizes that this is the perfect time to say something flirtatious. "I guess beauty does that to a man. You sure are enough to make a dude forget anything."

Jessie appreciates the compliment. She didn't expect him to actually fess up to him being distracted by her presence. He's never said anything more than hello to her. Most men are intimidated by her beauty and don't know what to say to her. If she weren't so upset about not receiving a letter, she may have humored him and responded kindly to his statement, but then again she knows he's married because she's seen him several times with his wife. Suddenly, her expression changes to that of an angry schoolteacher knowing that if she responds to that, he'll pour it on and make an attempt to take advantage of a rare exchange of words; so she remains silent. The doors open, and they both get on the elevator. Jessie pushes 11, and he pushes 12, but she knows he doesn't live on the twelfth floor. He lives below her, and she knows he is trying to figure out what he can say to spark up another conversation. He's such a little wimp. He's actually scared to say something to her without a reason, so he just keeps rubbing his hands together, trying to come up with an opening line. The elevator floor indicator is getting close to 11, the floor that Jessie lives on. He knows he's running out of time, and his heart is beating harder than it was before he got on the elevator. His mind is racing as he looks up at the indicator and then at Jessie. She knows he wants to say something to her and can hardly keep herself from laughing at him.

He's a short, squaint looking, balding dark brown fellow, and it's just comical that he would even think in his mind that she would give him the time of day. She shakes her head, giggles under her breath after looking at him and thinks, *Milk Dud.*

The door opens, and she quickly steps off. By now, her laughter has subsided, and she can breathe freely again. On the elevator she had to hold her breath because Milk Dud shortly must have been farting from nervousness. It got quite funky in there after the fourth floor. As she turns to head for her door, she glances down the long hallway and double takes, certain that she had seen a person's head disappear back into the exit stairwell at the end of the corridor. The sight was startling, and she keeps her eye on the edge of the wall to see if that head would peek around the corner again. It doesn't. Uneasy, Jessie takes a step back and then turns to get to her apartment as quickly as possible without running. Once inside, she feels safe but unsure of her security, so she puts the chain on the door. Something she never does.

She drops her things on the sofa and walks straight to the kitchen because she's starving. She pulls a long glass oven pan out of the bottom of the refrigerator and a table spoon out of a drawer next to the sink; she makes a plate of food from the leftovers from last night, and then plops it into the white microwave oven sitting on a counter next to the refrigerator. It's a small kitchen, and everything is within two steps of the other. After setting the timer and starting the oven, she skips around to the living room, past the small front door foyer and down the hallway to her bedroom.

In her bedroom, she snatches a gown off the back of her door and walks over to the bed and undresses. Before she can finish, there's a knock at the door. She instantly becomes terrified at the sound of someone knocking at her door, especially at this time of the evening. After seeing that head peeking around the corner, the knock is all the more daunting.

"Now, who on earth is *that?*"

Jessie tiptoes down the hall and looks through the peephole but can't see anybody. What she sees through the peephole is something red as her skirt, but it's not fabric. It looks like . . . a rose petal?

"Who is it?" she calls in a hesitant voice, turning her head to the side to listen for a response. When she doesn't get one, she comes close to running to the phone and dialing 911, but she will give it one more go at it to make certain that the person on the other side of the door can hear her.

"Who is it?!" she shouts out in a loud firm voice, then she looks through the hole again and can now make out the red object she had seen the first time she looked out. It *is* a rose. In fact, it's a bouquet of long stem red roses, and whoever it is holding them has stepped back away from the door and is hiding his face behind the flowers. From behind the roses, a familiar man's voice begins to sing an even more familiar song. And, only the man she yearns for would know to sing at a moment like this.

"Girl, you are to me-ee . . . all that a woman should be and I dedicate my love . . . to you always."

Jessie's emotion nearly collapses her, and her heart is now trying to jump out of her chest. Unlocking the door and sliding the chain free, she twists the knob and opens the door as she returns a love call back to her Romeo singing the song that is the theme of their relationship and has been their favorite song since they heard it being played on WHUR when they were heading to a restaurant on their first date.

"Your love is like a dove . . . It must have been sent . . . from up above . . . and I'm sure you'll stay that way . . . for all ways."

Benji is standing there before her, wearing an all-white, short-sleeve linen suit, holding the roses in his left hand and the gleam of dawn in his right. It's a diamond ring that has to be at least five carats. Their eyes meet, and Jessie has a tear streaming from her eye down the side of her nose, and they take a step toward one another. Benji steps across the threshold of the door and forces Jessie backward with his body while they continue to harmonize their favorite love song. In the middle of their singing, Jessie presses her mouth to Benji's and they begin to indulge in a most passionate kiss. The majority of the passion is coming from Jessie, who gasps and gags from all of the saliva her mouth is producing and how far she's sticking her tongue out of her mouth into his.

Benji pulls his head back and looks into her eyes once more. She looks like a sex-craving nymphomaniac who has just been told that she couldn't have any cookies. Her eyes plead with him to continue what they've started.

Benji tries to finish the song, "Come with me my sweet, and let's go make a fam . . ."

Jessie has heard more than enough singing, talking, and all other noise outside of sliding flesh and wet slushing fluids. A beast has been hiding in Jessie, and it has been dormant since he's been gone. In all actuality, she's never in her life unleashed this beast before, but today is the day it will make itself known and allow this woman to act in ways she would never had imagined. She's had many dreams of what she'd do to Benji if he were in her presence, and now she will perform all of those fantasies in real life, on the real thing.

Benji can feel her aggression, and it quickly becomes evident to him that she has waited a very long time to indulge herself in any type of sex.

The quiet agonizing sounds she is making as she kisses him in his mouth and bites him on his lips raises his blood pressure and gives him an erection so hard that it hurts.

With the door still cracked, Benji drops the diamond ring on the floor, and Jessie snatches the roses from his other hand and throws them somewhere behind her, still kissing passionately. Benji reaches for her buttons and tries to unbutton her top. Irritated with his clumsiness, she ferociously rips her shirt open, popping buttons across the room, and pulls the shirt franticly off her shoulders.

Benji puts his mouth to her neck and bites her like a vampire. She presses his head firmly to her neck, and he sucks and bites harder until she moans and caresses his head in satisfaction of the pleasurable pain he just gave her.

Benji can see that Jessie is not at all interested in making sweet love as they are accustomed to. She wants him to savage her, and that's exactly what Benji's about to do.

First taking her down to the floor, he pulls her brassiere over her head without unstrapping it and squeezes both of her plump round breasts; he then buries his face in them, sucking them where her cleavage shows and then gnawing his way to her hard brown nipples. He rolls his tongue around one of them with a mouth full of wetness, nibbling from time to time, and releasing it with a juicy smack and back down again.

The heat from his mouth synthesizes her thrills each time one of her nipples is consumed by his hot lips and tongue. She guides his head all around her chest and belly and his obedient head follows the lead of her hands all the while licking and biting wherever his mouth touches.

"Ooo . . . Aah . . ." Jessie whispers with her eyes closed while she enjoys the ecstasy of every movement and touch.

She releases his head and kicks her heels off while pulling her skirt off at the same time. Off comes her stocking and thong along with the skirt and the whole scene is comparable to two teenagers having sex for only the second time. The time when the nervousness and uncertainty is not there, but the same fervent desire is, as it was the first time.

Benji follows suit, climbing out of his trousers and shoes. He reaches down and slides off his socks, and Jessie pulls his shirt over his head.

They are both naked and meshed together on the floor of the living room, not realizing the front door is still cracked, and the female neighbor from across the hall had peeked out her door when she heard someone knock at Jessie's door and is now watching the whole thing unfold. She's quietly come out of her door and is standing at the crack in Jessie's door peering into her house and getting an eye full.

"Put it in, put it in, oh, please, hurry up," Jessie begs.

Benji has become somewhat flaccid during the clothes removal process, but the sound of her pleading brings Roscoe back to extra strength, and he spreads her legs around his hips while they kiss and places himself in perfect position to penetrate. With both his hands on the carpet in a push-up stance and his knees barley touching the floor, Benji allows his head to find its own way to her opening. When it finds a place that feels like the right spot, he applies pressure to her opening to make certain that he has the right hole, and when she reaches for his buttocks and tries to thrust him upward, he knows he is there. Teasing a bit, Benji rotates his torso, not allowing much more than his head to sink into her saturated vagina.

"Hoa, hoa, come on, Benji, get it," she murmurs "Take me, please."

Benji can feel her drenching wetness all between her thighs. She smells like pureed strawberries, and her yearning becomes stronger and more accretive with each thrust of Benji's third leg as it sinks deeper and deeper until he has reached maximum penetration.

Splash. Phererert, goes the sound of her tight womb.

"Umm," she grunts.

"Oh! . . . Ah! . . . Aggh! O . . . yes. Yes Benji. Don't stop. Harder. Harder. Give it to me."

Benji doesn't want to make it end so soon, but all the noise she's making and all the clawing fingernails digging into his back has brought him to the point of no return. He can feel himself about to explode.

Plap. Plap. Squck. Squik. Squish. Plap.

The woman at the door hasn't moved, even after some other people walked through the hallway. She doesn't care that she looks like a peeping Tom.

There is nothing that's going to pull her from the beautiful sight of Benji's chocolate skin intertwined with Jessie's reddish canary skin as they have powerfully passionate, hard sex. The sound alone would have kept her stationary but to see it is something she wouldn't trade for anything that she'd ever seen before.

Her pores are sweating, and she's running a river down her leg from the wetness of her own vagina. She wants to barge in and take part in the incredible workout, but feels she wouldn't be welcome, so she just stays riveted and silent, not wanting them to become startled and stop the peepshow.

Meanwhile, Benji has come and gone and still going and going and going, but Jessie doesn't at all meander with weakness. She's climaxed twice, but is still aggressively kissing and pulling on Benji.

Benji gets up and carries her to the bedroom and tosses her on the bed where he continues to ravage her in every possible position.

The room smells like sex. They're about as beat as they can be, and Benji squeezes out the last drops then rolls over on his back and falls asleep before Jessie can say anything to him. She lifts her head to look at him and then smiles a gratifying grin with the feeling that she's been filled up with all the loving she'll need for a week and that she's satisfied her man. She leans over toward him and kisses his cheek, lays her head on his chest and falls asleep too.

Three hours has elapsed since Benji walked through the door, and the two of them are sound asleep. Surely, they'll wake up in the morning and go at it again and again. The both of them will be in the Oakcrest Towers for the next three days making love and catching up on missed time together.

Jessie has already taken the phone off the hook and thrown it to a remote corner in her bedroom closet. There won't be any disturbance for this couple for a long time. If it were up to Jessie, that "long time" would be never.

Chapter 19

Potomac, Maryland is a haven for the ultra middle class and wealthy businessmen and women of the Washington DC area. Mornings in their communities are out of a Mary Poppins tale. The birds sing from branches of tall oak trees, and squirrels dance across lush-green lawns splattered with dew from the dense morning air.

The sun peeks through the openings between the trees that stand at attention like the royal guards of Buckingham Palace. No cars are stirring, but relentless dog-walkers, bikers, and joggers canvas the streets of this quaint suburbia, determined to savor every moment of resistance-free exercise before the ozone depleters emerge from their garages and concrete beds and fill the motorless serenity of these roads with vehicular chaos.

All is quiet at 10010 Peacock Lane as a yellow cat, which reminds you of Morris from the Nine Lives commercial, sits on the front doorstep licking the back of its paw and rubs the side of its face over and over again. The porch light is on illuminating the wall behind it, but it is too bright outside for it to make a difference beyond that. It's after seven o'clock in the morning, and the family inside this house has begun its daily routine of bathroom deeds and kitchen feeds. This is the Crawford family and Dr. Crawford is a surgeon who earned three million dollars last year in her medical practice, and that doesn't account for what her T. Rowe Price investments earned in dividends and interest payments.

She has everything she's ever wanted and more. A loving and supportive husband, three beautiful children, a big house, a pool, a

Volvo station-wagon, a dog, a cat, and good health have all contributed to fifteen years of earthly bliss since she's completed medical school and started working at Sibley Memorial Hospital, where she has operated on professional athletes from the Redskins, Wizards, and Capitals, congressmen, and presidents. She's fifty-eight years old and thinking about retiring soon to start a private practice. Her husband owns his own bike shop, and he enjoys fixing the bikes of his well-off neighbors and friends. He doesn't make much money, but he doesn't need to.

Peter Crawford is sound asleep, and his wife is in the kitchen fixing a cappuccino and bagel. The children are upstairs dragging themselves back and forth between their bedrooms and the bathroom as they prepare to go to school. The wooden banister in the hallway is lined with clothes that Andrew, the eldest son, has thrown across it in his daily morning ritual in an attempt to decipher what outfit he's going to wear today. Andy's seventeen and about five foot eight, very tall compared to his younger brother. He thinks he's such a mac with the ladies, so he takes much pride in his costume for the day. His blond hair, blue eyes, and handsome face isn't enough for the young gigolo's ego, apparently, because every morning, he has to empty out his entire closet to make sure he puts together the perfect outfit. If he doesn't do that, his family would think something is wrong with him, and his mother would check his temperature.

"Take that stuff in your room, Andy," says a little brown-haired, curly-head boy with bright red cheeks.

It's Andy's younger brother Winfield. Winfield is a few years younger than Andy and three years older than the youngest brother Robert, who is still asleep. Robert goes to school much later than his brothers, so he gets an extra forty minutes or so before his father's alarm clock is sounded. That's when Mr. Crawford gets up and gets Lil Bobby ready for school.

Winfield is standing in the hall waiting to get past his brother to get to his room. He hates that Andy has to impede on his flow of progress each morning. Usually he is able to time perfectly when he can walk through without his brother's obstruction but not this morning.

"Man!" cries out Winfield.

Andy steps back to the wall and waves Winfield by like a butler. "After you Cupcake. You may pass."

Andy was deliberately blocking the hallway and knew his brother wouldn't try to pass him because the last time he tried that, he got belted Even though Andy got grounded for his involvement in the assault, Winfield would rather not get elbowed in the belly and clumped across the back of the neck by his bully of a brother. His neck had been extremely sore for a week, and he couldn't go to football practice or play in the game that Saturday.

Winfield could sense Andy's movement and braced himself for a boot in the rectum.

"You play too much," Winfield says as he clutches his butt with a weaving hop forward but nothing happened.

Meanwhile, the good doctor downstairs is looking at the FOX 5 Morning News to get her dose of society gossip and traffic conditions while she drinks her cappuccino and nibbles on her raisin wheat bagel.

"We'll be leaving soon, boys. Andy, are you ready? You know you have a bus to catch. Let's get a move on," she commands in a polite authoritative voice, using her playful imitation of Princess Di.

Shortly afterward, one after the other, Winfield and then Andy stampede down the steps and come in the kitchen to eat some cereal. Andy eats Pops, and Winfield eats Captain Crunch. While they eat, their mom gathers her things and sets them at the front door, then waits patiently for her sons as she catches the last few bits of the news on the portable TV sitting on the kitchen counter where the boys are sitting on the stools wolfing down their food.

This is the weekday morning routine and has been since the both of them graduated from Potomac Elementary School. Dr. Leslie Crawford from her own perspective, truly, has a blessed and peaceful family. She wouldn't have scripted her life any other way. Her creator has certainly been good to her, and it's obvious that she continues to be showered with blessings.

✧ ✧ ✧

Perched upon a power line near the Cabin John shopping center a large black crow peers at the passing cars with an uncanny awareness. The bird only glances at some of the cars, but at others, it takes an intense glare and even shrieks from time to time. One never knows what goes on in the mind of a bird, or why they decide to sit on power lines above cars so they can drop white and purplish turds on them, spotting up their fancy paint jobs. Mindless animals. But this crow, however, has a conscious awareness that seems to be keenly comprehensive. It is apparent that this fine-feathered friend can distinguish the difference between each passing car.

"Awk, Awk, Awk," spews the black raven, becoming overly excited as a charcoal gray Volvo station-wagon makes its way down the street in close proximity to the nestled crow. "Awk, awk, awk, awk," he cries as the car drives under him. He swoops down and glides through the air above the moving car. The crow follows the car at an altitude just above the trees until the car begins to approach an intersection with traffic lights. As the car slows and stops at the red light, the bird descends and lands in the street right next to the driver-side window, revealing itself to the driver of the car.

It's Dr. Crawford; she has already dropped both of her children off and is on her way to the Bethesda Naval Hospital to console one of her former patients who is terminally ill and should die within the next couple of months. Little does she know that the bird that is staring at her from the roadside is actually Iblis, who has manifested himself into the form of a bird so he can seek out someone that might require a little calamity. He can sense the blessing of the Omega being showered down upon these puny humans, and he takes a special interest in those human beings who may seem to be receiving a lot more than others. He's facing the oncoming traffic, but the eye on the side of his face is focused directly on Dr. Crawford. He has a hard, sturdy beak incapable of any expression, but Dr. Crawford can't help but think that the unblinking bird that is staring into her eyes has a smirk on its face.

A deathly cold chill races through her body starting from her shoulders and spreads down her torso past her knees to her toes in a sensation equivalent to the striking of the funny bone. The sight of the bird's face is scary, but Dr. Crawford is a rational person, so she blinks her eyes to refocus to take a closer look to make certain that her mind isn't playing tricks on her.

How could a bird be smirking at me? she thinks.

Before she can refocus, Iblis takes to flight to avoid an oncoming car that nearly runs him over. A car behind Dr. Crawford is blowing its horn because the light has turned green, but she didn't realize it because of the bird. She tries franticly to get another glimpse of the bird that is flying away, but she is unable to. It's as if the bird just disappeared.

Bonk. Bonk!

She lets her foot off the brake and her Volvo drifts forward. Dr. Crawford is too shaken to oblige the driver stuck behind her with a quick takeoff; instead she lightly mashes the gas pedal and slowly accelerates to the speed limit.

Iblis is now flying high above Dr. Crawford, watching her and seeking to devour her. His sole mission is to bring destruction upon her as he scans the area below, pondering thoughts of evil. He spots another car traveling northbound to Old Georgetown Road, which intersects with Tuckerman Lane, the street in which Dr. Crawford is driving on. Inside the other car is Dustin Jarboe, a varsity stud that all the girls adore. His face is perfect, and his brown hair is spiked with a high top blend of blond streaks styling his head. He's on his way to school seeming to be in quite a hurry. He doesn't care that he's late. He only wants to see Julianne, his steady girlfriend, before she goes to her homeroom class. That's his inspirational reason for getting to school before the second bell.

Varoom, his engine hollers as he zooms past the Exxon gas station at the corner of Democracy Boulevard and Old Georgetown Road. He's in his black, 1970 Pontiac GTO Road Runner, a large heap of heavy metal with dual exhaust pipes poking out of the rear bumper and moving fast. He's blasting "Guns and Roses" out of his speakers and strumming his imaginary guitar with power strokes as he pumps his head with every smack of the drummer's snare.

By now, the crow is flying only a couple of hundred feet above the earth as Dustin approaches the intersection at Tuckerman Lane. The light is already turning yellow, and the brake lights are shining bright from the rear of the Road Runner. The crow glares intensely at the roof of the GTO trying to burn a hole in it so it can see the person sitting in the driver's seat. It's not possible, but Iblis sure tries. Inside the car, Dustin has his foot on the brake, but does not have much pressure on the pedal when he looks in his rearview mirror wondering if he should accelerate and fly through the yellow light. He looks back at the light, and it's still yellow.

Suddenly a voice in his head says, *Beat the light.*

His better judgment tells him that the light will be red long before he gets through it, but the voice continues to urge him to press on. *Man, there ain't no police behind you. Damn that light and the police too. They can't catch me in their wildest dreams. Yeah, I don't wanna miss my smooches from Julianne anyway.*

Dustin floors the gas pedal and the light turns red well before he reaches the white line, but the coast is clear, no police and besides, he's a rebel without a cause or a pause, so red, yellow, green; it's all the same to him. Black asphalt and white lines. It's *his* road.

His engine roars and the crispy purr of his Floor Master exhaust pipes rings through the air. The loud ferocious sound of his engine and pipes are melodious to any and all car lovers, and it actually makes Dustin feel like he's the king of the road. He approaches the intersection with his foot to the floor and a grin on his face when suddenly his face appears to have seen a ghost. His eyes are fully exposed, his mouth is wide open, and then his lips slowly back off his pearly white teeth as he grits them. Terror controls every muscle in his face, which is now as red as Rudolph's nose, and his eyes shrink to a Chinese squint. His teeth converge to form an ironclad lock as his neck widens from the way he's straining his muscles and pushing his head back in preparation to encounter his worst nightmare.

Skirrrrt!

Chapter 20

Being a surgeon, nervousness is something Dr. Crawford has grown to become immune to, but the feeling that complicates her thought process has her still wondering if she's just seen a smiling crow, which looked as if it were looking her right in the eyes, is disturbing to her because she's not used to feeling this way. She's a devout Christian who says a prayer every time she senses evil in her midst, and things aren't quite right around her now.

Oh, Heavenly Father, in Christ's name I pray that you wipe my fears away and protect me from this wicked world's evil. May your kingdom come, and may your will be done on earth as it is done in the heavens. Amen.

Leslie Crawford is a very fruitful person, and the blessings of the Creator are all around her. His blessings are with everyone, but more so with the righteous ones of the earth, however, unforeseen occurrences occur to us all, so one never knows what might happen next. Furthermore, Iblis is very much aware of her blessedness, so that makes her an automatic target of his powerful machinations.

She's approaching a red light. The street sign hanging from the power line over the intersection reads Old Georgetown Road, and there's no car in front of her waiting at the light for it to turn green. The Volvo is coasting at thirty-five miles per hour and Leslie is patient, not putting her foot on the brake pedal yet, allowing the weight of the car and drag of the tires to hamper the car's inertia. The car slows, but before she needs to come to a complete stop, the light turns green, and she's free to proceed safely through intersection. At least she should be, but not today.

Skirrrt!

"Awk," crows the black bird above the intersection as the black GTO driven by Dustin barrels down on the gray Volvo, which is already in the intersection.

The GTO leaves a trail of black skid lines and white smoke behind it just before it impacts the passenger side of the smaller gray car. The collision is so violent that the sound of it can be heard by people in nearby houses. It's the sound of metal thrashing metal, glass exploding, tires skidding and death.

The black GTO is wearing the Volvo wrapped around its frontend like a bumper guard, and the engine is still running, however, Dustin is unconscious and bleeding profusely from his brow after his body had tried to javelin out of the front windshield. As rebellious as he is, he did have on a seatbelt that has, without a doubt, saved his life, but in the Volvo? Well, she never had a chance to react to the squealing tires, not even to brace herself. Leslie dies on impact, unable to say a last prayer that her god would have heard and maybe spared her life in answer to her entreaties. One of Zion's beautiful, blessed children will return to her sooner than expected, wiped out by the power of influences—Iblis' evil influence. One down, millions to go.

"Awk."

✧   ✧   ✧

Here, in the lower realm, Iblis meets with his army of evil spirits to communicate with them in person so that he can heighten their awareness and diligence toward prolonging their hold on the current system of things and misleading the entire inhabited world to the broad and spacious road leading off to the lake that burns with sulfur and brimstone.

Iblis has just returned after roaming the earth, seeking the Omega's favored ones and doing all in his power to destroy or adulterate them—Leslie Crawford being one of the many. Iblis knows that since the time when animal sacrifice became a useless form of worship, all of mankind has an opportunity to become one of the chosen ones who will inherit the kingdom of the heavens or part of the great crowd of humans to inherit the earth. Those are the ones that are blessed, and Iblis is determined to make all those who follow "the path" a target of destruction. These ones will carry out the prophecies that will trigger a great tribulation upon the earth that will culminate in the great and illustrious day the Omega the Almighty and Iblis will be doomed to the abyss. That's why he is rampant. That's why he is relentless in the midst of the humans because they are the lock to the bottomless pit. Once the final prophecy is complete, the key will become useful. And at the appointed time "Apollyon will use the key."

The fathers of the Nephalim had returned to heaven but were exiled to the abyss because they forsook their original dwelling place by coming to earth and having sexual relations with the women of the earth. Iblis and his brethren dread the day of being sent there, and that's why they're here to discuss their assault against anyone and everyone that may help further the Omega's plan and purpose. Iblis is a cherub and so too are many of his followers while others are analim, and even seraphim, and they haven't joined together in this manner in hundreds of years.

Iblis is in his original form, beautiful as the day he was created. The other spirits fall down in worship of him for he is their god, and they are now reminded of what made him so influential at the time of his bringing them all to relative mortality since they will inevitably die as do mere mortals.

He stands before them and communicates. They remain in obeisance to him as he gives them their commands and warns them of the consequences of failure.

The one that will come along will be a motivator of the people, and he or she will join forces with the chosen ones to help them proclaim the message. Only, he is very different. He will defy all conventional methods and will escalate this great work to an unstoppable plague to my system of things. He will even put himself where he should not, in order to spread this virus. His people will continue what they have already begun long before him. Only the floodgates will be already ruptured, and this work will become ridiculous to my sight, and the ears of man will be open. Many will actually listen; most will turn away. Nonetheless, the prophecies will be fulfilled, and all will be lost. He must not be allowed to succeed! No, he must not be allowed to breathe! Find him! And bring calamity upon him, only you don't personally bring him harm, for it is forbidden for us to do so. Whosoever may be found that, remotely brings to mind the things you have just heard, sends calamity in his direction, and if deep in your soul you feel the blessing of Yahweh in the midst of the despicable creature, call upon me immediately my brethren, for he is most likely that one. Now go! You, sons of the Belial, students of the teaching of this wicked world, defy your Heavenly Father and curse him to his face! For you are already doomed to eternal destruction, and we must take the entire world to the lake of fire with us! Go you splendid deceiver of mankind. Go! Go! Go!

Chapter 21

The line is unusually long for twelve thirty-three at night at this Wawa
convenience store out in Annapolis, Maryland. Benji is standing at the
back of the line with his slippers on and a navy blue North Face ski coat.
His skullcap is covering the dome of his head in no structured fashion.
It's just on it, wrinkled up on one side and pulled down snug on the other.
He has a bunch of snacks and hygiene items cradled in his crossed arms.
There are Pop-Tarts, cheese-covered popcorn, strawberry ice cream,
symphony chocolate bars, cotton balls, and a tall plastic bottle of Deer
Park spring water.

Benji's eyes are bloodshot red, and he looks calm and expressionless
with his head tilted to the side, staring toward the front of the motionless
line. One by one the cashier sends the late-night shoppers on their merry
ways. Finally, Benji flops the bundle of goodies down on the countertop
and digs into his jean pocket and comes up with nothing but lint. His
eyes widen and his awareness rises sharply as he slaps and frisks his hips
and thighs, checking his pockets for money.

Man, don't tell me that I don't got no money on me.

"I know I didn't . . . leave the . . . ," he whispers as he checks his coat
pockets. The coat has an array of hidden pockets, and he's checking
them all.

He finds a fat, half-folded knot of money in an upper pocket that he
didn't even remember putting in there. He had forgotten the pocket even
existed. He knows that he had to be the one to put it in there because a
receipt is tucked between the layers of bills that has a number written on

the back in his handwriting. He remembers writing down the number but couldn't remember the name of the foxy lady that recited it.

"Alrighty then," he proclaims, dropping the receipt to the floor as he peels a couple of twenty dollar bills off the wad.

"Ten dollars and sixty-two cents," says the short, dark-skinned, nappy-head man speaking with a distinctive Central African accent.

Benji hands him one of the twenties and tucks the rest of the money in his jean pocket along with the change the man gives him. Byinga, the name of the man that is behind the counter, fills a white plastic bag with the products on the counter. Benji takes the bag and without any type of farewell bidding, he strolls out the door and hops into the forest-green Yukon backed up in front of the store. The truck's dual exhaust roars as the truck stabs out of the parking lot. He travels at a high rate of speed, tightly angling corners and running stop signs through the colonial style community where his house is located.

Once in the yard, he turns the headlights of his truck off because there is enough brightness shining from the sensor lights that illuminate the front and side of the house that Benji and Jessie bought together shortly after he came home. He knew it wouldn't be good for them to stay at the high-rise together. Not with Salina on the prowl. Jessie is in the house waiting for him to return. The driver's door swings open before the truck comes to a complete stop, and Benji emerges with a crunch of the transmission as he slams the truck in park while the vehicle is still rolling forward and then dashes to the front door of his huge colonial-style house.

"Jessie," he calls, entering the door. There's no answer, but she's certainly home. She's the one who sent him out of the house after he had fallen sound asleep. She's four months pregnant and is already irritable with abnormal cravings. She hasn't been too hard on Benji though, because he spoils her and spends lots of time with her since she became pregnant. He's a tireless father-to-be, always at her every beck and call but doesn't necessarily enjoy getting up in the middle of the night to go to the store.

All the lights are off in the living room, but the light over the stove in the kitchen is enough to allow Benji to see his way to the back without bumping into anything. He prepares a bed tray full of calories for Jessie and tips up the hardwood stairs to the television-lit master bedroom.

The room is spaciously cozy because, despite all the space in the room, there's enough furniture and plush carpet to make them never want to leave out for anything. There's a king-size bed. Actually, it's more like an emperor-size bed, and Jessie says that the bed is very comfortable but doesn't like the idea of needing a step stool to climb up in it. She hates to think of how it will feel if she ever falls out of it.

Above the bed in the ceiling are two sunroof windows that welcome the sunlight in the morning and the moonlight at night if they have the specially made curtain open. A loft furnished with a love seat and a stereo system triumphs over the bedroom, and a bay window adds to the beauty of the unique architecture. Benji had a wall built around the television to hide the ugly wires that run between the TV, DVD player, cable box, surround sound receiver, and speakers.

Jessie is sitting up, waiting for Benji. She has a scarf wrapped tightly around her head; also her gown covers her up to the neck. Though she's in bed, pregnant and undressed, she's pretty as she is on her way to work. She's also restless, so Benji may as well get prepared to be up for a while.

"Thank you, bae," Jessie says to Benji, who is accustomed to her gratefulness, so he doesn't answer. Instead, he winks at her, placing the tray down on her lap, and then peels his clothes off as he walks around the emperor-size bed.

"I'm about to go slam out," Benji says.

"No, bae," pleads Jessie, "don't go to sleep . . . I'm up. Keep me company for a while."

"Aw, bae, I was already asleep. I'm tired," he stresses.

"OK then, just watch TV with me for a little while. Let's turn to the Cartoon Network and see if the *Flintstones* are on."

"A'ight," Benji replies in a rather halfhearted tone.

He strips to the bone, boxers, and all, then climbs into the bed with his pregnant woman. They're not married, but Benji had put a rock on her left ring finger the day after he walked back into her life. The morning after they made sweet love, Benji got up to the smell of T-bone steak and popcorn-yellow scrambled eggs with melted Velveeta cheese, Hickory Beef Sausage, grits, toast, orange juice, and milk. He got out the bed and walked to the bathroom to kill the little man residing in his mouth with a shot of Listerine and then crept down the hall toward the aroma from the kitchen. The flowers, clothes, and ring he had dropped were still strewn across the floor. He picked up the ring and a rose and walked in the kitchen still wearing his birthday suit. He turned the corner and saw the love of his life standing over the stove with her back to him.

"Are you gonna eat breakfast before you leave me?" Jessie asked him without seeing him walk into the kitchen. She could smell him.

Benji paused then grinned at how she always seems to know what is going on behind her as if she has eyes in the back of her head.

He answered, "Bae, I ain't never gonna leave you. That means we're us from now on. I've made up my mind that you are the one I want in my life. You're the one who will be the queen to my generations. Jessie . . ."

She dropped her cooking utensil and whirled her body around to be face-to-face with the man she wants to say yes to. Her eyes are glossy and open wide. Her brow is arched high in anticipation of what he's about to say or ask.

Oh lord, please let him ask me. Yes, I'll marry you, Benji. "Yes."

Benji looked into her eyes and said as he handed her the rose and took her left hand with the ring in his other. "I love you, and I want us to be together forever. I got big plans," he told her, "I think you should be a part of them. I don't wanna go back home to Salina. She's not for me. You're the one. Your dreams have come true. I'm just sorry I took so long to make my own dreams come true. Let's do this, bae. Are you with me?"

The question, "Are you with me?" is not the one Jessie was hoping for, but it'll do for now and was enough to make her heart dance with joy. He hadn't let her down, and the smile that was shining on her face gave him every indication that now is the time to slip the large diamond ring on her ring finger. The ring slid onto her finger without resistance as if she had gone with him to get it fitted. Her soul was burning with fervent devotion toward the man that stood before her, and she wanted nothing more than to become Mrs. Benjamin Powell, but the gesture of solitude from him, even though he hadn't asked for her hand in marriage, meant that he had laid claim to her and had given himself to her in every sense of the word, making that the day that made the thirteen years of loyalty to a man that had belonged to another woman worth all the while in the world. She's finally become happy.

Yes. Yes. Thank you, Lord.

"I don't know what to say, Benji. I mean I've always been with you. I'd go to the end of the earth for you. I'm no gangster, but if you put it in my hand, I'll buss it. Damn right I'm witchu."

They embraced for a long while, and Jessie sighed a breath of relief and cried tears of joy, still in disbelief that that day had finally come.

Now, as he lies beside her and their unborn child, he knows he will make her his wife and has already purchased another ring and has given it to Bink, his best friend, who will be his best man at the secret wedding that he's planning for next week at the justice of the peace. He's even made all-inclusive accommodation for their honeymoon in Cancun, Mexico. He knows they won't be able to do all the things that they would like to do, but he just wants her to see how beautiful the sunrise is from the ocean-view suite at the top of the J. W. Marriott.

He wants to marry her before the baby is born because she's been talking a lot about living right and how she doesn't feel it is appropriate to continue to ignore family values and righteous morals and principles. Although she has never imposed the teachings of the Bible on him, she does mention from time to time that you must live right by God's standards. She's a Christian, and he's a Muslim, but that has never hampered their relationship. Benji just loves to be around her because she's respectful and fun, unlike Salina.

"So do you wanna play acey-deucey?" Benji asks.

"No . . . I just wanna talk . . . Do you think I'm getting fat?"

"Fat? You're already phat. Phat as a racehorse."

She faces him while he looks at her cheeks and neck.

"Bae, you're pregnant. Don't you expect to gain some weight? You're not fat. Don't worry about it. And if you do get fat, you'll still be prettier than any of them chicks out there."

"I *am* getting fat. I can feel it."

"Don't worry about it. You'll lose it after you have the baby. We'll get a membership to Bally's or something."

There's a long silence as they watch television, and then Jessie asks, "Benji . . . I remember you said something about starting your own business. I'm not trying to get all in your business, but I was just wondering if you were still thinking about doing that."

She's not afraid of upsetting Benji nor does she want him to think that she is suggesting that he stops doing whatever he's doing and start a business or get a job, but she's concerned about his welfare and knows that if he gets into any kind of trouble with the law, he won't be given much leniency by a judge, especially if it's a federal one because there are guidelines that they must follow, so she wants to try to coax him toward making moves to legitimizing himself for his future and hers.

Benji can recognize her careful approach to the question, and he makes a mental note not to get on the defensive should the conversation carry-over to him changing his life, stop selling drugs, and to start doing things in the best interest of them and the baby.

"I feel you, Jess. I know what you're getting at, and I've already started making moves toward starting my business."

Jessie's glowing smile spreads across her face, but she tries to hide it from Benji with her hand that is full of cheese popcorn.

"I've even come up with a name," he continues. "I'ma call it Scoop Trucking. I'll buy a couple of dump trucks, get two good drivers, an office, and find some contracts. Dump trucks are getting paid out there. At least that's what I keep hearing. I'ma try my hand. What the hell! Dudes I know with the brains of Martin Lawrence on *Love Boat* are gettin' money with just one truck, so how can I go wrong?"

"Oh well that's good. I didn't realize you were already getting things together. Why didn't you tell me? I can do some legwork for you, like get your business license, register the company name, and create a logo. All that."

"I was gonna tell you, but I decided to surprise you when I drove up in a big dump truck, but since you pressed me out . . ."

Jessie chuckles, "Aw nigga, ain't nobody press you."

"I know, boo. I'm just playing. But really, though. I wanted to surprise you. But it's okay because I do need your help. In fact, next week we can go up to the courthouse together and get some business handled. Can you take off next Friday?"

"Friday? . . . I suppose that'll be a better day than any. Plus it's the end of the week," Jessie agrees, "Yeah . . . Friday. We can do it on Friday."

Benji grins a sly smirk, knowing he has solved the dilemma that stymied him, his mother, and Jessie's cousin Denise. When he told them that he was planning to marry Jessie at the justice of the peace and whisk her away to a Caribbean retreat, if she would fly, They all wondered what would be a good way to get her there without drawing any suspicion. Well, Jessie has just offered herself willingly.

Jessie hasn't flown since 9/11 and has expressed a lack of interest in ever doing so again unless circumstances required her to do so. Certainly, a honeymoon to Cancun would be a justifiable circumstance, but no one can predict how she'll be, considering the baby that she's carrying.

"Can I go to sleep now?" Benji asks.

"No!" Jessie snaps, "We just got started. I've got a lot more that I want to talk about."

"Well, honey, talk to the head, because it's about to lie down and go to sleep. You can talk all you want, but I promise you, I'll be asleep in a couple of minutes."

Benji lies down and falls fast asleep. Jessie grabs her Bible and opens it to Revelation, her favorite book of the Bible. She reads for a while, then sets the Bible down on her lap, and starts to mediate on what's going to come of Benji's endeavor into the trucking business. She can see herself quitting her job at BET so she can help Benji manage a fleet of dump trucks. If she has anything to do with it, it's going to be well organized and will have a chance to grow. She can't wait until next week. A new life will begin, but little does she know how right she is. A new life *will* begin, and so will the drama, because Salina still hasn't let Benji go. She hasn't accepted that Benji has left her and the children forever. As far as she's concerned, he'll be back, but when she hears about the wedding, all hell's gonna break loose.

Chapter 22

The bed is unmade even though the dawn has broken, and it's not occupied. There are piles of clothes separated around the floor, and it's apparent that someone is preparing to wash them. But these clothes have been sitting around for three days and have only gotten kicked around, making the floor a pig sty.

The dresser is a mess with open cosmetic bottles, tissues, and all sorts of other items littering the open space of its white surface. The multiple doors of the closet are made of mirrors and are speckled with fingerprints and months of neglect reflecting a room of sorrow and desolation.

The radio on the bookshelf is playing an old Shirley Murdock CD, and the song is on repeat as it is every so often when Salina wakes up thinking about how much she wishes she could get some revenge on the people who she sees as the objects of her pain and suffering. The song that's playing cuts like a knife because it reminds her of the fact that her man is probably waking up with another woman this very moment. The name of the song is "Morning," and she actually hates the song with a passion but can't seem to stop listening to it regardless to how miserable it makes her feel.

The smooth melody of the song conjures up agonizing feelings inside of this distraught woman sitting in the adjoining bathroom of the master bedroom of the house that was once known as home to Benjamin Powell. It's now a forgotten resident where the Mama of Benji's babies live. Bink doesn't even come over to cut the grass anymore. He's recently become too busy for that, but Salina forces him to continue to come over to satisfy her need for sex, but his love-making skills are no comparison to Benji's.

She's sick that she hasn't so much as had a chance to share a passionate kiss with Benji, let alone feel his power thrust and warm caress. The thought of someone else enjoying the company of the man she loves twenty times more than she's ever shown makes her sick to her stomach and turns her whole world upside down.

She hasn't been the same person the world once knew since Benji smacked her in the face and walked out of her life for good. It's been several months, and Benji has vowed to never come back despite her pleas and tears. She's close to giving up, but defeat hasn't yet conquered her will and desire for the man who has made life so easy for her. She's never known what it was like to take care of herself. Benji's always been there since she left home. Though he was in lockup for years, his money wasn't.

She's on the floor of the bathroom talking on the phone to Benji now. This could be her last effort to convince him to come back home.

"But, Benji," she cries, "You're all I have. What am I supposed to do with the house?"

"Sell it. It's in your name. You can have the money and everything else. You can have the money I left for you too. You'll need it to take care of the kids, but of course, I'm going to get anything my kids need."

Little does he know that Salina has already spent most of the money he left at the house when he got locked up. The beauty salon she has isn't doing so well because she can't keep good stylist in there long enough to establish a solid clientele. Salina is really a difficult person to get along with.

"That money is gone, Benji. I had to pay for the materials to build the salon, all the equipment, and the advertising to get it off the ground."

"A hundred and fifty, sixty, or whatever it was is all gone? Sh . . . Man, I ain't got nothing to do with that. I can't believe you spent all that money. Oh well, I sure hope the business pays off."

"Benji, don't do this to me. I'm not going to be able to make it alone."

"If I wasn't home what would you do? Huh. You done spent all but who knows how much of the money I left. Now you don't know what to do and how you're gonna survive. And what really did you spend it on? Jack! You didn't spend it on nothing useful. I know damn well you didn't spend it all on that salon." Benji takes a deep breath. "You know. You're the biggest reason why I had no choice but to run the streets because you had to always be dressed in the latest fashions or go to every island on the planet. Then you got the nerve to tell me that you want me to get a job or else. Or else what!"

"I didn't mean it, Benji . . . *sniff* . . . I was just being mean. You can do whatever you want to do, baby. Just come . . . *sniff* . . . back . . . I'm sorry, baby. Please."

"It's too late Salina. I've made my mind up. I don't want to be with you."

Snapping to a viciously hysterical tone, Salina yells into the phone, "So what? You wanna be with that bitch?! Huh? That whore over me? . . . *sniff* . . . That's who you wanna be with?"

There's a silence.

"Yep."

Salina sighs a pitiful wail and bursts into a loud cry that makes Benji feel so sorry for her that he thinks of apologizing and telling her that he's coming home, but he knows that is something that he would regret for the rest of his life. Besides, he'd never leave his Jessie. As bad as he feels about making Salina feel this way, he knows that there is nothing that he can do for her but be perfectly honest.

"Sorry, Salina. I'm not coming back. I'm gone. Bye . . ."

He hangs up the phone, and that would be the last time he would talk to her outside of what the kids need. As time passes, he never returns to the house, and when his mother tries to pick the children up, Salina would rudely tell Mrs. Powell that if Benji wanted to see his children, he would have to come to the house himself. She'd also tell him the same thing whenever he would call, but Benji knew that was a trap. If he goes over there, he knows that she will seduce him into sleeping with her, and Benji has promised himself that he's going to do better with Jessie. He's determined to remain loyal to her. So instead of going to the house to see the kids, he goes to their schools and has told them to never tell their mother or else he would have to stop coming. Salina doesn't know, and it kills Nakeisha to keep the secret from her mother, but she knows it would kill her more to betray her father's wishes and not be able to see him at all.

Benji loves his children and has told Salina that she should file a child-support case, but she refuses to because she knows the judge will grant him visitation rights and possibly joint custody, and then she'd have to allow him to take the children with him. Benji's mother has told him to file for custody, but he doesn't want to take Salina to court for a judge to get involved in their business. If a judge is to get involved, it won't be because of something he initiated. Benji looks at that as snitchin', and he'd never go that route.

He believes Allah will work things out for him and is convinced that time will be the winner of this battle and the wounds will heal, allowing Salina to eventually get over him and go on with her life. How wrong he is!

Salina has all but withdrawn from the outside world. She does have to work. She may go to the children's schools if the teacher sends home a note for a conference, but otherwise she's in the car driving all around District Heights, hoping to see Jessie's car or the green truck with the dark tinted windows that Bink has told her Benji's driving. Little does she know that Benji and Jessie wouldn't be found anywhere near District Heights. They moved to Annapolis just as soon as they found a house that suited their taste. The only people that Benji has told are his mother and his two sisters. He doesn't know who told Salina what she found out about Jessie, but obviously it's someone who's close to him because there aren't too many people who knew about her in the first place. Benji wants to protect Jessie, so Bink doesn't know where their house is, nor does Richter, just to be certain that they don't leak it out to someone that would tell Salina. The last thing he'd ever conclude is that one of them would actually tell her themselves. Benji's mother and sister Pooh know that Salina has vowed to kill Jessie if she ever got hold of her, so they don't even talk to the rest of the family about where Benji's new house is. This is certainly the biggest secret they've ever had to keep.

If it were not for the photo of Salina in the guard's booth at the gate of the BET compound, Salina would have caught Jessie at her car months ago. Many days, she has waited outside the gate to try to see if she could follow Jessie's car but that's a waste of time because Benji has bought Jessie a new car and has tinted the windows. Salina has really been wasting time looking for Jessie, because she's looking for all the wrong things in all the wrong places. Her frustration sometimes makes her want to just kill herself.

As it is now though, she's still sitting in the middle of the bathroom floor crying her eyes out. Her face is in her hands, and the floor below is sprinkled with fallen tears.

Why can't I get over him? Come on, Salina. Pull yourself together. You gottta. Damn . . . You should have been sweeter. Benji is too good. Too nice. Oh god . . . Why? . . . OK, you gotta get rid of her. That's why it's so easy for him to let you go. I gotta find her. Where do they live? Her number started with 568, so she has to live somewhere off Pennsylvania Avenue on the Maryland side, but where? Bink's probably fakin' like he doesn't know. I'ma kill 'er ass. I hate her. I hate her.

"I hate her!"

She remains there on the floor for a good portion of the morning, and the song she was listening to is still repeating itself and becomes as unnoticeable to her ears as the oxygen that surrounds her in the musky air of the room.

Ring. Ring.

The sound of the phone pierces through Salina's heart because she knows that the voice on the other end of the phone will not be Benji's, though she is hoping that it will be. She'll never get over the father of her two children, the master of her bedroom, the king of her world.

Ring.

"Hello," she says groggily.

"Is that you, baby?" says an older woman on the other end of the phone.

It's Beverly, Salina's mother, checking in on her daughter as she does religiously every single morning since she found out that Benji had left her for good. Beverly has never known Salina to be so down and is concerned for her because she knows what depression can do to a woman. Salina's outgoing personality has all but vanished, and the confidence that she once bolstered toward a happy ending has become reduced to a bleak hope of even surviving.

The sound of her mother's voice is a dose of balm for her aching heart.

"Mama," Salina whines, "I'm so tired of crying, Mama. Make him come back to me . . . *Sniff* . . . Mama . . . *sigh* . . . He gone ma. He gone . . . What I'm gonna do?"

"Aw, Salina . . . You have to go on, darlin'. I know you hurtin', but life goes on. The babies are suffering to see you like this. And the Lord knows you killing your mother."

"I . . . can't help it. I wish I was just dead . . . ," she cries out in a loud voice.

"Please, baby. Don't' talk like that. You're scaring me."

"I don't wanna talk right now," Salina whispers in a broken voice and hangs up the phone not saying good-bye. She simply puts the phone down on the base, lies down on the bed, and stares at the spinning flaps of the ceiling fan.

Salina feels that she must do something, but knows not what to do. She does know that the other woman has won—won the prize that she once had locked in her own clutches—a prize of a strong, smart, handsome man who satisfied her in every way. She knows that another woman has everything that she once had, and the thought of it freezes her tears as venom enters into her thoughts. Treachery consumes her nervous system, and Iblis would be proud of the sinister schemes brewing in the mind of this mortal who has been influenced by him before and many of his dastardly creatures of plunder. But now it's all Salina, and no one is coaxing her at the moment.

All that keeps ringing in Salina's diabolical mind is a phrase from a movie that she once saw, but can't recall the name of it. She just hears the words and knows that she'll carry them out.

Murder. Death. Kill.

Chapter 23

At the corner of Kent Town Drive and Firehouse Road, Benji sits in front of his childhood home. There's a park that sits on the opposite side of a tall ivy-covered fence that runs along the entire length of the park, which is located behind the row of houses on his parents' street. The former white residence of the community once used the park as a driving range. There are still remnants of white folks speckled throughout the neighborhood filled with black families who fled inner city DC to find a safer, more peaceful community to raise their children. Well, Kentland hasn't been known as a safe and peaceful place since the early 1970s and has only gotten worse through the years, notorious for being one of southern Maryland's deadliest drug infestations. PG County Police have made national headlines for some of their worst brutality cases stemming from this neighborhood and other surrounding boroughs that make up the city of Landover, Maryland.

They call dudes from this area the NFL ever since the Washington Redskins moved their stadium here. "Niggas from Landover" has more Dallas fans than Redskin fans because of the way the late Jack Kent Cooks showed how racist he was and how inconsiderate he was toward the inhabitants of this little city. They didn't take too kindly to him telling the broadcast world to refer to their city as Raljon, Maryland instead of Landover. Overall, though, the Redskins have been a good thing for the people of Landover because there's been noticeable improvements all over the city—new roads, red-bricked crosswalks, new sidewalks, a state-of-the-art fitness center, a new shopping center that includes a plush multiplex movie theatre, courtesy of the famed Magic Johnson and a more aggressive approach to calls reporting emergencies and crimes. The latter has made Landover a much less attractive place for the not-so-good inhabitants of the city, and the FBI has built a field office right here inside of its city limits, which is where Lindsey Miles and Jeffery Faraday operate from.

The weather is brisk, and Benji's mother still has her Christmas lights from last year hanging around the windows and doors. The sun is shining bright and Bink's white Cherokee Laredo is bouncing the rays of the sun into the eyes of the couple of guys who glance at it as he drives up and parks. The leaves have long fled the tall trees that stand around the small townhouses of this block, and around the edge of the fence is a dust trail in the grass at the corner of the yard where people cut across the grass on their way into the park.

The two young men that are with Benji when Bink pulls up are leaning against the fence in front to the house. They're Amp and Bootemup, and they don't like Bink very much. There's no particular reason why—they just don't. Bink is a pretty boy who's not a gangster but dresses the part from time to time. He's also a bosom-buddy of Benji, so sometimes he's a hindrance to their time with Benji because there are things that Benji does with him that doesn't include his thugged-out buddies.

Bink has been to college and didn't get caught up in the street life when the two of them were coming up. Amp and Bootemup are a lot younger than Benji and Bink, so sometimes Bink shows that he's above them, and that really burns them up about him. He gets out of the truck and says, "What's up?" to everyone and then gestures to Benji to step to the side with him as if he has something to talk about that is so criminally inclined. They look at each other as Benji and Bink step off and shake their heads and shrug their shoulders before they pick up on what they were talking about before he pulled up.

Bink doesn't really have anything important to talk to Benji about. He just likes to appear as if he's up to something that's gangster. He's not a gangster, but he likes to perpetrate a fraud as if he is. Amp, who can see right through him, is sickened by this dude every time he comes around.

"That nigga is a bamma if I ain't seen one," Amp says as he glares at Bink.

Bootemup doesn't respond; he just sucks on his teeth and looks in the same direction that Amp is looking in. They aren't at all wondering what is so important that Bink had to pull Benji to the side because they already know that it's nothing. They know he's just frontin' as usual.

Amp and Bootemup are dressed in their urban gear that they have bought from one of the local clothing designers here in the DC area. Both of them have a closet full of HOBO sweats, and that's pretty much all they ever wear. If it's not HOBO, it's All Daz or Shooters. But Bink never wears the local designers. He's always got on Sean John, Phat Farm, or Iceberg. That burns them up too. Bootemup would like to beat him up just for the hell of it, and Bink can sense it. He makes Bink feel uneasy, and Bink doesn't like coming around when Bootemup is there, not because he's afraid of him, but regardless to the fact that Bink can fight and all that, he knows people don't fight like men much anymore. People squeeze and bang the gun nowadays, and Bink wouldn't be caught dead with a gun, so he would rather avoid a bad situation altogether. That's why he's asked Benji to get in the car with him because they were looking at him too hard. They just give him the creeps.

Benji had called Bink and told him to meet with him around the way. He had told Bink that he needed him to do a favor. Benji is preparing for the wedding, and he wants to give Bink the heads up on how everything is going to go down. Bink is going to be the best man and ring bearer.

"Married? To Jessie? Damn . . . I mean, that's good. I just can't get over how fast you're gonna do it."

Bink is really shocked and deep down he's hurt because he wants Jessie for himself. He was thinking in his own heart that it was possible if he just waited patiently for Jessie to get fed up with being Benji's mistress. His plan to get Salina to put pressure on Benji to leave Jessie alone has backfired on him. Benji has left Salina and is now going to marry Jessie. Bink tries to show that he's happy for him, but the smile doesn't come out right, but Benji isn't paying any attention. He's too excited to notice small deficiencies in his so-called best friend's demeanor.

"Yeah, we're getting married Friday, and I want you to be the best man."

"Friday? Damn slim. You ain't wasting no time, are you?"

"Naw, man. I've been wasting enough time in my life. It's time to get serious."

"So Friday. And what time do you want me to be there? Well, first, where do you want me to show up at?"

"At the courthouse in Annapolis. Be there at eleven, and have your cell phone on so I can call you and tell you where to meet us."

Benji can't stop smiling, neither can Bink, but Bink's smile isn't sincere. He's just putting on a good show. He's not at all happy. Bink hasn't altogether given up though. He knows how women are. Once they've got what they want, they have a tendency of changing. Maybe Jessie will become promiscuous and become susceptible to having an affair. His way of thinking has kept him from getting deeply involved with a woman and has vowed to never get married at all. That would all change if he could have Jessie, but that's a fat chance, and he knows it. But she's worth the wait even if it takes ten years just to get a shot.

"Humph, I guess you've done said the hell with Salina, huh?" asks Bink.

"Shid, I said that before I came home. I just didn't know how to break away from her, but the knife episode and her calling the police on me to get me arrested was enough. I knew then that she wasn't worth two cents. It was bad enough having to deal with her disrespect, but the police trick blew me."

"Yeah . . . That was messed up. So what came of that anyway?"

"Man, I have no idea, and I ain't askin' no questions. A nigga ain't tryin' to sit in jail for one hour. Feel me?"

"I know that's right," Bink agrees, nodding his head.

Nothing is said between the two of them for a moment as the music on the radio plays. Both of them take notice of Amp and Bootemup leaning against the fence.

"Are they waiting for you to finish talking to me?"

Benji shrugs his shoulders and says, "I guess, but I already told them that ain't nothing goin' on. I don't know what more they want me to tell them."

"What? You out of coke?"

"Naw, I ain't out. I ain't never out. But I know how to take breaks. If you're always selling coke, it's easier for them boys to clock your moves. Man, they catch me dirty again, I'll be a three-time loser. Feds'll definitely pick my case up and hit me with that career offender bullshit. That's twenty-five years off the top. Forget that. Them niggas can wait until I feel comfortable . . . We just had a three-month run. We had to have sold at least two hundred bricks. I know they stacked up by now."

"Man, you know them niggas ain't stacked no paper, Benji. All they do is spend their money on clothes and girls. Oh, I forgot. And their cars. I bet they're as close to being broke as you can get without actually being broke," Bink taunts.

Benji looks at the Jacob watch on his wrist then says, "A'ight player. Let me holler at these youngins. I'ma holler at you tomorrow or something."

Benji bumps fist with Bink and gets out of the truck. Bink skirts off with the bump of the horn; Amp throws up his thumb, and Bootemup up nods an acknowledging gesture and turns to Benji with a semismile on his face. Benji notices the aggravation on their faces and returns a similar smile back at them.

"What's up, fellas? I thought y'all would be gone by now."

"Naw, we still here," returns Bootemup, now looking more serious than he was before Benji's statement. "So when you think things gonna be nice again? A nigga tryin' to eat."

Benji shakes his head and raises his brow, "Ain't no tellin'. I'm still waitin'."

Amp smacks his lips and turns his smile upside down, looking away without a word. Amp is the silent assassin amongst Benji's young comrades, and he knows Benji is lying, but he won't say it out loud.

How can a nigga with all the bread this dude has got be talkin' 'bout he's waiting for somebody to send him some coke. That nigga can buy some coke from anybody. At least enough to keep us going. He needs to cut that fakin' *out before I punish his ass,* Amp thinks to himself.

Benji looks over at Amp and smirks at him. What he would really like to tell them at this point is to just wait until Richter calls them and to stop coming around harassing him about the matter, but that would be like telling them that they could go to hell and that they weren't close enough to him to come straight to him. He wants to take control of the situation, but that would require him to be rude, and that's not his way of doing things, especially not toward his foot soldiers.

"It's gonna be soon, trust me. Supposed to be in a couple of weeks. I talked to my man, and he mentioned next week, so I know that really means about a month. Don't worry. I got you. Trust me."

The reassurance makes them both feel a lot better, and their facial expressions return to pleasant. The three of them converse about people and rumors that never cease in the hood. Benji tells them of his intent to marry Jessie, and they congratulate him and wish him well. He knows the news will reach Salina, but that's not at all a worry of his. He's so proud of his future outlook that he would ride around with a bullhorn sticking out of his window announcing the good news if he wasn't concerned about being called a king bamma, which is the worst insult that someone could call a person like Benji, and to be called a *king* bamma really emphasizes the fact that the person should move down to the country far away from the city. The gesture indicates that he'd probably fit right in with the rest of the population of Alabama.

As their conversation begins to wind down, the sound of sirens can be heard echoing obnoxiously off buildings and hills in the distance. The sound is getting louder and closer and is becoming harder to distinguish from what direction the distracting squeals are coming from. The sound of howling dogs harmonize with the sound of screeching tires.

"That's them, boys. They chasin' the hell out of somebody too," Amp concludes. Bootemup loves to see somebody get out on the police in a high-speed car chase. He's smiling, listening intently to the sounds of the chase. "Damn, it sounds like they're in the Land." That's short for Kentland.

"Sounds like they're right around the corner," says Benji.

Skirrrt. Weeor, Weeor, Weeor. Skirrt!

The roar of the engines and the sirens of the cars involved in the chase are getting louder and definitely closer as if the person they are chasing is headed straight in their direction. From up the street, the sound of a powerful engine cuts through the scream of the sirens. The engine pronounces a striking similarity to the thunderous roar of the Corvette that Richter drives around town like a bat out of hell. Over the summit of the hill that divides the street, flies a dark blue bubble. Sure enough, the ZR1 that Richter drives bolts toward them and screeches to a stop with the passenger window down; he tosses a leather backpack in front of Amp's grape Impala and punctures a hole in the asphalt with the wide tread Yokohama low profile tires at the rear of his Torque Meister. The tail end of the car doesn't sway in the least bit to the left or the right. It just thrust straight ahead with the assistance of millisecond traction control and a firm grip of the stirring-wheel.

The three men standing at the edge of the curb watch as Richter whips his Vette around the corner and as three white police cruisers, one gray Lumina, and two unmarked Crown Victorias come flying over the same hill and make the left turn at the stop sign in hot pursuit of the navy blue Chevrolet Corvette, DC license plate: George-Ocean-Nora-Edward.

"You think they gonna catch him?" asks Bootemup.

The trio look at one another, and they all unanimously agree with a shake of their heads and an outburst of laughter.

"Naaah."

Chapter 24

At the top of the Firehouse Road, Richter stops for a moment and looks into his rearview mirror at the squad cars making their way up toward his idle car. He looks up out his open rooftop for a helicopter and sees none; then he turns right and drives smoothly over the traffic-calming hump in the road, then another before blasting his injectors with a shower of fuel that ignites an instantaneous combustion of mechanical action, reaction, and interaction from the cylinders to the drive shaft, which rotates so fiercely that the chassis struggles to keep from folding like a federal informant.

Richter handles the S-turn with the precision of a grand prix racer as he disappears out of sight before the pursuing police cars can even get over the first hump in the road.

The Vette, however, is spotted by another cruiser. This car is an unmarked detectives' car and is occupied by Miles and Faraday, who were at the original scene where the chase began. Richter was about to serve a half of a key to a guy named Kickstand whom he hadn't dealt with for a few months. The dude claimed he'd been out of town getting money in the Carolinas but in actuality he'd been sitting in a Federal holdover facility, awaiting trial for drug trafficking when he decided he'd work with the Feds to get some consideration on his own case.

He had set up a deal with Richter at the request of Special Agent Miles who is conducting an investigation on Benjamin Powell and wants to get some leverage against the only man close enough to him to help the government get enough dirt to make an indictment stick.

Richter could tell by the way Kickstand was trying to get him to say more than what was necessary to make the deal complete that he was probably wired.

"This time I'm just going to get half-a-key. Next time I'm going to get a whole jont."

"A what? What the hell you talkin' 'bout?" Richter put his index finger to his lips to signal Kickstand not to say another word.

"You got the coke with you?"

"Coke?" Richter brandished the butt of a wooden handle to his Taurus 9 mm handgun and stares at Kickstand with a cold heartless glare, daring him to say another word.

"Man, I'll tell you what! Follow me around the corner in your car, and I'ma take you over my people's house so you can get a soda. I don't think they got Coke though, but they got Pepsi."

"A'ight," Kick says defeated and nervous. He hoped the police wouldn't make a move on Richter, because he doesn't feel he'd done enough to put this guy away, knowing he'd never be able to continue to roam around the streets without getting his whole head blown off. He realized that Richter suspected him of being wired, so now he just wanted to get out of the car alive and as far from Richter as possible.

The door of the Corvette thumped shut. Richter immediately took off and attempted to leave the parking lot of the Dodge Plaza Shopping Center. He noticed a marked police car moving in a direction to head him off; also another one was moving in a parallel lane. He could see the "box-in" move from a mile away. He made an abrupt turn through an empty parking spot and darted across the parking lot toward a different exit from the shopping center.

Richter made it onto Landover Road and took the police on a wild goose chase though the streets of Landover into Glenarden and back into Landover again finally making it into Kentland so he could find somebody to grab his stash of drugs after he throws it out the window. Fortunately, Benji was standing outside of his mother's house.

Now Richter is bolting down Martin Luther King Highway toward the Washington DC line. If he can make it to DC, he knows he has a better chance of getting away because PG Police can't chase him into the district. Only four miles and he's safe, so he thinks, but little does he know that he's not only being chased by PG, but the Feds are back there too, and they won't be stopping at the district line.

Agent Faraday is driving and isn't usually the one behind the wheel, but Miles, the more aggressive and courageous of the two, insisted that he would be the one to get out of the car first when they descend upon Richter at the original bust location. Now that they're in pursuit of Richter, he wishes that he should have been the one driving because Faraday doesn't drive as reckless as Miles does, and Richter is stretching out on them. Faraday is almost embarrassed by the way he's eating Richter's dust. He stomps on the gas pedal as hard as he can, but it seems frivolous at this point because the ZR1 is getting smaller and smaller. It broadens its distance with every lane change and then hugs the curb at Sheriff Road. That is the last any of the pursuing police officers or the agents saw of the blue blur, and Miles is peeved at his partner for his amateur display of driving in a high-pressure situation.

"You can't drive worth a damn!" Miles slaps the dash. "You let the frickin' prick get away."

"Go figure, Mario Andretti! You try sticking with a road demon that can give a damn about his own life who is driving a car, all engine, and see how you do."

Miles looks at Faraday intently, wanting to respond to his remarks but decides against it, knowing that to do so would only have the two of them at each other's throats. So, Miles does the alternative. He bashes the dashboard again and hollers. "Shit!"

They continue down Sheriff Road and across the district line not speaking to one another, listening closely to the radio in case another car spots Richter.

Varoom!

Their car shakes from the gust of wind produced by the vehicle that just blew past them driving in the opposite direction. Miles and Faraday loop their heads around to get a glimpse of the blur that hinted their peripherals and see the word *GONE* on the license plate.

"Suck me!" exclaims Miles who doesn't bother to tell Faraday not to let him get away. He bounces his head off the headrest and reaches for the CB to make the call reporting the 10-15 sighting headed eastbound on Sheriff Road. Another request is put in for a helicopter, and Faraday has finally gotten the car turned around to travel in the general direction that they just saw Richter traveling in. Richter is long gone again, but they have a plan that'll put him and Benji in the middle of a conspiracy. All they need is one person to collaborate one story, and Miles has just the person in mind.

Chapter 25

A frigid breeze stings Benji's nose the moment he confronts the cold air outside his parked Cadillac Deville where he was wrapped in a blanket of warmth and relaxation. Today is a cloudy brisk winter day, but the air content is the sublime delight for people with sinus problems and nasal congestion. The weather is so crazy these days. One day, you can leave the house with a jacket. Another day, you need a Goose Down coat. The limbs of the nearby evergreens are cozy and equipped for the bitter cold weather, but the maple, oak, and cedar trees tremble in their nakedness against the gusts of wind that continuously wrap around their bark.

Cars passing by add to the power of the breeze that hits Benji in his face as he pauses to let one more car whisk by before he clear his car's ajar door, closing it and skipping around the front of the cherry-colored sedan adorned with Vogue white-walled tires around chrome mirrors decorated with gold Cadillac emblems in the center of each.

Benji is dressed in his favorite black suit and a red tie. His Stacy Adams hard bottoms call from the surface of the payment with every knock and skip. His London Fog overcoat makes him look like a high-powered executive in a rush to get his briefcase out of the passenger's side of the car, but the rush isn't for a briefcase; rather it's to open the passenger door for his lovely wife-to-be.

Jessie is on the opposite side of the treated glass that appears to have a greenish film over it. Benji can't remember ever owning a car without taking it straight to the window tinting shop after leaving the showroom floor, but this is the car Jessie drives, and she put up a Johnny Cochran case about why she didn't want this car to be marred with the relics of the street like the car she drives to work. Benji didn't give in easily and refuses to ride in the car anywhere inside the beltway. Nevertheless, Jessie got her wish and today, she's flaunting her fox fur coat, at the request of Benji, who has told her that the reason he felt that they should dress this way is because white people would respond to them better if they were dressed like they were already successful.

Benji doesn't always open the door for his woman, but whenever they go out on the town or are dressed like a million bucks, he does. Today, Jessie feels like she's very special because of the way Benji's treating her.

All this because I volunteered to help him get his business off the ground. Damn, imagine if I help him get a big business loan, she thinks, *he'll mess around and marry me on the spot.*

Benji pulls the latch, opening the door and reaches for Jessie's hand. She takes his hand, then gingerly lifts her right leg and drops it over the doorjamb, then turns her body before doing the same with her other foot.

"Take your time, bae," Benji advises.

"Back up a bit," she replies.

She grips his hand and with a tug she lifts herself up from the cream leather seat of the car. Benji pulls her gently to her feet and allows her to step up onto the curb before grabbing the briefcase out of the backseat. He closes the door and extends his elbow for her to take hold.

The two of them make their way toward the courthouse doors looking like the family members of a deceased tycoon whose estate is in probate, and they're about to rightfully claim their inheritance.

"Bae," Jessie looks down at their outfits. "Do you really think all this was necessary to get these people to help us get everything done we're trying to do?"

"Yeah, bae. We're in Annapolis. You know whities don't take niggas seriously down here, but dressed like this, they won't think we're regular old black folks, and we'll have them eating out of our hands. You gotta learn to play the game," he insisted. "Life's a big ass game. My Muslim brothers taught me that in the joint. Just stick with me. I'll show you."

Jessie nods with an expression of reassurance. Her eyes watch his lips in admiration, realizing she's affiliated with a smooth thug who has so much knowledge and understanding about the world and about the ways of life. He never ceases to amaze her, at times, displaying a boyish outlook toward simple social matters, then at other times, making her feel as though she was newly seeded green grass entering into the workings of this world for the very first time. He also makes her feel as though she is a professor learning from a teacher. After all, she works in the corporate world but not around many white folks.

The moment they walk through the courthouse doors, the special treatment punches them in the face. The young white courthouse security guard notices the two of them and is impressed by Jessie's striking outward appearance. Seldom does he ever see such beautifully well-dressed people, white or black, come through the doors of this courthouse. He also notices that she's pregnant.

"Excuse me, sir, could you direct the lady to this side? She's pregnant. She doesn't have to walk though the metal detector. I'll wand her instead." Jessie starts toward the man.

"Sir," the guard continues, "If you would like, you can put your case on the conveyor and come through this way as well."

Envious heads turn to watch as the well-dressed niggers get to skip the line and go on their merry way, while they have to stand in line and trickle through *one* metal detector. People in the line, both white and black become irate and can't bear to hold their tongue any longer.

"Oh, I see," says an elder black man dressed in overalls. "If you come to court looking like a lawyer, you get the red-carpet treatment."

"I guess the next time I come to court, I'll make sure that Tommy knocks me up first," says a younger white woman with long red hair.

Listening to the comments, Jessie looks at Benji and snickers, realizing how right he was about dressing the way they have. She's certain that if they were dressed in more comfortable clothing like blue jeans and sweaters, Benji would still be standing at the back of the long line of impatient people.

Benji walks over to the information desk and asks a lady for the whereabouts of the offices that he will need to go to in order to register his business name and get a tax number, while Jessie stands by his side letting her eyes roam around the prestigious reception area of the courthouse.

The lady at the desk points Benji down the hall, and he taps Jessie to get her attention. She grabs hold of his arm, and they make their way down the hall to take an elevator to the third floor where they find the comptroller's office. They walk in, look around, and then Benji turns to Jessie and says, "OK, you talk to the lady right there and find out everything we need to know, so we can walk right through the procedures. I'm gonna go down the hall and see about getting some information on grants and programs that might be set up for new minority businesses. The lady downstairs said something about that."

Jessie does exactly what he says unsuspecting that he's left to do anything other than what he's claimed that he's going to do. She walks over to the lady at the counter and talks to her with a smile on her face. A Colgate smile.

Happy to see that Jessie seems to have that task well under way, he takes off down the hall back to the elevator, wondering if everyone is on time and on point.

Denise and Marsha Powell, Benji's mother, met each other in front of Benji and Jessie's house and rode to the courthouse together in Denise's car. Benji has told them that he would wake up and take Jessie to the Double T Diner for breakfast at 9:00 a.m. and would be at the courthouse around ten thirty. By the time Benji and Jessie had entered into the courthouse, Denise and Mrs. Powell had gotten out of their car and followed behind at some distance just in case Jessie decided to look back.

Denise and Mrs. Powell go straight to the chapel room inside the courthouse's west wing and wait for Benji to walk through the door. Denise had been to the courthouse in Prince George's County where they don't allow cellular phones in the building and assumed that the policy was a universal courthouse standard, so she left her phone in the car. Benji has been calling it from his cell phone but keeps getting the recording.

Benji finally reaches the chapel room after walking down three different hallways, too stubborn to ask someone where the chapel was. He peeks his head inside the door.

"My baby, come here, sugar. Mama so proud of her baby. You gonna make me a mother-in-law. Praise the Lord."

Mrs. Powell has on her Sunday's best, a lavender dress with gold trimmings and her favorite broach. Denise is dressed in a hot red pants suit and a black blouse with the buttons open down to her cleavage. Marsha springs up and toggles over to Benji like he's a precious little baby just learning to walk and caresses both sides of his face. She puckers up and gives him a motherly peck on his full lips.

"My baby finally gonna do the right thing. Get married. Now all you need to do is get baptized in the name of Jesus."

Benji rolls his eye up to the ceiling. His mother knows that he's a Muslim, but she disregards that fact all the time. She tells him that Jesus is the Lord and that she doesn't know what on earth or who on earth Allah is. According to her and every other believer of the Trinity, Jesus is the only God.

"Ma, we're not gonna start that today."

"Oh, baby, Mama not gonna spoil your mood. I love you."

Denise stands up and waves at Benji shyly. He smiles and walks over to give her a hug, but she extends her hand, and they exchange a soul-brother handshake instead. Benji has an astonishing ability of reading body language. He could see that Denise was leaning slightly toward him as if she were prepared to finish off the handshake with a pound on his back, so he leans forward, and they embrace each other with their free hand, patting each other on the back.

Benji finds it very difficult to accept that a woman as fine as Denise is, with all the fragrances of a rose garden protruding from her clothes and flesh, could classify herself as a dom in a lesbian relationship. The cover of her book would mislead any judge and attract more men than most strictly-dicklies could.

Denise is different though. A person could never just look at Denise and come to the conclusion that she is gay. It's not until you take notice of her mannerisms that the truth comes to be told. Like a wolf in sheep's clothing, Denise can hoodwink the most observant scrutinizer. Benji himself can't help but take notice of Denise's sex appeal. He doesn't lust at her, but he does take a good look in constant amazement that a woman so attractive could be so gay. A dom at that!

"Have y'all seen Bink?" Benji asks, pulling a small gray jewelry case out of the inside pocket of his coat.

"Nope. I sure haven't," says Denise, "with his fresh ass."

Denise doesn't like Bink. He's a heathen in her opinion. She's noticed his undressing glares at Jessie, and it's been times she's had to put him in his place about slick little comments that he's made to her when the two of them would see each other at the mall or a show. She wants to tell Benji not to trust Bink with his woman, but she doesn't have a convincing enough argument on the matter to tell a man not to trust his so-called best friend.

"Well, what time did you tell him to be here, Benji?" asks his mother. Her expression is urgent. "Isn't he supposed to be your best man?"

Benji looks at his watch, "He should have been here by now. Let me call him right quick." Benji pulls out his phone and pushes a couple of buttons, then holds the phone to his ear.

Chirp chirp chirp. Chirp Chirp Chirp.

The sound is coming from the other side of the door, and then Benji smiles a semi-grin as he closes the flap of his Sprint phone.

"Hello? . . . Hello," says a voice outside the room.

Benji opens the door, and there is Bink wearing a brown leather overcoat and a pair of Tan Dockers with a walnut brown Hugo Boss sweater on. The letters are stitched across the front of the sweater with black thread that makes the sweater and shoes a perfect match. It's possible that they were made to go together since he bought them both out of the same Hugo Boss store when he was at the Tyson's II Galleria in Tyson's Corner, Virginia.

Bink reacts to the light that shines from the interior of the room. He turns around, eyes open wide; a smile spreads across his face upon seeing his friend.

"You're on time for a change," Benji praises Bink because Bink is notorious for being on black people's time, where a couple of hours mean later on tonight, an hour means three, in a little bit means within the hour and a minute means no telling how long they'll be. Benji himself often is on time for his appointments with family members and important legitimate engagements, but never is on time with dudes on the street. Bink, on the other hand is always on "nigga time"; he's always late for everything but work, and sometimes he's even late getting there, but today he's actually on time.

I don't believe it! Benji thinks to himself.

"Now, I know you didn't think I was going to be late for your wedding, did you, dog?"

"Slim, if it's up to you, you'll be late to your own funeral."

Bink thinks for a second. "I guess you have a point there, champ." Then he looks around to greet the ladies.

"Hello, Mrs. Powell. Now, don't you look ravishing today!"

"Oh, Binky! You sure know how to make a girl feel good." Mrs. Powell is blushing and acting like a bashful teenager.

"Yeah, I'll bet. Benji watch that boy with your mother," chastises Denise in a strong soulful voice. Disenchantment consumes Bink as he looks over at the pretty lady in red where the sarcastic remarks spews from but doesn't notice right away who the woman is.

"I know that's not who I think it is." Bink can't believe his eyes. "Niecey?"

"Put your tongue back in your mouth, Rover. I already told you that you don't have nothing comin'."

Bink takes a good look at her and can't believe his eyes. She looks even better in female clothes. Every time he's seen her, she was dressed in men's clothing. Today she's dressed like a stylish professional, and she is parading a wig with long auburn horsehair. She looks glamorous to say the least, and Bink wouldn't have noticed her in a million years, if not for her distinctive voice.

"Well, I'll be a monkey's uncle," Bink returns the cynicism. "It's the beautiful bull dagger. In the flesh."

"Let it go, Niecey," she says out loud to herself.

"All right, all right. Y'all love birds save your lover's quarrels for another time. This is my time and Jessie's time."

Benji is anxious to run down the plan because he doesn't want to leave Jessie alone too long. He figures she is close to being ready for his return, so he goes over the plan while everybody listens intently.

They all are so enthused to be a part of such an unexpected ceremony, a surprise wedding—not a proposal but a wedding. Benji can see their willingness to participate written all over their faces. His mother is praising the Lord in agreement with every intricacy of the plot. Bink has his hand under his chin as he rests his elbow on his other arm that he has braced under his chest. He laughs at the same things Mrs. Powell rejoices over. And Niecey just nods her head in appreciation of how well Benji has thought out his plan to surprise Jessie with a secret wedding. A surprise party is a wonderful feeling for the recipient, but a surprise wedding has to be the most incredible thing that a woman can ever experience. Niecey can't wait to see her cousin's face.

Benji reaches in his case and pulls out a digital camera and hands it to Bink. His mother and Denise already have cameras in their hands. The door swings open and everyone in the room is mortified that Jessie had foiled their surprise. How has she found them? What drove her to stumble into this room, at this moment?

They all turn to see the expression of the woman they wanted so badly to bring joy but see an imposing white man with a receding hairline, standing in the doorway, holding a Bible in his hand and wearing a cross over his black tie.

"Praise Jesus," Mrs. Powell exclaims. "Thank the Lord you weren't the bride."

"Ha-ha-ha . . . the bride? . . . No. I'm far from that," laughs the oversized priest, and says, "but if you'd like, I can make one of you ladies a bride of one of these fine young fellows here."

"No, Rev. These aren't the brides-to-be." Benji talks to the priest in a hasty tone as if he were a quarterback telling a play with time running out on the play clock. "Here's the deal. I'm about to go get the bride. She's upstairs. They'll tell you exactly what to do. You just stay out of sight until they give you the signal."

Benji looks nervous but in control. He looks over at his family, and the look on his face asks them if they are ready, without saying a word. They all nod, and Benji takes off in a flash.

Upstairs Benji sees Jessie sitting in a chair reading some papers. She looks up at him and spreads a subtle smile across her face. She has filled out the paper to register Scoop Trucking in the state of Maryland; now they must go get some papers notarized downstairs, and then to the tax office to file the company with the comptroller.

"All done?"

"Yep. We have to go downstairs now," Jessie replies.

"Okay. Let's go."

Benji knows people are waiting for them downstairs, so he knows he must initiate the conversation, so he can lead it to the topic of marriage before Jessie starts rambling on about what they need to do and insist on going anywhere besides to the clerk's desk for a marriage certificate.

The elevator opens and they get on. "After you, wifey."

Wifey? Jessie thinks. *He's never referred to me like that. I wish.*

"Why, thank you, hubby." She smiles then steps onto the elevator.

"Humph. Hubby, huh?" He repeats her trying to think of something else to say. "You wish I *was* hubby, don't you?"

"You wish I *was* wifey."

"I sure do. We might as well get married. We've been together all this time. We've got a house together, a child coming. What's left?" She can barely believe her ears, so she doesn't take him seriously. "In fact, let's go downstairs and get a marriage certificate, so when we decide to actually do it, we can just do it."

Jessie smacks her lips and cuts her eyes at him without turning her head toward him. "Don't play with me," she says then looks back at the elevator doors.

Ding.

The doors open, and Benji steps off the elevator, "I'm not playing."

Jessie is frozen, nearly allowing the elevator doors to close before she moves. She raises her hand so that the elevator sensors will reopen the doors; then she follows behind Benji with pep in her step that is uncharacteristic of a seven-month pregnant woman with pumps on her feet. She knows he's not playing by now, but she can't believe that she's hearing what she's hearing. She pinches herself.

I'm not dreaming. He called me wifey. I called him hubby and boom. We're about to be hubby and wifey for real. She shakes her head. *This can't be real. All right, let me pull his card.*

"Well," Jessie starts as she catches up with him, "where do we go to get the certificate?"

Benji clutches his fist in triumph and gives his fist a subdued pump. Jessie couldn't see that. He has successfully accomplished phase one of operation wifey boo.

Chapter 26

A trickle of salt water runs a river down the surface of the reddish complexion of Jessie's blemish-free skin. Her face is consumed with shiny wetness, and Benji's red tie is saturated with tears. Jessie was overcome by the sheet of paper that was handed to them moments ago.

Benjamin David Powell.

Jessica Ann Glockner.

Jessie looks at the marriage certificate again then looks up at the ceiling. "Thank you. Thank you. Thank you."

Benji is happy to see that she is so grateful to become his wife-to-be, and he knows that she's going to be even more pleased once she walks into the chapel and realizes that they're about to get married *immediately*.

Jessie wraps her arms around Benji and holds him tight for almost five minutes as she cries in his bosom. Benji leans back to get a look at her face. When she sees him, she laughs and buries her face back in his upper chest.

"Don't look at me," she giggles.

"Aw . . . My baby OK? She didn't fall down and hurt herself, did she?"

Jessie playfully slaps him on his arm. "I love you to death Benji, and I'm gonna be the best wife to you that you could have ever dreamed of having." She raises her head and peers deeply into his eyes and continues, "You're my world, my king, the father of my first child, Benji. I've never even been pregnant in all my life. I thought I couldn't have children, so this child is truly a blessing to me. I love you even more than you could imagine." She looks up at the ceiling again. "Thank you, so, so much."

Across the vast lobby area in a small room behind a slightly cracked door Denise can see Jessie and can tell that she's crying by the way that she keeps wiping her face with the pink tissue that the lady behind the counter gave her shortly after she handed them the piece of paper authorizing her and Benji to get married. She's happy for her cousin and wishes that she could feel the same joy. She doesn't like men, but she envies Jessie at this moment. How did Jessie escape their older cousin Lynn, who would molest Niecey every chance she got. For a whole summer, she was subjected everyday to being molested by Lynn. She soon came to enjoy what was happening to her until she couldn't imagine having it any other way. She was only eleven when it all started, and she's been doing it ever since. She just can't understand how it all got by Jessie, the prettiest of all her cousins. She really envies Jessie sometimes and now more than ever. Denise has never had sex with a man, but for the first time she feels an uncontrollable urge to have a man. Butterflies scrape the cavity walls in her heart as they flutter around inside her chest. She can feel her cousin's joy.

Will I ever feel such joy? Am I wasting my life away just to fulfill my sexual preference? Cuz has got a real live family now. Her own man. Her own baby. Niecey wonders if she could deal with going straight and being touched by a man. *Hell naw. Ain't no man gonna stick no nasty dick up in me.* She frowns and then realizes, *Well, hell, you've been stickin' those rubber dildoes up in you. So what's the difference?* She shakes her head. *A lot. Me and a man? Hell naw. Never that. I am a man. Now that would be some faggy stuff, and I ain't gonna never be a faggy.*

Denise dismisses the absurd thoughts of going straight and then steps away from the door so Benji's pushy mother can take a peek through the door to get a glimpse of the two lovebirds across the hall.

"OK. OK. They're walking this way. Get ready y'all," Mrs. Powell says as she peeks through the crack.

Benji consoles Jessie with kind words and occasional kisses on her forehead as they stroll across the lobby floor toward the chapel door. The door is usually locked shut, but today it's open for business, and Jessie is too preoccupied to realize that the door that they are about to walk through is the door to the chapel of the courthouse. Benji gives it a thought, and then comes up with another line.

"Look, bae. This is where they marry people at."

She looks up at the sign over the door. Tears still flooding her eyes, she's not impressed, but she flatters him and says, "Oh, that's nice."

"But we're having a big wedding in our backyard," Benji says.

Jessie is shocked to hear that and shows it.

"Well, maybe not our backyard," Benji recants, "but somebody's."

They walk slowly into the room and up to the podium. There's no one in the room, at least not that can be seen. Benji sits his briefcase down, and they look straight ahead at the stained glass window displaying a picture of Jesus. Benji's a Muslim but is nowhere near being considered devout because a true brother of Islam wouldn't consider making a bond with a nonbeliever, making her his wife forever. Nevertheless, Benji believes that eventually he'll be able to convert her, but he won't try too hard too early. Right now, though, the last thing on Benji's mind is religion and rituals. All he's thinking about is how happy he is about to be when he sees the expression on Jessie's face when the family comes through the door.

"May I have your coat please, madam?" The soft man's voice says from behind Jessie and Benji.

Jessie is startled a bit but not at all frightened, with her knight in shining armor standing next to her. Who could bring her harm or detriment? She turns.

Bink? She blinks her eyes tight and then opens them expecting that the appearance on the man's face will change. Beyond him another face comes into focus. *Niecey? What the . . . Mrs. Marsha?* Jessie's blood surges and her heart pounds an offbeat rhythm. Jessie can see a tall white man walking toward the podium, carrying a black Bible with metallic gold-trimmed pages in his hand. The man is staring at her with a casual smile as is everyone else in the room.

Benji? *What's going on?* She thinks to herself.

The light in the room turns into a haze in Jessie's sight, and the faces of joy fade into blank, open-mouth faces of concern that quickly disappear into a shroud of blackness.

Jessie can hear, but she can't see, nor can she respond to the swirling whispers of her name, Jessie, Jessie, are you all right?

"It must have been too much for the ole girl. She'll be all right. Give her . . ."

Chapter 27

A myriad of myriads of spirit creatures continue to behold the magnificence of their most powerful brethren who tower before them. He has been communicating with them all the words of the Most High since the time he first called out to them with a sound of great disturbance. The terror that took hold of them at that very moment still has a grip on their souls with the might of the Roman Empire, sixtyfold, but they are upright and steadfast as Apollyon conveys the message of the kingdom. All of this great multitude has known this information since the time before the Son of Man returned to the right hand of the throne, yet many have fallen impatient and have come to question the significance of the humans.

We all have our own part as do the mortals. They are the Omega's gifts to himself and his own kingdom. They must be nurtured, and he who created them takes much pleasure in providing this weak and feeble kind with all that they need to survive. Do not think that your existence is more significant and relevant than theirs, for it is not. And do not ask why we must wait to do away with Iblis and all of the enemies of our Father's Kingdom as if he needs you or me to do anything for him. The one who said things must happen does not and cannot tell a lie, thus the things that have not yet transpired will. So all things will become subjected to me except, of course, the one himself who has caused all things to be subjected to me. He who has given me the power will rest and prepare for the coming millenniums in order to expanding his kingdom beyond Zion herself. Have not my brethren labored abundantly to assist the hands of the Alpha and the Omega in order to spread the reaches of the universe to a great portion of the lower realm? Is there not still much more work to do before we have reached a completion of his work?

Before Apollyon can continue, he is summoned by the Omega, and he responds in an instant.

Yes, my father. How may I serve you? What is your will that I may carry it out? Have I not done as you have commanded? Have I missed anyone?

Apollyon, my son, I have not summoned your presence to squabble about such trifle deeds. Which one of your brethren would consider ignoring a warning from me for which I gave because of the thoughts of so few? Those to whom my concerns applied have long since prayed to me for forgiveness and have forever erased all doubts from their inner thoughts. I wish to advise you of a matter with a human child. One who will have the power of influence and understanding greater than most in his company, yet he is in grave danger and his current course is that of premature destruction that will cause such a snare that only divine intervention will be able to bring about the occurrences that must and will occur, but that should not happen. However, if not, too many will be led astray and Iblis will be allowed more time to bring more of the righteous to their knees, and they will certainly stumble and submit to his machinations, which will be the death of them all. There is a great dilemma, and you will have to make a decision for I have already given to you authority over all that you have to do with the things in existence.

Apollyon is spellbound and unsure of how to respond.

What must I do and what decision must I make to maintain the balance of the natural course of life mingled with the blessings of Yahweh? I fear not the outcome, but my concern is to produce a solution that will be pleasing to you, my father.

Apollyon will not ask the Omega what decision he must make. He knows that when the time comes, the decision must be his and his alone for the Omega has made him the supreme ruler over his entire kingdom. The Great War has not taken place yet, Apollyon has taken his stand and only the Omega does not fall under his dominion. Even Iblis will answer to the hand of Apollyon when he finally returns to the material realm as the one whom the entire world once knew but did not heed. It will be he who will fight the Omega's battle and after all of his enemies perish, the Omega will reassume his almighty rulership of all.

But for now, things are developing on Zion that will alter the course of events that will lead to the appointed time, and it has to do with a child. This child's life course must not be hampered or else countless numbers of the meek will fall prey to the evil influence of Iblis and a greater number of them will lose all faith and will commit grave sins that will seal their doom and bring eternal death upon them.

Apollyon muses over what wisdom he must muster in order to keep things on their proper course, and he knows that he cannot and must not fail.

Chapter 28

Benji knows that he must continue on the path he has set before him. It seems that there is nothing that can stop him from reaching his ultimate goal. His business is providing a formidable income for his new family. He's been married for close to five months and a baby is on the way. It's actually due any day now. The dump truck he is driving is carrying a load from a quarry in southern Maryland to Rockville, paying $500 a load, and this is his fifth load today. He has another dump truck following him with a buddy of his driving it carrying an identical load, and he's had enough calls requesting his company's services for him to consider purchasing another two trucks out of the want ads, and for him to tell Jessie to *never* return to BET even after she has had the baby. Things are really starting to snowball for Benji in a good way, and the only thing that jeopardizes him from reaching the finish line of legitimacy are the four or so kilos of Peruvian flaked cocaine he has stashed away behind the driver's seat of his dump truck. Well, that only if he doesn't make any more purchases from his drug connects.

He will be stopping at the old Landover Mall to meet Richter to hand these off to him before he continues to drop-off the load that he's carrying. Benji is well aware of the heat that he has attracted from the Feds since his release from jail because he has friends that work for both the PG Police Department and the Metropolitan Police Department who have told him about the surveillance that the FBI has on him, but he also knows that they won't touch him without an ironclad case. That's why he continues to drive around dirty stacking his chips, and then take breaks from time to time. Benji knows that they won't dare pull him over to do a routine traffic stop for the purpose of searching his vehicle because the last time they tried that, nothing was found in his car, and he filed a complaint against the force and promised to file a lawsuit the next time.

Benji is totally immune to the police who drive squad cars, because of the 'hands-off' flag that shows up beside his name in the computer system. There was already a flag by his name from when Salina had called the police on him and put a warrant out for his arrest, but now that the Feds are sure that he's trafficking, the flag has a footnote to go along with it. If a police officer gets behind any of the cars that he is known to drive and calls in the tag, they won't even pull the car over unless the vehicle is operating in an unsafe manner.

Today, it's mostly cloudy and traffic on the northbound outer loop of the Capital Beltway is thickening. The evening rush is about to be in full swing. It's already 2:45 p.m., and Benji will drop this last load before racing to his truck yard to get in his Yukon located in Hyattsville, Maryland. From there, he'll call home to see if his wife needs anything before he makes his way home down the newly expanded lanes of Route 50 to Annapolis.

The Landover Road exit is approaching, and Benji signals to get into the far right lane.

Beeeep. Beeeeeeep! Screams a Mazda Millennium that is straddling along the side of the veering dump truck.

"Get the hell on then," Benji barks at his blind side trying to see the car in his passenger side mirror.

The dump truck following Benji gets behind the Mazda and honks his startling horn, scaring the dog do-do out of the little diva behind the wheel of the car. The car speeds off as the dump trucks seem to be crowding it, and then Benji is able to safely get over and make the exit.

Bomp! Bomp! Benji honks his horn in appreciation of the driver in the other truck, who made it possible for him to make the exit.

Landover Mall is a desert. Only Sears is still open, but all the other department stores including Woodworth & Lothrop, Garfinkles, and Hecht's have all closed. Landover Mall was once the mall of malls in the Washington DC area. People drove from Annapolis, deep Virginia, and even Baltimore to shop at the prized Landover Mall. Then came a surge of development all around the fifty miles radius of the Monument. White Flint, Annapolis, Arundel Mills, Tyson's, Tyson's II, Pentagon City, Forestville, and Beltway Plaza malls all contributed to the death of Landover Mall. Now, its parking lot is only good for Redskin Stadium parking, a rest stop for truckers and driving lessons for rookie drivers.

Benji pulls into the parking lot and doesn't like the feeling that doing a drug deal in an empty parking lot gives him, so he gestures for the waiting Richter to follow behind him as he passes through the lot and back onto the road. He drives along Brightseat Road and then stops. Richter is back in his speed demon Corvette. He knows that they aren't looking for it anymore, but he's always prepared for a good chase. He thrives on those as long as he's in a fast car.

Richter gets out of the car and walks to the passenger side of the truck and climbs up into it.

"Wasup Rick?"

"Nothin'—Got some niggas waitin' on me." That's Richter's way of letting Benji know that he doesn't have time to be chit chatting.

Benji hands him the bag with the keys in it. "A'ight. I'll holler atchu tomorrow."

"Bet. Gone."

And just like that the drug deal is made. No words, no money, no conspiracy. Richter is Benji's lieutenant, and he handles 80 percent of all his traffic. There are only two other people that Benji will actually make transaction with, and those are cash- and-carry deals, far riskier than the deals he makes with his close friend who takes the drugs and brings the money back to him at a later time.

Richter, unlike, Tony, Amp, and Bootemup, is not dependent on Benji's supply of narcotics because Richter has money of his own saved up. He even has a totally separate operation going on. He primarily deals in heroine and makes a lot more money selling dope than he does selling coke. It's just that coke moves so fast that he can't resist making a quick twenty thousand dollars over the course of a couple of days doing virtually nothing. He profits off his direct sells to other heavy hitters in the area, and he makes money off all the coke that Tony, Amp, and Bootemup sell. Richter now owes Benji for ten keys. He has the money for half of them, but Benji likes to get the money all at one time.

Benji counts over a half a million dollars every week after he collects all of the money from drug sells during the course of the week. The birds fly as fast as they touch down ever since he's been back in full swing from the time he sent the first sixty thousand dollars out to his man Alamar on the west coast. Alamar sent back five keys, two scorpion cartels, and three from the three-clover cartel. The scorpion was all right, but the clovers crystallized into hard white boulders. The crackheads call it ice cream. The frontline soldiers call it the butters because the crackheads tell them that it melts straight down. Benji now demands the clovers, because the scorpion doesn't hold baking soda too well, and it gets a lot of complaints.

Benji's making a lot of money, and he knows how important it is for him not to be greedy and think he'll be slick enough to keep skating on the ice before the Feds thin it out enough for him to take a fall through the cracks. He has so much more than money and material rewards to live for. He has a lovely wife, two children, and another one on the way. He has a business that is turning a profit already and showing signs of being an extremely good investment.

As he drives down the road, his blessings come to mind and he begins to talk to his God and offer an acknowledgment of appreciation.

Allah, I know that it is you who have made all things possible. If not for you, I would be nothing. I'll correct my flaws and do right by my Jessie.

Benji is on the verge of giving up the street life. He doesn't care that his younger protégés have become increasingly more dependent on his supply and will suffer greatly if he should decide not to continue with his ongoing criminal drug enterprise. They all fell off, with the exception of Richter, while Benji was locked up, and he knows by their constant nagging and show of anxiety when he takes a two- or three-week hiatus that they have built up an extravagant lifestyle, which requires a steady flow of the narcotics that got them the prestige that they have regained since Benji's been back. What a shame it will be for them when the river turns into a stream, and they have to resort to buying or begging for weight from some jokers around town who won't nearly satisfy the price margin that they need to sustain such a lavish lifestyle. Situations like that drive people to all types to drastic measures, and if a game-show host were to ask *what do people depend on the most following a major loss of income?*

Undoubtedly, right at the top, the number one answer would be—the survey says, *Bing—robbery.*

Chapter 29

Iblis has taken on the form of his favorite mortal creature, the raven. And he's sitting perched upon a power line in the Montgomery County area. He frequents this area because there is a high concentration of blessed and holy individuals who dwell among the heavy population of its many wealthy and upper middle-class communities. In fact, he's not far from the very place he spotted Dr. Crawford.

"*Awk.*" He sees something that sparks his interest.

Along comes a purple Peterbilt dump truck with Scoop Trucking painted on the rear gate. Benji is driving and the load he was carrying is gone. He's now on his way to Hyattsville to pick up his SUV, so he can go home and be with Jessie for the rest of the evening.

Iblis swoops down from his lofty place above the road and takes special notice of the occupant of the dump truck. Iblis is confused. There is something very weird about the spirit that swirls about this individual.

There are evil spirits all about this man, but they do not seem to be able to overwhelm him. It seems that the spirit of the Omega is protecting this one, but I know this man. I've personally led him on many destructive courses. His life still holds on? His choices have not led him to sleep in deathly unconsciousness yet? It doesn't make sense that he has taken this sort of protective favor of this unrighteous one, who is not meek or forthright in his ways. I must know the secret behind this man and why he receives the blessings so strongly, despite his worldly ways that control his heart and soul. What is this man's true purpose that he should receive such undeserved kindness?

Iblis follows Benji and watches his every move. He has instructed his evil disciples to leave this man so that he himself can follow Benji and be the sole one to bring all peace in this man's world to an end. He recalls a man of long ago that had such a hedge placed about him, and that man served the Almighty and could not be swayed. But this man does not serve him, so there must be a very significant reason for this one to have the blessings as had the man Job.

I will come to know him and bring great calamity his way, so that his purpose will never be achieved. If your kingdom is to come, it most assuredly will not be through this one in any form or fashion.

"*Awk!*"

There is very little traffic for a late Wednesday commute down the long stretch of Route 50 between the Capital Beltway and the Parole exit that signifies the city limits of Annapolis, Maryland. Benji's almost home, and the sun is setting behind him casting a long shadow of his truck on the road before him.

The shadow of the bird flying high above him is not to be seen in the vicinity on the ground below, but darkness and gloom cover every soul in a three-mile radius, and the target of its evil is unsuspecting of what folly lies before him.

Iblis allows Benji to make his way with no outside influences to hinder his safe passage. At home, Benji walks up his stone-founded porch, and Iblis lands on the ledge of the porch with stealth accuracy and unmovable sturdiness, almost as if he just appeared from nowhere. The bird's sudden appearance startles Benji, causing him to rear back on his heels as he reaches the top of his porch. Benji stomps and flails his hands at the bird.

"Shew. Get . . . !"

The bird, all but, laughs at Benji, staring into his eyes with a blank motionless glare. Benji's brow wrinkles, and he feels apprehensive. Fear overpowers his heart. He steps back to reach for the knob of the iron storm door without taking his focus off the abnormally broad-breasted scavenger. His lip is hanging, and his blinkless eyes are riveted on the bird, unable to believe what he's seeing.

What the . . . ? I hope this bird don't turn into a vampire or something. Just don't make any sudden moves. He warns himself.

Benji fondles around for the knob and scratches at the doorframe until his left hand falls upon it. He turns the knob ever so slightly until it won't turn any more, then with a slow, muscle-clutching pull, he opens the door and backs up inside the threshold between the storm door and the wooden, round-topped front door of the house. Benji wants to just ring the doorbell, so he wouldn't have to fumble with his keys. That would require too much of his attention. He doesn't want to take his eyes off the imposing bird that appears to be stalking him. The only reason he doesn't ring the doorbell is because he knows that Jessie is more than likely upstairs, and he wouldn't dare drag her all the way downstairs just to open the door for him because he's too scared to use his key.

What are you afraid of? It won't hurt you.

Benji tries to convince himself that he's not scared, but he's actually terrified and is careful not to provoke an attack from the menacingly frightful creature. He slowly lifts his key to the deadbolt lock on the door and jams the first key into the top lock. The key is upside down and not even the right key. After dropping the keys, Benji panics, rushes to get the keys, gets the door unlocked, and then slips into the house slamming the door shut behind him. He runs quickly up the steps, and skipping two steps with each stride, he makes his way to the master bedroom to get his gun from under his pillow. He was too scared to go back past the bird to get the gun he has in his truck.

In the room, Jessie is leaning against the headboard when Benji rushes into the room and beelines straight for his pillow and snatches his .40 caliber handgun. Snatching it from its resting place, Benji leaves the room as quickly as he entered it. Jessie's heart skips a beat, fretting over what could have her usually calm, mild-mannered husband acting in such a way.

"My god! Benji, what's the matter?"

Benji is already halfway down the steps and is too shocked to make any response to his wife. But even if he'd have heard her clearly, he wouldn't have answered because the only thing that's on his mind is blasting the tail feathers off the insidious crow he left perched on his porch banister. In a mad dash for the front door, Benji looks through the window in the living room to see if the bird is still bold enough to be sitting there. It is.

Benji can hardly wait to reach the door so he can see this bird explode from the blast of his gun. He can almost taste the fury inside of him. He feels violated.

Damn bird!

Benji snatches the door open and then pushes the storm door open raising his gun all in one motion. The crow is gone.

"Damn it!" Benji looks all around. Up in the trees, on the lawn, everywhere, but no black bird. He'll shoot the first black bird that he sees, even if it's not the right one. It doesn't matter. If it is black with feathers, it's a goner. "You lucky!"

He takes a deep breath, and his heart slows to a mellow beat after it had scorched his veins with fast flowing blood making him sweat feverishly.

There hasn't been many times in Benji's recollection that he has gotten so filled with rage and terror, but he recalls that he's in a quiet neighborhood where the white neighbors wouldn't take too kindly to him blasting his gun in the middle of the day while their children are coming home from school and playing in the streets. He's glad that the bird was gone; otherwise, he would have done something rash.

There was only one other time that Benji has had such an agonizing desire to use his gun, and that was when he was twenty-one years old. He had just come out of the Tropicana Caribbean Food Carry-out on U Street with his food in his hand when he was ambushed by two young black men brandishing a nickel plated revolver. They took his eighteen-carat gold herringbone necklace, the nine hundred dollars that he had in his pocket, a two-carat diamond pinky ring, *and* his food.

When it was going down, all he could think about was staying alive. He didn't care one bit about the things they were taking from him. He just wanted to be able to walk away without being shot. The robbers did the job, and Benji stood there and watched as the two men skedaddled around the corner up Ninth Street toward Howard University. Once they were out of sight, Benji's fear changed into blinding rage, and he ran for his car, jumped in, and peeled off out of the parking lot in the direction that the assailants went.

The two dudes were wearing dark-colored clothes and were easy to spot. They had heard the screeching tires, so they were well aware that the candy apple red Beamer with the spoiler kit and fancy BBS rims wasn't some cat from across Key Bridge looking for a trick. They took off running and Benji, with his passenger window rolled down, driving with one hand and shooting with the other, let loose a palisade of 9mm rounds from his Glock 21 pistol. One of the guys stumbled and fell against the fence that encases the WUST parking lot. The other guy never broke stride, running to Georgia Avenue where he turned and saw the red BMW stop in the intersection. The driver got out and ran toward him, shooting his gun. This robber wasn't the one with the gun, so all he could do is take the rounds of hot ball to his chest, leg, and abdomen, then watch as the gunman walked away and speed off into the night. That was all the revenge Benji needed to make him feel vindicated for being violated. He probably would have taken his stuff back, but there were too many witnesses. As he drove off, he turned his lights off so it would be more difficult to see his license plate. That was the last he heard of the matter.

Benji was hoping to have a chance to relive that moment of gratification with the sight of the pesky bird being exploded like a Gremlin in a microwave however, Iblis is nowhere to be found, at least not by the wondering eyes of Benjamin Powell. Iblis is not seen but is not gone anywhere either. He is watching Benji with great interest and bewilderment because there is enough Holy Spirit being showered down upon this household to cleanse the soil in the yard. Yet, this man has a spirit of his own that is violent, wicked, and cruel.

There is something in connection with this one that has to do with the enormous importance in the unfolding of monumental events relevant to foretold occurrences. I must alter his course and learn what will bring swift destruction to him. He must not be permitted to survive.

Iblis has transformed himself into a loathsome cockroach and has taken the liberty of crawling into the house while Benji continues to seek out the crow.

Inside the house, Iblis observes the many blessings bestowed upon this earthling who, obviously, in Iblis' opinion, deserves nothing more than eternal death. There is another life force in the house; actually there are two that Iblis can sense, and he feels a concentration of the Holy Spirit in their vicinity—even greater than that which envelopes Benji's soul. Iblis is almost certain that he has stumbled upon something of enormous significance, but he will remain patient to see if there is somehow a way that he can use Benji to carry out his bidding. Benji's a weak-hearted man and can be easily influenced to do bad things, and if it is true that whoever it is upstairs holds a key to any part of the Omega's plan, then Benji will need to be used somehow to manipulate an intricate web of sinful snares to invoke disaster over all that is righteous in this house.

I shall bring destruction to anyone who stands, and hopefully death to the ones who may serve a kingdom purpose.

Jessie is mortified by the slow drumming sound of feet climbing the stairs outside the room. She was expecting to hear gunshots after Benji reached the bottom of the steps, but instead she heard nothing but the door shut. Her mind started to race.

What is going on? I hope that's Benji. "Benji?" *Call 911,* she thinks.

The footsteps go mute as an indication that whoever it is coming up the steps has reached the top and is walking on the rollout rug that runs down the length of the hallway. Jessie grabs the phone and dials 911. The muffled sound of footsteps approach the room, and Jessie raises her brow and grits her teeth tight anticipating on seeing a person who doesn't belong in her house coming to tie her up. That is her greatest fear, that one day, the stickup boys will catch up with Benji, and she'll be the one that they'll use as leverage to force him to give up the stash of money.

"911 Emergency," says the woman on the other end of the phone.

Jessie begins to speak, but no words come out of her mouth. She is not sure of what to say at this point. Is it a prowler, a killer? Who is about to make themselves known from behind the wall?

"911 Emergency," repeats the woman in a more assertive voice.

Benji walks into the room and glances at Jessie whose expression changes from terror to sublime relief. She whispers a word in to the phone and responsds to the questions of the person on the other end so that Benji cannot hear her, and then she hangs up.

"Bae, what is going on?" she asks him, frowning up her face watching him return his gun to its place under his pillow.

He looks at her with a very serious expression on his face; then the muscles in his face relax, and he spreads a chuckling smile across his face. The thought of telling her that a bird spooked him to the point of making him sweat and run for his gun strikes him as ridiculous.

"This damn crow . . . It just landed on the porch and stared at me. I think it even said something to me, but now I think I'm just being paranoid. I need a vacation. My mind's starting to play tricks on me."

Chapter 30

Deep inside, Benji knows that he wasn't imagining things at all. That bird gave him a glare that he could feel, and it scared him out of his wits. It was as if Benji heard a voice in his head that wasn't his own. It didn't even seem to be English, so he knows it couldn't have been him talking to himself. That's what really spooked him.

Jessie rolls her eyes in relief and snickers at Benji in an undertone. She knows that Benji can get very paranoid at times, and that's why he sleeps with a loaded gun under his pillow already cocked and ready for action. All he has to do is take off the safely lock, aim, and shoot. He's never shown much belief in the supernatural until today. He's just made somewhat of a joke of the situation, but Jessie knows that he is veiling his true emotions. If he didn't really think that he saw what he thought he was seeing, he wouldn't have gone through so much to do away with his fear. Jessie doesn't recall ever seeing such a horrifyingly distressed look on Benji's face during the fourteen years that she's known him.

"Now, you know goodness well ain't no bird talk to you." She's only prying, trying to get more out of Benji concerning what he saw or heard from the bird to make him react the way he did. "What did it do?"

"Nothing. It just stared at me. I stomped at it trying to shew it away, but that stupid bird just looked at me like, nigga . . . what's up? Was that supposed to have scared me or something?"

"Humph," Jessie snickers and dismisses the topic as irrelevant. "Oh well . . . I'm glad you're home anyway. How was your day?"

"Fine until that crazy bird came along."

"Well, baby, don't let that spoil our evening. Come over here to Mama and let me rub your temples. Get some of that tension away . . . Come on, bae."

Benji's heart melts as he begins to undress. It's been almost a week since the last time they've had sex, so Benji's primed and ready.

"OK, bae. Let me take these dirty clothes off first and go take a quick shower before I lie down in the bed."

"Alright. Hurry up, though. Mama been waiting for you all day. I got a treat for you."

Benji's face brightens, and his movement hastens. He knows what that means. A treat. It's on now. He's given her enough time to rest her pregnant body, and he knows that he'd better move fast because, right now, she evidently isn't experiencing any pain, but he knows that could change any minute. She's due to have the baby any day now, so she hasn't been in the mood to do anything, especially not anything that might trigger another labor attack. Benji has been very considerate of Jessie's wishes during her pregnancy, so he hasn't put any pressure on her to allow him to dip into her pool of wetness between her legs. Since she's been carrying the baby, her vagina has been extra wet, and he craves to get a shot of it whenever he can. He realizes that tonight might be the last chance he'll get for nearly two months, so he hops in and out of the shower before the next commercial break of the Oprah Winfrey Show. Jessie was watching it when he came into the room.

Jessie pulls her night gown over her head and takes the four pins out of her hair that was holding it up in a ball on the back of her head. The sun is shining bright through the open blinds and the light cast a shadow of Benji's muscular body on the floor. His third leg sticks out from the silouette of the shadow and Jessie points at it.

"All that for little ole me?"

Benji, still dripping wet, says, "It sure is."

He plunges gently into the bed and overwhelms Jessie with a kiss. They kiss and talk to one another about their day.

"I love you," Jessie tells him.

"I love you too," he replies with a kiss on her nose.

"Did you see your kids today?"

"No . . . but I did see Lil Benji yesterday. I forgot to tell you." A thought comes to Benji's mind. "Humph. And guess who I bumped into."

"Who?"

"Salina," Benji says.

"Salina? You lying . . . Where? What happened?" Benji hasn't had an encounter with Salina in months since he had to change his cell number because of the way that Salina started harassing him once she found out that he had married Jessie. "How you forget to tell me about that?"

"You were asleep last night, and I didn't feel like talking about it anyway. But . . . when I stopped by Benji's school to check in on him before school let out, I saw him and had a word with his teacher. She was surprised to see me, because she was expecting his mother."

"His mother? Why?"

"Well, she had scheduled a parent-teacher conference for after school, and it just so happened that I had popped up."

"Oh, shoot. And Salina got there before you left," Jessie summarized.

Benji shook his head and rolled his eyes up to his eyelids then back to Jessie. "You wouldn't believe all the names she called me in front of all those elementary school kids. It was ugly."

"What did she say?"

"Man, she went on and on about how I was gonna pay for leaving her and how she was gonna get you if it's the last thing she does. She said that I would never see my kids again, and how she's been screwing all my friends—all kinds of bull."

"Did she say who?"

"Naw, she's probably lying. Just trying to say anything to make me mad . . . She didn't look so good either. She looks like a crackhead if you ask me."

"Aw baby. I feel sorry for her," Jessie said remorsefully almost with a tear in her eye.

"Sorry? . . . Man, the hell with Salina. She'd see me and you dead if she could . . . Besides, I'm your man and always was. I just had children with her, so that kept me from marrying you years ago."

"Yeah . . . but, I know how she feels right now, and it's just sad. That's all."

Benji is silent for a while letting Jessie finish sulking, and then he kisses her in the mouth. She doesn't respond, but he doesn't care. He sticks his tongue between her lips to stop her from talking. She can't resist the warmth of the kiss, and she joins in the intimate mingling of their tongues and lips.

They embrace and caress each other's back and buttocks as they engage in passionate foreplay, arousing their sexual organs.

Jessie's stomach hinders them from all-out lovemaking, and Benji is ever so gentle. He kisses her arm and neck then the tips of her breast before he slides himself into a position behind her and finds the cervix between her thighs and butt muscles. He plunges into her pool of vaginal juices.

Squuk, sik, plap, squk.

The sound her vagina makes every time Benji's slab fills her hole brings him closer and closer to an ejaculation with each and every pulsating stroke. He winds his hips around as he pulls back and reenters.

"Um," Jessie murmurs with her eyes closed and her mouth open. "Oh . . . yes . . . Um hum . . ."

While Benji continues his subdued performance, his eyes fall upon a large bug that looks a lot like a roach standing on the wall facing him and Jessie. It's been a long time since he's seen one of those.

What the . . . Shoot man, let me hurry up before Jessie sees that.

Benji starts to stroke a little more rapidly and digs a little deeper. The sight of the roach took his mind slightly off concentration. He was trying to keep himself from exploding. His adrenaline is rushing harder and harder, and he can feel himself climbing higher to his climax. Jessie is starting to move a lot more, holding her stomach all the while. She wants to rise to her knees, but she knows that would not be a good idea. The pleasure she is feeling has her disregarding any pain as she bounces her torso in rhythm with Benji's back and forth, in and out stroking.

She opens her eyes and raises her head up off the pillow and looks back at her hip to see how it shakes from the increased violence of their humping. Her eyes roll and she leans her head all the way back and moans and groans in harmony with Benji's increasingly louder grunts and slurs.

"Agh!" Jessie spots the roach and screams, pushing back into Benji's chin nearly making him bite his lip. "A roach! Benji. Get it. Kill it!"

Just what Benji had feared has happened. Jessie has seen the roach and nothing will calm her down until it is dead and flushed down the toilet. Benji has gone limp, and his chin smarts from the head bunt. If Jessie's head hurts, she doesn't show any sign of pain, just loathsome disgust for the insect resting on the wall.

"Benji!"

"OK. OK."

Benji rolls out of the bed and clamors around for a shoe. Finding one, he casually walks over to the wall where the bug is standing, and he cocks the shoe back behind his head then swats.

"You missed him, Benji! Get him. Get it," Jessie exclaims now up on her knees pointing in the direction that the roach fled. "Don't let him get away."

Benji starts moving things, trying to see where the roach had run, but doesn't see it. He moves the nightstand, still nothing. He gets down on his knees to look under the bed. Nothing.

"You let it get away, Benji." Jessie is very upset, because she knows that one roach means more. "All right, we gotta clean up. We gotta clean this house from top to bottom with bleach. I'm not bringing my baby in a roach-infested house."

"Roach infested? Man, you saw one roach, and you trippin."

"One roach means more. It probably done laid some eggs and all that. Get the bleach and go to the store and get some Raid Max."

"Raid Max? They still make that?"

"Just go."

Benji knows that there's absolutely nothing that he can say to drive her from her mission to get rid of that roach. It would be a waste of time and breath to ask if they could finish what they started. She might slap him or something, so he surrenders and mopes over to his drawer for a pair of boxers without a word. Benji's about to transform into Mr. Belvedere.

Chapter 31

It's well after midnight and Benji is still slave to Jessie's commands. He's scrubbed every tile floor in the house with bleach on his hands and knees, disinfected the two and a half bathrooms, all but rebuilt the kitchen, moved furniture so Jessie could vacuum in between her overseeing duties, and threw out all excess paper in the whole house.

"Spray over there, then take that bag outside . . . Aw . . ." Jessie winces and doubles over clutching her stomach.

"You OK?" Benji asks reaching for her. "You need to go lie down. You've been on your feet all night. You know you shouldn't be standing up."

"Whew . . . Oh, boy. Agh!" She cries out again, clenching up her face in agony still holding her stomach.

Benji and Jessie stand in the threshold of the kitchen doorway. Benji appears to be in as much pain as Jessie as he tries to keep her from falling to the floor.

"Is it moving around? Is it coming?" Benji desperately inquires.

"I . . . don't . . . Uhh. Don't know," she whimpers.

Benji struggles to keep her on her feet, helping her over to the kitchen table. He eases her down on the chair, and she leans her arm down on her thigh and continues to hold her stomach with one hand while gripping Benji's shirt with the other.

"Hold on, baby. I'ma go get your coat. We're going to the hospital."

"OK," she whispers.

Jessie reluctantly releases him, and then he scuffles around the corner to the closet. He returns with her coat and puts it on her. He leaves the kitchen again, this time returning with his own coat and pants. He bows down in front of Jessie and slips her slippers off her feet and lifts them into the cotton pajama pants that he brought from upstairs along with a pair of thermo socks and a blanket.

Once he has bundled her up in warm clothing, the two of them leave out the house into the darkness of their front porch. The sensor lights illuminate the front yard once they take a couple of steps beyond the slamming door behind them. Benji assists the ginger-footed Jessie down the steps then to the truck.

Chirp. Chirp. The truck alarm sounds as they approach the passenger door. The truck also starts up automatically.

✧   ✧   ✧

The room is cozy with wood paneling on the bottom half of the wall, while pink paint and a border decorate the top partition. There's a lamp in the far corner of the room. It's set on dim, giving the room an intimate feel, and the palm tree plant next to the lamp adds a touch of life to the atmosphere of the room. There's a chair that has an extended seat, and Benji is stretched out on it knocked out cold. Next to him on a maternity bed, Jessie is also sound asleep. She's just given birth to a seven-pound baby boy. They've already agreed to call him Asa—named after a great king over the nation of Israel, a descendent of the wise King Solomon.

Benji had prayed countless times to have a boy. Though he already had a son, a son by his rightful queen makes Benji feel as though this is the start of a lineage, and this son would be the primary benefactor of the greater portion of his estate. Benji sees this son as a prince who will carry his torch and be second to no one. Even Jessie will have to take cautious notice of how highly Benji will exult in this child, but he's not the only one who foresees a meaningful future for this child.

Iblis is nearby and has been since the time they left the house eight hours ago. Iblis has not taken on any form at this time. He's in his spirit form and invisible to Benji and Jessie, and he's listening, watching, musing.

Blessed is the child. He is healthy and strong. I don't believe sudden death will befall him. The spirit is strongly in his midst. Enlightenment is certain. He is a strong possibility. I must destroy him or bring him to my side if calamity escapes him. But death is the only safe remedy.

Iblis can sense that the child is the source of all the blessings that this couple is receiving from above and knows that he must do away with this child and has taken no time to figure out the fastest most sure way of accomplishing his mission. *Salina.*

Iblis remembers the things that Benji told Jessie concerning the deep hatred that Salina has for Jessie and the vow she made to be the cause of Jessie's demise. Iblis wishes no longer to be annoyed by the bombarding spirit of his father above, so he removes himself from the quaint quarters of this blessed couple in search of the tool he shall use to bring about detrimental harm to yet another candidate for being the one who will or might be responsible for bringing about his own demise. Salina will be his friend. Salina will prolong his authority over this world's evil system of things, but there must be others that he can use. So he summons two of his analim to focus on the workings of Benji and Jessie, while he focuses on the main ingredient to his plot against the Omega's likely sacred one.

Benji wakes up under the watchful eyes of Quazibub, Iblis' arch servant. Benji cannot see Quazibub, but an inexplicable smell is in the air. The smell wasn't there when he awoke an hour ago. He sits up and peers over at his wife, then stands up and walks over to the glass baby crib. Asa is in it sound asleep. Benji bends over and sniffs the air above his son's body.

That's not do-do. What the hell is that smell? Damn. Smells like sulfur 8.

It's actually the scent of Quazibub. He is in his spirit form, but his covetous gaze at Jessica has him in between a spirit and material manifestation. He's contemplating bashing Benji's head brainless so that he can have his way with the fleshy creature that is sound asleep in the bed. Though he knows it is extremely forbidden for any spirit to take on a material form for the purpose of interacting with human kind ever since the Nephalim wreaked so much havoc upon the earth in Noah's day, his lust has him at the breaking point. The only thing that is keeping him from doing it is the thought of the punishment that he will receive afterward. First Iblis will command that he manifest into flesh so he can be dipped into a pool of molten lava deep in the earth's crust, and then Apollyon will banish him to the abyss before the appointed time. At any rate, he's a lustful spirit and his body is giving off a nasty stench, and Benji is perplexed by it.

He walks out into the hallway and down to the nurse's station, saying to the chubby white woman sitting at the computer, "Look . . . y'all gonna move my family out of that room right now. There's a smell in there that might be some of the electrical equipment about to catch fire or something. The room stinks like hell."

The woman jumps up from her seat and moves quickly toward Jessie's room. In the room, the woman sniffs the air, but there is no strange smell. Benji walks in and can't smell the scent anymore either.

"It's gone. I don't get it. I could smell it just before I left out the room a second ago, but now I don't."

The woman walks around the room but smells no sign of what Benji could have been talking about. She looks at him raising both of her eyebrows high on her Tyra Banks forehead.

"I don't smell anything. Do you still want us to move you all to another room?" the woman asks politely, almost being sarcastic in her overly cordial consideration of accommodating his wishes. "There are three rooms available."

Benji doesn't detect the sarcasms because he's starting to think he's seeing, hearing, and now smelling things. "Naw, that's OK, but I could have sworn I smelt something . . . I guess I was lunchin'. Thanks anyway."

"Are you sure?"

"Yeah. That's a'ight."

The woman smiles then turns away from Benji scrunching her face and thinking *coo-coo,* as she walks out the room. *Give me a break. Guess he's never smelled potpourri before. Figures. He's probably from Barry Farms anyhow.*

Benji walks over to the baby lying in the clear plastic crib. Jessie wakes up and watches her husband marvel at the young child. She's so elated to have been able to bless him with a child. She can see that he's proud, and it's written all over his face. He's so happy. A tear drops from the corner of her eye, and her life finally feels complete. There is nothing more she feels that she needs. She knows she has been blessed.

"Good morning, bae," Jessie whispers.

"Oh. Good morning." Benji glances at Jessie, and then returns his full attention on the baby.

"He's beautiful, isn't he?"

Benji nods silently; he then turns and leans over to kiss Jessie on her soft red lips.

"Thank you, Jess. I'm sorry I made you wait so long."

"No, you didn't make me wait. Things couldn't have worked out any better."

They shared a smile and another kiss.

"Bae, I'm about to go to the house and shower and then change clothes. I'll be back later on. I know you'll be having company in and out."

"Yeah, go ahead, sweetie. I'm fine. Go celebrate with your friends. I'll see you tonight."

"Tonight? You sure?"

"Keep asking me so many questions, and I just might change my mind."

Benji knows that he can't take being cooped up in a hospital room, watching soap operas all day, doing absolutely nothing. "A'ight. A'ight.

I'm gone." He surrenders. "Call me if you need me for anything, even if you get bored. OK?"

"OK . . . now go, before I change my mind."

Before leaving, he holds his son and talks to him for about twenty minutes. He kisses his wife, and then leaves the hospital. After going home and changing his clothes, he goes to the liquor store and buys three bottles of Cristal, a case of Moet, a bottle of Hennessy, and a case of Heineken and throws them all in a big cooler in the back of his truck.

He drives uptown and meets his man Geech at the Juice Joint across from Howard University to buy an ounce of the "Heezee for Cheezee," that's Hydro, marijuana grown under water. After leaving from uptown he calls everybody under the sun and tells him or her to meet him around the way. Around the way is always in Kentland in front of his mother's house. He tells each person he calls to bring some chicken, crabs, or ribs and informs them that he's just had another baby by his new wife. For most, this is news to even find out that he's married.

He makes one stop at CVS to buy a bag of Backwoods and goes straight to his mom's house. His father lives there too. But in the hood, as long as a man's mother is alive, the house he returns to is referred to as his mother's house, and with some, it'll still be called Mom's house after she's dead and gone.

There are people already out in front of the house by the time Benji gets there. Even though the weather is not exactly picnic weather, Benji and his friends still find a way to have a gathering that closely resembles a cookout, complete with folding chairs and tables. It doesn't take long before half the neighborhood knows that the boys are back in town. There's smoke in the air, drinks being downed, and food being chomped. The music from the back of Benji's Denali drowns out the conversation of the people's voices from across the yard, and Benji's parents look outside from time to time hoping that the police won't come harassing their son and his friends while they rejoice over his firstborn child by his wife. The police come, but they never stop, and Benji and his crew celebrate well into the afternoon. It's only 1:00 p.m. on a Saturday afternoon and obviously quite early for a gathering, complete with food and drinks, but with a guy like Benji, a party could spark at any time. Life is real good for the young fellow—at least at the moment.

This gathering will draw more and more people as the day moves on, and it's sure to drag well into the night. It's almost like a holiday for Benji. All of his appointments have been cancelled, and he is only prepared to move if Jessie calls him. Otherwise, this is where he'll be until it's time to return to the hospital. Hours pass by and so do several joints of hydro. Before long, the sun is setting and the crowd of people has turned over multiple times. Benji hardly notices. He's too high and drunk to be concerned with anybody that he's not talking to, and boy, is he doing a whole lot of talking.

Little does Benji know that every single word he utters is being recorded in the perfect memory of Quazibub who will report these things to Iblis. But Quazibub is focusing on not only what Benji is saying, but he's focusing on everyone. Every single person who has come through is marked by Quazibub and will soon have one of Iblis' wicked spirit creatures suffering their every move to determine how they can use them to destroy Benji, his wife, and most importantly, his blessed child, who, no doubt in Iblis' mind, has a divine purpose.

The day is aging and the sky has turned royal blue. Soon darkness will dominate the western hemisphere, and secret thoughts of the heart will be pronounced so that the spirit of the air can know the evil that men seek to do. What's in store for the happy Benji, he does not know, but he's surrounded by calamity and the power of a roaring lion seeking to devour him.

Chapter 32

Jaspers is filled with the regulars on this Saturday evening, mixed with the anytime, any day drinkers who don't work, drive fast cars, and prowl around all day and night looking for a sex partner to give them another notch under their belts. Fatts and Daryl sit at the bar, drinking two Bonecrushers. Fatts is eating stuffed flounder, and Daryl is sloshing down chicken wing after chicken wing, licking the barbeque sauce off his lips after each swipe of the meat off the bone. A gluttonous pig in every sense of the word.

"Hsslp . . . look at. *Smack* . . . Papi, lil funny lookin' ass," mumbles Daryl with a mouthful of chicken. "Think he a . . . *smack, chomp* . . . pimp, don't he?"

Fatts looks across the room until his eyes fall upon the long-haired Mexican breathing on the shoulder of some chocolate brown cutie. He gestures his approval with a semi-smile. "Humph, yeah." He laughs under his breath and nods his head satisfied that his homie knows how to pick 'em.

"Man, whatever nigga," fires Daryl. "I get more broads than him. And they look way better *and* phatter than his. His chicks ain't got nothin' on mines."

Fatts peeks at Daryl out of the corner of his eye and chuckles defiantly under his breath at the statement that his main man just made. Daryl, not appreciating his buddy's denial of what he feels, barks, "What? You sayin' I ain't got no bitches?" He waits for Fatts to reply, and then asks him again, "You sayin' I on't got bitches? Shid nigga . . . You better ask somebody. I on't know what kinda games you playin'. You need to check my record."

The overly confident fat boy Casanova is mad now, mumbling to himself under his breath and jealously clocking Lil Papi's moves, resentfully cutting his eyes back and forth at Fatts. He's really in his feeling about Fatts' implications.

Sucka ass nigga gon stop playin' with me. I'm the one who got bitches for real. That nigga Papi fakin'. He ain't got bitches for real. That broad looks like a chicken head anyway.

"Man, I know you ain't over there trippin'. Man, you trippin?" Fatts ask.

"Naw, you trippin' . . . I gets my man, joe. Humph. Ask Tish. Ask Nee-Nee. Yeah . . . Ask Adrian. Ask your sister, nigga."

"Oh my god! Man, you are trippin'," Fatts surrenders, looking away from Daryl toward the entrance, hoping to see Luther coming down the steps into the bar pit. "Where's Luther? He supposed to been . . ."

Just as Fatts is finishing his sentence, Luther bends the corner and skips down the steps to the bar area and sits in the empty seat between Fatts and Daryl. He doesn't look so happy, but he greets them as normal in the usual ultra cool salutation he always uses, "What's up on it, dog on it?"

And they respond to him with the usual reply. Harmoniously "Shit."

"What's goin' on, moe?" Fatts pries into Luther's lackadaisical demeanor, noticing that something is troubling his mood. "Everything a'ight?" He sucks a piece of meat from between his two front teeth.

"Um huh . . . Aye Jacob, let me get a VSOP straight. Double. Twist of lime," Luther calls to a bald-headed white guy behind the bar.

"Remy?"

Luther nods.

"You eating?"

He shakes his head.

There's a long silence after Luther makes his order. Daryl isn't even talking to himself about how many girls he's got. Even he senses the tension in the air. He hates the feeling he gets when Luther comes around in silence. That usually means trouble, and his stomach is churning causing him to lose his appetite and bounce his leg. He hasn't had this feeling for a long time, and the thought of drama has him pooting and sweating in his palms. He only has three more chicken winglets to eat, but he doesn't have the stomach to off them. It's not that he's full; just eating right now has become a task. He's fighting to swallow what's in his mouth right now.

Fatts ponders over what the problem might be. He's praying that Luther isn't about to tell him that he has taken a loss. Luther owes one hundred and eighty thousand on his bill of four hundred thousand dollars. Money's been coming in slow from Luther lately, and that's unusual. He's the one who moves a majority of the bricks, but for some reason, he's been in a slump and moving the least of them all.

"I on't know, man. Ain't nothin' movin'. Niggas getting coke from somebody cheaper than I can give it to 'em," Luther confesses angrily. "I'm waiting for one of my men to come up here to holler at me now. Today was the first time he's called me in weeks. He usually gets like three or four by himself."

"Who?" Fatts asks him.

"Kan Quick," blurts Luther.

"Oh, Quick?"

"Yeah . . . He said he's been gettin' with some dude named Amp. I on't know."

"Amp?" Fatts wonders where he's heard that name before.

"Amp. That's one of Richter's youngins," reveals Daryl. "You know Richter with the Vette."

"Yeah." Fatts knows him well. They used to gamble against each other back in the day. Richter used to bring piles of money to the Riverdale Bowling alley to shoot dice. The only reason he didn't try to rob him was because he always had a mob of guys standing around, toting big guns under their jackets.

"They say he's gettin' it too," Luther tells them in a tone that has remnants of larceny in it. "He's supposed to be in real tight with some Maryland bamma named Benji. They say this dude Benji is doin' the damn thang." That means he's getting a whole lot of money and moving a lot of weight. "I say we find out who he is and rob his ass blind. He's cuttin' into our business. *For real.*"

Just then Kan Quick comes into the bar area. There are no seats at the bar where Fatts, Luther, and Daryl are sitting, so he just stands there behind them. No one greets him as he approaches, but they all swivel their bar stools around in order to face him. Luther extends his hand, and they soul shake. The short version. Kan Quick looks at Fatts, who up nods as does Daryl.

Kan Quick is a feared man in his own right and always has been. He's the same Quick that used to box, and who got tamed by his now good friend Amp. The Kan has been added to his name since the two of them fought because he gave up boxing and bought a gun. He learned how to box so that the average dude on the street wouldn't stand a chance against him in a fist fight, but after the tune-up that Amp gave him, he decided that fighting was for the birds. He'd rather put some hot balls in his enemies and has taken many opportunities in doing so over the years. He's been known to kill a nigga Quick, and somehow over the years he's gotten away with doing just that.

Even still, he has a fear within him for Lil Papi, who is making his way toward them. He can't understand why this guy strikes up such an uneasy feeling inside of him. He just knows that he's terrified of him.

"So what's been up, slim?" begins Luther. "Your main man done run out, and now you're crawlin' back to me?"

Kan Quick leans his head to the side and looks to the floor. *Here we go*, he thinks to himself.

"It ain't even like that, dog," Kan Quick explains checking the expression of the two men's faces beside Luther, and then focuses back on his interrogator. "I've been dealin' with that dude way before me and you hooked up."

"That wasn't the story you . . . Hold up." Luther pauses, realizing that this conversation is leading into a negative direction. He doesn't want to scare off his best clientele. "It's all good, slim. You got the right to deal with whoever you want. I'm just glad you call me too. My bad."

Kan Quick analyzes Luther's veil of deceptive apology and deems that he shouldn't trust Luther anymore, but he can't back off now. That would result in a sure enough beef. Luther and his relentless mob of hustlers, killers, bitches, and street spies would have him packaged and delivered blindfolded as well as duct taped in the back of a trunk in a heartbeat. He has to play his cards right or fall victim to the streets.

"Yeah, I know what you saying," Quick says but doesn't really believe that everything is actually cool. "Wasup killer?" he says to the approaching Lil Papi as he extends his hand.

Papi tugs at his hand and they meet chest and pound one another on the back. "You the killer," Papi acknowledges.

Quick surveys Papi's gear then continues, "But ah, wasup though, Luther? Can I holler at you?"

Luther gets up, and they walk up the steps leading out the bar pit. Lil Papi sits down on the stool that Luther was sitting on and digs into Daryl's plate grabbing two of the last three pieces of chicken.

"Man what you doing?!" Daryl snatches at the chicken, but Papi plays keep away and plops one of the winglets into his mouth.

"Igh high. You missed," Papi taunts.

Highly upset, Daryl snaps, "I told you. Y'all niggas play too much, man."

Fatts and Lil Papi share a teasing laugh as they lean against each other getting a kick out of Daryl's overreactive temper. Fatts is laughing, but in the back of his mind, he knows that Luther is plotting a scheme and the thought of them resorting back to their old ways against a powerful clique that knows them well since they've come out of the shadows to become well-known drug dealers doesn't settle well in his mind. He knows that

Luther has no problem with it, so how can he tell him, *forget those dudes? Let 'em make all your money.*

Somebody's gonna have to pay. And Luther has already said out of his mouth that the target will be some Maryland bamma named Benji.

Chapter 33

Night has fallen on Fifty-eighth Street NE, where some of Washington DC's most notorious extorters, hit men, and street hustlers have roamed. At the top of the hill on the southeast side, Amp rides shotgun with Richter in his blue Vette. The street is bustling with the living dead, transacting with the young merchants operating their open-air cocaine strip. No one pays too much attention to the surveying vehicle crawling through their pumpin' narcotics depot. Richter and Amp are searching for motorcycles up on the curb or the faces of Luther and Fatts. Richter knows them both well, but who doesn't know Luther? He's arguably the prime candidate for dead man of the year. Every year, people talk about how somebody's gonna kill him and "dump them thangs" in his head, but at the end of every summer for the past eight years he's managed to prepare for the coming kidnapping season when stick-up boys gear up in big coats and carry big guns. Well, he hasn't actually needed to do things like that for the past year and a half because he's been on the other side of the fence for a change, and the city's many kingpins have been somewhat at ease, knowing how rich Luther and the rest of his mob have been getting without robbing.

Even though Fatts is without a doubt the leader of Luther's so-called mob, Luther's name is known by people who aren't even street people. Kinda like Rayfus a.k.a Rayfel Edmonds and Matt Dilinger who were made into criminal gods from the way their names were kicked around in everybody's daily conversations.

Luther's no god, and he sure isn't dead by a long shot, but if Richter has his way, he'll be dead by the break of dawn.

"Man ain't no tellin' where them niggas are at. They don't have any reason to be hangin' out here no more," Richter assures Amp who is only knowledgeable of their possible hangouts through grapevine sources.

A week has passed since Kan Quick informed Amp of all the questions that Luther was asking about Benji and the rest of them. Quick had emphasized that Luther doesn't ask questions about people unless he's set on bringing them a move. He threw Luther some curveballs, but he knows Luther never relies on the information of one source when it comes to a move that is worth a couple hundred grand or more.

Amp goosenecks to make sure the person behind a parked Jeep isn't Luther. Realizing that he isn't him, he turns forward and sits back in the leather bucket seat as Richter taps on the accelerator launching the car toward the stop sign at the corner of Southern Avenue.

"We've been lookin' for them bammas all week. I'm wasting time. I need some coke," Amp complains.

"Shorty, it ain't gonna be no coke as long as these niggas on the prowl for our man. We've got to take care of this business first. As long as these niggas breathin', Benji ain't trying to do nothin'."

Amp sucks his teeth. "Man, that nigga act like we ain't got no bills to pay . . . He keep . . ." Amp is furious but knows to keep certain things left unsaid. Richter is loyal to Benji and would turn on Amp in a second if he thinks Amp would raise a finger against his friend. Amp shakes his head and goes on, "I'm sayin', though, Benji knows we depend on him to keep us rollin'."

"I don't," Richter interjects quickly taking his eyes off the road to glance over at Amp.

"I know *you* don't. I'm talking 'bout me, Tony, and Bootemup. We *need* the work. My daughter's in private school. I got a car note, rent, all that."

Richter nods his head in understanding of what Amp is trying to say. "Every time the goin' gets good, the goods get goin' and then they're gone. And y'all don't even let us flip the money. We just gotta wait till God knows when for Benji to decide to get some more. That's not right. That's all I'm sayin'."

Richter feels his pain and knows he's not lying, but there's nothing he can say about it. He's just Benji's middleman. "I feel you."

✧   ✧   ✧

Amp stands at the door of apartment number 918. The music coming from the other side of the door is very loud, and he doubts that anyone can hear his riotous banging on the metal door besides all the neighbors in the other three apartments on the floor and the other six apartments downstairs. He turns his back to the door and cocks his right foot forward and kicks back striking the door as hard as he can.

Dooomp. Doomp. Doomp. Doomp.

He maintains his position, and then raises his leg again. This time raising his butter-colored Timberlands up to the level of his crouch area and kicks back again. Before his foot reaches the door, the music blasts in his ear and his foot swings back further than he had expected it to and lands against something that moves upon impact. Amp quickly swings around to see what or whom he had just kicked. It's Tony hopping around his living room reaching for his left knee. Unbearable pain is written all over his face, and the anguish he's enduring is too excruciating for the anger inside him to show. His mouth is open wide, but no sound is coming out of it. His eyes are closed. His brain believes in mind over matter, but his leg doesn't know what the hell that's supposed to mean. He's in pain.

The music drowns out all of the "sorrys" and the "my bads" that Amp offers as condolences for all the suffering his friend is going through as a result of his power kick to his knee.

"Are you OK?" Amp asks, but the music is too loud for Tony to hear him.

"Serial Killer . . . Serial Killer," the rapper on the radio says repeatedly with a deep monstrous voice over the hardest drumbeat imaginable. The music has been the culprit of countless picture frames and ceramic ornaments on Tony's neighbor's walls and bookshelves falling to the floor and breaking into pieces. The band's name is Backyard, and that's exactly where this band got its start. In somebody's backyard, and now they have become something like a local Grateful Dead band with a crowd that will pack anywhere they perform on any day of the week, seven days a week. It's been that way for years, and the voice is that of legendary Genghis.

Genghis is the lead rapper of the band and is a gangster to the bone. There are so many stories that surround the fact that this guy is a true gangster. Once he jumped off the stage in the middle of a performance when a fight broke out in the crowd. The music stopped, and the crowd formed a circle around him and the two guys who were fighting. With the mic still in his hand, Genghis scolded the two dudes for messing up the party, punched both of them in the face, and the guys looked at him as if he was crazy. Everybody in the whole joint was shocked and nobody said anything. The entire place went mute. Genghis looked at the two dudes, daring them to retaliate. He mean-mugged them, then raised the microphone to his mouth and said, "Gotdamit, y'all make the call." The music dropped back into a pocket, and the crowd went wild as Genghis danced in the circle with the two guys he had just punched, singing along with the dancing crowd who was chanting, "Nowhere to run to, baby. Nowhere to hide."

Scenes like that have labeled Genghis as the Ghetto Prince and have made him legendary with a growing popularity far beyond the DC Go-Go scene. A scene Amp, Tony, and Bootemup will invade tonight if Tony is able to walk without a crutch.

Amp walks over to the dining room and clicks the light switch, turning on the light and the ceiling fan. He walks over to the black entertainment center in the living room and turns down the volume to a near hush.

"Dog, my bad, man. I was at the door knocking for like twenty minutes." He's lying. "I knew you were in here, and I didn't even hear you open the door. You a'ight?"

The sympathy on Amp's face allows Tony to forgive him sooner than he wanted to. He wanted to call him all kinds of stupid m-efers first, but Amp's pleading and remorse has extinguished the fire that was raging in Tony, and he can only hold his knee and shake his head. He knows his knee is going to swell, keeping him from going to see "Back Yard" tonight.

"Damn, moe," Tony says, "You busted my knee up," wincing and frowning.

Bootemup comes from the back room wondering, what's keeping Tony so long from returning to hit the Bob they were smoking before he stepped away without any explanation. Bootemup didn't hear the door either, so when Tony got up to go answer it, he didn't know why he had left the room.

When he sees Tony holding his knee and Amp just standing there looking down at him, he figures something ridiculous had just happened, and he immediately starts to chuckle.

"Ha . . . What happened? What'd you do, clip him up?"

Amp can't help himself. He burst into laughter too.

"Man . . . ha-ha . . . you always laughing at something." Amp wanted to laugh from the start, but he didn't want to make Tony mad, but now that Bootemup has set it off, it's open season. "It . . . ha . . . ain't funny . . . ha." Amp looks at the expression on Tony's face who is looking at him. "What? He's the one laughing."

Amp tries to explain to their agonizing buddy sitting on the floor. Amp wasn't going to laugh at all, but he can't stop laughing since Bootemup got him started. The more he thinks about Tony and how he was hopping around like Tonto, the harder the laughs, and the less he can explain why he's laughing so hard. Tony is promising to get them back, provoking them to laugh harder and harder with every threat until tears start running down the sides of their faces as they roll around clutching their stomachs. Bootemup didn't exactly know what he was laughing at, but wouldn't pass up an opportunity to clown one of his two best friends for nothing in the world. He can't wait to get the full story so he can laugh all over again.

They finally start to get headaches to the point that they don't want to laugh anymore, but when Amp tells him the story, they end up laughing all over again, but Tony isn't laughing. His knee is slowly swelling up, and he doesn't feel much like going to the go-go tonight. They sit there, and no one says anything for a while. It's like everybody's in their own world. Tony and Bootemup fall asleep, but Amp stretches across the couch gazing at the ceiling with his forearm raised across his brow. His mind is wandering, thinking about his shortage of money. He doesn't want to dip into his savings that he has stashed away, but if some drugs don't come through soon, he'll have no choice. The very idea of it angers him, and bad thoughts cross his mind.

I should rob his punk ass. Can't stand that ole faggy anyway. He thinks he's all that . . . Nigga don't care about me. I should get him before somebody else does.

Amp looks over at Tony and can see that he's not asleep anymore, but he's not saying anything.

"Hey, Tonto. You all right?"

"Humph . . . You got jokes," Tony suggests calmly.

"I'm just trying to make sure you a'ight," Amp recants jokingly.

"Yeah. That nigga's a'ight. He's just got a lent ball for brains," garbles Bootemup.

Amp and Bootemup share a subdued laugh then silence fills the air again. Amp doesn't know how to say what he wants to say to his friends, but he feels he must. He longs to tell them how bad he wants to grab Benji, tie him up, and take him for all the money he has. Amp is also a known gun busser, but it's been years since he's had to resort to that type of violence, so murder isn't part of the nasty wishes he has for his drought-imposing drug supplier. What he does know, however, is that he needs the support of both of his friends in order to get away with it.

"You know me and Richter was ridin' around, looking for Luther and 'em last night and earlier."

"Yeah? So what happened?" asks Bootemup.

"We ain't see 'em . . . So you know what that means . . . We ain't getting' no coke till we murk them niggas," Amp informs them.

Bootemup raises his head up off the love seat situated adjacent to the sofa that Amp is lying on. "That's what he said?" His eyes are filled with animosity and concern. He smacks his lips. "Man, that nigga Benji a bitch, joe. How that nigga gonna hold us up 'cause some niggas askin' some questions about him?"

This is the reaction Amp was hoping to get. Now, all he has to do is see where Tony is before he starts rambling off ideas of larceny against the man who feeds their kids and appetite for the finer things in life. Tony is closer to Benji than they are, but none of them considers themselves good friends of Benji. Benji is a few years older than they are and looks at them as his youngins. He likes them but doesn't invite them to hang out with him as he does Richter and Bink.

Richter, on the other hand, loves them all and sometimes even joins them at the go-go. Richter's actually older than Benji by three or four years, but he has become known as a heavy hitter since he's been hanging with Benji over the last ten years or so. Back in the 1980s he was only known as a compulsive gambler and a stick-up boy. He kinda looks up to Benji and would never betray him. Benji's been caked up since the mid-1980 as a young teenager putting him light years ahead of most of the people around him. He likes them, Amp, Tony, and Bootemup, but he doesn't show them much love.

"Tony, Why don't you holla atchor boy? Tell 'em to break us off so we can pay some bills before we focus on getting at them niggas," Amp encourages Tony, testing his response.

"Shid. That nigga ain't my boy. The hell with that nigga for real. If I thought I'd get away with it, I'd hem his ass up myself."

Amp's heart rejoices and a smile gleams across his face in the same way he's spread across the black leather sofa. (What is it with black people and black furniture? Seems that's all they know.) Amp sits up and tells them his true feeling about Benji, and they discuss how they can use the Luther situation as a patsy to cover-up their own caper, but they know they'll have to act fast because if Luther is back to his old tricks, Benji could be snatched first thing in the morning. Then, they'll really be up the creek.

The clock is ticking. The race is on.

Chapter 34

Benji has been very uncomfortable with his surrounding since it has been brought to his attention that the most infamous thugs in town have been asking questions about him and his whereabouts. He does, however, find a lot of comfort in knowing that practically no one has information about where his new house is. He has Salina to thank for that. With all her meaningful threats against Jessie, they haven't entrusted any non-family members with their new address. In fact, their driver's licenses and tags to their cars are not registered to the residence, so writing down their tag numbers wouldn't help a stalker or an investigator for that matter.

It's very late and Benji would usually be home at such an hour, but tonight he's creeping. There's a lot unusual about Benji's actions tonight. He would normally be driving his truck or one of his many hoopties that he has stashed around town, but tonight he's driving Jessie's car, the Cadillac. He hates the car because it doesn't have tinted windows That means that everyone he passes by will see that it's him in the car. He feels like a sitting duck behind the wheel, and considering his circumstances, he can't understand why on earth he's even driving it in the city.

He's in NW Washington DC, blowing his horn outside of a rowhouses.

Whose house is this? He wonders to himself and why am I here?

He really has no idea. The door opens to the house that he's sitting in front of, and a young lady comes out of the door, wearing a pair of Daisy Duke short-shorts that are so tight that Benji can see the camel's foot sitting between the bow-legged stances that the young lady is sporting as she poses at the top of the steps leading to the front door. She waves for him to get out the car leaving it double parked in the street.

Benji still has no idea who she is or why he's here, still he obeys her request and as he approaches her gate, he begins to see her face a little better than he could while he was sitting in the car. The closer he gets the more he starts to recognize her face.

Now I remember her, he says to himself. *That's the girl who told me her number, and I wrote it down on the receipt that I dropped on the floor that night in the Wawa. What was her name . . . Damn. I can't remember.*

Benji wrecks his brain, trying to visualize the name that he had seen when he pulled that piece of paper out of his pocket with the bundle of money that he found that night. How will he greet her without calling her by her name? She'll surely realize that he doesn't even know her name the moment he calls her baby, or sweetie, or anything along those lines.

He sizes up her incredibly proportionate body figure and feels a sinful chill of lust and desire enter his bloodstream. But he doesn't understand. He hasn't thought of another woman besides Jessie since he came home. He only took the girl's number in the first place to show Bink that he could still book any girl he wanted to, no matter how much of a dime piece she is, or thinks she is. He never intended on calling her, so how could he be meeting her at her home? Whatever the case, Benji feels that if she shows any indication of giving him the green light, he's going to go.

He gets a little closer and stops as she turns to walk in the house. He says to her, "Let me park the car." When he turns around, he sees a head duck down behind a car parked across the street and another person in the shadow of an overgrown shrub in her next-door neighbor's front yard. *It's a setup!* He thinks, but it's too late. Still another body emerges from the opposite side of the street.

Benji knows he won't be able to get to his car before the man coming across the street has him in point-blank range, so he jumps the fence, escaping out of the yard and races up the street. The three men take chase, and there is no telling how many more there are. Benji cuts left at the corner of North Capitol Street and runs north against the southbound traffic. Benji runs down an alley and can hear his predators' feet pitter-pattering the ground close behind him.

"Damn, one of these niggas is fast as hell." Benji realizes that he's not going to get away from these dudes and wishes that he had his gun on him. Why is it that every time he needs his gun, it's in the car or under the pillow?

One of the men tackles Benji from behind, and Benji goes down scraping the side of his face on the concrete.

"All right, you got it. You got it. I'm not strapped." Benji surrenders and hopes these guys are only going to beat him up for running.

"Get up."

Benji can see the gun that the man is holding, and he can also see the others coming toward him while his captor holds him by his collar from behind. Benji stands up on his feet, and then comes the sound he has always dreaded the most.

POW!

Benji sees his world turning sideways, but he can't hear a thing. He falls sideways and lands on his shoulder.

"Don't khhi . . . ," Benji mumbles, waking up in a cold sweat. His heart is hurting, and his brain feels numb.

He looks around and sees Jessie beside him. She raises her head from the pillow and looks at Benji. The look on his face startles her, and she becomes instantly wide awake. She jumps up and looks over at the baby's carriage beside the bed.

"What's wrong, Benji . . . Asa?"

Benji takes a deep breath. "Hum da Allah! I was only dreaming . . . Um, um, um, it's nothing, bae. I was having a terrible dream."

Jessie turns to him and wipes his sweaty brow. He kisses her wrist. "I love you, Jess."

"I love you too. Now, go back to sleep and don't scare me like that—no more, boy. I thought something was wrong with the baby."

Benji gets out of the bed, walks over to the baby's carriage, and kisses Asa on the cheek then gets back in the bed. He doesn't fall back to sleep right away. He just lies there with his eyes open, peering into the open bathroom door. He knows he must find Luther and Fatts as soon as possible. There can be nothing else in the world more important than that. It's them or him, and he doesn't plan on going out like Willie Lump-Lump.

The sun is shining bright from the east. The morning dew is glistening atop the grass blades of a perfectly manicured lawn. There's a tree bearing fruit, and Jessie is picking the ripest of them from the branches. Asa watches as his mommy carefully examines the fruit. He is in a pouch that she is wearing on top of her belly. They are in an open field, and the only thing other than them and the tree is a door and its frame, but the house that belongs to the door is absent. Beyond the door Asa can see the top edge of a hill and appearing from the other side are four wolves. Asa remembers seeing something like them on his parents' picture box that his mommy watches all day until his daddy comes home, and his parents talking is to him as if they are *making noise at one another every time one stops making noise at the other. He doesn't understand that they are communicating; it's just noise to him.*

The wolves start to slowly make their way down the hill toward the unsuspecting mommy and her child. Asa watches them. Jessie doesn't see them, but she looks down at her agitated son.

"You don't wanna see Mommy pick fruit anymore? Are you bored, honey?"

Asa doesn't react to her voice like he usually does because his attention is fixed on the four animals that are headed in their direction. Jessie realizes that something has got her son's attention, and she looks to see what it could be that has him so captivated. When she turns, her jaw drops, and panic takes over her mental capacity. She makes a mad dash for the door.

Asa's vision is distorted and can no longer focus on the world around him because his mother is bouncing him all over the place. The wolves are no longer visible. He can only she the cleavage of his two food sacks under his mommy's shirt when suddenly he can feel himself free fall and then stop with a thudding bump on his back. He can hear his mommy scream louder than he's ever heard anybody scream including himself when he's hungry. He can also hear the sound of growling and snarling wolves. A bone-crunching sound is followed by a wailing cry from his mother that tells him that something is very wrong.

He looks over his head and can see the gnashing fangs of a wolf gnawing at his mommy's head and neck.

He can't see, but there are two other wolves mauling on Jessie as the fourth wolf sits at the door waiting for them to finish. Jessie is balled up protecting her baby from the thrashing teeth of the wolves, but there is nothing that she can do to save herself.

Asa starts to cry like a child who has just gotten hit in the nose with a football. Jessie and Benji hop down out of the bed together, and Jessie snatches their son out of the crib. Asa is damp with perspiration and trying to cry his head off. His eyes are still closed, and her bouncing has no effect on his consciousness.

"All baby . . . baby, don't cry." Jessie pleads. "Mommy and Daddy are here." Asa continues to cry as hard as ever. He finally opens his eyes, but that doesn't make much difference. He continues to cry for fifteen minutes until his throat gets hoarse, and he realizes that his mommy's nipple is in his mouth. That's when he stops crying and starts to suck on it. He falls back to sleep within three minutes of nursing on his mother's milk, and Jessie lays him down in the bed between the two of them.

Benji lies on the other side of Asa and knows he won't be able to go back to sleep now, so he gets a notebook and a pen and decides now would be a better time than ever to write to his little buddy John. He hasn't written him since he moved to his new house, and he's sure Salina would have thrown away any letters John has sent to his old address. After that dream that Benji had, many of the things that he's been neglecting to do have come to mind, including thanking John, that is to say,Lil Chucky for all the things that he did to help him get back in court. John had helped Benji research his case and even typed it up. He was of a lot of help. John can't help him with the problems he has now, though. Benji's a survivor, but still, tomorrow scares him, because for the first time in his life he feels that his life and well-being are in jeopardy. He'd rather have the Feds catch up with him than the streets, and unless he does something about it, the streets will take him under.

Chapter 35

Dear Chucky,

Sorry, I haven't written you in so long. I haven't forgotten about you, buddy. It's just there has been so much happening in my life that I haven't taken much time to do the small things that mean so much. I know you've probably written me at the house, but I haven't been in there since the day after I came home. I left Salina's crazy ass. I'm with Jessie. You told me that you thought she was the one that it seemed like I should be with. You were right. Are you ready for this? I married her. Yeah. I sure did. And we bought a house. A big jont out here in Annapolis. But wait. There is more . . . we have a son. We named him Asa. I'm so happy. You wouldn't believe how well things have been going for me. I have you to thank for so much though. I can never repay you, but I'll never leave you hanging as long as I have been home. I wish I could have gotten your letters. That would have kept you fresh in my mind, but don't worry. From now on, I want you to send me your letters to the return address on the envelope. It's not the address of my house because I don't want them people down there to have my address, but where the letters will be going, I'll definitely get them. You know that letter to the judge was the last time that I wrote a letter. No, I take that back. I did write you once, but I put that old address on it. You might have written me back. Dag, how'd I forget about that, man? See, that's what I'm talkin' about. There's just so much going on that I don't know what I did last week sometimes. I probably could have gotten your letters, but I didn't want to even go around Salina because I knew what that would have led to. I didn't wanna give her an opportunity to weasel her way back in my heart with her sweet talk and sex. That has reeled me back in before, and I wasn't about to allow her to do it again. I love Salina, but not enough to spend the rest of my life with her. Now Jessie, on the other hand, has a soft spot in my heart. I love her like no other, even more than my mother and kids, and you know how much I cherish my kids. I haven't had much time with them since I left Salina, but hopefully, she'll take me to court for child support, then I'll be able to demand my visitation rights, but she's conniving enough to go without the money just to make me suffer in that way. I do see them though, because I go to their schools. I give them money to buy clothes and pay for their needs in school. But you know money is never enough. They really miss me in their life and beg me to come home.

Anyway, enough about me. What's up with you, shorty? My men taking care of you? I've sent you enough money to last you another six months to a year, so spend it however you want. When you get low, let me know, so I can send you some more. I've got plenty of money. I forgot to tell you about my truck company. I bought two dump trucks and got more work than I can handle already. I'ma buy a few more trucks as I stack some more Gs. You dig? I call the company Scoop Trucking. The trucks are mean. You know me, joe. I'm like that. Nothing but the best. First class all the way. Anyway, shorty, my life couldn't get any better. I just have one problem to take care of. But it's nothing to a mere giant. I'm way on top of it. Really, it's nothing. I just wanna make sure I stay on point. Life's too short to be half-steppin', you know. Anyway, much love. Take it light and holla atcha boy! Gone.

Benji

Chapter 36

The sound of the early bird chirps, breaking the dead silence of the early morning dawn. Benji opens his eyes and looks at the white ceiling above his mountainous bed. A cringing sensation grips his heart and then travels through his stomach down to his anus. He feels as though he's lost his appetite, but he wasn't hungry in the first place, so the feeling is nothing more than a warning from his body that he shouldn't even consider eating anything right now.

Jessie is already up reading her Bible. She hasn't noticed that her husband has opened his eyes, and he doesn't say anything to inform her that he's up. He just lies still thinking about his dreadfully daunting situation.

I'ma have to carry my hammer everywhere I go now. Damn. I hate carrying that joint everywhere. Police be pressed, he thinks. *But what choice do I have? Can't let 'em catch me slippin'. I need to put a price on them niggas. I can't live like this.*

Benji blinks and shakes his head.

"Good morning," Jessie sings to him with a kiss on his forehead. "Did my baby sleep tight after all that dreaming woke you up?"

Benji doesn't respond, but he acknowledges her kindness by squeezing her on the calf. She sees his thoughts are elsewhere and doesn't interrupt his process. She goes back to reading her Bible after cross-checking on Asa, who is sound asleep in his crib. He has a much larger crib in his own room, but he's been kept close to Jessie since coming home from the hospital.

Benji lies in silence for at least another hour before he gets up, goes to the bathroom and sits on this throne until his legs fall asleep. Every morning, it's the same routine except for mornings when he wakes up in a hurry to be somewhere.

He comes out of the bathroom after taking a shower, and he's still dripping wet. Jessie hates it when he does that because he always leaves a trail of cold, wet carpet, and Jessie can't stand it when she steps her foot in it. She complains, but he always gives her the same lame excuse.

It's hot in there, he always says.

I guess it is if you set the water on hell, Jessie says sometimes.

Benji dries himself off and still appears to be in deep thought. He's thinking of his need to call on Allah for protection. He's ashamed to approach him in prayer since he hasn't prayed since he left jail. He feels he'll be acting as a hypocrite, and his prayer might be in vain. But he remembers reading in the Quran that Allah is merciful and forgiving, so he lays his towel on the floor, clothes himself, and gets down on his knees and puts his face to the floor.

Jessie gets up to go to the bathroom, and when she comes around the bed and sees Benji down in this strange position she pauses.

"What the . . ," she whispers under her breath.

Benji is murmuring in a foreign language that Jessie had no idea that he could even speak. The sight is startling to her. She is highly convinced that something is wrong. Something has him acting far from the norm, and she is going to stand and wait for him to finish whatever it is that he's doing so she can ask him what his problem is. She's not going to take "nothing" for an answer.

Benji finishes his never-before-seen prayer ritual and rises to his feet. He knows that Jessie is looking at him, and he's not at all in the mood to be doing any explaining, so he carries on as if nothing is to be explained.

"Don't think that I'm just gonna let you go without asking you what on God's green earth that was all about," Jessie demands with her hand on her hip still posted at the foot of the bed.

She's in her white and lavender nightgown and her stomach is still poking out from her pregnancy. Benji puts his socks on, irritated by Jessie's persistence, he turns and snaps, "Mind your business." Jessie knows that Benji had become a Muslim while he was in prison his last visit, but she has no idea what goes into being a Muslim, and Benji realizes that, but he's more than offended by her staring and prying.

Jessie didn't expect a sharp response like that and didn't ever think that he'd tell her to do such a thing as to mind her business. She usually doesn't have a defiant bone in her body where it involves Benji, but he *is* her business. Something has him disturbed to the point he is subjecting her to abnormal behavior, and in the middle of the night, he is having nightmares. She knows something is wrong, and she wants to know about it. It takes everything in her strength to hold back her own version of blowing a fuse. Calmly, she endeavors to compile a string of words that won't ignite a bomb between them, blowing their usually respectful communication exchanges into a shouting match which they've never experienced before.

"Benji . . . I'm not trying to get into your business," she pauses to make certain that he absorbs that fact. "I love you . . . and I see . . . something . . . I see something is wrong. Me and the baby live here too . . . so if something is wrong . . . don't you think you should tell me?" Her eyes are glassy, but there are no tears welling up, yet. Her feelings were hurt by his outburst, and she isn't enthused about being in a confrontation with him.

Benji looks at the seriousness on Jessie's face, and it breaks down his unwillingness to share with her that something is *very* wrong, but what should he tell her? That the most ruthless and relentless gangster in DC are out to get him, and he has to revolve his life around getting to them and murdering them before he himself is claimed a victim of the streets. No. He certainly can't tell her that.

"Naw, bae, it ain't like that. I just got some haters, that's all. Niggas just be puttin' your business in the street, and bammas get to talkin'. That's all. I hate that kind of stuff. I'm just trying to figure out who told somebody where my stash house is."

Jessie isn't satisfied that he's being perfectly honest because if it was that simple, he wouldn't be down on all fours praying like he never has before. At least, not as far as she's ever known him to do.

"Well, I'ma say a prayer for you. The Lord'll be with you." Benji doesn't find any comfort in her telling him the Lord will be with him since he knows her version of the Lord isn't the same as his.

"The Lord?" he asks resentfully. "Who is the Lord?"

"Oh, you know what I mean, Benji. Stop being so difficult."

"No, I'm not trying to be difficult. I'm just asking who you mean when you say Lord."

He knows exactly what she means when she says that, but now is his chance to talk to her about that.

"God. The Lord Jesus."

"Jesus ain't God. See. That's what you have to learn."

"OK, Benji. Let's not get into that right now. You have your beliefs, and I have mine. I didn't mean to upset you."

"Upset me? The only thing that upsets me is that you won't make it into paradise with me if you believe in a falsehood."

Now she's mad. "Wait, just a cotton pickin' minute. You taking things a little bit . . ."

"I ain't takin' nothin' too far," he interrupts.

"Well, tell me who said that Allah is God, and that you and the Muslims are the only ones going to paradise. I don't remember the Bible ever saying that Allah was God's name."

"Well, for one thing, you need to get it straight. Allah is not his name. That's what we refer to the Most High as instead of God."

"OK. Then what's his name?"

"Nobody knows his name for sure as he has many names, but it sure ain't Jesus."

"Look, Benji. I don't want to argue with you about this. Just, I'd appreciate if you don't offend my beliefs; I won't offend yours. I wouldn't ever tell you that Allah wasn't God."

Benji smirks and arrogantly looks toward the ceiling then back at Jessie. "That's because you can't. Allah is the God of Abraham, the God of Isaac, and Jacob. Allah is the God who led Moses and the Israelites out of Egypt. You can't say he ain't God . . . I'm just trying to save my wife. That's why I say to you what I do. I'm not trying to offend you."

"Well, you need to save yourself and find out who Jesus *really* is."

Jessie speaks boldly, then walks away from Benji, and gets back in the bed covering her legs with the blanket. They go on and on that way until Benji has his work clothes on and is standing at the bedroom door. Jessie isn't as knowledgeable about Islam as Benji is of Christianity, so she's no match for his overwhelmingly convincing statements that argue his points and make her nearly question her own faith. But she stands strong and dismisses her husband's words as the work of the devil.

"Benji," she interjects, trying to shut him up, "the electric bill is on the table. I ran out of checks last week. Could you take the bill to your office and write a business check and send it in before they cut the electricity off?"

Benji knows that they're not going to cut the electricity off. She's just trying to run away from his bombardment of religious facts. The fact is that he knows three times more about what she believes in than she does.

"All right. I'll send it . . . But I'ma say this, then I'm gone. I was born a Christian. My parents are Christians. I'm not totally against it, but I know that there are too many conflicting things going on in it. I want you to answer this one thing for me. Is the Son a subject of the Father now that he's back in heaven?"

"See, that's the part you won't accept. The Son is God in heaven," Jessie snaps.

"OK, so you're saying the Son doesn't have to answer to God?"

"How could he if he's God. When he was in the flesh, yes, but in the spirit, no."

"Well, read 1 Corinthians chapter 15, and after you read it, if you can explain to me how on earth Jesus is God, then I'll become a Christian myself. No bull."

After saying that, he walks out the door and down the steps without saying good-bye or anything. He's just gone. Jessie ponders over what the scriptures might reveal to her and is almost afraid to read them for fear that it might tell her something that she didn't want to know. She repeats the scripture in her head and to make certain that she doesn't forget it, she decides that she should read it right away. She grabs her Bible and opens it up to 1 Corinthians chapter 15 and reads what the Apostle Paul has to say to the congregation in Corinth.

She slowly reads verses 1 through 19, but when she gets to verse 20 she slows her reading to a crawl and backtracks several times before getting to verse 29. The wording is confusing, but the meaning is very clear once understood. The scripture clearly puts the Son as a subject of God, and what is even more outstanding about the scripture is that the Son and God are two distinctly different individuals. This reminds her of what the Jehovah's witness lady had said to her when she gave her two magazines that they used in their field ministry. She reads the verses again to make certain that she has read it properly and begins to wish she had never read it because now she feels as if she has been misled all her life to believe that Jesus and God are actually the same person.

Now, I'm really confused.

Her faith in Christ hasn't changed, but her understanding of his part in the overall theme of things has her asking herself questions with no one to answer them. She forgets all about finishing the chapter. She doesn't read any further, instead, she goes downstairs to the office they have set up in the back of the family room and picks up their blue *Oxford Dictionary and Thesaurus* and looks up God. What she reads in the thesaurus part collaborates with what Benji has said but gives some support to what she has been taught all her life. According to this book, the alternatives to God are the Almighty, Jehovah, Yahweh, Allah, the Creator, Supreme One, Lord, and Most High. Likewise, she looks up Christ and finds Jesus, Messiah, Lord, the Son, Son of Man, Chosen One, Michael, Redeemer, Archangel, and Savior as alternate words.

After returning to her room, she doesn't want to read anymore, she just wants to sleep. She just wants to forget all about the things on her mind that are trying to destroy her faith and confuse her, but she can't fall asleep. Thoughts of Bible scriptures swirl around in her head. She prays to God using no name at all and no other titles. Just God. She prays until she fades into a settling blackness. She never had a chance to say amen.

Chapter 37

The nine-foot gate at Scoop Trucking is secured with a chain and Masterlock. There is only one of its two dump trucks parked in the yard with a small trailer that Benji uses as a corporate office. He thinks big, so he's structured his company as a limited liability company complete with bylaws and a corporate structure with him sitting high and mighty as the chairman of the board. His other truck is already on the road. Fernando, his reliable driver, had left the yard over an hour ago. Benji never sees him in the morning at the yard, but during the course of the day they honk horns at each other along the route between the work site and the quarry, or sometimes they catch each other at one place or the other.

Benji pulls up to the gate and gets out of his truck with the music blasting his favorite CD. It's the Scarface release. The "Diary and the Mary Jane" song vibrates the inside panel of the open door. Benji uses his extra lock key to unlock the gate and swings the gate out, then gets back into his SUV, and pulls into the yard. He backs into his regular spot, gets out, and walks across the yard toward his dump truck parked right by the entrance.

Swerve! Scurrd!

A white van swings into the open gate stopping just short of knocking Benji off his feet. The doors open before the van driver can put the vehicle in park. Three passengers emerge from the vehicle. They emerge from the van like a young swat team pointing two assault rifles and a very big handgun at Benji before he could recuperate from the shock of nearly being hit by the front grill of the GMC utility van.

"Get down! Get your ass *down!*" hollers one of the gunmen. They're all covered from head to toe in identical swat-team apparel. Their faces are covered with masks that don't reveal any part of their skin. The masks have mesh veils in the front, and cotton hoods that fits loosely over their heads. The veils are black and appear opaque from the outside looking in, but is virtually transparent to the person who is wearing it.

Benji can't make out whether the men are white or black, but from the sound of the one man who is doing the talking, they're black. The other masked men don't say a word; they just point their guns and kick him as he drops down to the ground holding his hands in the air.

Damn, joe, I let these sucka ass niggas catch me slippin! Benji is more disgusted with himself than he is scared for his life. He brought his gun, but didn't feel the need to carry it around in the dump truck. It's sitting in the console compartment of his Yukon. *Damnit!*

After being frisked carefully for a weapon, one of the men yanks him by the collar of his sleeveless *HOBO* T-shirt.

"Get up, nig! . . ."

Benji remains calm. He's never been in a situation this helpless, but he has already prepared his thought process to cope with it if it ever happened, but he *never* thought it would happen so soon. All he can do is shake his head in disbelief and do whatever these guys tell him to do. All he wants to do is kill every single one of them, and he's looking for a window of opportunity. That's until they pack him into the van and shut the door and one of them pulls out a pair of handcuffs.

Clank. Clank.

Now, Benji has a hair-raising paranoid feeling bouncing down his spine. The blindfold magnifies his trauma and reduces his lion's heart to a whimpering mouse's organ. He has no idea what these silent men are planning.

Allah, please . . . I'm sorry for all the wrong I've done. I've tried to be a good person. Please don't punish me like this. Don't let these men leave me somewhere dead. My children need me. My wife . . . Please. Why won't they tell me what they want? Maybe they're corrupt cops and not Luther and 'em at all. Well, that'll be good. At least, I'll live. But what if . . . Naw, it's Luther. I'll tell Richter to get together a hundred and fifty. Naw . . . I gotta let them tell me how much they want. Whatever you do, don't take 'em to the house. I ain't takin' these bammas to my house. They'll just have to kill me.

Benji can feel somebody's hands digging into his pocket for his wallet. The person pulls his wallet out.

Oh my god! The bill. Where's the bill?

Another hand digs into his other pockets and pulls something out of his back pocket. Benji can hear a whisper and then the sound of paper being passed from one person to the next. A pat on his back assures him that the paper being celebrated by the silent kidnappers is the bill that he was hoping that he left in his truck. Tears began to soak the blindfold and Benji knows that he must give them whatever they ask for. He wants them out of the house as quickly as possible.

The van drives for a while before coming to a stop. One of the men gets out and goes into the 7-11 convenience store and returns to the van with an ADC map, and they examine the map to find the street that Benji lives on, assuming that he is carrying a utility bill that belongs to his current residence. Seems like a perfect place to start.

After scanning the pages of the map, they finally find the street. "Boom. I found it. We . . . out. Hit 50."

That's Route 50, the main highway that leads to Annapolis. The only person Benji hears talking has a voice that Benji has never heard before. He only hears whisper from the other three men, and it's aggravating him to death.

The van backs out of its parking space and drives off. Benji remains as silent as these men have been during this whole ordeal. The silence is driving Benji crazy, but what is he to say? Talking might incite them to violence, so Benji opts to keep his mouth shut to avoid any brutality. If they're gonna torture him, it won't be from anything he's provoked.

It's not long before they make their way into Annapolis, and Benji can tell that they're close to the house because of the turns the van is making after taking the exit off Route 50.

We're here already? I don't ever get home this fast. Damn.

"We're almost there," says one of the men. "Take the right at the stop sign."

✧　✧　✧

Jessie's car pulls into the yard after driving past the white van sitting at the curb in front of the house between their house and the next-door neighbor's house. She doesn't see that a man is sitting in the driver's seat of the van, nor has she so much as taken a second look at it. As far as she's concerned it's a contractor doing work at one of her neighbors' houses. She could care less what type of business they're into, or who would be sitting in the van. Jessie's just upset about not being able to reach Benji since he left for work earlier. She has called him several times, but Benji's phone just keeps on ringing until the answering service picks up. She wanted to remind him to take the bill to the power company.

She had left out shortly after Benji left, because Asa woke her with his relentless crying. She didn't hear him at first, but when she did, she jumped up to see what was bothering the child. His problem was that his diaper was wet, and when she went downstairs to get his baby bag to get a diapers, she found that there were only three diapers in it. Those were all that were left in the whole house, and she knew that that wouldn't be enough to make it to noon. She dressed the baby after cleaning him up, and then she got dressed. The two of them left out and went to the pharmacy and are now returning to the house about to turn Benji's world upside down, because by now, he has realized that they were not in the house when they arrived there, and that was a relief. Jessie has no idea that the reason that Benji hasn't responded to her call is because he's bound with duct tape to a chair in their house.

Now you know this don't make no sense. I sure hope he's not gonna act like this all day. She thinks he's still trippin' off the conversation they had before he left, and that's the reason why he's not answering her call. *I'd never ignore him like this, regardless of what's happened between us. I could be having a real emergency or something. He doesn't know . . . it must be something for me to keep calling him like that.*

Now, Jessie wishes she had a four-door car. This is the first time she's left the house since she's been home from the hospital. It's been over three weeks, and the last thing she wanted to have to do was to be forced to take the baby out of the house. Benji was supposed to have gotten some pampers a couple of days ago, but as usual, he forgot like he does everything else unless he's reminded. He has so much going on. Now, Jessie has to struggle to reach the backseat to get Asa out. It's not that much of a struggle, but she knows it would be a lot easier with a four-door car.

She carefully scoops Asa out of the child seat, waking him up from a light doze. "Hi, precious," she whispers smiling at how cute he looks in his baby cap and blue outfit. "Look at that, there, boy. Him so adorable . . . yes, he is." His mouth just hangs open and his eyes glow with excitement.

"Uh . . . Un," he utters.

Jessie kisses him, and then rests him on her shoulder; she hangs his sky blue and white baby bag on her opposite shoulder, then closes the door, and walks toward the house.

Asa sees everything to his mother's rear. There's the car, a tree, a mailbox, some shrubbery, a beautiful lawn, and a white van. Asa doesn't know what time of day it is because he has never been outside before, but there is something familiar about what Asa is seeing in the distance as his mother climbs the first step to the front door. The fruit tree. The grass. They both are familiar to him, but he doesn't know why. He realizes it but doesn't have the slightest ability to reason with himself as to get an understanding. He isn't able to understand that the feeling that he's experiencing is déjà vu. He scans the scenery more, and his eyes fall upon the man sitting inside the van.

Their eyes meet and the coldness Asa sees in the distant glare of the man's tiny eyes causes an image to flash into Asa's mind that reminds him of something that had made him feel very unsettled. The vision in his mind has him unsettled now; the vision of the wolf sitting at the door in his dream. The sight of the wolf instantly terrifies Asa, and he starts to cry in such a way that Jessie thinks she has hit the boy with the storm door as she swung it open. She steps back from the door, puts the baby bag on the patio chair, and looks at Asa with motherly concern.

"Aw, baby. Did Mommy hurt you?" She asks in an apologetic tone. "Mommy so sorry. Don't cry."

Asa will hear none of it. He cries just like he cried last night after waking up from that horrible nightmare. Now, Jessie is really concerned and wants only to get him in the house and check his head or arm for a bruise.

"OK, honey . . . Mommy comin'." She bounces him on her forearm and unlocks the door leaving the baby bag outside. Once in the house, she walks straight back to the kitchen and sees a chair missing from the table. She notices it immediately because she knows that it was there before she left.

That chair was there when I . . .

"Hhhuh!" Jessie inhales heavily, nearly having a heart attack.

There's a ninja standing behind her pointing a stainless steel handgun with a pellet-size hole in the barrel at her temple.

"You move, you dead."

Jessie turns and looks down the barrel into the bottomless pit, staring at her, and then she says a silent prayer for her husband, Asa, and herself. Never blinking her eyes, trying not to panic and faint as she did once before, she walks out of the kitchen and into the family room to the right of the entrance of the kitchen. As she leaves it, Jessie holds her whining baby close to her bosom. Asa cannot see the man walking behind his mother, but he knows someone is there, and that someone isn't his father.

Inside the family room, Benji is tied to the kitchen chair that was missing from the table, and his cuffed hands behind the back of the chair tells her that this in not going to end well. She can see that he has a lump on the side of his head, and blood is flowing from it. As she continues past him, she doesn't look at his face because the sight of it will bring her to tears of deep sorrow. Benji is conscious, and his face is brutalized from the beating he's received from the men. No one is saying anything to him or her. They're just pointing their guns in silence and now that Jessie and the baby are present, it will be easier for them to get more than the hundred thousand or so that Benji has already given them. They know that he has a lot more than what he's given them, and he's taken quite a beating trying to hold out on them.

The shorter man of the three snatches the baby from Jessie quicker than she can tighten her grip on Asa's body.

"Not my baby . . . Please," she begs the man. "There is your money. Why don't you just take it and go? Why do you want to hurt us? Benji," she turns to him, "give them what they want! What do you want? Don't hurt my baby."

Jessie pleads with the men, but they say nothing. Then finally, one of them says, "We've tried to be on our way, but we know your man is holding out on us, and we want it all." Then he points his gun at Jessie, who falls to her knees—face filled with tears. Benji speaks.

"In the shed, under the floor—there's an alarm. The code is 1329."

One of the men goes outside while the other two stand guard with Jessie and Benji. They're pointing their guns at Jessie to show Benji that she will be the one who gets it if anything goes wrong.

Ten minutes later, the man walks back into the house, carrying two brief cases the size of a medical doctor's, filled with hundreds and fifties. He gestures that it's time to go, but one of the men has a different idea.

He's been lusting over Jessie the whole time his comrades have been outside and has already made his mind up that he's going to rape her the moment they get what they came for.

He sits his gun down and pimp smacks Jessie with the back of his hand hurling her down to the carpet. He pounces down on her and starts ripping her clothes off in plain sight of Asa, who is leaning in the corner of the armrest. Benji can only look on but would rather not, so he closes his eyes and painfully listens to his wife's hopeless pleas for mercy.

"Shut up," the man says garbling his words so that his voice cannot be recognized. He punches her in her face, making her whimper like an injured puppy. She goes silent and stops resisting.

It doesn't appear that the other men are interested in joining in with what he is doing to Jessie, but the sight of her long thick legs pull them closer to the scene. One of the men, the one who was carrying the moneybags, comes over to take a closer look as Jessie's panties are pulled off her feet. He sets the cases down and drops his pants.

Jessie is then ravaged by all three of the men; none of them uses a condom. She is raped repeatedly in the presence of Asa, who only watched with curious glimpses at his mother and the three rummaging men clamoring over her body like maggots. Jessie's crying and lying limp on the floor taking the punishment from the savages until the last one finishes.

They leave her lain out exhausted and stretched out on the floor as they buckle their pants and prepare themselves to walk out the house.

Benji opens his eyes and sees his naked wife flailing her leg then clutch her stomach as she curls up into a fetal position. His hurt is beyond the pain he felt when his grandmother died when he mourned for over forty-eight hours. Rage would be a useless emotion to conjure at this time seeing as how there's absolutely nothing that he can do about what has just happened to his wife, but he hates the three men walking past him enough to want to see them all dead. He looks the last one in the mask with a vengefully piercing eye nodding his head as if he knows who it is behind the mask. He actually thinks he does. As far as he's concerned, it's Luther and Fatts. How wrong he is!

What the hell you lookin' at? The masked man says in his mind as he walks past Benji. *Man, he might have recognized my voice when I told her to shut up. You gotta kill 'em.*

"Hold up," says the man to the other two men who were leaving out before him. Benji recognizes that voice.

"You little . . ."

POW!

Chapter 38

Special Agent Miles walks into the front door of Benji's house followed by his partner, Faraday, who is exasperated and showing signs of repugnance at what has happened to the primary target of their investigation. Benji is brutally murdered, and Faraday was supposed to have had surveillance on him the first thing this morning. If Faraday had been on his job, none of this would have happened. They were closing in on him and only a reliable informant short of indicting him on federal drug charges. Now he's dead, and they can all but shut the book on this investigation, but they'd like nothing more than to find out who is responsible for this. Who is it that has killed their bread and butter?

Miles walks past the stairs and stops at the opening leading into the family room and sees the back of a man's head blown clean open. The gore and brains splattered all over the floor behind him is flagged with white pieces of paper with writing on them to identify the particles. The putrid stench of copper and warm flesh turns Miles' stomach nearly turning him back toward the doorway that he walked through to get in the midst of this atrocity.

He doesn't enter the room; instead, he continues into the fresher-smelling air of the kitchen, where the anguishing Jessie sits sobbing and prostrating over her son Asa is sitting in his baby chair on the kitchen table. They are surrounded by detectives and police officers in uniforms, holding pads and pens like a group of anxious news reporters waiting for a scoop. No one has had an opportunity to get any line of questioning going with the hysterical woman, hastily turned into a widow, after being demoralized and savaged at the hands of her beloved husband's executioners.

"How dare you fools keep asking me questions after I've had to sit there and get raped and messed over by them dogs while my baby and husband watched!" Jessie was in a demonic state, screaming at the detective at the top of her voice, who had arrived on the scene shortly after the police officers had entered the house and found her naked holding her baby in her arms. "I ain't answering none of your damn questions. They were covered up with ski masks! Just leave me alone!" Jessie doesn't use such foul language, but anything was liable to come out of her mouth at that point in her life. She's nearly out of her mind with sorrow and pain.

The officers asked her no more questions, and she has done nothing but cry and sigh. All the while, they've stood around her, waiting for her to calm down, up until now. Miles and Faraday have walked in the room, and she has calmed her wailing down to an exhausted whimper of sobs and deep breaths. She looks up at the two white men in suits and feels that the authorities have pulled out the big guns to get to the bottom of this insidious plot against her and her husband's life. They look different from the other men. They move more assertively than the other men other men who in suites, and they seem to have more influential power over the men that she perceived to be in charge.

Faraday walks over to the round, fat, white detective standing by the stove. His name is Lieutenant Buchannan, and he's five foot ten about 285 pounds. His mustache is salt and pepper and his crew cut is freshly tapered. The gray suit jacket he is wearing is a bit too small for his wide body and doesn't go well with his light blue slacks. He's the detective in charge of the crime scene, and he's waiting patiently to talk to Jessie about what has happened. Faraday flashes his badge at Buchannan, and they step out of the kitchen to have a word with one another, out of the presence of the mourning woman.

"Ma'am, now is not a good time to talk to you I'm sure, but here's my card," Miles offers her a card, speaking in a tender tone. "Feel free to call me if you find out any information about what has happened to your family. We'll do all that we can to bring those responsible to justice."

Jessie looks at the card and then up to Miles. His face shows that he is genuinely sympathetic to her woes, and she appreciates his courtesy, so she takes the card and nods at Miles as another stream of tears flow freely down her face. She is sadder than she's ever been in her life and wants nothing more than to have these people out of her house, so she can sleep and try to relieve herself of the pains weighing heavy in her heart. She doesn't want to stay in the house at all but has nowhere to go. At least not anywhere she would like to stay.

After lots of examination throughout the house, the police and officials clean up the grotesque murder scene. Jessie tells them, after coming around, what little she remembers. After she answered a few questions, they determined that she wasn't at all familiar with Benji's street life, so they asked her if she would stay at a relative's house for a while, but she insisted that she had nowhere to go and if they were going to do any further investigation, they should stay as long as they wanted to. Most of the police left shortly afterward but forensics stayed, and the ambulance took Jessie and the baby to the hospital to get some DNA from her. If any of the men had been locked up in the past ten years, they'd have a way of matching the semen to a suspect.

After returning to the house from the hospital the following morning, Jessie wants to leave the house right away, but for a reason she cannot explain to herself, she doesn't. She goes upstairs and gets in the shower, while Asa lays sound asleep in his crib. After getting out of the shower, she calls several people to inform them of what has happened to Benji. She doesn't tell them that she was raped but does give the heartbreaking news of Benji's death. One of the last people she decides to call is Benji's best friend, Bink.

"Hello?"

"Hi, Bink . . . puah," Jessie begins to cry as she has done with each person she's called to break the news. "Benji . . . Benji . . . is . . . puah . . ." she *cries* . . . "dead."

"What you say?" Bink didn't hear her correctly and doesn't want to believe what he thought he heard, so he asks her to repeat herself. "I didn't hear you. Say that again."

"Benji is dead."

"Dead!" Bink hollers. "What happened . . . Who . . . All man!"

"Uh hun . . . ," Jessie whimpers, "I can't talk no mo . . . more."

"All man," Bink continues. He doesn't know that Jessie has hung up the phone while he was trying to absorb the blow that the news of his buddy's death has dealt him. "Who did it? Did you see what happened? Were you there? Who told you? . . . Jess? . . . Jessie?"

He hangs up his cell phone and calls the number back that Jessie had called him from. He's never seen the number before because Benji had never called anyone but his mother and sister from the house phone before. The answering service comes right on after just one ring. He tries again but gets the same result, so he comes to the conclusion that Jessie has the phone off the hook and doesn't want to talk to anyone. He dials another number and listens for an answer.

"What's the deal, Bink?" says the person on the other end.

"Richter! Did you hear?"

"Hear what?"

"All man . . . They ain't tell you . . . Benji's dead."

"Dead? Whatchu mean dead?" Richter knows exactly what he means, but takes it as a joke. *Benji can't be dead*, he thinks to himself.

"Whatchu mean—what I mean dead? What part of *dead* don't you understand? . . . Jessie just called me and told me."

On the other end of the phone, Richter is speechless. He can't believe those niggas done got to his man that quick.

Gotdamn! He scorns himself. *I knew I should have been with him everywhere he went until we smoked them bammas.*

"Richter? You there?"

"Yeah," Richter replies with a sullen response. He would like to hang up on Bink as Jessie did, but he is preoccupied with what he must do next. Thoughts of revenge bubble over in Richter's head.

Man, I'ma kill all them niggas. All of 'em. He smacks his lips like a nine-year-old that just dropped his ice-cream cone. *Damn! Benji.*

"Damn," Richter whispers. "Look, joe. I'ma holler. I got some things to do."

"Alright . . . If you need me, hit me . . . You know that was my man," Bink reminds Richter, who knows Bink isn't a punk but also knows he's not a killer either.

"A'ight, I'ma hit you."

Bink can tell the difference between, "I'ma hit you, and I'm definitely gonna hit you." Richter's not gonna call him at all. Not even to tell him that the culprits are dead. All that's on his mind is finding Luther, Fatts, Daryl, Lil Papi, and Blue. Those are the people he knows are responsible for his main man's murder, and those are the ones he and his crew are gonna lay to rest. Whoever is seen first is the first one who's gonna get it. Punished!

Richter calls everybody under the sun and tells them to meet him around the way. He doesn't inform anyone of why he's calling this meeting, but when he calls for a rendezvous, no one ever questions why; they just come immediately, because he never calls them to meet unless it's very important. Of course, Amp, Tony, and Bootemup know exactly why he's calling this meeting, and they've already discussed how they must react to the news.

They're already together when he calls them, and on the way they discuss the situation again.

"Aye y'all. We gotta act like we're shocked about this. I know Richter is on a nut. That dude loved slim," Amp tells them.

"Man, slim sounded like he was trippin. Did he sound like that to y'all?" Bootemup ask.

"Yeah," answers Tony. "He's probably calling everybody in DC, Maryland, and Virginia to find out where Luther and 'em is."

"We might as well get ready for war," Bootemup warns them, "because Richter is gonna wanna put it out there that we gonna kill them dudes, and you know they got a lot of people too."

Amp blankly stares into the distance knowing that Bootemup is so right. War is in the wind. He only hopes that he can survive it so he'll have a chance to enjoy the three quarter million dollars that he got from Benji.

Richter and several other guys are standing in front of Benji's parents' house as Amp and Bootemup pull down the street in Amp's SS Impala. Tony has taken the long way to the spot in his own car to make it seem that they weren't together.

All right, how would you act if somebody told you that Benji was dead and you didn't do it? Amp muses. *First you gottta kirk out. Naw. You wouldn't kirk . . . Damn . . . A'ight. You gotta make a face like you mad as hell. OK . . . Then, you gotta start talkin' 'bout killin' somebody . . . Yeah . . . Then let it flow.*

Meanwhile, Bootemup is preparing himself to receive the news as well, but he's a good actor. He doesn't need much thought on it. He already knows how to react, and what he's gonna say. Amp is parking the car, and they're about to be face-to-face with some of Benji's cousins and older friends, distraught and filled with ghastly inclinations of revenge. Murder is written all over Richter's balled-up face. Richter's bottom lip is poking out like a little boy who's mad at his babysitter, and his eyes are distrusting of all he looks upon. He can't see through the dark tints on Amp's car, but the guilt that Amp and Bootemup hold gives them the feeling that Richter is looking them dead in their eyes. They look at one another as would two cops who know they're about to be reprimanded by their commanding officer, then they reach for the door handle, and try to gain their composure before Richter can see the lost puppy dog expressions on their faces.

Once from behind the veil of the tints, the race for the academy award begins. Bootemup puts on a face of suspense, looking around at all the unusual faces, and Amp puts on a face of anticipation. He walks over to Richter from around the driver's side of his car and asks him immediately, "What's wrong? Where's Benji?"

Richter can no longer hold the mean mug on his face at the mention of Benji's name. He bows his head and closes his eyes. By the time he raises his head and looks back at Amp, water has glazed his eyeballs, and they have turned crimson red. He tries to speak, but the frog in his throat might ribbit, making his words break, proving to the world that the mighty Richter is human.

Amp shifts gears and moves toward an Oscar-level performance when he probes the eyes of the other onlookers searching for someone to give him an answer to the question that Richter has failed to answer.

"They killed Benji at his house yesterday," says a tall brown-skinned guy who can pass for Benji's brother. He's actually Benji's cousin Eric. Eric is a friendly person but would do anything for Benji, and that's just what he's here to do.

Amp drops his jaw and looks at Richter in a state of shock. He looks as though he can't believe what he's just heard, and Richter confirms it with a remorseful series of slow nods as his eyes connect with Amp's. Bootemup does not need to act. He just frowns, turns his back, and leans on the car. Silence is the best performance from his vantage point.

"What?" Amp shouts, "They kilt Benji! . . . Naw, naw, joe. He 'on't mess with nobody. Man, I 'on't know about chall, but I'm gettin' ready to kill me a nigga."

Amp paces back and forth for a few minutes and rants and raves about how he's gonna blow somebody's brain out, while he marvels at how big a weller he is.

A weller is a person who lies about what he's done, what he's going to do, what he has, or what he's going to get. The lies come from so deep down in the well that after a while, the well runs dry and if he's really a good weller, it's not a problem to dig a little deeper to come up with more lies. In Amp's case, however, he's not welling about what he's done, or what he'll do, rather his welling is more indirect about what he hasn't done.

He's the one who initiated the robbery, the rape, and the one who pulled the trigger. His whole performance is a "well," and no one suspects a thing. On the contrary, he's rallied everyone to seek and destroy Fatts, Luther, and the rest of their posse. He's effectively made them a patsy of his whole diabolical scheme.

"Anybody can get it!" exclaims Amp as he walks around his car and gets in. He's about to go find one of Fatts' boys to set off the war. Bootemup gets in the car, and as they pull off, shortly afterward, Tony pulls up and gets the news about Benji. His act is not as convincing as Amp's was, but Amp was so good that he doesn't draw any suspicion from anyone. No one is actually paying Tony any attention anyway because everybody's busy calling people on their cell phones trying to gather as much information as they can about their targets. Tony listens and tries to show some emotion, but he's no actor, and remorse is something he didn't even show at his own brother's funeral, so no one who knows him would suspect a thing.

But now has come the time to show allegiance because the men around him are galvanizing and preparing to commit mass murders. Anyone around their targets will get blasted: men, women, children, and cats. It doesn't matter. Somebody's got to die.

Chapter 39

There is no grass, but the sculpted shrubs and palm trees bring life to the U-shaped driveway in front of Trump's Taj Mahal in Atlantic City. The lights and Alladdin-style decorations that adorn this majestically fabulous recreational retreat flash in a sequential array of red, yellow, white, and purple. The busy terminal of taxis, cars, trucks, and limos is alive with people moving to and fro, calling for bell caps and taxicabs alike. There's no need to call for valet attendants because they are like Johnny on the spot. The moment a player steps out of the driver seat of his car, they're already standing at the rear bumper awaiting instructions. Service at the Taj is impeccable, second to none on the whole strip, and the tables are gambler friendly as well, if you know how to bet.

Fatts and Luther know this all too well. It's a bright sunny day, but the sun can't see them from where they're standing with big smiles on their face after coming out on top during one of their many overnight excursions to the City. They visit Atlantic City like women visit the local mall. Twice, sometimes three times a week they make the trip bolting to exit 3 off the New Jersey Turnpike to Atlantic City. Their game is Baccarat, and the pit masters lose their swagger when they see these two sharks coming. Seldom do they get up losers. And today is no different from others; they've come out on top and now wait for valet to bring Fatts' pearl white 600 Coupe Benz so they can leave and head back home.

Between the two of them, they're carrying over two hundred and thirty thousand dollars in crispy one-hundred-dollar bills. They came with fifteen thousand a piece as they always do and are two happy campers unaware of the blame they've received back home for the death of Benjamin

Powell who was killed yesterday morning while they were preparing to leave town to gamble.

"We hit their ass good this time," says Fatts with a full belly glow on his face. "I know they can't *stand* to see us niggas walk down into that pit."

"Humph. I know that's right," Luther agrees.

Ring. Ring.

Luther snatches his phone off his hip and flips it open, "Yo." Fatts can hear the voice on the line but can't quite make out what's being said or who the person is, but the tone of the man isn't pleasant.

"Man, what the hell are you talkin' 'bout?" Luther returns to the man on the phone. His face is puzzled, and he looks over at Fatts who has already raised his eyes to Luther's.

"Joe . . . first of all, you gonna calm down," Luther replies calmly snarling his upper lip. "Second of all, nigga, I don't know nuffin' about no Benji getting his wig split. If I'da did it, you'd known about it, 'cause I'da got chor bitch ass too! So don't *call* my phone no more talkin' that *nonsense*, slim." He pauses and listens for a moment. "Yeah? . . . A'ight, moe. Have it chor way. Get chor wig pushed back too. Gone."

Luther hangs his phone up with nothing else said.

"Who was that?" For the first time, Fatts can see a hint of fear or stress on Luther's face. Luther doesn't say anything to Fatts, rather, he muses over the ramifications of being responsible for the death of a well-known big timer, but not actually being guilty of anything.

Damn! I just asked a couple of questions about the dude and just like that, I got the beef. A murder beef at that. Luther smacks his lips. *I done robbed I don't know how many niggas and ain't heard nothin' of 'em since. Now, out the clear blue sky, a nigga gets his boots smoked and they wanna blame us . . .*

"Who was that Lu?" Fatts reiterates.

Luther snaps out of it with a blink and a slight shake of his head. "Kan Quick . . . He lunchin'."

"Somebody killed that dude Benji?"

Luther is startled by Fatts' knowledge of the matter. "How'd you know?" He's wondering did he have anything to do with it, but that's impossible.

"I heard him say his name."

Oh. Luther thinks then says, "Yeah, I guess."

"So what's he tryin' to say?"

"It ain't what he's tryin' to say. It's what he's sayin' that everybody else is sayin' . . . We did it."

Fatts looks into Luther's eyes hoping that he's not taking it seriously. He figures if Luther doesn't seem too alarmed, then it's not that big of an issue. Luther returns a depressed look that a neighbor gives a man when they have to be the one to break the news that his dog just got hit by a car. Now, Fatts is starting to realize that it's about to be a very long ride home, and all the money in the world couldn't make them feel any better. They're sure that other men are preparing for war, and that means money is about to get low because during a street beef, nobody can make much money due to the fact that the mere task of leaving home and making it back becomes a death-defying endeavor. Luther has never really had a stable, but he's recently gotten his mother to purchase a condo for him in her name. It's the first time he's called a place other than his grandmother's house home.

The valet pulls their car up behind a platinum-colored Lotus, but they don't see it. They're not at all paying much attention to their surroundings. Both Fatts and Luther are stagnantly lost in their thoughts or worse yet, fears. A young white man with dark brown hair, cut neatly, wearing a purple vest trimmed with gold around the collar and sleeves walks up to them. His nameplate reads Tess.

"Sir, your car is ready," Tess says, pointing over to their left, holding the car key in front of Fatts with his other hand.

Fatts peels a bill off the first bankroll his hand touches in his pocket and hands it to the valet attendant. He and Luther step off toward the car, leaving the bottom of Tess' chin lying on the ground.

"Abda . . . Abda," Tess stutters, unable to say anything coherent before Fatts waves his hand gesturing for him to keep the change.

The big face Benjamin Franklin in Tess' hand comes as a nice surprise to him, especially coming from a black man. Regardless to how nice a car is that a black person is driving, they're seldom good for anything over twenty dollars. A hundred dollars is unheard of even for white folks. Tess has suddenly come down with a bad case of the flu bug and asks to have the rest of the day off.

Meanwhile, Fatts and Luther whiz past Trump Plaza toward the Atlantic City Convention Center. "Aye, stop at McDonalds." Luther is craving an egg McMuffin, but Fatts drives right past the McDonalds as if he didn't hear Luther, and over the bridge they go on their way home.

Phroom. Like a torpedo shot out of a cannon, the white Benz blast past cars as though they're standing still, and all Fatts is concerned with is getting back to DC with hopes of clearing his name of this dreadful and dangerous farce.

Chapter 40

The small J. B. Jenkins Funeral Home is filled to capacity with black folks paying their respects to the mourning family of Benjamin Powell. The weather outside of the building reflects the mood of the people who sit and stand in sorrow over the unexpected death of such a vibrant young member of their generation. No one is smiling, most women are crying. Most of those who aren't shedding any tears have already done so at one time or another since hearing the news of Benji's death. Men and children alike have cried, but women close to him have barely stopped.

Jessie is sitting in the middle of the front row, holding her baby Asa. She has on a black dress and a pair of dark sunglasses to hide her running eyeliner and bloodshot red eyes. The agony her heart has experienced has made her wish that she would die in her sleep. She hasn't contemplated suicide or anything of that nature, but relief from her pain and endless crying via eternal sleep would suit her fine.

Oh god, please give me peace. Dear Lord, I can't take it no more. I know my child needs me, but I feel that I may go insane if I continue to live in this evil, wicked world. Those disgusting heathens destroyed me. Why? Why Lord, have you let this happen to me? I'm a good person. I know I'm not perfect but why? Why? Why?

Jessie has put the house up for sale and has slept there only twice. She's been staying with Niecey, but there's been too much activity in her house for Jessie to get any peace of mind. Between the music videos that blast from the surround sound of the television set and all of Niecey's pretty lesbian girlfriends hitting on her, Jessie doesn't know which has her wanting to be alone at home, but yesterday, she stopped trying to figure it out when she moved all of her belongings back to her house in Annapolis and savored the quietness of being in seclusion. The only problem with that is her thoughts became louder and her sanity began to unravel faster. All she did last night was pray, talk to Asa, and sleep. She woke up several times and went through the same changes all night long until she noticed that the sun had come up.

Most of the people in the funeral home have no idea who she is because she's been only a name to them. They've never been privileged with her acquaintance. Not even Benji's closest cousins have ever met the famous Jessie. They've heard that she's existed over the years, but seeing her face-to-face was thought to be impossible. Her beauty has been thought to be exaggerated. *The woman sitting in the front row, holding the baby must be Jessie,* many of the passersby think as they scan the faces of the front row. She's the most outstanding person in the whole place with her long black hair adorning her head and shoulders.

Next to her sits, Poah, Benji's younger sister. She's a dark brown-skinned young lady with a smooth tone on her face. She has a gorgeous set of pearly white teeth that can be seen each time a friend of the family greets her. She'll return a friendly gesture and slightly smile to show her appreciation to those who extend their condolences. She's the only member of Benji's immediate family that all of Benji's friends know on sight because they've been tight all their lives, and she looks a lot like him, so people know right off the top that they're closely related.

The room is already overflowing; still, curious people stand shoulder to shoulder against the walls trying to see which of the who's who of Washington and Maryland will come through the door to pay their last respects to Benji. The females are all dressed in their best outfits showing off their figures but not revealing too much. After all, it is a funeral, so they try to show a little dignity by not coming down the aisle, wearing a little more than a thong and a bra. They all actually have on clothes that show a touch of class. Well, a majority of them do, but there's a hoochie mama here and there bursting at the seams.

None of the young men have on suits with a tie; rather all are wearing some sort of linen suit or black T-shirt with a pair of jeans. Some are wearing sport coats and dress shoes, but most are not distinguished at all. They're in the same type of clothes that they'll have on when they hit the block for the rest of the day. Gangsters and thugs are side by side with the well-to-do family of the deceased Benji, and they all share the same common ground today. Sorrow.

The roving eyes of three federal agents are also amongst the people in this crowded room. They are black men, two wearing suites and one of them blending right in with the hoodlums, watching intently for people in conversation so that they can slide into position close enough to hear gossip of who may be responsible and whether or not there is any plan of retaliation. No one suspects that the men are police. There are so many people in the room that don't know each other, and everyone is accepted as one of the countless people that Benji showed love to and never asked for anything in return. Benji was well loved and respected, so his untimely death came as a shock to even his jealous haters. They are here just to show off their outfits and cars or to let people think they were friends of Benji even though people know they're full of cow manure. Of course, the guys knew that Benji was a lady's man, so the women would be wall to wall, and they are.

It's difficult to make out what anyone is saying because everyone who has enough composure to speak is whispering in the ear of the ones who are listening. Occasionally, someone will call another person's name out to notify them that they are in the building, but besides that, the room is fairly quiet. There are still people making their way toward the coffin in a line that is snaking out the door. The coffin was supposed to be closed up ten minutes ago, but the line was still out the door, so there was no way they could close the coffin with all those mourners trying to get a final look at Benji.

Big Country is in line grieving like he's one of Benji's brothers. Country is a fly guy with a grain of hair that'll make you seasick if you look at it long enough. He's much darker than Benji's complexion and the rolls of fat around his torso is a dead giveaway that they don't share the same genetic structure, so he's either a secret lover or the biggest phony in the whole joint. Rest assured, it is the latter, and everybody knows it.

Look at this fake ass nigga, thinks Richter. *He needs to cut that bullshit out.*

Poah sees him and has some thoughts of her own. *Oh, I can't stand his fat ass. He's the same one who tried to do it to me and then tried to do it to Salina while Benji was locked up. He needs to stop. He better be lucky I don't have my knife with me, 'cause I'd stab his ass in front of all these people. Fakin' like he loved my brother.*

Poah's anger flares up inside as she pierces her eyes toward Country. Country and Poah's eyes connect, and instantly he knows that he's been made.

Damn! Poah is lookin' at me like she wants to kill me. I ain't trippin'. He looks away from her and commences to put on his spectacle of teary-eyed condolences for the sad audience only now in a more subdued performance. He doesn't want to make Poah jump out of her seat and pull his card in front of everybody for making a mockery of their family.

The line is down to the last few stragglers and the funeral home ushers are at the end of the line waiting for the people to get a look at Benji for the last time so they can shut the coffin and begin the homegoing ceremony. Benji's mother, Mrs. Powell, looks around as she's been doing the entire time. She's sitting in the front row, two seats from Jessie. She's been looking for Salina and Benji's other two children, Benji Jr. and Nakeisha. They haven't come through the line to view the body yet, and the casket is about to be closed forever giving them no chance to ever see their father again. Other members of the family start to look around in the same way, but there is no sign of Benji's babies. How saddened they've become at the thought of Salina being so cold to her children to deprive them of having one last glimpse of their father. It's painfully obvious that they're not going to walk through the door before the coffin is shut, and as the woman wearing the white gloves reaches for the coffin door to close it, howls of heartbreaking crying commences and even the roughest of characters can't hold back the welling tears in their eyes. The much-loved Benji is about to be no more, and the reality of that is kicking in as the lid to his eternal bed is about to be shut.

"No!" screams out the voice of a young girl crying, "Wait! . . . Daddy!" It's Nakeisha crying out as she stumbles past the people sitting in the front row.

Little Benji follows her closely. The sight of the children pushing the lady, who was about to close the coffin, to the side and climbing all over Benji's dead body sends the entire family into a crying frenzy.

"My daddy . . . my daddy . . . they . . . killed . . . my daddy." Nakeisha is agonizing and can hardly get her words out of her mouth.

They lay over the coffin like two resting heaps of leaves, and then they are flocked by Benji's mother, sister, and cousins. They all cry together on their knees hugging the children. There isn't a soul in the room who doesn't shed a tear. Even the undercover detective can't hold back their emotions and empathy for the hurt children. They've never seen anything so sad in all their lives. No one has.

Then, a rolling rumble of mumbling voices sweep through the funeral home as someone, accompanied by an entourage of well-dressed women and children, comes down the aisle of the parlor. Salina and all her female relatives have come not only to pay their respect to the once loved Benji, but also to make the widow feel very uncomfortable and threatened. Jessie doesn't see what is stirring up all the commotion, but she has a good idea that it's Salina and no telling who else. She doesn't have much of her own family there because they weren't close to Benji, though they knew about him.

Salina enters the viewing area and then stops front and center, staring at Jessie daring her to muster up enough gall to return the same venom that Salina is displaying. Jessie's face starts to tingle from the hole Salina's eyes are trying to burn through it, and she can see other people in her peripheral vision stopping behind the indignant woman.

"Look Salina," starts Poah, "I love you, but if you come in here with that mess at my brother's funeral, I'ma whoop your ass myself. Trust me."

Salina knows that Poah means it too. Her brother meant the world to her, and she's been known to put the crucial beat down on quite a few broads before, so Salina whispers to Jessie, who looks up at her and her troublemaking posse, "Watch your back."

Jessie reads her lips loud and clear, and the hairs on the back of her neck stand up. Jessie says another prayer that she might get home safely. Nothing will keep her from going to the cemetery, so if Salina plans on hanging around until Benji is placed in his grave site, there's no telling what might happen in between now and then. Jessie just hopes that the people accompanying her and Asa won't let this woman pull any drastic stunts. At least, she's sure of two people, and that's Poah, who has already spoken her mind, and Denise. They all watch Salina and her mob of young heifers that she's brought along just for the purpose of kicking off some drama. Even Salina's fifty-three-year-old mother looks like she's game for some drama to kick off.

Little does Jessie know that she has the entire room on her side because everyone knows how much Benji loved the woman that they only knew as Jessie; so Salina and her hood-rat posse would do best just to leave well enough alone, pay their respects, and get the hell up out of there. Salina has no intentions on staying around to hear the eulogy or joining in on the long procession of hymns and funeral line to Harmony Cemetery located right here in Benji's hometown of Landover. She does, however, intend on sending one of her relatives on a spy mission to find out the whereabouts of Jessie's home. Before she grabs her children to take them away from their father, she takes a final look at the man she loved as long as she's known how to love.

Her knowledge of him being shot in the face made her wonder why there wasn't a closed coffin ceremony for Benji. Once she was able to approach him, she was able to see why the coffin was still open. Benji had been shot only once in his face, and the bullet entered his head through his eyes socket and his brains exploded out of the back of his head through a gaping hole produced by the large bullet shot out of the .45 caliber gun used by the murderer. His left eye is covered by a pirate's patch, and his face was not marred in the least bit from the ordeal. Benji looks like Benji, only lifeless.

Mrs. Powell stands up from where she was on her knees consoling her two grandchildren, and Salina turns to her. Salina has no gripe with Benji's mother for what her son did. Mrs. Powell has always taken Salina's side when it came to her and Benji's quarrel, and she had even reprimanded him for leaving the house and kids for Salina to fend for on her own. Benji didn't listen to his mother or anyone else for that matter. His mind was made up. Jessie was going to be his wife and no one on earth could have changed that. Not even his kids!

Salina looks into Mrs. Powell's swollen eyes and feels her pain. Her hate for Jessie and Benji's abandonment hasn't allowed her stone heart to feel any remorse over his death; she figures he's gotten what he deserved, but seeing the look on his mother's face reminds her of how much she used to love him too, and she slowly breaks down. A single tear spills from her eye, races down to her chin, and drips off, falling to the cleavage of her breast. Mrs. Powell steps toward her, and they hug each other and cry together.

Richter is standing near the entrance into the room and steps out of the doorway. He feels himself getting teary eyed again, and he'd rather not show his soft side twice in one day, so he joins Amp, Tony, Bootemup, and Quick out in the parking lot where they've been since they came out of the building from viewing the body.

At the far end of the parking lot there is a green and tan conversion van with tinted window. Inside are Lindsey Miles, Jeffery Faraday, and Lieutenant Buchannan of the Annapolis Police department. There's another detective with them, and he's taking pictures of everybody who comes out of the funeral home. These men don't resemble any of the three young black undercover agents inside of the building. They all look like cops, so they'd never be able to intermingle with black folks to get any real undercover detective work done; therefore they hide behind a shield of black glass and photograph all possible suspects and potential retaliators in this case.

As Richter approaches his younger buddies, he looks at the van but doesn't suspect anything out of the ordinary. He's always wanted a conversion van, and this one looks just like something he'd love to have himself.

"What's the word, moe?" Richter asks Kan Quick. Quick is supposed to be helping them place Luther, but after doing his own investigation, he's skeptical about them having anything to do with any of this.

"Man, I was just tellin' them that I think somebody else might have done this."

"Nigga, that's some bull, and you know it! You tryin' to cover up for them bammas," blasts Amp in an angry tone with an equally angry expression on his face.

Kan Quick smirks his lips to the side because he can't believe this dude has just made such a ridiculous accusation about him after all he's done to put himself in harm's way by the way he's threatened Luther with paying the price for Benji's demise.

"I can't believe this! Them niggas tryin' to hit my head 'cause I called Luther and told him that they did it, and they'd better watch out, so you need to check yourself. I'm witchu, not against you" Quick assumes that Luther and his crew will be looking to get at him for his accusations, so he's prepared himself mentally for their fiery rebuttal.

Amp knows better than to jump out there too far with Quick because he's already in fear for his life, so he's prone to kill the first person who shows the slightest inch of animosity toward him. He wishes he hadn't made the remark, but he had to try to throw Richter off from believing that anybody besides Fatts and his men are responsible. If they aren't, then the next question is who is?

Richter doesn't feed into what Amp has said about Quick covering up for Luther and Fatts, but also isn't interested in hearing that they aren't responsible for what has happened to Benji. They're the scapegoats, and as far as Richter is concerned, they're the ones who are going to pay for his friend's death.

"Why do you say that, Quick? Why the sudden change?" Richter is wondering if, maybe, Quick has heard something on the streets.

"Because Luther and Fatts were in Atlantic City on the day that Benji got hit. My lil' man told me. And he wouldn't lie to me because he don't even know that I deal with y'all like that."

"Humph." Amp doesn't say anything, but he's still trying to imply that Quick is trying to cover up for them.

Quick doesn't like that this dude is putting him on the spot like that and becomes irritated. "You keep poppin' slick . . . What you tryin' to say, slim?"

Richter cuts him off. "Look. I ain't trying to hear all that. Bottomline—them niggas was askin' questions. My man got hit. They tryin' to hit you now, probably all of us, now that you put them on point. So we gotta hit them first. Ain't no other way around it. Find out where them niggas are, and let's do the damn thang."

After the funeral, people go their separate ways, but Richter and the rest of the crew stick together. Everyday they are on the job of tracking down Fatts, Luther, Daryl, Papi, and Blue. They chase every lead known to man, but these guys are like phantoms. Nowhere to be found. But finally, a word on Daryl leaks through the grapevine, and they've finally found something to go on.

Chapter 41

It's been a week since Benji's funeral, and many still are trying to recuperate from the sting of watching his coffin sitting under the canopy as they drove away in their cars. The sight of it all has his friend Bink fighting with himself for being untrue to Benji by screwing around with his children's mother. Now that he sees a chance to make his dream come true about getting close to Jessie, consoling her and keeping her company in her misery, he's generated mixed emotions and wishes to make amends with his friend by being loyal to him in his death, so instead of plotting to move in on Benji's wife, he opens a college fund for Benji's two older children and leaves Jessie alone altogether because he knows there is no way he can be around Jessie without falling in love with her and trying to make her his wife.

Bink is in his truck, and he's just got off work and is on his way home listening to the radio on full blast when he sees the screen on his cellular phone light up indicating an incoming call.

He turns the music down. "Hello! . . . Huh! . . . Hold on." He mutes the radio because it's still too loud. "Hello?"

"What's up, slim?" It's Richter, and he sounds tired. Either that or very sad. Bink is surprised to hear from him because he knows that Richter doesn't think that he would be useful in retaliating.

"I'm straight. Everything all right?" Bink inquires.

"Naw, not really. We need you."

Bink's anal sphincter tightens and he starts to sweat in the crack of his butt. His thoughts are doing cartwheels in his mind wondering what on earth they need him to do.

Need me. For what? They want me to kill somebody. I ain't never kilt nobody. I don't think I wanna get involved. But if I say no they'll label me as a sucker for life. I'd never be able to show my face again. But what if I kill somebody and get caught? I'll have to do life in prison. All damn! Damn! Damn!

"Whatever, dog," Bink says confidently, sucking up the punk in him.

"Well, we can't find nay one of these jokers, so we need you to meet this girl who works at Footlocker. She's a friend of Daryl. That's Fatts' buddy. They be together every day. If we find *him*, we find Fatts."

"But I thought Luther was the main one."

"He is, but Fatts is the main, main one."

"Oh . . . OK." *Whatever,* thinks Bink relieved that all he has to do is meet a girl. That should be easy enough. "So what's the girl gonna do? She gonna tell me where Daryl lives or something?"

"Naw. She doesn't even have any idea what's goin' on. I just want you to get her phone number and find out where she lives. Daryl is supposed to be trying real hard to impress her, so he's bound to come over her house. That's the only lead we have on these dudes, so let's just try to make the most out of it. Pour it on thick so she'll think you're tryin' to really get with her. I don't care what you do. Just find out where she lives."

Bink agrees to go to the Footlocker on H Street NE today. Richter gives a good description of the girl but doesn't remember her name. His source told him that the girl was a pretty redbone with hazel eyes, about five foot six and phat as a Georgia Pine. She wears her hair short and gets off at eight thirty at night, but Bink doesn't plan on waiting until then. He heads straight there from the Rockville area where the computer software firm he works for is based.

After finding a park on Ninth and H Street, he walks into the Footlocker and spots a pretty young thang behind the counter with golden eyes. A real jaw dropper. Bink's a real live ladies' man and is always bragging about how big his dick is, so he has no cut-card when it comes to going straight at the ladies. He says whatever comes to the mind once he has them laughing and joking with him.

He looks at her and thinks, *Oh, I got her. She looks nasty too. What you gonna say?*

He doesn't have to think what he's gonna say past the first line. The response to her response will come naturally depending on what she says to counter his first liner. He heads toward the shoe stand against the wall near where she is standing. The whole time he's maintaining eye contact with her while wearing a devilish grin on his face. She is putting some shoes in a plastic bag and slows her motion to a pause and returns a slight smile and says, "Don't tell me you know me from somewhere."

Her pleasant sarcasm catches him totally off guard sending his original plans to the abyss, but Bink's a professional womanizer, so her little ploy to shoot him down before he could even launch an attack is no match for his volley.

"Naw, I was just coming over here to tell you that I was taking you to dinner as soon as you get off, propose to you around ten, marry you around eleven, be on our honeymoon by midnight, and go half on a baby by three in the morning."

Everybody in the whole store chuckles including the young lady he is talking to. That comeback was too strong for her to think of something to say that is time enough for what he just said. He's got her.

"Now that takes the cake," she jokes. "Humph. You got jokes."

"Well, I can't marry you if I can't pronounce your name," Bink is looking at her nametag but can't pronounce it.

"Kaisha," she tells him, with a smile on her face.

"Kay-sha. Oh. OK. That's pretty. Sorry, I can't say the same for you. Damn, I would get stuck with an ugly broad, wouldn't I?" he teases.

"I bet you won't be saying that on our honeymoon."

"Oooo," says a young lady who is listening to the exchange.

They go that way for a couple of minutes, then she asks her manager for a break, and the two of them walk outside and down to the carryout as they continue their conversation. Bink has her eating out of his hand by the time they get back to the store, and she never notices that he came into the store with no intentions of buying anything. She's just in a daze over being swept off her feet by a perfect stranger. He jots down her number and promises to call her later, and then leaves.

Then, like a woman who left her purse on a park bench, she sprints for the door chasing after Bink. She catches him at the corner.

"I forgot," she says, "Tonight, there's gonna be a big party. Chuck Brown's at the Sphinx on K Street."

"The Sphinx? Where's that?"

"In Northwest. At thirteen and K. It's a nice spot. Why don't you meet me there about twelve, then after that we, can go get some breakfast? I'll ride with my buddies, so I can leave with you, if that's cool with you."

Bink doesn't like to go to go-gos, but he's on a mission with a cause, so he has to do whatever it takes to get the job done.

"Yeah. I'll meet you there, boo. How should I dress?"

"No tennis shoes. No boots."

"All right. I got you. See you at twelve."

Chapter 42

The high cathedral ceiling looms magnificently over the two-story ballroom. There's a six-inch-high stage that the band is performing on, and Chuck Brown plays his guitar to the baseline and to the drummer's beat. The dance floor is jammed with soul brothers and jitterbugs, pretty ladies with some pretty smiles all decked out in the belated styles. There's only one bar, and Moet bottles are just about the only things being passed from the white bartenders to the big spenders who are showing off for the ladies. That's the only expensive champagne being sold. The rest of the champagne is garbage.

Kaisha and three of her female friends are among the party people playing the bar close. The light is on over by the bar so people can show their outfits off a lot better. Kaisha, however, is not thinking about any of the guys hounding her because she's all prettied up for one man, and that's Bink. She had planned on wearing a less revealing outfit but has opted to wear a short draping pink and white dress buttoned down to her navel so the onlooker can see her pink bra and firm breast; she mainly wants to incite Bink to sexual violence, which, at the time, is doing just that to men and women watching her.

Bink has just turned the corner, where he's in Kaisha's line of sight. Her passionate juices rise to the surface of her skin, making her flesh feel moist and warm. She can feel her womb open up and the thin strip of satin between her legs becomes moist. She doesn't understand why she feels this way about a man she has just met, but whatever it is, she's never had such an animal magnetism toward a man like this before. And without a word to her friends, she steps away from the bar and beelines toward Bink, but the closer she gets, the more her passage way becomes hampered by people bolstering their way to the overcrowded bar.

Bink doesn't see her approaching because there are so many sexy ladies crisscrossing around him that he has forgotten that he's already meeting a female here and already contemplating what he's going say to another young lady in his sight. There's so many to choose from, and he's like a dog in heat.

"Enjoying the view?" says a familiar voice behind Bink, making him turn around. "You all in her butt. What about mine?"

Bink turns and sees Kaisha and can't believe she's the same cute little chick he met earlier at the Footlocker. Blood swells his third leg making him have to shake his leg to give it room to budge, but that doesn't work, so Bink is standing there with a peculiar bulge in his crotch. Fortunate for him, there are too many people around them for anybody to see it, but he has to keep his distance from Kaisha because it might poke her in the stomach if he tries to give her a hug right now.

Damn! Bink says to himself as Kaisha wastes no time, showing him some affection.

"Damn, Boo! What you got, a gun?" Kaisha steps back slightly and looks down toward the source of the poke she just felt in her stomach. "Damn! It's like that?" She's smiling, because by the looks of it, Bink has quite a hammer on him, and she has all the intentions in the world in giving in to any sexual advances he makes toward her.

Bink is beyond embarrassed, but he's always at the top of his rap game, so he replies, "I ain't know you was gonna be looking so good. You caught me off guard. I though you would have on a wedding gown, but you already have on your nightgown." He looks down at his bulging pants and continues, "I'd like to introduce you to my best friend. I don't go anywhere without him. This is Him. It's a pleasure for you to meet Him."

They both laugh out loud while she reaches down and grabs a hold of *Him* to shake his hand, so to speak. Bink's embarrassment has turned to aggressive compulsion, and he wraps his arms around her and gives her a hug. She enjoys the embrace; that is until she sees Lil Papi. Lil Papi doesn't see her, but she doesn't want to take any chances on him stumbling upon her being cozy with Bink. She turns her head the other way and casually pulls back from Bink's clutches. Bink noticed her reaction to seeing somebody across the room, and realizes that it must be somebody that she's involved with. Hopefully it's Daryl.

"You act like you just saw a ghost."

"No . . . worst . . . One of my friend's buddies."

"Your boyfriend?"

"You can say that. Really he's just a friend, but we've been going out. I don't need the drama. These guys act real simple. I don't see my friend, but that don't mean he ain't here. Damn!"

"So does that mean you ain't leaving with me tonight?"

"Shid. Naw, that only means we're about to leave now. Let me go tell my girlfriends I'm about to leave." This isn't his type of party anyway. He's more the Love Nightclub type. He likes partying with the "booshee" and college crowd. Once outside the building's basement, his cell phone gets a signal and he calls Richter immediately.

"Rick, they here! They here!"

"Here where? Who is this? Bink?"

"Yeah. The broad, she told me to meet her down here at some joint. I don't even remember the name of the place. Chuck Brown down her."

"The Sphinx?" Richter always knows where Chuck Brown is playing. That's his favorite band.

"Yeah, that's it."

"She near you?"

"Naw. She told me to leave out. She was ready to go after she saw one of them."

"Who's down there? Who did you see?"

"I didn't see anybody, but I could tell by the way she was acting that it's them. I did hear her say Daryl's name."

"A'ight, bet. Good shot, joe. You go ahead. We'll be down there."

Back inside, Lil Papi is with a couple of his younger road dogs, Ears and Buck. They sell drugs for him and will do anything else he tells them to do. To Ears and Buck, Lil Papi is a god, and they'd do anything to make sure their hero has smooth sailing everywhere he goes. He doesn't stand in lines; he doesn't drive unless he's by himself, nor does he need to tote a hammer, but he does because that's just how Papi lives. He doesn't go anywhere without a gun. He's aware of the so-called beef they're supposed to be having with some dudes, but Lil Papi and the rest of his mob don't really take the beef seriously. As far as they're concerned, Benji and his crew are some Maryland bammas, and the only real nigga on their side is Richter, but he's not enough to make them run scared.

Lil Papi and his two companions are swarming through the crowd not at all interested in what the band is playing. They're here on business. One, to run into some fools that owe the crew some money, and two, to find little freaks that look good and are up to the task. Everywhere they turn, girls are shaking their ass—some are backing that thang up to the first good-looking dude that appears to be on the prowl. There are candidates all over the room.

There are girls everywhere. I gotta get me some drink in me homes.

"Papi!" he shouts to Buck, "to the bar!" He gestures with a point to the back of the spacious room. They walk to the back, where Lil Papi sees Angel, Kaisha's friend. He's seen her a couple of times before but has never pushed up on her because the situation didn't ever allow for it, but now would be a good time, and she looks hot. And not the sweaty kind either. "Ain't you . . . ?"

"Kaisha's friend." Angel is aware that most people can't ever get Kaisha's name right, so she helps him out a little bit. She's always wished he would say something to her when she went around Fifty-eighth Street with Kaisha to meet Daryl, but he would always be in the middle of something. "Lil Papi, right?"

"Yeah."

"You gettin' ready to go to the bar?"

"Yeah. You and your girlfriends drinkin? I got y'all."

"Oh, you so sweet." That's what all the girls say when somebody offers to buy them a drink.

"Where's Kaisha?"

"Oh, she's at home, asleep. She said she didn't feel like coming out tonight."

Papi nods as he looks at her other friends, thinking that he's probably accomplished one of the tasks that he set out to do in coming here. There's one problem, though. There are three girls, but one of them looks terrible. No; aweful. He'll leave that for them, Ears and Buck, to squabble over which one of them will end up with the ugly girl. He has the best looking one out of the litter, so he can care less. Both Ears and Buck go over to the bar to get the drinks while Lil Papi leans back on the wall and puts his mac down on Angel. They share a few laughs, and once the fellas come back with the bottles and the glasses of apple martinis for the ladies, they all get drunk together. Ears ends up with the nice-looking girl sitting on his lap, and Buck looks Medusa up pad down and finds that even though she is ugly as sin, she's the most attractive, bodywise, out of the three; only he'll have to hit it from behind because he'd rather look at her butt than look at her face.

Little do they know, they will have to walk through an ambush to get to their cars, so the night of protected sex they're planning will never come to fruition. The assault being mounted against them outside the doors of this building is formidable enough to have been used against Uday and Quassay, Saddam Hussein's sons, when they were killed.

Lil Papi is sitting by the bar alone with a dark green Moet bottle sagging in his hand. He's waiting for everybody to come back off the dance floor so they can leave. Lil Benny is on the stage relieving the aged Chuck Brown as the band starts its finale that sends the dance-crowd to the exit doors once the last drum roll sounds and the lead rapper says "good night."

Angel is the first to return, then Buck, and then the rest of them come back, and they all leave out together. Outside, there are police in full force to help the promoter's security force disperse the large, highly intoxicated crowd. Lil Papi isn't that drunk, but that can't be said for Buck and Ears.

"You ridin' with me, right?" Papi whispers to Angel.

"Where we goin'?" she slurs playfully.

"Oh. I don't know. I guess to get something to eat, then . . ."

"Please . . . You know damn well . . . You getting ready to take me somewhere and try to take advantage of me . . . hiccup . . . while I'm drunk."

"Well, Mami. If you insist, hey."

"Aye, Buck . . . Ears," Papi calls in his Spanish-American accent, "Me and shorty about to go get straight to it. I'll catch you vatos luego."

"*Luego*?" shouts back Ears. "Well, *hasta luego* to you too, ha-ha-ha."

Lil Papi and Angel get lost in the crowd and Ears and Buck walk off with the other two girls toward their car. Ears drove his own car, so Buck, who came with Lil Papi , hitches a ride with April, the ugly chic, and Kim rides with Ears. They'll all end up at the same motel before the night is over because that's mandatory when these two get together, once they finish with the one they started with, they swing partners. Sometimes their dates are game, sometimes they're not, but always they try their hand.

It's after three o'clock in the morning, and all the street lights are lit bright on the streets of Downtown, Washington DC, where Lil Papi and Angel are walking. The two of them cross the street only a block away from the party spot they just left. Cars line both sides off the street on Thirteenth Street. Papi's Hummer is parked on I Street, the next street over, and they're almost there when Papi hits the alarm, which unlocks the doors and starts the truck's engine.

"Damn, you got it like that?" Angel acts as if she's in awe at seeing Papi start his truck with his alarm, but she's actually seen that before and is only trying to make it seem like she's never been with a baller before. "Um. I guess next you're going to take me to a mansion that looks like Buckingham Palace."

Papi doesn't comment but does smile and look at her through his squinted eyes when he hears footsteps that sound like they're scampering toward him. He turns to see who or what that is, and he sees two men fast approaching brandishing guns and another guy not far behind. When the men see him turn around, they raise their guns and start shooting at Lil Papi. Papi pulls Angel in between him and the shooters, and a bullet rips through her blouse and into her chest.

"Aaagh!" she screams.

Lil Papi runs to the side of his truck and opens the door before the men can get too close, and he pulls a .45 Magnum from under his seat, turns, and starts bussing back.

Dhoom! Dhoom! Dhoom! The Magnum explodes spitting a stream of fire out of its barrel. *Pow, pow, pow, pow,* returns the other guy's guns.

It's Amp and Tony, but Lil Papi has never seen them before, but he's a hundred percent sure that they're some guys that Richter and Kan Quick have recruited to go to war for them. They are nowhere near being the chumps Lil Papi thought might be on the opposing side of the street beef his crew has found themselves in.

Lil Papi can hear one of them slapping another clip in his gun as well as the sound of Angel moaning from the rear of the truck. She steps from behind the truck soaked in her own blood, and Lil Papi comes extremely close to blowing her head off her shoulders.

"Help me . . . Please. I don't want to die."

In the distance, Lil Papi can see someone stoop down behind a car, and then sparks fly. Angel is shot several times in her back, and she falls into Papi's arms. He shoots back, releasing all the rounds he has left before his gun goes *click*. He climbs up into his truck while he holds onto Angel with all his might. He snatches the truck into drive and rams the rear end of the car parked in front of him, carrying it away from the curb along with the front of his truck. Gun shots shatter his back and side windows as he pulls away, and the weight of Angel's limp body is too heavy for Papi to hold. He loses his grip on her; she falls down to the moving surface of the street below, and her arm is run over by the truck's rear tire. The black H2 Hummer roars out of sight, and the shooters dip off into the shadows of the night. Police sirens can be heard bouncing off the buildings several blocks away. People are screaming and running wild everywhere, while Angel lay in the middle of the street lifeless and bloody. Several cars have blocked the road, and the drivers of the cars are out of their cars, shocked and speechless at what they are seeing.

Death and utter chaos on the streets of our nation's capital, and this is only the beginning!

Chapter 43

Apollyon muses. He's troubled over what the Omega has to communicate to him since he was summoned. He has had no mention of what the matter concerns. The Omega has only called for him but has remained in meditation, if that's even necessary for the All-Powerful. No one can start to imagine what goes through the thought process of the Almighty unless he himself makes things known. If something is impossible to imagine, one can bet the farm on it that the Omega has already thought of it and discarded it as nothing. He can see the future for a thousand generations, and man's entire past began only a week ago to him, so that's why when He says, *"in just a little while longer,"* those who expected to see the fulfillment of His word perish. Their children's children become the ancient ancestors of the people who actually live to see his word come true.

Apollyon recalls the last time that his Grand Creator mused in the way that he is musing now. It was a period before the time the Omega informed him that he was sending him to the material realm to serve his purpose for mankind. That was a very difficult decision considering that mankind doesn't deserve the air that they breathe and doesn't compare to Apollyon's significance in the kingdom. Apollyon means to the Omega what the heart means to the body of a mortal, what gas means to the sun, and what light means to sight. For the Omega to risk his only begotten son to the influences of darkness, by being in the vulnerable state of human flesh, is a testament for all to take note of, and is evidence of the love he apparently has for mankind, yet much of mankind still has not submitted to his will.

Apollyon, begins the Omega, *I shall now reveal to you another sacred secret that I have not already made known to you. I have not made it aware to you because it has to do with the appointed time and no one is to know of that time but I. But you must know now because I have given you authority over all things and something unforeseen is about to happen that will cause all to be lost on the earth. As you very well know, the time of the Great War has matured, and Iblis is quite aware that his time has been cut short. It is known that a prominent individual will contribute to the culmination of the signs that must occur, but who that individual is, no one knows but I. And now you shall know because you must not allow Iblis to destroy mankind's only hope. Another child has been born into the world, which will perform zealous works marking a sign of the times that indicate the eminent conclusion of Beelzebub's wicked system of things. And he, the god of this evil world's rulers, kings, and leading clergy, has wandered upon this child and has already sent destruction toward this glorious one who must come of age and be able to follow his course, or the prophecies will not be complete at the appropriate time in order to save the righteous ones from being swallowed up by the jaws of the great dragon. I shall not allow my spirit to intervene for I have given you authority over all the universe; therefore, you must decide what must be done to preserve the life of this child. The adversary will not rest until both the child and his mother are brought to ruin, and he has already found the likely evildoer to bring about total destruction of these righteous ones. Truly, I say to you, unless he is stopped, the child will die, and then so many of the meek ones of the earth will perish because Iblis will have more time to influence the weak fleshly creatures to do evil, so they, like him, will be thrown into the lake of fire.*

"I, Yahweh, the Almighty have spoken!"

The Omega speaks in a thunderous voice, sending all other heavenly creatures to wonder what is so important that his majesty has spoken out. Apollyon wants to ask for the advice of the Omega, and who the subject of this whole matter is, but after having his spirit paralyzed by the outburst of the Omega's voice, he dares not to ask any questions of the Great Lord but knows that there is no other way to find out who on earth he must persevere. *O, Holy One, I have not . . .*

The child's name is Asa. The Omega already knows what question Apollyon will ask. *Son of Benjamin, son of Richard, son of Lester, son of Charles, son of Edward, son of Toby, son of Bootsey, son of Soji, son of Kuntakinte.*

Apollyon is immediately aware of the child and the danger looming. He knows the child's father has just been slain and the concubine of the father wants to kill Asa's mother. He also understands that if the child or the mother is killed, the course of the child's life will not unfold in line with the fulfillment of the prophecies. Apollyon muses in the presence of the Omega. The Omega awaits a question to come up into Apollyon's mind so he can answer him; meanwhile, Apollyon recalls the history of Benjamin and Jessie. He visits the history of all their friends and loved ones as well as their enemies but cannot see an answer to the dilemma of preventing Salina from carrying out a deadly scheme to murder Jessie for taking away her prosperity. Then all of the sudden he has an idea!

What if . . .

No! Interrupts the Omega, t*hat should not be the remedy. How can he be trusted to do right and not wrong. What makes you think he won't avenge his death and kill rather than preserve? How could bringing him back save the woman and the child? Tell me, my son, tell me the answer to these questions and hope that your resolution can receive my blessings. And if it does, I shall allow my spirit to influence the things that must happen for the sake of mankind and for the sake of my glorious kingdom.*

Apollyon explains to the Omega why he feels that resurrecting Benji would preserve the life of the woman and the child. He also explains that there was a great probability that Benji would take revenge on his murderers and that he would be judged for all his deeds on Judgment Day. He explains that if he preserves the life of the child, then his life would be preserved and those he kills will be resurrected after the Great War in order to give them an opportunity to become righteous in the eyes of the Great Lord and have their names written in the *Book of Life.* But if he doesn't preserve the life of the woman and the child and many have to die as a result of his selfish vengeful ways, then he shall suffer the effects of the second death along with those who killed him. For his deeds in the world, he will be judged accordingly, and his part will be eternal unconsciousness, forever and ever.

The Omega agrees with Apollyon and his reasoning. He gives him his blessing to resurrect Benjamin back into the world and promises not to hold his sins against him, but he adds, *Truly, I say to you, I have given you my blessing, but it is only for a short period of time. I will allow this sinner to be risen after the dawn of the day of your liking; however, he must not be allowed to carry on indefinitely. Therefore, at the dawn following the third day of his resurrection he must be back to his resting place when the cherubs return to lay him to rest in his grave until you call him and all the others after the Great War. If he is not in his proper place by the rising of the third sun, he shall be judged immediately wherever he stands, and I myself shall be the one to determine his reward or punishment based on all that he has done. This is the covenant I am making with you.*

And it is so. Benji will be raised, and he will have three days on the earth to accomplish what Apollyon believes he will do, but first he must somehow be given a sign of when he should return to his grave because Apollyon doesn't want Benji to have to fall into the hands of the Omega. Not that the Omega is not merciful, but Apollyon knows that Benji's judgement will be according to his way. However, death will acquit him of all transgressions, opening the way for him to be given another chance at the appointed time.

He will not know why he has been raised, but he will be very aware that he was dead, and he'll remember that his so-called friends killed him. What he will do will be his own choice, but whatever he does, he only has a short time in which to do it. Salina has been told the whereabouts of Jessie and Asa's home, and she is wasting no time following the constant urges spurred on by the influences of Iblis to lash out at Jessie. Apollyon knows that there is no time to hesitate, so he summons two analim to carry out the task of releasing Benji from his bondage in Sheol.

Chapter 44

The wooden framed entrance into the family room where Benji and Jessie were assaulted is covered with a multi-toned comforter that is hanging from three nails. There are boxes everywhere and the kitchen counter is filled with canned goods, condiments, and jars. Where pictures and paintings once hung on the walls are lone nails left abandoned by the framed prized possessions that once brought life to the Powell residence. Now there's nothing but dead silence and empty, lifeless moments for Jessie when she ventures into this house.

She's upstairs in the bedroom, packing clothes and is about to be in for the surprise of her life when she sees who is coming up the stairs and into her room. It's Benji, and he can't wait to see his wife face-to-face again. He loves her so much and knows she has suffered a great deal after losing the man she had waited so long to have. As he quietly climbs the steps, his heart flutters with excitement at the prospect of hugging and kissing his Jessie once again. His clamoring movement is causing him to make more noise than he'd like to make, but Jessie has the music on in the room to soothe her mind and keep her from thinking too much about the things that make her cry.

Benji reaches the top of the stairwell and turns left to walk towards the master bedroom. He takes a deep breath, closes his eyes, and then reopens them before he walks into the open bedroom door, where the tones of Anita Baker flow out of the doorway.

With all my heart, I love you, baby.
Stay with me, and you will see
My arms will hold you, baby.
Never leave, 'cause, baby, I believe
I'm in love. Sweet love.

Got me calling out your name.

I feel no shame. I'm in love. Sweet love.

Benji enters the room and sees Jessie who turns to him after seeing him out of the corner of her eye while she was rummaging through a drawer. Benji watches her as her face goes from shock to horror. Jessie clutches her chest and falls to her knees. She is in obvious pain but doesn't scream or cry out in agony. Her body falls sideways to the floor, and she squirms while she holds her left breast. Benji's feet become cement blocks and his head feels light. He moves toward Jessie but falls to his face before he reaches her. He reaches out and grabs hold of the chest at the foot of their enormous bed and pulls himself up, but there is nothing he can do for Jessie. He crawls over to her and grabs her arm, but she offers no resistance. Her arm is like a rag doll. It falls to the floor the second he releases it. Jessie is not moving.

"Jessie!" Benji is devastated by what he's seeing. Jessie is unconscious. She doesn't answer him, and he's thinking that she has fainted again, but she has not fainted. She's had a heart attack and after a few minutes, her heart has stopped beating altogether. Jessie is dead, and Benji doesn't realize it until he feels for her pulse. He's not sure if he's doing it right, so he presses his ear to her chest. No heartbeat. He franticly shakes her, and then attempts a rudimentary CPR procedure, but it does no good. Jessie is dead. Finally he realizes that it's no good. Nothing he does will bring her back to coherence, and he agonizes at what has happened to Jessie, feeling it's all his fault.

What made me think that she would be able to handle this? She couldn't even handle a surprise wedding. Why Benji? What have you done?

He slumps over her lifeless body; he then lifts his head up and looks out of the window and sees there are three suns in the sky. The three suns shine so brightly that he's blinded and everything turns white. Benji can also feel himself getting hotter and hotter while his breathing becomes shorter and shorter. There is death all around, and Benji has just tasted life again after experiencing death, but he's starting to feel like he's about to eat it again if those luminaries in the sky have anything to do with it.

"No. I can't die again. I haven't even seen my kids!" He can feel himself blinking out slowly but surely, and then he thinks of the irreversible tragedy he's brought upon his poor Jessie, and he screams out loud, "Whyyyyyy?"

Suddenly, it was pitch-black. He's not sure if he's still alive or dead all over again. He's sure that his eyes are open after he blinks them a couple of times, but he still can't see a thing. His quarters are tight and condensed as if he's in another place far away from his house. It's hot and stuffy, and the air is starting to choke him. He's lying flat on his back, yet it feels as if the ceiling is rested gently upon his forehead and nose. When he goes to reach for what is so close to his face, he finds that he can't lift his hand up because whatever it is above his face is also restraining his hands. Benji's strength is fully restored and much more than it ever was before, but when he goes to push whatever it is before him or above him, it doesn't budge. He's trapped, but where? He was just in his bedroom mourning the death of his wife that he literally scared to death, giving her an instant heart attack; so how could he be in this dark secluded place that feels like the inside of a . . . ?

A coffin. Benji realizes. *No. It can't be real. What the hell is going on?*

Benji doesn't know it now, but he'll soon find out that everything that he had experienced with Jessie was a dream. No, not a dream—a vision. Benji is trapped in his coffin losing oxygen with each breath he takes. He's been alive for a while, and the oxygen that had gotten trapped in his coffin when he was buried is now running thin. He had been asleep for nearly an hour, so his breathing has poisoned the air around him.

"Allah, the beneficent! Why have you awaken me up from my sleep only to let me die again from suffocation? Please le . . ."

Before he can finish his sentence he hears several thumps against the outside of the coffin, and then it starts to move. The sound of scraping rocks and rumbling earth can be heard while Benji feels the tomb in which he's trapped being pulled or pushed deeper below the earth's surface. For about ten minutes, the coffin inches deeper and deeper. Benji is starting to get-light headed from the carbon monoxide he's breathing that has been expelled out of his own body. He takes shorter breaths and holds them before exhaling, trying to buy himself some time. The coffin is moving in the wrong direction, but the fact that it's moving is hopefully a promising sign for the resurrected Benji, trapped in Sheol, soon to be liberated from his eternal resting place.

After the coffin travels about four feet deeper than it was before the rumbling, it stops and Benji can hear the sound of a click near his head and another one coming from the direction of his feet. The analim of the Most High have been dispatched to release Benji from his prison by pulling his coffin deeper under the heavy soil on top of his grave. Now that they've also unlocked it, it's now up to Benji to figure out that he's free and make his way to the surface.

Benji pushes on the coffin lid once more, and this time it gives. He pushes it fully open but doesn't find any more air outside of the coffin than there was inside, nor is it any lighter. Benji still cannot see his hand in front of his face, but now he has more than enough room to move. His blood is flowing through his veins, and his muscles are fully functional, but he's as stiff as an amateur weightlifter who has bit off more than he can chew, but as a matter of life and death, Benji must loosen up quickly or else he'll die again before he gets a chance to escape his grave. He's not sure which would be worst; dying before he was about to get out of his mother's womb or dying before he can dig his way to the surface of the ground above his own grave, but there is no time to consider anything besides clawing and scratching at the hard soil, imprisoning him in the earth's crust. Dirt is falling on his head as well as an occasional stone as he piles the dirt below him so he can reach the high ceiling he is creating as he digs like a hound trying to uncover a bone. Exhausted, Benji finally feels a cool breeze blow against this grabbling fingers indicating that he's struck air, and with a mighty tug of the grassroots and topsoil, Benji creates a hole big enough to allow a sea breeze of lung-refreshing oxygen to shower down in the open space around him. He takes a deep breath and exhales it out of his mouth. He looks up at the royal blue sky through the small opening and can see that it is either very early in the morning or early evening by the appearance of the subdued glory of the sun against the layers of the atmosphere. Stars can still be seen, but it is probably not evening time, considering the restless sounds of singing birds.

Benji can see clearly, but he cannot understand why he can't open his left eyelid. He reaches for his face and feels the pirate's patch over his eye, then he touches himself on the back of his head, and he feels the bandage that covers a hole in his head left by the bullet that exited his skull after blasting his eye out and ripping through his brains. Benji's heart grieves over the thought of Jessie having to see such an atrocious sight of her husband. He can just imagine how terrible a sight it must have been to witness. His brains must have been all over the place. His emotions began to stir and he, for a moment, begins to feel sorry for himself, then a tear drops from his eye, and his emotions transcend from pity to sheer rage and then diabolical thoughts of revenge.

I'ma kill all those suckers!

He commences with his digging frenzy piling enough dirt beneath him to stand on and push the layer of grass and dirt above him with his hands. He reaches out of the hole for a handful of earth so he can pull himself out of his prison. He looks around before climbing out of the grave and sees a car driving toward a small building about three hundred yards away. In the clearing between him and the building, there are a few trees and a gently sloping lawn to his north, east, and west. There are only a few tombstones in sight because Harmony Cemetery uses plates to identify the occupants of their graveyard. Benji is amongst the few that have one.

Benji's been to many funerals in this graveyard, so he's quite familiar with where he is and in the distance, he's reassured that he's in Harmony because he can see the townhouse community of Village Green. He has several friends who live around there, not to mention girls he used to chase when he was young.

Certain that no one can see him, he pulls the rest of his body out of the hole and places the clumps of grass back over the hole to make it look like no one has been in or out of the hole. He doesn't want to attract any attention to his grave and have people looking for his body. Not that anybody would think that he dug himself out of the ground, but no need to alarm the family with the news that someone has stolen his body.

Benji's parents only live a mile from where he is, so he starts toward their home, wondering how he should approach his family, or if he should at all. He's not the handsome fellow he once was before the coroner, morgue, and funeral parlor people got finished with him. Benji's head is wider and features on his face look swollen. His skin is leathery and dark. He's alive, but in all actuality he looks undead. A real scary sight! Fortunately, his dressers fully clothed him as requested by the family. They even put his shoes on his feet, but his swollen feet hurt, and the alligator Ferragamos he's wearing are making the walk to his folks' house excruciating.

When he gets there, he sits in the park and waits for both his mother and father to leave out the house on their way to work. The last one to leave is his mother and once he sees her pull off, he walks over to the house and approaches the basement window at the rear of the small townhouse. The window is locked, but he knows how to maneuver it until the lock slides to an unlocked position. He climbs inside and goes through some bags that he had left in the basement filled with old clothes. He changes into something more comfortable and even finds a few pair of tennis shoes in another bag next to the door of his old bedroom now made into a storage room for his mother's junk. There is a black Redskins fitted cap atop a wig manikin head; he grabs it and carefully places it on his head, covering the bandage on the back of his head. The black jeans and the white Aja Armani T-shirt will allow him to look normal in public as long as no one looks at his face in the light. The gray New Balance running shoes are perfect for his aching feet. They're fitting a little tight but walking won't be a problem.

Benji can think of nothing as much as he thinks of Jessie and his children, but he knows that revealing himself to them would be a tremendous mistake considering the vision that he had. And just when he thinks of the engraved tragedy of his wife, he recalls the dream he had before his murder. The nightmare when he went to visit the pretty girl who set him up to be ambushed by those men who chased him down the alley where he was shot in the head. The thought freezes him, and he wonders if that was a sign from above of what was about to happen to him, and was his dream of what happened to Jessie when he walked into their room a warning sign to keep away from her? But how could he be so strong not to visit his wife? How could he be let back into the conscious world and not hold her in his arms once again? That alone would have been the one thing that he would have asked to come back for if he had a choice in the matter.

I can't stay away from her. I must go see her. I've got to go. His heart won't allow him to stay away from his love. Apollyon knew that this would be the case, and that's why he's back on earth alive and well in the first place.

It was foreseen that he would covet the life he had before he died such an untimely death, and in him doing so, he would certainly see the things going on around his wife and child that will eventually cause them some harm. Though Apollyon orchestrated the idea of bringing him back, it's the Omega who is driving Benji along with the visions. The Omega is wise enough to know that Jessie will not be able to handle seeing Benji under normal circumstances; also if he's to succeed in accomplishing his mission, there is no time for any type of reunion and bonding.

Benji heads from the stairwell, leading to the rest of the house. At the top of the steps, he opens a white wooden door. It's very flimsy, and he nearly rips it off its hinges on his way out of his parents' cozy little home. He does have hunger pangs but isn't sure if he should eat anything, seeing as how he's fresh out the grave and everything. He looks into the kitchen but turns for the front door determines not to submit to his belly's call to be fed.

Benji bypasses the front door though. He wants to see his face in the mirror, so he goes up another flight of stairs to get to the bathroom. He has touched his face and is curious to know how it looks. He's not prepared for what he's going to see. He just hopes it doesn't look as bad as it feels and that he doesn't regret seeing himself in the first place. The bathroom is at the top of the steps straight ahead. Benji can see himself in the mirror before he even enters into the bathroom, but since the blinds are closed and the other doors in the hallway are all closed, he cannot see just how horrid he really looks.

Upon stepping beyond the threshold of the door, he can make out his ghastly appearance. His skin is dark and discolored and its texture is glossy. The uncovered eye is sunk in and his nose appears to have been broken. Benji stares at himself in disgust and curiosity.

"Shhhit," Benji whispers in a low voice, wondering, *what the hell is going on! I've got to be dreaming. I'm dreaming. Wake up, Benji. I must be in a coma or something and can't wake up. Jessie's probably sitting beside me right now, 'cause I know what I think just happened at the graveyard didn't really happen. I didn't just dig my way out of my grave. I'm not dead. I'm dreaming. Open your eyes, Benji. Wake up.*

Benji closes his eyes and repeatedly demands himself to wake up, but the familiar scent of his mother's perfume that is still lingering in the air brings him to the reality that his worst nightmare is not a nightmare at all. He was dead; there's nothing he can do about it, and the ugly patch he has on his eye is real. The hole in the back of his head is real. The fury building up inside of him like a raging bull is causing his face muscles to have spasms is real. The blood in his head is rushing to his eye. His brows arch with anger, and he grits his teeth, exposing them through his crusty shriveled up lips. His fists are clutched tight and murderous thoughts are wandering across his mind.

I'ma kill 'em all. I won't leave nobody. I'ma cut their children up in tiny pieces for what they've done to me. Richter, Amp, all them bammas. They did this to me. They did it.

The more he recollects his ordeal and that of his wife's before his death, the madder he becomes with those whom he knows are responsible. He turns and storms down the stairs and goes around to the basement door back to the window he came through. He left the basement door open as well as the window he exited on his way to find his former friends. It's only been twelve days since Benji was buried, but people's schedules have gone through a complete transformation during this time, so he'll need a car and a cell phone if he's going to find anyone. And he *will*, if it's the last thing he'll do.

Chapter 45

The Sunoco gas station on Martin Luther King Highway in Landover is always crowded in the morning, and today, under the gloomy overcast of gray clouds, it is a sequel to yesterday's morning rush. There are two bays covered by a roof to protect the patrons from the looming threat of rainfall that would destroy women's hair-dos and ruin a dude's opportunity to strut with a pimp showing off his outfits.

There is a car at every pump on both sides. One of the cars is a black Lincoln Town Car Signature Edition. An older gray-haired black man is standing at the rear of the car. He has his eyes glued to the woman, wearing a green skirt and multi-colored shirt, who is pumping gas into her Toyota Camry. She's not very pretty, but the man isn't looking at her face. None of the men at the gas station are looking at her face as they make their way between their vehicles and the building where they pay for their gas. They're all looking at the backside of the woman. It wouldn't be a problem to sit a hot cup of coffee on it without spilling a single drop. That's how much back baby has got.

Baaaabe. Thinks a young fella who hops out of his silver Bronco. He has plats dangling from his watermelon-size head, and he's about the same height as Little Arnold on the TV Show *Different Strokes*. He thinks he's a gangster but considering the way he walks, he probably wouldn't bust a grape in a food fight. Little pip-squeak.

"Wasup, shorty?" he calls in an overconfident "mac" tone. "What's a pretty young lady like yourself doin' pumpin' that gas by your lonesome? Your man didn't fill it up for you last night? Here, let me get that for you."

The woman smiles. *This little two-feet tall wanna-be gigolo. He thinks he's all that, too. He is cute though. Probably got a little dick.*

"Now, who told you I had a man? That's where you're wrong. On top of that, you wait until I've already paid for it and pumped most of it before you come over here to help? You've got to do better than that, boo."

He's not actually as short as he looks from a distance. He's about five foot two and they see eye to eye, so she's thinking that maybe he'll do.

"Baby, I got you. If you were my girl, you wouldn't ever pay for gas, food, smokes, nothing."

"You smoke?" She's a weed smoker, and the question opens up the door for him to be as raw as he wants to be.

"Do I *smoke*?!" he asks, giving every indication that he does.

She laughs a bit and they converse while her gas finishes pumping. Meanwhile, Benji who was hiding in some nearby shrubbery hops into his truck and hopes he's left the key inside, but he doesn't see them. He strikes the steering wheel as he looks around for the guy who has just gotten out of the truck. He groans a grizzly sound in frustration and decides he'll just wait for the guy to return to his truck and strong-arm him for his keys. Benji climbs into the backseat and ducks down just in case the guy walks in front of the truck and sees him through the clear windshield.

Casanova is writing down the number of "Miss Coffee Table Butt" on a dollar bill, and then they exchange good-byes as he walks away, now with more of a tiptoe in his strut. Bennie Hill would be proud.

After paying for his gas and buying his daily prescription of weed-smoking paraphernalia, including a thirty-two ounce bottle of water, some salt and vinegar potatoe chips, a honey bun, a pack of Big Red chewing gum, a pack of Backwood blunts, and a single Dutch Master cigar to smoke with his main girl, he returns to his truck in a hurried scamper, because he's supposed to be in class at PG College in ten minutes. He's already going to be late, but he figures no need in missing the whole class.

Inside his truck awaits Freddie Kruger's nephew who is going to scare the living daylights out of him. Shorty's name, according to what he told Ms. Hourglass, is Jermaine, but he's lied to her. He never gives his real name to the girls he meets. He doesn't want his name to somehow get back to his woman at home.

He's another one of those wellers, always lying about something he has, and has a tendency of trying to put on like he's ruff, frowning, and mean—mugging at people until he runs across a real nigga who mugs back. That's when he'll nod his head so as to say "wasup" and then looks away. Anyway, Jermaine's finished fueling up. He snatches the nozzle out of the tank, slams the gas tank door-panel shut, leaving the cap on top of the back tire, then jumps into the truck. He throws the bag filled with goodies across to the passenger seat then digs into his pants pocket for his keys.

"Gotdamnit! *I hate when I get in the car with the keys still in my pocket.*"

He pulls his keys out of his left pocket and puts the key in the ignition. Before he pulls the gear shifter down to drive, he glances into his rearview mirror. A quick glance followed by a long glare. He raises his head and opens his mouth. Terror consumes his entire body, and the sensation of crawling roaches tickle the surface of his skin from head to toe.

A deep groggy sound comes from the red-eyed monster behind him, "Get out."

Petrified, Jermaine can't move, but when he sees Benji's eye flare-up, he comes to his senses and says, "Alright . . . y . . . you . . . you got it, man. I'm gone, joe. You got it. You want my money!"

"Yeah," groans Benji. *This nigga's a clown*, Benji thinks. "Your cell phone too."

And just like that, Benji is on his way, a truck filled with high octane gas, a phone, and a wad of cash. That was too easy. The hard part will be finding his killers. With all the money they took from him, they have no need to hang around the usual spots. They've split over a million dollars between four people, much of which was bill money that had to be sent to Benji's connect in California. Benji doesn't know that Richter had absolutely nothing to do with the jape, so as far as he's concerned, Richter's on the list too.

Damn, I wonder if the dude has a gun in here. Knowing him, he probably doesn't. Where should I start looking for these niggas. Richter ain't never home. Let me check the breakfast spots first.

Benji drives all over town. First he goes to Ms. Murry's on Kenilworth Avenue. He doesn't see anybody's car, so he sits there for a while to see if someone will come out or show up. After an hour, he leaves and travels to White Corners on Southern Avenue, another popular breakfast spot. He stays there for a while, but no one shows there either. He rushes uptown to a spot where Richter frequents called Goins. No Vette, no Richter. He hangs around for a while hoping to get a chance to see Richter's car jet pass on Georgia Avenue but no show.

He could call them, but he doesn't know one single number because their phone numbers were stored in his cell phone, and that was the only way he called them. There was never a need to memorize anybody's phone number. Just program it in the phone and search for it by name. Now he wishes he had dialed their numbers when he called them, then maybe he'd have remembered them. But really what good would that do? What would he say? How would he lure them to where he wants them to be? "What's up, man? This is Benji, and I'm back from the dead to kill your ass." No. That wouldn't work, but there is someone he can call who'll be able to help him out—Bink.

So Benji takes off from Georgia Avenue toward Maryland, through Silver Spring to the Capital Beltway, and then around to Old Georgetown Road. Bink works in an office park on Democracy Boulevard by Montgomery Mall. Benji pulls up in front of Tower II of the complex and calls Bink's cell phone.

"Hello?" Bink answers.

"Bink," Benji musters from his hoarse vocal cords. He sounds like a frog with a cold. "This is Ben . . . ji."

"Who? . . . stop playing? Who is this, Richter?"

"I'm d . . . ownstairs. Front chor . . . building."

Bink thinks it's Richter being silly. "Humph. You play too much. What, you wanna holler at me?"

"Yeah."

"A'ight. I'll be right down. Give me about five minutes."

Benji hangs up the phone without another word. He doesn't like to talk because his throat feels like it's been sanded with a fresh pad of sandpaper coated with Tabasco sauce. He's glad he didn't have to explain too much over the phone, even though he knows Bink is going to get into the truck expecting to see Richter and not a walking corpse. Benji muses over what he'll say to keep Bink calm or from jumping back out of the truck and running back into the building to call the police.

I'll keep my head turned until he gets in and closes the door.

Benji hasn't been listening to the radio because he's been concentrating on what he must do, so the truck is quiet and the sound of people's shoes can be heard as they strike the white concrete sidewalk. The sound is wrecking Benji's nerves. It seems he can hear their shoes and what the people are saying to one another. It's as if he is walking with them. The longer he sits there in silence, the louder the sounds outside of the truck bounces off his eardrums. The sounds are getting louder and louder, and Benji can't seem to get any control over it; then suddenly he returns back to normal and can no longer hear far off sound, but the phenomenon has Benji spellbound in amazement yet again at what he's become.

Why have you done this to me? Why am I alive?

He sits there in silence, again hoping that what happened a moment ago will happen again. He tries to make himself hear what the people standing by the glass door of the building are saying to each other, but he can't. He tries to concentrate but still nothing. He has no control over the miraculous power, which is more frustrating than not knowing why it happened.

He looks at the building again where the people are standing, smoking cigarettes and sees his friend Bink coming out of a revolving door, wearing a white shirt and tie. His strut is aggressive, not lacking any confidence. He cast an unsure gander upon the silver truck, having never seen it before. He's reluctant to approach it without a signal from the occupant notifying him that it's safe to open the door. He doesn't want to open the door of someone's vehicle he doesn't know. Benji can see his reluctance by the way Bink is piercing his eyes in an attempt to look through the tinted windows as he reduces his trot to a creep.

Bonk. Benji honks the horn, and Bink continues in his previous demeanor. He reaches for the handle with his right hand; Benji turns and looks in the other direction as Bink hops in the passenger seat and closes the door. Benji turns back toward him.

"*Agh!*" Bink is startled and screams in an act of cowardice. He reaches for the handle with his face still looking at the creature in the driver's seat; then Benji moves to reach out for Bink's arm, and Bink pulls back slamming his back to the door with his arm against the door and his hand gripping the dashboard. His face is showing no courage whatsoever; his eyebrows and his hairline are synonymous with one another, and his eyes have lost their eyelids. How stupid he looks! "What . . . the . . . ?"

"It's me, Bink." Benji says in his deep groggy tone. He swallows some saliva but is afraid to drink any water, still wary of the effects it may cause. The water Jermaine left behind has been calling Benji, but he's afraid, however, if he's going to talk to Bink in any lengthy capacity, he'll have no choice but to take a swig or two considering how painful it is just to say one word.

"B . . . B . . . Benji? What tha . . . fa . . ." Bink is in total amazement and can hardly believe his eyes. Bink relaxes, but is not at all comfortable and is wondering how he's going to get out of the truck before Egor grabs him.

God, please forgive me. I'm sorry for all the wrong I've done. I didn't mean to do it to Salina. Please don't let him kill me. I promise I'll never have sex again.

Benji looks at Bink with the only eye he has and says, "I don't know how to start, man, but I need you. Them niggas kilt me and I gotta find them."

Bink is still speechless, but he's starting to feel like this thing isn't going to kill him.

"Bink. Did you hear me? I said it's me. Benji, man. Snap out of it. I'm just as confused as you are. I don't know what the hell is going on either, but all I know is I'm alive. Don't ask me how. But really, I need your help."

Bink is certain that he's not seeing things now. It *is* Benji, and he's asking him to help him.

"I'm sorry, man." He still doesn't feel right calling this thing Benji. Furthermore, he's speaking in a trembling tone. His words are coming out of his mouth, yet he hardly knows what he's actually saying. "I don't mean to be acting this way. It's just . . . well . . . you know. It's hard to believe that you're actually sitting here in front of me. Could you start all over again? I didn't really catch what you said about 'them niggas.' You're talking about Fatts and 'em?"

"No. I'm talking' about Richter, Amp, Tony, and Bootemup. They're the ones who kilt me."

Bink is astounded to hear what Benji has just said. "No way. Why do you say something like that? Richter is trying to do everything in his power to find the dudes who killed you." Bink is frowning in confusion and still delirious about talking to a corpse.

"That's the whole thing, they're frontin'? They did it and are using Fatts and Luther as scapegoats. I know what I'm talking about. I was there." Benji gasps and reaches for the bottle of water on the floor by Bink's foot.

Bink curls up lifting his leg so Benji can't touch him. He thinks he's reaching for his foot. Bink is on the edge and can't hide his fear, but he's even more afraid of trying to escape. Once he realizes that Benji was only reaching for the bottle of water, he rests his leg back down but remains snake-like cautious, watching Benji's every movement. He watches Benji guzzle the water out of the upside down bottle like a ground troop on his way to Baghdad. All thirty-two ounces of it, and then he continues, "Ahh . . . I know it was them because I heard Amp's voice just before he shot me."

Benji continues to utter his words in a very deep voice, but the sting of speaking is gone. The water made him feel rejuvenated with each gulp, and he feels much better than he did before, but Bink is still in a state of shock and hasn't responded to what Benji has just said because he can't grasp the fact that he's talking to a man who has been killed, knows who did it, and now wants him to help kill them. It's all a little more than he can handle.

"Bink. Don't be afraid. It's me, dog. Your man. You know I wouldn't' lie to you, and I certainly wouldn't hurt you. I need you, man."

Bink stares off into space for a moment. "Have you seen Jessie?" Benji takes a deep breath, then turns away from Bink, and looks down to his lap. He visualizes Jessie in his head and sorrow fills his heart. Oh, how he wishes he could go see his Jessie. Nothing else in the whole world would matter, not the killers, not his thirst, not even the kids—just his wife and holding her in his arms one last time. He doesn't know if he's immortal, or if he'll drop dead again, but he does know that seeing Jessie would be his greatest joy, but unfortunately his worst nightmare should something happen that he'll regret. He's already seen his worst nightmare and has no desire in seeing it manifest.

"No. I can't let her see me like this. It might kill her."

There's a long silence between the two of them, broken only by a sniffle from Benji. Bink can't see the tears, but he knows his friend is weeping and remorse has taken the place of fear. Regardless of how strange the situation feels to him, Benji has come to him and nobody else, showing him that this man loves him even from the grave. Bink's guilt begins to eat away at his conscience. He's been only half the true friend that Benji has thought that he was by sleeping with Salina, and he feels now would be the only chance he has to clear his conscience by telling the truth to Benji.

"Benji," Bink starts in a calm sincere voice, "I have something to tell you on another topic that I've wanted to tell you before . . . Well, you died before I could tell you. I couldn't muster up the courage."

Benji has no idea what to think, but he braces himself to hear bad news from his friend. The thought comes to mind that he's about to tell him that he's slept with Jessie.

I'ma kill him right here, right now.

"I had sex with Salina."

Benji breathes a big sigh of relief.

"I don't care about that, man. For real, you can marry her and take care of my kids for me if you want."

That's not the response that he was expecting, but he hasn't told him everything yet. "Yeah but, this was going on while you were locked up. I felt *real* bad. Real bad."

"Hey, a ho gonna be a ho. Nigga gon be a nigga. I ain't mad atcha."

Now Benji will attempt to see if he can get any information about the night Bink crashed out at Jessie's house. "Aye. What about the night you fell asleep over Jessie's house? You hit that night, didn't you?"

"All hell, naw. Jessie loves you to death. That girl wouldn't cheat on you to save her life. I didn't hit that. I ain't saying I wouldn't have, but I never tried, and now I wouldn't touch Salina with a thirty-foot pole. That's how bad I feel about betraying you. I love you, man. I miss you."

Benji feels the sincerity pouring out of Bink's words, and he nods his head in approval of their friendship. He feels no anger or resentment.

Bink continues, "As far as Amp, Tony, and Bootemup, I wouldn't put it past them, but Richter . . . Not him. You got it wrong. This man is on a rampage. He's been losing weight and everything. That's all I think he's living for. To find Luther, Fatts, and some dude named Lil Papi. I think they almost caught up with him, but he got away. Another dude named Daryl too. Last week, I went to some club called the Sphinx and met this girl that Richter put me on to. That's where they caught up with Lil Papi. Like I said, he got away, but two dudes that were with him got hit along with his girl. Well, maybe not his girl, but some girl he was with. But what makes you think . . . or so sure it was Amp you heard?"

"I know that lil' nigga's voice. It was him and the others, but you might be right about Richter because I didn't see anybody that fit his size and build."

"Man, I'm telling you. Richter is on a nut trying to find those dudes. I thought you were him. In fact, I'ma call him right now."

Benji is not totally convinced that Richter had nothing to do with it, but listening to him talk may help sway his conviction. There is no answer on Richter's phone, but Benji has an idea on where to find him around noontime. Right by the university campus of Howard. He's usually down there circling the blocks of Seventh and T Street by the old pool hall.

Richter goes there to collect his money every day. The morning rush of dope customers who fatten the pockets of his runners get him more money than he was making selling cocaine. The only reason he was selling it in the first place was because there is no one else that Benji could trust to handle so much of a load without messing up the bill money. Richter's a seasoned veteran in the street game. He only needed somebody like Benji to give him a real chance to flaunt his talents. Well, this seasoned veteran is about to either get the shock of his life or slice of his life from the huge Rambo knife that Benji took from his father's tackle box that he carries with him when he goes fishing. Whether he lives or dies, Richter is sure to be shocked.

Chapter 46

There are very few blocks in America quite like this one and none to be found in the whole Washington, D.C. area. It's not that this intersection has something visibly extravagant or superlative about it, or some overly violent crew that shoots at anybody they're not familiar with, including the police when they drive through, and it's not even because it's filled with the sexiest women on earth. What makes this particular intersection so unique is the diversity in the people that inhabit each side of the street, and the signs of the arteries that lead from this intersection all bear different names. Northbound is Georgia Avenue traveled by Howard University College students, inner-city ballers, honies, and suburban midlevel government Blacks, Whites, and Hispanics on their way home. Traveling southbound, in the opposite direction, the street is called Seventh Street, and those who head in that direction are mostly professional on their way downtown to their offices or overpriced condos. The eastbound direction is named Florida Avenue, where the notorious dwell. In the cars that commute along this corridor every day, you will find mostly the people from the hood. DC's most shady as well as the ordinary working class from boroughs in Northeast, Southeast, and Prince George's County, the richest black county on the planet, and one of the most dangerous. Florida Avenue becomes U Street on the other side of the traffic light where the Ethiopians, wealthy Whites, Hispanics, and other foreigners roam.

This is the crossroads of Washington DC and the place where dope fiends come to get their fix. There's always a lot of activity on the four corners of this block, but to the naked eye, it's life as usual. Even the roving eye of the law has a very difficult time recognizing who it is that is receiving the thousands of dollars that exchange hands in the drug trade every single day. The pool hall that was once the haven for the lieutenants of the drug lord and the drug lords themselves is now closed, but that hasn't slowed productivity in the least bit. Two blocks away is the Tropicana Jamaican carry-out's parking lot on Ninth and U Street, where Benji is sitting and waiting to spot Richter. Like clockwork, the blue Vette emerges. Benji springs into action and puts the truck into drive. At least he tries to, but the truck is off, so the shifter doesn't budge. Once he starts the truck, he dances it off the curb, forsaking the driveway and Humphrey Bogards his way across the lane of oncoming traffic to get to the light before he could be blocked by other cars from making the turn to trail Richter.

Already, the Vette is out of sight, but Benji is not alarmed. He's sure that Richter has only bent a left onto T Street to circle the block in search of his lieutenant. Sure enough, Richter has pulled to the curb in front of the old Howard Theater, where Motown's original alumni made their marks in DC. There's an old-timer named Ball Bell wobbling over to the passenger window of Richter's car as Benji turns onto the block. Benji quickly pulls to the side of the road behind a U.S. Mail box truck. He can't see the Corvette as long as it is parked, but he'll be able to see it once it pulls into the street. He watches and waits patiently. In less than a minute, the Corvette is on the road again, and Benji allows it to get to the stop sign at the corner and start its turn before following suit. But by the time Benji gets to the stop sign and looks to see how far the Vette has traveled, it has put some distance between them. Benji disregards any traffic and is nearly hit by an Isuzu Trooper filled with Orientals who instantly start pumping their fist and shouting what is more than likely profane words that Benji can hear but can't understand. He's just had another one of those sound surges he had experienced earlier, but he has other more important things on his mind like running this red light in front of him and trying to keep up with the aggressively skilled driving of Richter.

Man, this dude is off the richter. Benji can hardly stay close enough to keep an eye on Richter, and it reminds him of how he got his name in the first place. Everything he does, he does vigorously. Especially driving!

After cautiously crossing the red light, Benji floors the truck and speeds down Florida Avenue, hoping to catch the next light at First Street before it turns red. He barely makes it. Richter continues to drive like Speed Racer, and Benji comes no closer to getting into a comfortable trailing position. Richter hangs an illegal left turn at North Capitol Street, and Benji loses sight of him for a moment. In fact, that's the last he sees of the blue speed demon.

"Damn it!"

Benji's blood boils, and he's blocking traffic behind him and ignoring the sounds of hollering horns, insisting that he gets a move on. There's too much traffic traveling in the opposite direction, so Benji can't make the turn, but there's no use in trying, anyway, because Richter is long gone, and calling the number that Bink gave him wouldn't help much. Richter never answers the call from strange numbers unless they leave a message and indicate that the number that they will be calling from. Benji knows, with his voice, leaving a message would do no good. Besides, Richter can't know that he's back from the dead. If he had something to do with his murder, Benji doesn't want to announce that he's coming to slaughter the wolves responsible.

Dejected, Benji takes a final look up North Capitol Street and releases the brake, allowing the truck to roll forward. He decides that he will drive around town and hopes to bump into Amp or Bootemup. He knows where they live, but doesn't know where Tony lives. He knows they spend a lot of time over Tony's house, playing Madden or Live, so he doesn't expect to catch up with anybody, but he'll try.

He heads for Southeast Washington to a neighborhood called Barry Farms where Bootemup stays with a girl named Cassandra. Cassandra lives smack-dab in the middle of the weed strip on Stevenson Street, a block that has more niggas standing around than the Million Man March and enough guns lying in bushes and patches of grass to make the North Viet Cong proud. But Benji doesn't care. He's already dead. What more can they do to him? One thing he's not confident of, and that's scaring anybody in Barry Farms into a mad dash. If anything, he'd get the fur blown off *his* ass, so pulling up and jumping out like Rambo is totally out of the question.

When he arrives, the scene is nothing like he expected. There are black guys on the sidewalk, waving for him to stop signifying that they have weed, but Benji is certain that they don't belong here. They look nothing like authentic drug dealers and just as he suspected, they aren't. At the opposite end of the long street sits several unmarked police cars. There had been a raid not long before Benji came and those guys back there are really undercover police officers, trying to entrap somebody with purchasing drugs. The Feds don't play fair, and it's a good thing that they weren't conducting a roadblock as they often do on this street after one of their raids, or Benji would have had trouble. The sight of those police really shook Benji, making him forget all about why he even came to Barry Farms in the first place. Once he finally gets out of the neighborhood, he comes back to his senses and drives around the area for a while to give the police some time to leave before he returns to sit in front of Cassandra's house. He'll sit there until he gets restless, waiting for Bootemup to show up.

Chapter 47

The high-rise apartment that Jessie used to live in is within a three-mile radius of 2 Exquisite, the beauty salon that Benji bought for Salina a few years ago; so how they never bumped into each other was a mystery to both Jessie and Benji. Benji had tried to talk Salina into finding a spot for the salon inside the city, but she had fallen in love with the building, the landlord, and the parking lot of the Silver Hill Shopping Center to accommodate all the clientele she had envisioned. Her client base once reached a very high profitable level, and six other stylists rented booths from her each week. But with the fall of her private life also came the fall of her ethics in business.

Reality has finally caught up with Salina, who right now, is in a back and forth argument with one of her stylists that keeps complaining that supplies are never stocked, and there are never enough clean towels. The once elegant salon boutique with mirrors on every wall, brass statues, and purple carpet in the waiting area is now marred with deficiencies. The mirrors are always spotted with fingerprints, and the carpet hasn't been cleaned for eighteen months. Salina can't afford to pay the clean-up man, who is responsible for keeping the place clean, to come in every week, so she's assumes the duties herself.

Salina was never much of a professional or a people's person, but when things come easy for a person, it's a breeze to deal with people's complaints and to correct your own iniquities. The problem for Salina is, now that things have gone south because she doesn't have the support of Benji, she can't maintain the home front, and there's no way she is able to adequately satisfy the needs of the salon. She's in a real bad shape.

Salina's chair sits behind the cash register, and the woman she's arguing with is closest to the front on the opposite side of the room. Her name is Keisha, a short woman who also sports a Tyra Banks forehead and a wide body physique. Her hair is in crimps, and her juice cooler lips have been rolled with glossy red latex paint. Her fat cheeks don't move much while she talks, but her lips flap continuously even when she's not saying a word. Between huffing and puffing and disrespectfully smacking them at the end of each one of Salina's sentences, Keisha's mouth never stops moving.

"If you don't like it, you can take your fat ass to another salon." Salina has just gotten personal with Keisha and has probably opened up a can of whoop-ass.

Oh no she didn't go there. I ought to whip this bitch's ass on my way out the door, Keisha thinks to herself before firing back. "I got your *fat ass,* bitch! . . . Yeah . . . Slut! What! . . . What!"

Keisha has put down the hot curlers that she was holding and is standing in the middle of the isle, wearing her black apron, gray sweatpants, and white Reebok Classic tennis shoes. Her hands are held out at her sides with her palms facing Salina, and her fingers are inviting Salina to come to her to get some of whatever she has in store for her. Salina's more mouth than anything, and fight is not in her vocabulary, so why she called this weight-conscious woman a *fat ass* is beyond her, knowing the drama it would bring.

"Look," Salina begins, thinking of what she should say next, "I didn't mean to call you out your name. I apologize, but you need to . . ."

"I need to do nothing but come over there and show you that I ain't the one. Yeah, slut, come on. You got all that mouth . . . What you gonna do?" Keisha isn't interested in her apologies, nor is she trying to let Salina off the hook so easily.

All the other women and Buster, the faggy, stop and stare at Salina, anxious to see if Miss High and Mighty is going to back up her Queen "B" ego. There are only four other stylists because the other two had gotten fed up with the way Salina has been running the shop and have packed up and left. There are also seven customers and a hair-wash girl, all stunned at the outburst between the two ladies and are hoping to see a fight. Salina knows that everybody hopes that she tries to fight Keisha, so they can watch Keisha beat the crap out of her. She's no match for big Keisha, nor is she mad enough to try her hand. Salina's moment of truth is over before it began. She looks around, rolls her eyes at Keisha, and continues styling the head that she was working on before she made the remark that started such a fire.

Keisha now has her fist balled up, and she can see that Salina has just punked her way out of getting waxed.

She called me fat. Fat ass at that. Naw, she ain't skatin' like that.

Keisha mosies over to Salina like nothing is wrong, but Salina is watching close and pauses waiting to see what Keisha is about to do. The lady in the chair in front of Salina is an older woman, and she is looking right in Keisha's face and can sense that she is about to lash out. Everyone in the whole salon is motionless. They're barely breathing and as bad as they want to see Salina get her butt whipped, no one wants to see Keisha be a bully and pick a fight with someone who obviously doesn't want to fight. Especially not over the top of a very respectable client.

"Keisha, I said I was sor . . ."

Prrtch! Keisha's hamburger-helper-size fist pummels Salina across her temple.

"No!" screams Buster who jumps from his station like a gay gazelle and grabs Keisha while she beats Salina down to the floor. Punch after blistering punch sends Salina sliding down the counter next to her station. She never had a chance to fight back after the first crushing blow, but that didn't stop Keisha, who seems possessed by an evil spirit filled with pure hate and rage.

"You . . . wanna . . . call somebody . . . fat . . . do you?" Keisha grunts with alternating words between hacking blows to the already unconscious Salina, who is bleeding profusely from her mouth and nose. She also has lumps on her forehead and eyes, and Buster can't stop Keisha from committing overkill.

"My god!" screams the older woman in Salina's chair. "The poor child is dead, for crying out loud. Why is she still beating on her like that?"

The word *dead* strikes a nerve in Keisha that flips her anger to fear. *Dead* means a long time in jail, and Keisha has too many children to be doing twenty years in prison, so she stops all movements for a moment to see if she can tell whether or not Salina is breathing. She is.

Thank the Lord, Keisha thinks before taking a sigh of relief. Buster, clumped over Keisha's back, may as well had stayed where he was before the fight broke out because the only thing he did was add weight to the heap of flesh and bone already taking its toll on Salina's petite body.

Keisha shoves Buster for him to get off her back. She's no longer scared; instead, she is full of vindication. She's wanted to do that for a very long time but never had much of a reason. She's got all the reason in the world today, and she took full opportunity to relieve her stress. Now, her work is done.

"Makayla, finish her head for me. I've gotta go," Keisha tells a tall, lanky stylist who works opposite of her at the front of the salon to finish what she had started on her client's head. She's about to leave 2 Exquisite for good.

"OK," responds Makayla.

Not another word is said while Keisha gathers her things before Salina comes to consciousness. Keisha walks out the door carrying a large white trash bag and a Samsonite carrying case filled with the tools of her trade. Buster and the woman whom Salina was styling shake Salina for her to wake up. She got knocked the f;@!k out, and when she finally comes to life, she is totally embarrassed and extremely angry with everyone because they're just standing around, looking at her, yet no one helped her while she was getting all the crap beat out of her, at least, not as far as she knows.

"What y'all staring at?" she slurs through her bubbled lip as she stands up to her feet to look at her lip and eye, which is also swollen. "Y'all, just sittin' arou . . ." Salina sees her face. Her mouth sags, and she reaches for her face in slow motion but doesn't touch it. She appears to have just gone seven rounds with Iron Mike Tyson from 1988. "My . . . face," she murmurs. "Y'all let her beat on me like *this*?"

"We tried to stop her, but she was like a crazy person high on some love boat," Buster tells her in his feminine tone. "Her big ass was strong like Hercules or somebody. Shoot. My little ass ain't equipped to be wrestling with a she-rock."

Salina can't believe her eyes. Her blood has stopped pouring, but what's to stop her heart from bleeding? Things aren't going well for her at all. She hasn't been able to pay all her bills on time, supplies are never stocked, the children are doing bad in school, her body's attractive features are sagging from excessive loss of weight, and her stylists are leaving one by one. Now she's down to three, and they'll be leaving her soon if things continue on their current course. Not to mention she's lost her most prized possession to another woman and then to the crypt keeper. The only good thing that she's had going for herself is her pretty face, and now that's in ruin and a source of ridicule and disgust.

Salina burst into tears and puts her face down in a towel that she had grabbed to wipe away the blood. The sorrow is too much for her to bear. She wishes Keisha would have just killed her and put her out of her misery. Life since Benji left her has become a bungee jump into a bottomless pit; Salina wonders if the cord will ever catch.

The woman in her chair stands up and puts her hands on Salina's shoulders, consoling her. "Honey, everything's gonna be alright. Just pray. I know you're going through a lot, but you need to sit back and evaluate things. There's a reason why you're going through so much. Why don't you figure it out and do something about it? Whatever it is, honey, which has you in such a fickle, take care of it or leave it alone."

You know what, girl, Salina's voice says to her, *she's right. You know why you're going through so much. That whore took your man. Things ain't been right since. You know where she lives. Go kill her ass. Stop procrastinating. She's got everything I'm supposed to have. She's living swell while I'm suffering. Uh-uh.*

Salina raises her head, inhales deeply, and then lets the air slowly out of her nose. She turns around and walks over to her jacket hanging from a hook on the wall, reaches in the pocket, and grabs her cell phone. She calls her sister, Hifeeza, who answers after two rings.

"Feeza, ask Kevin if I can use his car. I'll let him drive the Lexus. I need to pick some things up, but I need a station wagon or a truck." She pauses. Then continues, "OK . . . When you talk to him, tell him to come to the salon and leave the keys in the glove compartment. The keys to the Lex will be under the car mat. Tell him to just take the car because I won't be in the salon when he comes."

Of course, she will be there; however, she doesn't want him to see her face. She pauses and waits for her sister to finish.

"Thanks, boo. I'll call you later."

Kevin has a Buick Roadmaster with tinted windows, so that would be the perfect car for Salina to hide in. She plans on going to Jessie's home and sitting in the back of the car until she sees Jessie, then she'll jump out of the car and shoot her with the handgun that Benji's kept in the house for protection. He's even taken her to the gun range several times, so she's no spring chicken when it comes to bussin' off a ghat. It isn't twenty minutes before Kevin pulls up in front of Salina's shop, itching to joyride in the Lexus. He can't wait to pull up around his buddies pushing a house. Salina sees him and runs to the bathroom.

"If he comes in, tell him I went somewhere with somebody and that I told him to just take the car."

He's already been told that Salina won't be in the shop, but he goes in anyway because he can't pass up the chance to be seen by the women in the shop. Makayla tells him what he already knows; he walks out of the salon, forgets to leave the key to his car, brings them back, then leaves out again to get into the Lexus, and is gone before the engine can warm up.

Meanwhile, Salina waits in the bathroom, peeking through a crack in the door. The light is off inside the bathroom and the scented aroma of Morning Fresh permeates the air. She can see nothing inside the windowless bathroom but can see straight to the front door, watching Kevin come and go and return again with the keys to his car. He gave them to Makayla and then skipped out the door to his prize in which he was happy to receive, even if it's only for one night. She waits a couple of minutes before she exits the bathroom to make certain that he doesn't double back. While she waits, she allows her mind to wander, but really it's Iblis putting evil thoughts in her head.

Jessie is going to die tonight. She won't see another day. I'ma kill Keisha too. Both of them whores gonna get it. I hope they don't think it's sweet, and they gonna to get away with what they did to me. Whore! You took my man. I know where you live, and I'ma make you wish you never met Benji. Think you gonna live off my money. That's my money. My house. My car. Everything you got is mine! You gonna die tonight.

One of Salina's cousins followed Jessie home from the repast gathering after the funeral, so she is well aware of how to get her hands on Jessie. She calmly walks out of the bathroom, walks to her station, grabs her jacket and phone, and without a word to anyone, not even her client, she walks out of the door and gets into the Roadmaster with nothing but malicious intents. She's off to her house to get the gun and then to go lay in wait for her victim. Tonight, it's Jessie and whoever might be with her—namely, Asa.

Chapter 48

Jessie sits on her Pacific Ocean-size bed, which is covered with clothes, hangers, and hat boxes from out of the closet which is empty with exception to an unused set of TaylorMade golf clubs that Benji bought for a measly one hundred dollars from a crackhead kleptomaniac, who can steal the Pirelli tires off your rims at a red light. Asa is leaning back, sunk into a pile of oversized goose-feather-filled pillows. He's as snug as a bug in a rug and has enough strength to lift his hand up to his mouth but not strong enough to lift his head, so there's no chance of him falling forward and rolling off the bed.

Surrounded by a plateau of stuff on all sides, Asa presides majestically as king of the bed, while his mother jibber jabbers with her own mother on the cordless phone. She has been receiving prank phone calls all day from a wireless phone according to the built-in caller ID on her phone, and they have been driving her crazy. She's called the number back, but the answering service keeps picking up. There is no one speaking a greeting, rather a rap song plays for so long that she hangs up before she gets a chance to leave a message. The phone has been beeping indicating that she has a caller trying to reach her on the other line, but she dares not answer it again just to hear the person on the other end inhale every three seconds.

She thinks, *if it's important, they'll call back. I ain't answering any calls unless I recognize the number.*

"Mama, I'm tired of being here. I can't wait until the apartment comes through. Being here makes me sick to my stomach, and I refuse to go back over Niecey's house. That's like living in the Amazon forest. Nothing but horny women having orgies with each other all day, every day. Then they don't have any respect. They make it a point to leave the door open so I can see, like it's gonna turn me on or something."

"Oh no, child. You don't need to be over there with all that mess," her mother warns, but how can she talk? She's married to her own cousin, who is Jessie's father, and he's having an affair with her mother's sister and has two other children by her, and Jessie's mother is still with him. Their family has practiced incest for nearly fifty years, but Jessie refuses to have any part of the heritage, and as a result, she's been disowned by most of the family. Her mother, however, secretly maintains a close but discreet relationship with her lovely daughter. "God don't like ugly. I'm just so sorry Paul won't soften his heart toward you. I would have you here with the baby in a flash."

"I know ma, but I definitely wouldn't want to come there. I think it would be *worse* around the rest of the family. You know how all the men were fighting over who was going to get me as their wife. Lester tried to rape me, so I'd never come back around that."

"Yes, baby. I understand," her mother says sadly. "Would you at least bring the baby to me for a weekend? I know I'm going to see him tomorrow when I come to help you pack, but I would like for him to grow up knowing who his grandmother is. He does have *two* you know."

"I know ma, but—"

"But what? Do you think that once every six months will be enough for the boy to get to know and love me?" her mother, Loretta argues. "I won't allow the boy to be influenced by the family and their ways."

"Ma. You have no control over that. You won't be there every second of the day. And the moment you turn your back, they'll say things *and* do things. I know. I went through it. There's absolutely nothing you can do."

Her mother sighs on the phone because she knows that Jessie is right. It has always been that way; the immorality is not going to change now, so she accepts the fact that she'll never have a close relationship with Jessica's only son. The revelation pierces her heart making it feel as though it is bleeding, but the stress wanes off after another heavy sigh.

"Well, Mama, I'm about to go. I'm hungry. I haven't eaten since noon and it's already nine. Me and Asa are going to the Double T Diner, so I can fill my belly on some stuffed flounder and greens."

"Child, it's late. You need to put that baby in the bed."

"Ma, it's Friday and he's been asleep all day. He's entitled to stay out late on Friday," Jessie jokes. "I'll make sure the car doesn't turn into a pumpkin. Ha-ha."

"OK. You be careful, and I'll see you tomorrow."

"See you tomorrow. Bye."

Jessie hangs up the phone and immediately starts preparing to leave, talking to Asa about the good food he's about to smell and the fact that she's taking him out on a date as if he can understand the adult conversation she's having with him. Little does she know that outside, parked across the street from her house, in a station wagon and hiding behind dark windows is her assassin. Salina's been there for sometime now.

It's dark on this quiet street with exception to the porch lights on Jessie's neighbors' houses that are widely spaced due to the enormous yards that everyone has. There is one street light two houses up from Jessie's house, but it sheds no light on her front yard and offers no measure of security against prowlers who might lurk in the shadows of the trees and bushes that drape the suburban street.

Salina, inside the car, is staring at Jessie's house ready to wait all night if she has to, but she knows that a woman with a young baby isn't going to leave the house once it gets too late. She looks at her watch and strains her eyes to see what time it is. It's nine seventeen, and she's been sitting in this very spot since six forty-two, and Jessie's Cadillac was sitting in the yard when she pulled up, and she's watched lights turn on and off in the house, but there's been little to no movement for the past hour. Salina's vengeful anger outweighs her patience, so she hasn't considered leaving until now.

She looks down at the handgun sitting in her lap and then leans her head back on the headrest for a moment. She looks at the house one last time before reaching for the ignition and starting the car. She puts her foot on the brake, but before she can put the car in drive, out of the corner of her eye she sees what looks like floodlights brighten the entire set of where she has planned to commit the perfect murder. She turns and sees a woman, whom she's sure is Jessie carrying her child toward the lack-luster Cadillac sitting in the yard.

Damn! She's right there. Just get out the car and shoot her! The little voice in Salina's head is urging her to stop hesitating, but another voice is making excuses for why she hasn't made a move yet. *Don't do it. It's too much light. Someone will see you. I know you ain't sit here all this time for nothing. Damn the light. Damn whoever sees you. Kill the bitch now. Ain't nobody around.*

Salina looks all around wanting to get out and run to Jessie and unload on her, but twice in one day, the punk in her is prevailing. Iblis is in her midst, and he's doing all that he can but take possession of her body to make her kill Jessie, knowing that there is nothing that the Omega or Apollyon can do to change her mind from wanting to see Jessie dead. The problem is Salina, and now that the opportunity presents itself, she's accepting every excuse that her cowardly mind is presenting as a reason not to go through with the hit.

She puts her hand on the handle to open the door as she watches Jessie at the front door locking the deadbolt lock. She's breathing hard. Her adrenaline has caused her to break out in a sweat, and she's fighting with her fear.

Ain't nothing to it but to do it. Why am I scared? I got the gun. She's walking to the car.

Salina has overcome her fear and is now ready to launch, and just when she is about to spring, Jessie looks over at the running car. Salina's courage nestles between the crack of her ass like the tail of a mutt about to fight a Rottweiler. She watches Jessie get into the car and back out of the driveway.

Whimp.

Salina waits until Jessie gets some ways up the long street before she pursues her. She turns her lights on as she passes the street light in the middle of the block. Disgusted with herself for not getting this over with when she had the chance, she strategizes that she'll catch Jessie when she gets out of the car once she gets to where she's going. Salina is still making excuses though. She really doesn't have the guts to walk up on somebody and pull the trigger. Shooting a target thirty yards away is one thing, but pumping lead into a real live human being while others are bound to be watching is quite another.

Salina smacks her lips. *I can't do this. But I gotta see her dead. She's not just going to get away with ruining my life.*

They've left the community where Jessie lives and have come to an intersection where Jessie turns right at the light. The Ford Bronco that Benji's been driving around is making a left turn at the light while she bends the corner. The Bronco hesitates in the middle of its turn and tries to make a U-turn but has to swerve to keep from hitting the Buick that barrels around the corner in a hasty rush.

Bommmp! The wagon sounds its horn as it swoops onto Volcan Mill Road. Inside the Bronco, Benji is livid, cursing and insulting the driver of the Roadmaster in the same manner that Salina is babbling about whoever is driving the truck. Meanwhile, Jessie is in her Cadillac at peace with Asa listening to the Quiet Storm on WHUR, not aware of the road rage unfolding behind her. She doesn't know that she's being stalked by a desperate, jealous lunatic who's out to make her fatherless child an orphan, nor does she have an inkling of a thought that for the last fifteen hours or so she hasn't been a widow and that her undead husband is right behind her too.

Jessie has made several turns on her way to Route 50 but hasn't noticed that she's being followed, and once on Route 50, the volume of the traffic has made it impossible for her to recognize that she is being trailed. Salina has positioned herself into the middle lane next to Jessie when suddenly before Benji's very eyes, the large station wagon rams into the car that his wife is driving. Not once but three times the two cars do the bump, and each time, the Cadillac comes closer and closer to being run off the road. Benji is in a state of shock and awe, unable to gather his composure enough to stomp on the gas pedal, knowing that he'd never get there to prevent the wagon from hitting Jessie's car one last time.

Sparks fly and the Cadillac careens off the roadway onto the shoulder where a cloud of dust consumes the air. The other cars began to break hard unable to see clearly. Benji can see the Cadillac in the midst of the cloud, and it appears to have driven off the road completely and hit the guardrail where it slopes from the ground, causing the car to upend on the driver side, nearly capsizing. The station wagon presses on, and as badly as Benji wants to chase that car down, he can't imagine not stopping to make sure his wife and baby are all right. However, he's unable to pull to the side before passing the place of the accident.

About four hundred feet up the road he is finally able to muscle his way to the shoulder where he puts the truck into reverse, but because other motorists who have also stopped to help are blocking the shoulder, Benji hops out the vehicle, and in a rampant stampede, he bolsters his way to Jessie's car, not hoping but praying that neither of them is hurt.

The people around the accident get a look at Benji's face and become terrified, running back to their cars as if they have just seen a grizzly bear. As Benji approaches the smoking car, his senses become keener, and the sounds around him intrude his thought process. The sound of passersby commenting on the accident, the sound of the baby's cry, the music from the car radios, the treads of tires rolling on the pavement, and engines are all starting to become increasingly louder and more nerve-racking to Benji. His sense of smell has also become noticeably more sensitive as well. Benji can even feel a strange sensation come over his entire body as if his muscles have just been rubbed down with Ben-Gay or even tea-tree oil. They're burning, but no pain is present.

Benji gets to the car, then climbs up onto the side of it and grabs the handle of the door, but the door doesn't budge because it has been bashed in from the impact of the larger car's weight as it smashed against the delicate sheet metal of Jessie's luxury sedan. Hearing the baby in the backseat cry with all its might, Benji, without any regard to himself being injured, punches the window of the driver's door and shatters the entire glass to bits, then grabs the door and with one mighty tug, rips the door from the car, and tosses it over his shoulder as if it were made of aluminum foil.

Inside the car, his beloved Jessie is vaguely conscious, but mindfully Benji gives her a shot to the chin to send her back to la-la land. Benji doesn't want her to gain her consciousness only to see his face and go into cardiac arrest as she did in his vision. As badly as he wants to hold her and to have her return the same affection, he knows that the outcome could be very unpleasant. Jessie undoubtedly wouldn't display tender loving care toward a walking corpse claiming to be her estranged husband, rather she'd more than likely become exasperated, so therefore Benji's knock-out tap on her chin should be really considered as an act of mercy rather than a love tap or an insane display of brutality.

After releasing her seatbelt, he looks to see the situation with the fiercely crying Asa. He's still in his car seat and appears not to be injured, but just in an uncomfortable position. So Benji yanks Jessie out of the car by her waist with the ease of King Kong carrying Jane, hops down, and places her several feet away from the car. He sneers at bystanders and rubberneckers as they cringe and move for cover.

He returns to the car and rescues his son, pulling him and the chair out of the car. He takes him to the sleeping Jessie and falls to his knees still holding Asa in the chair against his belly. Joy has his heart fluttering, and the desire to be with his family is penetrating his flesh from his head to his toes. His Jessie is so beautiful lying on the ground. Oh, how he wants to kiss her! Asa has stopped crying and is focused intently on the face of the stranger that is holding him. Benji turns to him and can see the likeness that he once shared with the boy before his facial structure became mangled and disfigured.

It won't be long before the sirens that Benji can hear in the distance will be upon him, and they will be asking questions, or worse, trying to arrest him. He can distinguish the difference between emergency vehicle's screeching sounds. The fire engines, being the loudest with the trumpeting blasts from their horns make them easy to recognize, but ambulances sound a lot like police cars, yet to the trained ear the two can be distinguished, and Benji can tell that the sirens headed his way is a squad car. He is having a hard time getting up and leaving his family behind, but he can now see the source of the shrilling sounds in his ears, and he sits Asa down beside his mother and pulls himself away from them with slow backward steps. As badly as he wants to stay, go to the hospital, and then home with his family, he knows he can't. A tear rolls down his face and pain wrenches his heart.

Bye Jessie. Bye Asa. He's holding his right hand up like a man being sworn into public office. *I love you.* He turns and leaves.

Chapter 49

The night is silenced by the suburban quaintness of this Valley Estate community clustered with ramblers and split-level houses assortedly decorated with painted bricks, siding, and stone. It's the wee hours of the morning and nothing is stirring about, not even a squirrel.

Benji is standing close to the garage door of a red rambler. The bricks of the house, however, are not painted; rather they're still the natural reddish brown that they were when the house was built. There is no car in the driveway, and from the looks of the spotless, white concrete under the moonlit sky, there has never been a car parked here. The occupants of this house most assuredly park their cars in the garage at night, whereupon in the day, if they do happen to park in the driveway, the car they drive must be a Norstar, because it obviously never leaks any fluids.

To Benji, the clean driveway comes as no surprise since his friend Richter, whose house this is, stays in the street all the time, and probably doesn't even take time to even clean his car in his own driveway. Benji isn't quite sure if Richter is home right now for he never sleeps and when he does, there's no telling where he ends up. Where he lies his head is his home; he's a rolling stone, but regardless to that fact, Benji's about to break and enter the garage door. He turns the handle until it pops and the door rises.

He knows Richter has a state-of-the-art alarm in his house considering all of the conspicuous ADT signs that are posted, but even if he had no signs, Benji has been here many times before with Richter, and there was never a time that Richter didn't enter the house and walk straight to the alarm's keypad control center. Also, Benji can recall his friend mentioning that he has motion sensors all over the house and that he can tell where an intruder is in the house just by looking at a motion indicator that is in his room. He realizes that he's sure to get his head blown off again, but he's the undead, so what peril could possibly put fear into his cold heart? This man is responsible for the rape of his wife and for his untimely death. There's nothing going to keep him from rioting on his enemies. His own personal Judas Iscariot.

As expected, the alarm system is not connected to the two-car garage door, but he can be sure that the door leading *into the house from out of the garage will trip the alarm and startle whoever is inside. Benji waste* no *time making his way around the dark-colored Corvette as he* hurries *to the access door of the house, but it's locked, so he tries to turn and break the lock as he did with the garage door, but that doesn't work. Picking the lock is not an option, so with a mighty kick, the door burst open and the alarm sounds immediately.*

Once inside the dark house, Benji walks toward the back rooms. The door to Richter's room is at the end of the hallway, and it's already open. Visibility is minimal, but Benji is certain that walking straight down the corridor would prove to be suicidal. Taking the necessary precautions, he ducks into the first open door in the hallway and stands completely still so that he can listen for any movement. Richter is here unless someone has picked him up because both of his cars are in the garage.

The irritating sound of the whining alarm is coupled with the ringing of the telephone. Evidently, the alarm company is checking to make sure it's not a false alarm before they dispatch the proper authorities.

Benji peeks out into the hallway just when the phone stops ringing. He can hear the sound of a voice coming from Richter's room but doesn't see anyone. He hones in on the voice and miraculously can make out the whisper of his friend's trembling voice and the voice of the person on the phone.

"Are you sure?"

"Hell yeah, I'm sure. I heard a crash. Sounded like my door was kicked in. Somebody's in here."

"OK, sir, remain calm. The police are . . ."

"Remain calm?" Richter interrupts. "I'ma show these niggas calm. It's about to be a bloodbath!"

Clunk. Benji hears the sound of the phone drop to the floor. He can also hear the sound of metal against metal. Certain to be the sound of a soldier preparing for war. Now he can see movement on the floor, and a red light flashes and then disappears. It was the light from Richter's laser beam built into his Smith & Wesson as he tested it to make sure that it is working properly. Benji doesn't know how well Richter can see down this dark hallway, but he's about to find out. He crosses from the room he's in to another room closer to where Richter is.

Pow. Pow. Pow.

"Come on, niggas. I got something for your ass," Richter shouts hysterically. "You goin' down big today, boy. Yeah! You goin' down today."

That answers his question about Richter's ability to see. Now he has to figure out how he's going to get to him before he is shot to death for a second time in his life. He gets down on the floor to his knees and pokes his head out to see if Richter responds with another hail of bullets. Nothing. Benji slowly ventures out into the hallway below the angle of Richter's visibility, so he thinks, but suddenly shots ring out again.

Pow. Pow. Pow.

Benji is shaken, so he stops, but little does he know, Richter is only shooting because he is looking at his motion indicator, which has detected movement in the hallway. He can see no one; but he is only reacting to his indicator.

Richter unleashes another two shots when Benji raises his head. Benji thinks back to what Richter had told him about his alarm system and understands why the shots are flying high above him even though he's a sitting duck in the middle of the hallway floor. Without any further ado, Benji, like a predatory feline, starts to crawl toward Richter who is now standing up reloading another clip into his gun.

Reaching the threshold of Richter's bedroom, Benji prepares to enter the room and bum-rush the armed and extremely dangerous adversary before him. Still out of visual contact, Benji pulls the ten-inch hunting knife out of its harness that is strapped to his belt.

Shrret.

Richter franticly jams the clip into the gun, snatches the hammer back, and starts bussing off like a blind maniac; Benji lunges for the gun, and just before the flaming cannon can find its proper aim, Benji is able to put "the big hand" on it and forces Richter to point it in another direction while still franticly pulling the trigger.

Click. Click.

The gun is empty, and Benji releases it. Richter, though he is in a defensive mood, can't put himself in motion to lash out at the beast that the minimal light coming through the window reveals. The sight of Benji's grotesque face is discernable and a state of shock consumes the entire nervous system of Richter's body.

Facing his suspected assassins' co-conspirator Benji says, "I thought you were my friend Quake." That's a name only Benji called Richter, which tells Richter who has a firm, powerful grip on him.

"Benji?" Richter tilts his head to the side as a befuddled pooch would toward his master if he were to quack like a duck. "You're . . ."

"Yeah. I'm back."

Benji thrust his left hand to Richter's neck, clutching it with enough might to nearly dispatch his head off his shoulders, and with even greater force, his opposite hand, wielding his father's knife, is hurling straight for the shirtless chest cavity of his most loyal comrade.

The knife enters into Richter's solar plexus and continues through his heart followed by the knife's handle and Benji's hand and wrist. It doesn't stop there either. Out his back goes the knife and Benji's hand along with Richter's spinal cord. Richter's eyes are open as wide as they possibly can manage as he slowly begins his descent from consciousness, but before he can fall limp he mutters, "It wasn't me, dog." Then he dies.

The sun peeks over the horizon, bringing sunlight to the ground, trees, and the few Saturday morning shoppers already on the road, headed to the grocery store or to work at one of the occasional places that opens early for business on the weekend. Benji doesn't have anywhere in particular to go and, at the moment, doesn't even know where he is or why it feels like his blood is starting to literally feel as if it's boiling.

He's somewhat asleep in the truck and sweat is dripping from his nose and racing down the side of his face. His eyeballs are rolling under his closed eyelid as he twitches from the aggravation that his sweating glands are causing him. He opens his eyes and then leans forward to look at the scenery around him. After concluding that he's still parked in the same place he parked in last night, the parking lot of the Run N Shoot in District Heights, Maryland, he asks himself, "Damn. Was I dreaming?"

He's not sure if what happened last night actually happened at all. It seemed surreal, enough so, that he recollects the smell of gunpowder and blood, but he doesn't remember leaving Richter's house, nor does he remember falling asleep, but he knows that this is the same place he parked last night.

"Why am I so hot?"

Benji almost wants to pinch himself to make sure he's really awake. He knows that something is very wrong with the way he feels, and the anxiety is getting worse and worse.

The dawn is already broken, but the sun is on the other side of the building; so it hasn't prevailed over the entire morning sky, but as soon as the first ray of light shines upon Benji, he immediately looks up at the sky, and the magnificence of the bolstering sunrise seemingly blinds him and cooks his body like it does in a vampire movie. Though it does him no real harm, and the excruciating pain only lasts for close to thirty seconds, it's the worst pain he's ever experienced.

The trauma is over shortly, and he is laid back in the reclined seat of the truck totally exhausted as if he's just come down after taking three ecstasy pills, snorted some coke, had sex all night, and came six times.

"What the hell was that?" Benji says out loud, trying to catch his breath.

There was no violent convulsion or anything like that, but the feeling that just went through his body was enough to make him wish he were still dead. Hoping that was the last time he'll ever go through such a tumultuous ordeal, he sits there, wondering what could have brought on such an attack and if it had anything to do with the sun. After all, it didn't happen until the sun rose and blinded him for a moment and made him feel like he was sitting in an oven.

Benji also calls to mind last night's episode. He feels as though he were actually dreaming, but to confirm the notion, he pulls the knife out to see if it shows any signs of bloodshed, and it doesn't. It's as clean as it was on the day it was bought.

Benji breathes a sigh of relief because after what Bink told him and hearing Richter tell him in the dream that, it wasn't him, he doesn't believe that his loyal friend had anything to do with his demise, but as sure as he pulled himself out of his grave, he's gonna dig one for Amp, Tony, and Bootemup.

Chapter 50

Jessie is back at home, lying in her bed. Loretta, her mother, is there by her side sitting next to her, Indian style, holding young Asa in her arms. She's a fair-skinned woman with long black hair just like Jessie. She's not as gorgeous as her daughter; nonetheless, she's an attractive middle-aged woman in her mid to late fifties. This is the first time she's seen her only daughter in a whole year, and holding Asa in her arms brings her such joy that only a first-time grandmother could explain. Loretta hasn't taken her eyes off Asa in the past fifteen minutes or so as she cradles and rocks him ever so gently. Asa is sound asleep as is his bruised and battered mother. Jessie, however, wakes up at the sound of the telephone.

Ring. Ring.

"Hello?"

It's Special Agent Lindsey Miles. Jessie had called him and left a message on his answering service, telling him that someone had made an obvious attempt on her life. Lindsey is anxious for leads to who could have killed her husband, in effect, foiling his long-standing investigation. He called her the second he heard her message.

"Oh, hi! I didn't expect you to call so soon. I was just sleeping." Jessie's mom sits motionless trying to get an idea of who it might be on the phone. She knows that Jessie's had called the police and that they should be calling soon.

"Yes . . . No . . . They tried to run me off the road . . . Route 50." Jessie answers his questions deliberately in a tattle-tale tone, much like children who tell their father how someone took advantage of them. Loretta is certain that it is the police on the phone.

"No, I only bumped my head, but I was out cold for a while. They say someone pulled me from the car . . . No . . . Oh, it's a wreck . . . I have no idea. I'll have to call the police station . . . Yes, I'd really appreciate it . . . OK . . . I'll be here recuperating . . . Thank you so much. Bye."

Jessie pushes the phone button on her cordless phone to hang it up and lays it down next to her pillow.

"Who was that?" asks her mom.

"That was the FBI detective that I told you about. He's investigating Benji's murder."

"FBI!" Jessie didn't actually tell her that she was calling an FBI agent. She said police, but FBI just slipped out of her mouth. "What on earth are they doing investigating his murder? Was Benji a drug dealer?"

"No, ma. Dag, you sure are nosy."

"Honey, nosy has nothing to do with it. I just know that the FBI don't have no business investigating no murder way out here in Annapolis unless that person killed was of great interest to them. That's all."

Jessie can't argue with that because she hadn't thought about it, but that couldn't be anything but the truth. How she hates it when her mother analyzes things like that and is able to read right through her lies! She used to be able to do that to Jessie when she was young, but now she wishes to leave well enough alone. But no, her mother has to ask a hundred and one questions along with it. That's what Jessie hates the most.

"Ma!" Jessie whines, hoping that her mother won't force her to be any ruder than she's already been.

"Well, what did he say?"

"He said that he was going to check on my car and see if he could get any information about the other car, and that he'd call me as soon as he found anything out."

"Well, bless his heart. So now all you have to do is get some rest. I'll take care of Asa. Are you hungry?"

"No ma," Jessie whispers, relieved that she didn't have to go through any more explanation. "I'm just sleepy. Answer the phone for me."

"OK, honey. Go to sleep. Get you some rest."

Jessie doesn't say anything else to her mother because she knows that one thing might lead to another. She just closes her eyes and falls back into a deep sleep. And while she's asleep, the phone rings several times, but the person on the line says nothing. It's Benji, and he wants only to hear Jessie's voice to know that she's alright, but she won't answer the phone, so Benji keeps trying only to continue to hear the voice of a person he's not sure of whom it might be. He's heard the voice before, but he can't place a face or name with. He wants to ask for Jessie or at least ask if she's OK, but his voice might scare the person on the line and make them never answer the phone again, so he just listens to the background sounds to see if he hears Jessie's voice speak or Asa cry . . . Nothing.

✧   ✧   ✧

Elsewhere, Miles and Faraday are seeking information from the local authorities concerning the incident that occurred last night on Route 50. They are told at the police station the same information that witnesses told the police—a station wagon rammed a Cadillac several times forcing it off the road. No one got a tag number, and no one could see who was driving the car. Also, a bestial man came from out of nowhere and ripped the door off the Cadillac and rescued the woman and the baby inside. He was driving a Ford Bronco with Maryland license plates ZZKV06. It turns out that the truck is stolen, so that is a dead end lead not worth pursuing according to Faraday. Wrong. If he does investigate how the car was stolen, he would get an idea of whom or what stole the truck!

Miles tells the lieutenant that he would like for him to have the door fingerprinted because he believes that whoever rescued Jessie may have gotten the tag number to the station wagon that ran her off the road, and it seems that it is the only lead that he can pursue to actually turn up a clue in his investigation. Lieutenant Buchannan assures him that this request would be taken care of immediately.

Miles and Faraday return to their office to wait for a call from the lieutenant while they finish up some work on other cases they've been working on.

"What do you make of it, Jeff? Who would be trying to kill Powell's wife? They robbed him, killed him, and raped his wife. Why not kill her *then*? Do you think she knows more than she's saying?"

Faraday ponders the question for a moment and then replies after taking a deep breath, "With these type of people, you never can say. She may know but is too scared for her life and the baby's life to come forward, but then again, she hasn't given any indication of withholding information. She *was* pretty vivid with what happened according to the initial reports. I personally don't think she knows a thing. I don't even think she knows how big a drug dealer she was involved with. I could be wrong, but that's what I think."

Miles nods several times in agreement and then says, "I don't know why the hell I asked you, anyway. I was hoping you'd say, 'Yeah, I think she knows. In fact, she set the whole thing up, let's tap her phones and watch to see if she starts spending time with the shmoe who knocked her up while her husband watched and now that she's got the big stash, she's holding it back from her sportcoat and feeling guilty, so now she's talking about coming clean and revealing to the police what really happened, and sportcoat is not havin' it.' But *nooo*." Miles continues, "She knows nothing, so basically, we're up the creek without a paddle with nothing to go on . . . Sheesh!"

Faraday peers into Miles' stony blue eyes, wondering if his partner has been drinking too much lately, and Miles is glaring at Faraday to see if he'll show any sign of positive discernment of his far-fetched speculation. Miles doesn't really believe that the thoughts he has just conveyed are true, but maybe if he can get an amen from his partner, he'll start to think so. Fat chance.

Slowly shaking his head with an expressionless look on his face, Faraday lovingly warns his good friend, "You know, you should see the shrink. She'll help you, pal. I don't think you should have ever cancelled the appointments you scheduled last year. I don't think you're gonna make it."

The response is a sobering blow to Miles' ego, and he wants to recant his own hypothesis, but he's said it with strong conviction, and his partner has succeeded in showing him how absurd he sounds.

Shrugging the ridiculous notion off, they both, in their usual manner, go about the process of making files, comparing notes, listening to phone taps, and planning follow-ups on leads. Hours pass by, and then the phone rings.

"Special Agent Miles."

He pushes a button on the phone console, then hangs the receiver up, and a voice from the intercom says, "Those results are back on the prints. You ready for this?"

They both pause looking at the phone. Miles says, "Let's have it."

The person on the phone exhales and blurts it out. "Benjamin Powell." An eerie chill rolls across the two detectives' necks. Faraday swallows. Miles smirks. He's a skeptic, so any ghostly thoughts he had quickly vanishes from his mind.

"Benjamin Powell," he blurts, "nothing else? Just him?"

"Well, there's a print from what is most likely Jessica Powell's but no other big hands or fingerprints on the door where it appears to have been snatched from the car."

"Well, that's impossible, he's dead as a doornail. I saw him with my own eyes. Brains and all."

Faraday leans forward at his desk. "Yeah, me too. It must be his print left behind from when he was alive. It *was* his car, too."

"Well, that's what we got. Nothing else. Just Powell. A dead man."

Miles is disgusted not wanting to accept that he's come to another dead end, literally. He has to call Ms. Powell, but what will she say? *Your dead husband saved you. Have you heard from him?*

Chapter 51

Campbell's Barbershop sits in the middle of an area that is filled with some of the most notorious people who have walked the face of the earth. Fifty-eighth Street and Dix Street NE isn't a drug strip, gambling spot, nor any type of haven for gangsters or snatch men, but it is the crossroads of killers, bosses, and extortionists. Amazingly, many of these criminal predators pit stop here at Campbell's Barbers shop along with ordinary pedestrians, working-class citizens, famous boxers, and local fiends without ever causing a ruckus. No, that seldom ever happens at Campbell's because of the respect everyone has for Mr. Campbell's business.

It's like any other barbershop on the inside. Chairs line a wall where waiting customers sit and talk about everything from women, to cars, to world news. Campbell's chair is the second barber's chair, and it is always occupied. This morning a well-known heavy weight boxer from Ray Leonard's gym named Moe Gray is sitting in the chair, and he is feeding the three barbers that are working information that will keep their adept gossiping skills sharpened. Sony, a longtime friend and barber of Mr. Campbell used to work in the corner where he'd cut hair and beat the brakes off somebody in a game of chess at the same time. His chair sits vacant now. No one has worked in his chair since he hit the high road, and Campbell doesn't seem anxious to fill it with another barber. Sony was a one of a kind. Nobody could replace him.

Chess players from all over the area would come just to try their hand with old Sony. Some of the regular customers would bring guys, who just came home from jail playing chess for years, to the barbershop and bet hundreds of dollars on their man. Others would side bet on Sony, and he'd never let his fans down. Sony would stand over his customers' head and cut away, casually glancing over at the board until his opponent made his move; then he would take a long pause, stare the board down, go back to finishing the line he had started, and once he'd finished, he'd step to the board, look it over for about five to ten seconds, and then make his move with an aggressive thud of the piece on the board. Then, he'd go back to cutting. Before long, his opponent would be scratching his head and taking a long time to move, but Sony wouldn't be looking at the board anymore. He'd already know his next move, and shortly after, the game would be over. Whenever Sony stopped looking at the board, it was pretty much over with.

Moe was quite fond of Sony, and he often reminisces over how Sony would beat those guys, cut hair, and talk trash all at the same time, but today Moe has something else on his mind. It's Benji. He wasn't close to Benji, but respected him and liked his style. Both of them are from Landover and shared many of the same acquaintances, so when Benji was killed, naturally Moe was emotionally affected by it.

"Yeah, them suckas did it. Cruddy jokers." Speaking of Fatts and his crew. It's a known fact that they've been robbing and killing dudes around town for a few years now. Moe knows them too but never had anything against them. They always gave him his props and never bothered any of his people until now, even though they're not at all responsible. But Moe doesn't know that.

"That's a shame," says Campbell. "Benji was a good young fella. He came through a few times. So you say ole' Luther grimy ass got to him, huh?"

"Yeah, but Richter is on a nut. He gonna kill all them niggas," Moe replies.

"Richter? Is that Benji's buddy?"

"You know Richter, Mr. Campbell. Everybody knows Richter. I know he's been through here."

"No . . . I don't think I know him."

"Well, yeah. That's Benji's main man, and he's looking for them cats. Him and my man Amp."

"Oh yeah?"

"If I see one of them bammas, I'ma knock 'em out my gotdamn self."

"Now, now Moe, you don't need to go getting yourself caught up in that mess."

"Man, shid. I'ma punish one of them niggas."

And Moe means it too. Moe is one of those boxers who is more of a street thug than he is an athlete and hasn't been bashful when it comes to bashing somebody's face in. Moe's not worried about the fact that these guys carry gun either. He's been shot numerous times and hasn't been tamed *yet*. So he feels that he's invincible and no man can stop him Besides that, he carries a .45 caliber of his own and doesn't have a phobia of shooting it.

Moe was once shot seven times in his upper body by a terrified young boy who he had slapped around, but that didn't stop Moe from grabbing hold of the kid and beating all the crap out of him. Another time Moe hit a dude on his chin and broke his neck, paralyzing him from the neck down. The man is still in a wheelchair to this day.

His worst injury though didn't come from a bullet wound, but from a knife. That knife put him in critical condition and almost brought it all to an end, but Moe is resilient; he recovered quickly and returned to the ring with the same tenacity he had before he was hospitalized.

"Hold your head down, Moe so I can finish tapering your neck." Campbell is one of the few people who can talk to Moe like he's a child and get away with it.

Moe drops his head as he continues to talk, "Luther comes here to get his hair cut sometimes, doesn't he?"

Mack, the barber next to Mr. Campbell's chair, who cuts Luther's hair from time to time, answers Moe, "Man, you never know what barbershop he's going to go to. He might come in here and get his hair cut one day and not come for a couple of months, and when he does come, it seems like he just got his hair cut, so I know he has another barber. Dudes like him don't ever make a habit of nothing but being cruddy."

Beside Mack's chair is a partition that creates a foyer on the other side for people walking into the front door. The door opens and sounds the bell that hangs from a nail at the top of the door. The mirrors on the opposite wall from the barber stations allow them to see who is entering through the door. It's Luther, and he's by himself. Mr. Campbell's heart drops, and he lowers the clippers in his hand to his side.

Gotdammit. This boy would come in here at the damnedest time. Damn it Moe, don't start no crap boy.

Luther walks into the main area of the shop and looks around the shop as he always does but now in particular because he's well aware of the fact that people are out to get him and the rest of his posse, so he's ever conscious of his surroundings and always ready. He's wearing a safari vest to conceal the Magnum he is carrying under his T-shirt. Moe is sizing him up and is certain that Luther is strapped but could care less. Moe's adrenaline has sped up and has him perspiring already.

Luther catches sight of Moe but at first thinks nothing of it. He's more preoccupied with the way everybody in the shop who knows him is looking stunned as if he's bleeding out of his eye sockets or something. It's as if they can't snap out of it, and then it dawns on him that he was apparently the topic of an unpleasant conversation that they were having before he walked in the barbershop. His eyes travel back toward Moe, whom he remembers is from the Landover area, which means he was probably a good friend of Benji. Now, Luther is on heightened alert and offended at how they're looking at him as if they've taken sides against him for doing something he really didn't do.

These faggots think I did it too. Man, I don't owe these niggas no explanation.

"What!" Luther is noticeably irritated and immediately jumps on the offensive. "Y'all dudes are like some henpecks sittin' around gossipin' about some stuff y'all don't even know about."

Mr. Campbell knows why Moe is asking if he's finished. It's because he's going to get out of the chair and carry out his plans of brutality on Luther. Luther knows Moe is a boxer, but what he doesn't know is Moe is ten times more aggressive than he is and crazy enough to attack a known killer with a gun with no regard to his own outcome.

"Naw, Moe, I got a little more . . ."

Moe leans forward in the chair and gets up before Mr. Campbell can finish. He's actually done all that he was going to do, but he was trying to keep Moe in the chair a little longer. Maybe Luther would leave. But now there's nothing he can do. Moe is already pulling the barber's cloak off. He tosses it in the barber's chair in a hasty rush so he can get close enough to Luther before anybody can do or say anything that will give Luther a heads up to what's about to happen to him.

Luther is still standing in the same place he was standing when he came around the corner from the front door, and with no warning, Moe delivers a crushing left hook that flings Luther into a tailspin down to the floor after banging his head on the arm of one of the chairs. Fortunately there was no one sitting there because it's still early, and all of the barbers aren't yet at work.

The punch caught Luther clean on his chin, and he never had a chance. He never even saw from what direction that Mack truck came from, but he knew he'd been hit, but now he is conscious of nothing at all. He is out cold, and Moe doesn't intend on leaving him there. He knows several people who are looking for Luther and his gang, so they can put them to sleep permanently. Moe is not in the killing business, so he pulls his cell phone out of his pocket and calls Amp. He and Amp have been friends for years and Amp has told him that they've been trying to find the dudes. Now, Moe is going to make sure that Luther gets what's coming to him.

"Moe, man, you can't let that boy lie in my floor like that. I've got customers comin' in here. Man, you've got to respect my business, man."

"You're right, Mr. Campbell. My bad." Moe hangs up the phone and steps toward Luther; then he bends over, effortlessly hauls him over his shoulder and carries Luther outside.

Once outside, Moe trots to the corner of the building and flops Luther down, carelessly banging his head on the ground. Luther makes a dreadful groan but is still out cold as Moe makes a phone call on his cell.

Amp answers the call on the other end of the phone in a playfully chipper tone. "Moe? What's up, nigga? Holla at chor boy."

Moe smiles, he's always loved Amp because of the honor and respect he always extended toward him. No matter how many fights Moe has lost, Amp still treats him like he's a champ, and that's the main reason he's put himself in the middle of a street war that most certainly will cost him his life if the other side gets wind of his antics.

"What's up, shorty?" Moe answers.

"Aw snap! Where you at, dog?"

"I'm up Campbell's."

"Yeah? Come around the way. I got some green. You training for a fight? Can you smoke?"

"Naw, shorty. Not right now. In fact, I got somebody up here you need to see . . . Why don't you come up here real quick? Bring your girlfriend."

Amp's stomach instantly turns upside down, and he starts pooting and passing gas. He knows what Moe means by bring his girlfriend, and he pats his hip to make certain his Nina is with him. She's there. Now he's wondering who Moe is talking about and how many people there are.

"Well, how does it look up there?"

"Oh, you cool. Everything is already taken care of, basically. You know how I do, shorty. One hitter quitter."

Amp realizes immediately, that whoever it is, Moe has already subdued and there's not going to be any type of threat when he arrives.

"All right, bet. We'll be there in ten minutes."

"A'ight, hurry up, shorty."

Moe looks around, sees a Benz truck parked at the curb and figures that Luther must be driving it. He decides that it would be best to put Luther in his own truck to keep from drawing unnecessary attention. He puts his phone away and digs into Luther's pocket on his vest. Finding a set of keys, he points the alarm remote at the truck and deactivates the alarm; then he picks Luther up again and whisks him into the backseat of the truck. He walks over to his own car and digs into his gym bag and returns to Luther's truck with a roll of hand tape and ties Luther's hands behind his back and then goes back into the barbershop to get his jacket.

"Moe," begins Mr. Campbell in a reserved, fatherly voice, "I hope you haven't gotten yourself into something that you can't get out of . . . Writing a check that your body can't cash."

"Naw," Moe replies. "As long as y'all don't say nothing, who can tell it? Dead men don't tell lies."

Everybody perceives that Moe has already killed Luther, and they look at him in disbelief, but no one says a word. Moe knows what they're thinking and doesn't intend on telling them anything to make them think differently. He likes the idea of being thought of as a killer. It's one thing to be known as a man who will knock a person out, but quite another to be known as a man who will kill, so Moe figures it's no robbery to be thought of as such.

He says his good-byes and leaves out of the barbershop. Shortly after, he sees Amp's Impala creeping down the street. He walks to the curb as Amp pulls up.

"What's the deal?" Amp asks.

"Park," Moe says calmly as he walks toward the Benz truck.

Amp parks and gets out the car while Moe motions for him to come to the passenger side of the vehicle that Luther is in. Inside the truck, Luther is vaguely conscious, bewildered, and disoriented and doesn't know where he is or how long he's been out. Realizing he's become a victim of his own brand of making acquaintances with people, he squeezes his eyes tightly together, then pops them back open, and shakes his head, trying to regain his coherency back to normal.

Damn! He wishes he'd never shaken his head so violently because the pain due to the headache spikes him like an Olympic volleyball champion.

Wincing in pain with his head resting on the backseat of his truck, he feels the door giving way to his foot and light floods the backseat of his truck turned into a personal holding cell. With his hands bound behind his back, he feels pessimistic about living to see tomorrow and wonders why he's still alive to this point.

Whoever it is that has opened the door isn't saying anything, and Luther knows better than to raise his head and try to see. In the business that he's been in for years, he knows that the fastest way to die is to keep looking at your predator. That's not to say that you won't die anyway, but if you do die, it's better to die quick not knowing that it's coming than to die slow and painfully. Besides that, he doesn't want to see the means of death. *If it's going down, let's get over with it.*

The feet of a couple of other people can be heard approaching the open door.

"What the f . . ." Amp is shocked to see a body laid across the back of the seat. He wonders if the person is dead. "Who is that!"

"Luther," Moe says with a grin.

Now Amp is really in disbelief. He looks up at Moe with his eyebrows raised high on his forehead and his jaw dropped to his chest; then he turns to Tony and Bootemup who can't see the body, but they did hear the name and are in somewhat of a frenzy themselves wondering what on earth is going on.

"He dead?"

"Naw, man. I'm letting y'all handle that. I know you said you was lookin' for them niggas, so when I saw him, I knocked his ass out."

Amp can't believe it. "Damn, Moe, you a beast. I mean you a beast, for real!"

That is all Moe was looking for. A little glory and appreciation. He already knows Amp will see him straight because Amp gives him money for nothing. All he has to do is ask, and Amp will pull out a wad and hand it off to Moe like it is nothing. Moe is sure to get a nice lump for this.

"Aye, Moe, you mean to tell me," Bootemup says "Luther allowed you to get close enough to him to knock him out without you getting shot?"

"Shorty, you don't know how vicious my left hook is," Moe laughs and says, "he ain't never see it comin'."

"Yeah?" Tony adds.

Moe, trumped up with pride and conceited arrogance, nods his head in answer to Tony, who is getting a kick out of seeing Luther packed in the backseat of his own truck. He thought he'd have to risk his life just to get in position to kill Luther in order to make it seem he had nothing to do with Benji's death, but now he's relieved to know that it's almost over now. They've got the most dangerous member of their rivals, and Amp is already thinking of a scheme to inflict upon the rest of Luther's counterparts in order to rid themselves completely of all their woes.

Luther is surprisingly unconcerned about what is about to happen to him. He's been on the other end of his current situation all too many times, and he's not about to let these chumps put fear in his heart as if they really have the upper hand. He'll simply cooperate with them until he sees a small window of opportunity. He's sure they'll slip somehow and when they do, he'll be waiting.

Chapter 52

Fatts is becoming irritated because it's been two whole hours since Luther was supposed to be here at his house to meet up with him and the rest of the crew, but he hasn't even so much as made an attempt to inform them that he'll be there late. Fatts hates to be waiting around doing nothing, and if the agenda weren't so urgent, he would have been gone a long time ago.

"Man, this is getting ridiculous." Fatts blurts out. "This nigga supposed to have been here a long time ago. What the hell?"

"Yeah, but this ain't like Luther. He knows we're waiting for him. What's really goin' on?" says Daryl.

Lil Papi is sitting in the recliner not saying a word. He's just gazing into the wall-size TV screen, glued to the reverberating movement of Beyonce's butt cheeks. He always goes into a zone whenever Beyonce's videos come on. He's in love with her like most men who watch music videos on BET. At the moment, he could care less about what's going on with Luther or anybody else.

The only other person that's missing besides Luther is Blue, but no one expects him to show up. They have barely seen him since their last robbery, and he doesn't care much to get involved in any further street activities. He's taken his share of their licks and has bought two vans for his carpet cleaning business and is doing extremely well. He's a family man anyway, and the streets would be in the way of everything he has going on in his life. Nobody really wants Blue to come even though they could use the extra gun.

Today is not a day in which they plan on snatching some unsuspecting drug dealer off the street and pilfering him of all his cash. Nor are they preparing bundles of money to package up and give to their coke connect for the next shipment of drugs. They're on a mission to seek and destroy any and everybody remotely connected to Benji and Richter. Luther's people have informed him of all of their hangouts and even where some of them live, so today is a day that they plan on paying some people a visit. They're sick of hearing people saying that Richter and some Maryland bammas are trying hard to get at them, proving it by nearly getting to Lil Papi at the sphinx last week.

"Call him again, Fatts," Daryl says anxiously, "I'm saying . . . you think something is wrong. This ain't like Lu."

Fatts realizes that Daryl has a good point, and his own stubborn attitude has distorted his thinking until now. He's never known Luther to be so irresponsible when it came to a rendezvous or anything else for that matter, so it's highly likely that something *is* wrong.

Damn Luther. What's going on? Where you at? I hope you ain't let nothing happen to yourself. Answer the phone. Answer the phone. Fatts bites his bottom lip as he waits for an answer.

The phone is ringing, but after five rings the answering service comes on as it has for the past eight to ten times that they've tried to call him. Fatts hangs up the phone, puts it down on the coffee table, then stands up and walks over to the stairwell leading up out of the basement. He scampers upstairs, and Daryl drops his forehead down to his fists as he looks down at the floor between his feet, barley able to see the texture of the carpet in this dimly lit room. He raises his head and looks over at Lil Papi who is still watching the television as if nothing on earth is a matter except the rumps that are shaking in front of him. Daryl's attention is directed to Fatts' vibrating phone on the coffee table. A sound of thunder rolls down the steps followed by Fatts, who heard his phone vibration from way upstairs. He picks up the phone, looks at the screen, and then there is frown on his face.

"Come on, man, you jivin'," Fatts hollers into the phone at Luther, who, on the other end of the phone, is still tied up sitting in the back of his truck with a gun to his neck. "You got us sittin' 'round waitin' on you, and you ain't even answering your phone."

"What's up, chief."

Suddenly, a gut wrenching feeling pierces through the abdominal area of Fatts' body. His scrotum sack shrivels up tight as a prune, and for a moment he's at a loss for words. Luther has just calmly called him chief. Chief!

This is the day they've always expected would eventually come but never thought it really ever would—the day when somebody would turn the tables on them and would try to use one of them as a lure for the others. Chief is code word for; they got me hostage.

"Can they hear?" Fatts asks.

"Naw, I'm just chillin. Where you at?"

"A'ight . . . Feds or Bammas?"

"Yeah," Luther responds.

"Feds?"

"Naw, I need to get with you over shorty's house."

"Oh, all right." Now Fatts knows that he's not up against the police. It's some guys who have Luther hemmed up. More than likely, it's Richter and his little crew. "So what's up?"

"Look, I need you to go get Lil Papi and y'all meet me over Bunny's house. I need y'all to ride with me to handle something. I ain't gonna talk about it on the phone. Just meet me over here. I'ma be waiting for you."

Richter has told him what to say and to act as if it's something urgent and illegal, knowing that real niggas don't talk about things that could implicate them in a crime on the phone, especially not a cell phone. Little does he know, however, that the message has already been sent, and Fatts is well aware that somebody is setting a trap for him and Lil Papi. Daryl and Blue aren't at all a concern, after all, nobody really knows them, and so their reputations on the streets don't warrant great urgency. Neither Fatts nor Lil Papi on the other hand can be left alive to have a chance to retaliate.

Fatts' facial expression tells everybody in the room that things aren't going to be peaches and cream. He swallows and then looks around at everyone without a word. His stomach has an upside down feeling, and he has no idea what they're going to do. All he knows is what they *have* to do. Head over to Bunny's apartment located on a very busy street where there are sure to be witnesses to the murders Fatts hopes he and his men will be committing rather than being the victims of somebody else's crimes.

"So what'd he say?" Daryl doesn't like Fatts' silence. It's making him feel nervous.

"He said them niggas got him. He wants us to meet him over Bunny's house, so it's a trap. At least we know he's alive. They won't kill him until we get there because they probably know we're gonna call him again."

"So what you sayin'?" Papi interjects. "They tryin' to bait us in?" He laughs. "Man, let's go. I gotta go get my other baby for this one."

They all make a move for the stairs and stomp angrily upstairs and out the side door of the house.

"Wayne!" Fatts' mother calls from the other room, "Don't you slam that gotd . . ."

Slam!

"Damn you boy!!"

Chapter 53

There's a rubber tube running from the yellow double lines in the middle of the street across to a metal box atop the curb. The tube is filled with air, and it's counting the times that air is disturbed by the vehicles that run over the tube. Since 3:00 p.m., when the tube was filled with air by the compressor in the metal box, over ten thousand vehicles have passed over this survey spot, and it's only 4:35 p.m.

Luther has been forced to call Fatts' phone several times to see what's the holdup, and Fatts has told him each time that he hasn't been able to catch up with Lil Papi. When Luther told Richter the reason why they were taking so long, Richter emphasized that he should tell him time to make sure that Lil Papi was with him because he needed to talk to both of them. Fatts already knows that Papi is just as big a threat to Richter and his men as he is, so this excuse is perfect because it allows him to round up as many reliable soldiers as he can who would not only kill at will, but would also keep their mouth shut if something went wrong, should the police get involved.

The only person that he could find that would be willing to walk into an ambush to rescue Luther and that would fit the criterion was his old friend Gargamel, a tall lanky dude who's not your typical Billy Dee Williams, but he's not needed for his looks. Just his legs, finger, and gun.

Richter, Amp, Tony, Bootemup, and Benji's cousin Eric have been babysitting Luther inside of Bunny's apartment for hours, and now that it's getting late in the evening, Luther is afraid that Bunny will be coming home soon, and he would hate to drag her and her children into this mess, so he speaks up.

"Hey, look, man," he says nonchalantly, "I don't know what y'all plannin' on doin', but you need to get it over with before my folks come home with her kids."

There's a stony silence for a period while Richter digests the thought of having to kill everybody, kids included.

Naw, man, we ain't killin' no kids. Damn. What now? These niggas takin' all day. It would be perfect if they walked up in this joint right now.

The sound of keys is in the hallway, outside the front door. Everybody tenses up and stares at the door. The keys stop jingling and the sound of somebody opening the next-door neighbor's door brings an opportune time for everybody to exhale and for Richter to realize that now would be the best time to go.

"Come on, man, we just gonna have to catch 'em outside. We ain't killin' no kids," says Richter as he crumbles under the pressure of his conscience.

Bootemup is glad to hear that because ever since he saw the movie *Scarface*, he's had this thing about doing anything that would jeopardize the life of a child. He, like most guys in the Black and Latino community, is an Al Pacino disciple. Although Scarface isn't the greatest role that Al has played, it doesn't matter what role he's playing; his role as Face and the things he stood for has had a permeating impression on millions of young men around the world—if not around the world, at least in the hoods of America and Mexico.

Scarface refused to blow up a car that was occupied by his target and his children, so Bootemup has the same sentiments. Whether or not that's Richter's reasoning is not even clear to him, but whatever the case, they're all headed out the door, carefully concealing a dog leash that is attached to a belt loop at the back of Luther's blue jeans.

Outside, the relentless sound of passing cars rip past the apartments of Fairfax Gardens, each car making a *thump thump* sound as they speed over the rubber tube laid in the street. Amongst the cars traveling eastbound on Pennsylvania Avenue through the light at Southern Avenue into Maryland are Fatts, Lil Papi, Daryl, and G-mel. They are in an inconspicuous hoopty, and Lil Papi is driving. They've been riding around for the past forty minutes trying to see what they can see, with hopes of pinpointing where their adversaries might be poised in wait of the rest of Luther's crew.

They've avoided calling Luther because they don't feel ready to go up against an undetectable enemy. These guys could have snipers sitting in cars for all they know. They're courageous not crazy. As they approach the front of Bunny's building, the door opens and several men emerge. Lil Papi clenches the steering wheel with both hands and Fatts sits up in his seat on the passenger side.

"Look! Look! It's them," shouts Fatts.

Papi practically slams on the brake, and the car behind him nearly rear-ends them, while the driver lays on the horn. They all are startled as they look back at the swerving car blasting past them on the driver's side. Everybody is discombobulated, and no one knows what to do.

"What we gonna do?" asks G-mel.

"Come on, man, they lookin," Papi says.

There is tint on the window, so Richter and his men can't see how many people or what type of people are in the car. The street is quite a distance from the front of the building, plus there are cars parked parallel at the curb, but the horn attracts their attention, and since they're up to no good, the slightest ruckus is noticeable. They're not suspicious of the blue Oldsmobile with the tinted windows, but Richter, Amp, and Eric have their eyes glued, all the same, as it continues to the corner and turns right at Southern Avenue.

Luther is elated but confused. *Where the hell are they going? They should have jumped out.*

Just as he is finishing his thought, he sees Fatts, Daryl, and some dude he's never seen before coming back around the corner running at top speed. The guns they have in their hands are like black batons with firing pin and mix-match bullets in them.

Eric is the first to see them, and he's also the first to draw his gun. He reacts without saying a word.

Pow! Pow! Pow!

"Man, what the . . ." Amp says as he ducks and pulls out his gun all at the same time.

They all look to see who is shooting and who he's shooting at, but by that time a barrage of bullets rain back in their direction. They have no cover and are somewhat disoriented from the shock of a guerilla-style assault. They thought they were the ones that were going to launch a sneak attack, but quickly they find themselves at the brunt of their marks counter initiative.

If it were not for Luther walking in the midst of them coupled with Eric's alert response to the silent raid, they all would be dead, but now they are shooting back. They're not aiming yet, but at least, their gunfire has succeeded in halting the rush.

Luther is lying on his stomach, looking for an opportunity to mug one of his captors for their gun. He's afraid to try to run because that might remind someone that he's there, and that may result in many flesh wounds, but at the moment, no one is even thinking about Luther, so he stays put and watches as Daryl looks at his gun that has just run out of bullets; then he gets up from behind the tree that he was shielded behind and tries to run to the corner where they came from.

Pow! Pow! Pow! He doesn't make it.

Next to run out of bullets is Gargamel, but that's to be expected because he's an average street thug who has no need for extra clips for his gun, but Daryl, on the other hand, has extra clips for all his guns, so there's no excuse for not coming prepared. G-mel looks around and sees Daryl trying to get up off the ground before he flops down to his belly and sways his legs a couple of times, and then he doesn't move anymore.

Fatts slaps another clip in his gun and opens fire once again at Richter's small group of mercenaries whose guns never seem to run out of bullets. Fatts, realizing that he's the only one on his side of the volley that has ammo to shoot back, knows he has to take better aim. Instead of *pow pow pow* his gun now sounds like POW . . . POW. He knows he only has about nine more shots, and then he's through.

Where is Lil Papi? He should have parked the car by now. Run, Luther, get out of there. Why are you just lying there? Fatts is wondering.

Eric is about twenty yards away, and he is reloading his gun. He has no cover except the rounds that Richter and Amp are firing. They too are low onto bullets, but Tony has run to Amp's car to get the two guns they left under the passenger's seat. Bootemup is holding on to the leash that's connected to Luther's pants, and he hasn't shot a round since the shooting commenced because his gun was one of the ones left in the car.

Tony returns with the guns and tosses Bootemup his gun. He squats down to look for a target but the only person he sees in the distance is a fat man laid face down on the sidewalk near the corner, and he's not moving. No shots are being fired because no one wants to waste any bullets.

"Where they at?" Tony asks Amp.

"One of 'em behind the big tree, and the other one between the two cars down there. See him? By the green joint."

"Naw, I don't see him."

Tony then looks over at Luther.

"This nigga still alive?"

Luther looks over at Tony, who raises his gun to fire; then all of a sudden, what sounds like a 1920 Tommy gun explodes into a shooting frenzy, sending bullets whizzing through the air like shrapnel bursting from a pipe bomb.

"Uhhg!" Tony is splintered in his arm. His gun goes off shooting Luther in his lower rib area. Luther rolls in agony; Tony drops his gun and takes off running, as does everybody else on the receiving end of the new foray of burning missiles piercing through the air.

Lil Papi has a hundred-shot Calico in his hands, and after the first spray of bullets, he focused his attention on the most hittable target. Eric. He pummels Eric with enough lead to fill fifty number-two pencils, and he dies before he even hits the ground. He then turns his arm toward the fleeing squad of kidnappers. The man they used as bait, Luther, is bleeding out of his side. He'll survive if he makes it to the hospital in time, but as for Tony, he's been hit in a main artery in his forearm.

The bullet went straight through, so the blood is running from both sides of his arm. He doesn't realize the extent of his injury, so when he gets into the car he raps it up with a T-shirt.

"I got shot," Tony says as Amp pulls off.

"Where?" asks Bootemup. "You all right?"

"Yeah. I just got hit in the arm. It went all the way through. I'll be all right."

"You sure, man," Richter says. "Man, you might need to go to the hospital."

"Yeah, but if one of them niggas died, they gonna give me the beef. I ain't tryin to go to jail for murder. Aw shoot! Where's Eric?"

Everybody's eyes bulge as they look around. They have to drive past the scene and as they do, they can see Eric slumped over the very place he was shooting from.

"Damn," says Richter.

"Oh, he's dead," Bootemup responds to the motionless body in the middle of the courtyard.

"Man, this joint bleedin' like a mutha." Tony has panic in his voice but still doesn't want to go to the hospital, and he insists that Amp doesn't take him there. "I'll be all right."

"Go to my house," Richter says. "I don't live that far from a hospital. If we have to, we'll take him from there."

Tony takes a deep breath and tries to calm his nerves. He doesn't want to die, nor does he want to go to jail. There's a tug-of-war going on in his mind. Does he take the chance and hope he lives through this wound or does he go to the hospital, and then most assuredly go to jail? He decides that he'll ponder over his decision until he gets close to Richter's house. He figures, by then he'll be able to determine what he should do by how much blood he loses between now and then.

It takes about twenty minutes to get to Richter's house. Tony has been silently looking out the window the whole time. He's leaning against the door, holding his arm in what appears to be a comfortable position.

"You all right, Tony?" Amp asks, looking at him through the rearview mirror as he pulls into Richter's driveway.

Tony doesn't respond.

"Tony," Bootemup reaches for his leg to shake it. "Tony, you all right, man?" Urgency inflects in his voice.

Tony is dead, and everybody's head drops, but that's only their second concern. The first is *what are we gonna do with his body?*

Chapter 54

It's been more than five hours since Tony died in the backseat of Amp's Chevy Impala, and he's still sitting in the same place. The car is backed up into Richter's garage to conceal the dead body that's sitting in it because they don't have the nerve to dump it anywhere, and considering how forensics seems to be able to come up with these impossible clues that lead to the culprits responsible for all kinds of homicides since the O. J. Simpson case, they're afraid to even try. They're also trying to harden their hearts enough to dump a friend.

They're sitting between a rock and a hard place because if they report the death, then they'll surely be connected to the murders in town, but if they don't, they'll have to do something dastardly to get rid of the body, risking leaving behind evidence that links them to the crime. Either way they'll be charged with murder, unless of course, no one ever finds the body—unlikely.

Amp and Bootemup are getting pissy drunk at Richter's dining room table. Richter's been back in his bedroom since nine. It's a quarter past ten now, and they haven't heard a peep out of him since. They take it as he's asleep or on the phone talking to some chick.

"They kilt my man, man . . . hiccup," Bootemup slurs in disgust. He's just got up from the table and is standing, hunched over a bucket of chicken that they found in Richter's refrigerator. It's been in there for almost a week, but they were so drunk when they found it that they couldn't even tell that it's cold let alone old. They've drank a fifth of Remy, a fifth of Hennessey, and all the Michelob's they could find in the refrigerator. Neither one of them is a heavy drinker; so they're charting uncharted territory.

"Man, shhhit man," Bootemup slurs slowly, "gotdamnit, man. It wasn't supposed to go down like this, man. We had the upper . . . *hiccup* . . . man, hand . . . I mean . . . hand, man."

Amp isn't saying anything. He's just as hurt as Bootemup is, but he's afraid if he tries to talk, more than just words will come out of his mouth.

Please go back down. I feel like throwing up. Take a deep breath. Aw, man. Go, sit in front of the toilet.

Amp struggles to get up, and then he hobbles back to the bathroom. He doesn't turn on any lights, but the twilight coming through the small bathroom window is enough to illuminate the white porcelain bowl that Amp slumps over until the geyser blows.

"Hugh! Hugh! Oh god. Hugh!"

He continues to puke until nothing but white saliva and stomach enzymes spew out of his mouth. The little pieces of chicken skin that's mixed in with the mucus makes him think that he's throwing up stomach tissues.

"God, please don't let me die. I promise I ain't gonna never drink again. Please. Just let me survive this one. Ohh, my head," Amp agonizes. "I don't want to throw up no more . . . hugh."

Tears are dripping off his face into the toilet, and his last heave produced nothing but air. There is absolutely nothing left in his stomach to vomit. He sits hugging the toilet relieved that it's been five minutes and nothing has happened. He slowly stands to take a leak, and then pisses out a river.

Meanwhile, Benji has finally made his way down to his old friend Richter's house. He's been lurking around for fifteen minutes trying to find a way in without attracting any attention. He knows Richter's home because his Vette is sitting in the driveway. He never parks it there, so he assumes he's just here for a moment. Maybe just to pick something up.

At the moment he is standing outside a bedroom window. He sizes up the window before catching a glimpse of a hexagonal ADT sign posted in a small flowerbed to his left. Standing in the front yard, Benji looks very conspicuous, and it's apparent that he feels a bit apprehensive because he looks both ways to see if anybody is watching him before he reaches for the window.

The alarm system is probably off since he's home and more than likely about to leave soon.

Benji is right to think that the alarm system is off, but Richter has no intentions of leaving until well after midnight. He figures that would be the best time to try to dispose of a dead body.

Benji tries the window. To his surprise it slides upward. He pushes it until it goes up as far as possible. He's sure that the room is empty because he recalls that this is Richter's weight room. And if he was working out, the light would be on. From the outside, the only light that appears to be on in the house is the dining room light. There is a soft blue television glow coming from a window on the far side of the house where the master bedroom is located, so Benji figures that this room is the farthest room from any occupants in the house.

As he climbs through the window, he has to dodge a stack of barbells untidily placed under the window. Unable to clear all of them he steps on one.

Clink Clump.

He holds onto the window sill and listens for any movement outside the room. A toilet stool flushes just outside the room. Amp heard the noise, which snapped him out of the drunken nod that he fell into during the incessant leak he was taking.

Amp opens his eyes still holding his jimmy, with his head leaning slightly back, and his mouth gape wide open. He cuts his eyes toward the direction the sound came from. His head is throbbing, and he prepares to use everything he's got to turn his head in the direction his eyes are peering. Slowly he turns his head and looks at the door across the hallway. Watching the door, he jingles one time, then jingles twice, and then he tucks Roscoe away and wipes his urine-splattered fingers on his pants. Giving no thought to zipping, he erects his head and turns toward the door while reaching for his gun on his hip. He knows that it's empty or maybe he's forgotten; nevertheless, he clutches the handle tight and cocks the hammer back slowly.

Amp steps softly, listening closely for another sound to come out of the room across the hall. He is unequivocally certain that the sound he heard didn't come from the back where Richter is, nor did it come from the front where Bootemup is, and he also knows that there shouldn't be anyone else in the house, so he approaches the door in the semidark hallway with caution. He slowly grabs hold of the doorknob, turning it without pushing the door open. Once it stops turning, he carefully opens it, then listens.

He's on edge and supremely alert. His high is blown, and the headache that was pounding on his temples a minute ago has vanished. It's amazing how fear makes a person forget about pain, and how slow he runs, his girl, and even whether or not he has bullets in his gun.

He peeks through the crack in the door, but he can't see much because there's a short wall to the right of the door, obstructing his view. He inches the door wider until he's able to point his gun barrel through the crack. Amp proceeds behind his gun into the room. There's a light switch on the wall to his right. Now he can see most of the room. The window on the opposite wall is wide open, but there's no sign of anyone in the room. He hits the light switch, and a small lamp sitting on the dresser drawer illuminates the room. There's a weight bench, a rack with several free weights beside it up against the wall, a gym bag sitting in the middle of the floor, with the handle of a tennis racket sticking out of it, and a bunch of barbells strewn across a small area of the floor under the window.

The only part of the room that Amp can't see is to his right beyond the wall that houses a small closet that takes up part of the area in the room. Amp is still looking out the window when he steps past the end of the wall. He tries not to look like he notices, but in his peripheral he can see what is most certainly the stature of a man. He instantly begins to hear the sound of his blood thrusting through the veins in his head, and his breathing gets heavy.

Amp whips the gun in the direction of the man standing in the corner. He sees the patch. All of the sudden, nothing seems real. His mind flashes. He sees an open coffin, then the look on Jessie's face when he slapped her and told her to "shut up." Then he sees the hole his gun left in Benji's eye socket when he shot him in the face.

The vision of that face morphs into the face he's looking at now although the resemblance is discrepant, there's no doubt in Amp's mind that the person he's looking at is the same person that he shot.

"B-B-B," he can't get his words together. "B-Benji? . . . You supposed to . . ."

"Yeah. Dead. Thought so too. But I came back to rip your heart out."

Benji's own mind flashes back to the infamous day he died. All he can see is his wife's legs slung apart while those three masked men's hind pots pounded back and forth between them. He recalls her faint wailing and whimpering as they ravaged and pummeled her one behind the other. Benji's anger ignited inside of him, and he becomes infused with energy and vigor.

He takes a step toward the trembling Amp. Amp pulls the trigger and the gun clicks. He wants to run, but he panics. He can't move, holler, or scream. Benji reaches for his gun and grabs hold of Amp's wrist. Amp becomes hysterical and hollers as loud as he can. He tries to ward off Benji with his left hand, but Benji grabs hold of his other wrist and pushes Amp back up against the dresser. Then he raises his foot up to Amp's chest and pushes his body back with his foot and pulls his arms with a mighty heave, ripping both arms of Amp along with his sleeves away from his torso. Blood gushes from both his shoulders like a fountain, and Amp makes a gurgling sound.

Benji takes Amp's right arm, which didn't lose its grip on the gun and begins to beat Amp in his head with it. Each time Benji hit him with his own arm, the gun gashed his skull and face.

"Kill yourself! Kill yourself," Benji bellows.

After five mind-blowing cracks across the cranium, Amp's body lies lifeless. Ironically, his blood is, literally, in his own hands.

Benji stands over Amp, then drops the arm, then looks to his left, and Bootemup is standing in the doorway in a state of shock. Benji goes after him. Bootemup doesn't hesitate. He runs directly for his gun he left lying on the dining room table. It's full of bullets because he never got a chance to fire it before Lil Papi sent them running for cover back at Fairfax Gardens.

Like a Rottweiler chasing a cat, Bootemup can feel Benji hot on his trail. He dives for the gun and crashes into the wall. He fumbles, trying franticly to get the gun situated properly for shooting but not before Benji pounces on him, knocking the gun clean into the kitchen and pins him to the floor by his neck.

Benji snatches his father's Rambo knife out of its holster and raises it high above his head.

Kabloom!

Benji's body is knocked into the wall, and he can feel a burning sensation under his arm and in his shoulder. He knows he's just been shot. Again. And he knows another shot is soon to follow. There's only one thing he can think to say to buy himself some more time. He doesn't want to die again without, at least, getting a glimpse of Jessie.

"Quake, it's me. Benji."

Richter has a clear shot at the monster on the floor and his finger is already applying pressure to the trigger. But the sound of the name sends shockwaves through his body. Nobody calls him Quake. Nobody even knows that he would respond to that name except for Benji. It was a name that Benji affectionately called him when no one else was around. Richter loved that name and wished it was the name everybody knew him by, but since it was a special name that Benji gave him, he never presented it to anyone else.

Man, what the . . . Richter, wake up. You gotta be kiddin' me. He sniffs. Naw, you ain't trippin.'

"Benji?"

"Yeah man, it's me, dog. They did this to me . . . Amp and 'em. They kilt me and raped my wife right in front of me. They did it. What's up, man? Was you in on it?"

Richter doesn't respond because he still can't believe what he's seeing and hearing. He doesn't feel he has to explain anything to a zombie. In fact, it angers him to think that all his problems stem from him taking revenge for his friend's death, and then to be accused of having something to do with it really burns him up. But then again, to find out that the very dudes who actually did the murder had led him astray enrages him even more.

Man, this nigga think you had something to do with it. I gotta kill 'em. How you gonna kill somebody that's already dead. Where you gon put all these dead bodies? Them niggas did it all the time. Them little cruddy jokers. That's who you need to kill. Sh . . . Just kill everybody.

Richter looks at the two men on the floor.

"Don't listen to him, Richter. Kill him, man. Kill him," Bootemup shouts.

Richter raises his shotgun.

Chapter 55

"I don't believe a word of it. It doesn't make any sense. Not only does it not make any sense, but this is also ludicrous. I don't even know why I'm sitting here listening to this cockamamie. You just hold him right there, and we'll be right over to question him ourselves," Lindsey Miles yells into the phone.

He hangs up the phone and then flops back in his office chair slapping his hand on his blood red forehead with his eyes closed. Faraday sits across from him flustered by his partner's own agitated demeanor.

Miles drags his hand back through his hair. He opens his eyes and peers over into Faraday's eyes. Faraday doesn't want to know. The last time Miles looked so distraught after getting a phone call was when they received a call notifying them that the key figure in their bread and butter case was shot to death. Faraday can't even start to imagine what could top Benji's murder. That was the lowest point in their careers since they became partners.

There is nothing said while the two FBI agents stare blankly at each other. Actually, although their eyes are set on the others, neither can see the other. The both of them are daydreaming until Miles snaps out of it.

"Just when you thought you heard it all."

Faraday refocuses his vision on his partner but remains silent.

"Do you believe in ghost?"

✧　✧　✧

Richter sits in a 4 × 6 room with a table and two chairs in it. He's been in this room for more than nine hours. It's almost 10:30 a.m., and he's been questioned relentlessly about all the dead bodies in his house and the two bodies found on Pennsylvania Avenue in Southeast Washington. He hasn't mentioned anything about the gunfight at Pennsylvania Avenue and has maintained that he's been home alone since 3:00 p.m. yesterday up until 9:00 p.m.

As regards to the dead bodies at his house, he's blamed everything on Benji. He figured that he may as well because it's not like they can do anything worse to Benji that hasn't already happened to him. Naturally, no one believes him, but he's sticking to his story repeating it verbatim to every detective that tries to come in and catch him in a lie. He's repeated his story so flawlessly, that they are starting to think he really believes he's telling the truth.

Benji was such a large dealer in the area for so long that all of the PG County detectives are at least familiar with his name, and they know for a fact that he was murdered in Annapolis, Maryland, so no matter how convincing Richter may sound at times, they all refuse to consider any notion that he may be telling the truth.

Richter is asleep in the chair he's sitting in when the door to the room is opened. He wakes up, but he doesn't open his eyes. He's sick and tired of being questioned and refuses to answer another question. He knows his story so well that he'll remember every detail months from now, but for now he's through. He doesn't care what they do with him at this point. He just wants to get to bed.

"Vincent Taylor?" Faraday says, not asking a question; just pitching his voice as if he is about to ask one.

Richter doesn't respond.

Miles and Faraday exchange looks. They both know he's not asleep and that he heard his name called.

"OK, Richter," Miles continues, "we'll just tell your friend Benji that not only are you blaming his ghost for what you did, but that you've gone crazy and to top it off, deaf."

Richter is stunned by the sound of his nickname being called out in a Maryland police precinct. He seldom ever does any criminal activities on this side of the district line; therefore he's virtually unknown to police in Maryland. He's been questioned by more than ten different detectives and unidentified by twice as much, so Richter is anxious to see what homicide detective they've summoned for across the line to try to get him to break.

Richter begrudgingly opens his eyes. His head still hanging forward, he looks at the shoes of the two officers on the opposite side of the table.

He raises his head like Lurch of the *Addams Family* and has no idea who these two white men are, so he wonders again how they know his name and how long will it be before he gets to see a bed.

"Look, man," says Miles, "I've already heard your story, and you sound pretty sure of what you're saying. I know you're lying, but even if you weren't, no jury would ever believe it, so these are your options."

"Suck a fat one," blurts Richter.

Miles pauses, clears his throat and then continues, "As I was saying, you can either go to jail for life, go to jail for forty years, or you can try to plead insanity, but I don't think that'll work in your case seein' as how you're black. To tell you the truth I could care less what you do. I'm sick of this crap."

Miles turns and walks out, leaving Faraday alone with Richter. They look at each other. Faraday shrugs his shoulders and then takes a seat. He doesn't try to pry any information out of Richter because it's perfectly clear from the hours of recorded interrogation of Richter that he and his partner have listened to, that Richter has an ironclad story and is sticking to it.

"OK, you say the two dead guys in your house showed up around 6:00 p.m., and they asked you to park the car in your garage?"

Richter nods.

"You let 'em, but because of the tint on the window, you were totally unaware that there was a dead man in the backseat. Is that correct?"

Richter nods.

"Then you go back to your room because you weren't feeling well and the next thing you hear is somebody screaming and hollering in the next room."

Richter doesn't respond. His mind revisits the sound of the vicious thrashing and the hysterical yowling he heard after Amp's arms were ripped from their sockets. When he came out of his room, he nearly vomited at the sight of his armless underling gushing out pools of blood on both sides of his body.

Down the hall he could also see Bootemup being pounced upon by some dude that had no business in his house, and if that was the person who did what he saw done to Amp, there was no need in grabbing a handgun. Richter scurried to his bedroom closet and grabbed his shotgun that he had only used for skeet shooting. He immediately cocked it to make sure it was loaded and then stormed down the hallway toward the two scuffling men by the dining room table.

When he saw the man on top of Bootemup raise a very large knife above his friend, he took aim and shot him in his shoulder, knocking him against the wall, and splattering brown gunk on the wall.

Quake . . . Quake . . . Quake . . . Benji's groggy voice echoes in Richter's head when the sound of a white man's voice breaks the trance.

"Mr. Taylor. Are you still with me?" says Faraday. "I'm just trying to make some sense of it all. If you ask me, I believe you saw what you saw, but as far as the man being Benjamin Powell, well, I don't know."

"Man, look! It was him. I know my friend." Richter suddenly turns hostile, and if he were not cuffed to the chair he would have stood up and pounded his fist on the table. "I'm not lunchin'. I know what I saw. It was a man, but . . ." He pauses and becomes averted by his thoughts. "His skin . . . it was . . . like cowhide. He spoke to me." This is the first time he's given such details about his encounter with Benji. The detectives outside the room all stop what they are doing and listen intently to Richter. This is the first time he's said anything outside of his "story."

Richter gazes to his side, recalling what Benji said to him, ever conscious that what he's about to say must collaborate with his story. He knows he's venturing out of its framework, but it's killing him to keep it inside. "He said they killed him."

"They who? Who killed who?" Faraday slips in.

Still speaking as if he's in a daze, Richter continues, "Amp and Tony . . . and Bootemup. He said they killed him . . . and raped his wife."

"So that's why he killed them? It's likely he killed Tony before they got to your house then."

"Naw . . . well. I don't know. Maybe, but he definitely killed Amp and Bootemup."

Faraday recognized Richter's slip up and is now convinced that he knows what really happened to Tony, but he doesn't address it now because he doesn't want Richter to clam up.

"So why do you think he didn't kill you?"

Richter takes a deep breath and thinks before he speaks. He doesn't want to speak on impulse again.

"He said that he thought I might have had something to do with his death, but somebody led him to believe that I didn't. I guess after he looked in my eyes he really believed it."

"You mean someone else has seen him? Who?"

Faraday leans forward. Richter knows, but he's not about to bring Bink into this investigation.

"I don't know. He didn't tell me."

"Who might he have talked to?"

"I don't know, man. I don't know."

Faraday runs his fingers through his hair in frustration. He actually is starting to think Richter is telling the truth. He doesn't want to believe it, but Richter's eyes are highly convincing.

"I shot him."

Faraday's face turns to stone. Richter has just confessed to killing Bootemup. This is disappointing to Faraday because Richter really had him believing his story.

You lying little shit. Faraday thinks.

"Well, why didn't you just say that hours ago? Why'd you have to come up with this elaborate lie? You know, you're going to rot in jail. So how'd you cut his arms off?"

It isn't until Faraday mentions the arms that Richter realizes why he flicked off in such a way.

"I'm not talking about Bootemup. I'm talkin' 'bout Benji. I shot *Benji.*"

"Oh . . . well, I apologize. Please do forgive me for that outburst."

Miles and the other detective are riveted to the speaker, and some of them are jotting things down on their pads. This is all new information.

"Continue."

Richter is reluctant to go forward but speaking the truth is giving him a lot of comfort—although he has no intention on telling the whole truth.

"Yeah. Where was I?"

"You shot him."

"Oh yeah. Well, that's the brown stuff on the wall. When I shot him, some brown stuff splattered instead of blood. The only reason I didn't shoot him again was because he called me Quake . . . Nobody but Benji knows me by that name."

"So how'd he get the gun? You said that he was the one who shot Bootyup . . . or Gettemup, whatever. How'd he get the gun? Did you give it to him?"

Now, Richter starts lying again.

"Well, I was kind of disappointed to hear that he could have thought that I would ever do anything to hurt him, so I threw the gun down to his feet and told him, 'If you think we had something to do with it, then handle your business.' So he grabbed the gun and blew Bootemup's head off."

"Well, how'd he get in the house?"

"I'm not sure," Richter says. "I think maybe through the window where Amp's body was because I remember wondering how that window got opened. He had to come through that window."

Meanwhile, the call was already being made to check the window for fingerprints, and also to get a sample of the brown blots on the wall. Detectives were also sent to the neighborhood to ask the neighbors if they might have seen anything after the gun shots were fired. Everybody now believes that there was somebody else involved. But who? That's what they hope the further investigation of Richter's revised story will reveal.

Chapter 56

Salina has all but given up on life. Her bills are mounting up on her. Her business is on the brink of total collapse, the kids can't stand her, and her appearance has fallen down to crackhead status. She doesn't look in the mirror much anymore. She's afraid she might want to commit suicide.

It's almost noon, and she should be enjoying brunch with her children on a Sunday morning. If not that, maybe taking them to some religious service, but instead, Salina is sulking in her misery. The children are confined to the upstairs because Salina is smoking a joint of marijuana. She hasn't smoked in years, but the stress is too great to bear with a clear head. She tries to stay high as much as she can. Soon she'll be drinking too.

Misery is her cosmetic, and slipshod is her kitchen's decor. The cloud is perpetually over this house, and there is not a vestige of cleanliness left anywhere in the house except in Nakeisha's room, where she spends most of her time nowadays.

All Salina ever does is grunt and complain. Her malevolent disdain is even more toxic since she called the information desk to the hospital in Annapolis to inquire about Jessica Powell. When she was told that she was discharged this morning, Salina nearly gave way to tears.

Damn! She said before hanging up the phone in the receptionist ear.

Now she's toiling over how cowardly she was acting when she had the chance to do away with the person who is the cause of all her misery and pain.

Iblis is watching her from atop the stove. He's in his spirit form, so he's invisible. He wants Jessie dead even more than Salina does, but more so than Jessie, he wants Asa to be done away with. The Omega's spirit engulfs the child, and Iblis is sure that he somehow works very prominently in Iblis' own demise.

He enters into Salina and with silent voices he talks to her.

I should have shot her. I should have shot her when I had the chance. I'm a punk, man. I let that big fat bitch beat me up, and I didn't do a thing. Now this whore is still alive 'cause I was scared to get out the car and walk up to her and blast her ass.

Salina slaps down on the table.

"That's all right, you ain't getting away yet," she says.

She ain't do nothing but go right back home. And that's what I'ma do. Set the whole house on fire. Uh-huh!

Salina is aghast at the thought that just came to her mind. She has never thought that she could be so sinister and hateful. To shoot somebody is one thing, but to set the house on fire with them in it, not to mention a newborn baby is beyond Salina's capacity to do evil. For a moment she ponders how wicked she's become ever since Benji refused to ever come back to the house. She's progressively becoming more and more diabolical as the days pass by.

What is happening to you, Salina? A thought that she conjures up herself. Iblis, although inside of her cannot hear her own thought, nor read her heart, but he doesn't need to because her heart is treacherous; therefore, the strings he pulls she'll follow with little to no resistance.

Yeah, that's what I'll do. I'll burn her house down and if she comes out alive, I'll be waiting with the gun. I just gotta wait till nighttime.

Iblis leaves her and hovers over the kitchen table. Salina takes another drag of her joint. It's really too small to even hit.

"Ouch, gotdamn it."

Chapter 57

Some people don't like to hear distressing information on the telephone, and Lindsey Miles is one of those types of people. Unfortunately he's in the kind of occupation that 99 percent of incoming information comes through some type of communication device, and all too often, it's bad news.

At the moment his cell phone is ringing, but he refuses to answer it because he knows it's a call from the Prince George's County Police precinct that is holding Vincent Taylor. When he left there, their forensics team also left en route to Taylor's, or rather, Richter's house. The entire day has passed by, and now he's on his way back to the precinct.

This is a call he's been waiting for all day, so whatever information they have for him, he'll hear it when he gets there. The only good news they could possibly give him is that everything Richter told them was fabricated; he strangled himself, and the case was closed. But he knows that is not going to be the case. He's only afraid that, if Richter is lying and didn't kill himself, he's going to have to move to take over a stupid murder case because it transcends multiple jurisdictions.

His phone rings again. Now, it's Faraday. He picks up. "Meet me at the precinct."

He hangs up before Faraday can say a word. It's not the first time he's done that to his partner, and it certainly won't be the last. Miles knows that if it's something that can't wait, Faraday will call right back. Faraday hasn't called, and Miles is pulling into the Prince George's Police Department of District III. He knows he'll be able to dodge the bullet of getting bad news over the phone for a change.

Inside, a Major Morrison comes from the back through a double door and escorts Agent Miles down a hall he had been lead down earlier. The precinct is unusually vibrant for such a late hour. Well, it's not really that late: 9:38 p.m., but still. Officers and detectives dart from room to room calling to one another with leads; Miles is noticeably disturbed by the near pandemonium ensuing around him.

The Major he is following stops at a door and yells inside. "The fed is here." Then keeps on down the hall. Never looks back. Just leaves Miles behind to figure out for himself whether or not he should stop here or keep on following him.

Miles steps to the opening and turns his head to look in. He sees one of the homicide detectives that was at the District 4 precinct who had told him that they would be transferring Richter here to the headquarters.

The detective waves him back sporting a sullen expression on his face as if he has to be the one to tell Miles that they just found his son floating in a river. All kinds of thoughts are brewing up in Miles' head, and none of them are realities that he is prepared to entertain. The least of them all, that Benji is on the loose, but what else could be so disconcerting?

The detective meets Miles halfway. His name is Bigelow. His body fits it well. He's a pudgy fellow—a 230 lb Danny Devito, with a head full of hair.

"Mr. Miles," he shakes his head. "We just might have a dead murderer on our hands."

The sound of that sends a chill that grows from deep within Miles' body that spreads down to his feet making his toes feel numb. All of a sudden his bowels feel loose, and he's no longer the 'in control, take the lead on the investigation' FBI Agent Miles. He's lost, scratching his head. He's not breathing.

After gasping for air, he asks, "OK, where do we go from here?"

"What do ya mean, 'Where do we go from here'? Guy! Did you hear what I just told ya? We have a *dead* . . . murderer on the loose! For all we know he's immortal. You know, like, some kind of demon that can come and go in an instant. The guy Taylor wasn't lying. He shot this thing, whatever it is, and that . . . that frickin' crap on the wall. It's more like mud than blood. But the DNA matches what we have on Benjamin Powell. And we found Powell's fingerprints on the wall in the dining room. Not because of any oil in his skin but because of the blood he had on his hands after he massacred the kid who lost his arms. If he came in through the window, whatever oil he had in his skin is now too dried up to leave any prints behind, but somebody left a scuff mark on the siding when they climbed in the window, so more than likely, he *did* enter in through the window."

"Where is the Taylor boy?"

"Oh, he's on his way to Upper Marlboro. We've got all we need from him for now. The commissioner didn't even see him yet, so if he does get a bond, it won't be until after he sees the judge in the morning. But he won't get a bond, not tomorrow anyway."

"OK, good. Now the first thing we need to do is . . ." Miles contemplates what he's about to propose and then ardently exclaims, "Jeez! What the hell is this? We're actually plotting on how we're going to track down a ghost! You can't track down a ghost. This is ridiculous!"

Miles laughs out loud. It's not that it's funny to him but so unbelievable that the whole thing has put him in a state of delirium. He feels light-headed and out of body. He stops laughing and shakes his head. Bigelow is just standing there looking at the impetuous shifts of Miles' behavior from serious to delirious to uneasy—biting his thumb—darting his eyes in a mad scientist kind of way.

"Are you all right, man?"

"Hell no! I'm not all right. I mean what are we looking for? A ghost, a zombie, or what! Has anybody even dug this guy's grave up to see if his body is even in the coffin?"

"Well, no. We didn't involve the cemetery ground keepers. The last thing we want is the media to get wind of this."

"Damn the media! We've got to know just what the hell we're dealing with. Can we blow this . . . this *thing* to smithereens or what? I'd feel a whole lot better knowing that we're dealing with something we don't need the Ghostbusters to kill."

"Well, OK," says Bigelow, "you get it authorized."

Miles looks around for Faraday, but he's forgotten he came alone. He opens his Sprint but can't reach his partner on the direct connect, so he calls his phone.

"Faraday, I need you."

Chapter 58

Killing comes easy for some folks, but for Benji it's not, at least it wasn't. He's never had a problem with paying somebody to take care of his problems in much the way he took care of Koca Moe for his friend John, but to get his hands dirty in that way, was just something he could never bring himself to do, except the one time he did when he was robbed.

He's been riding around all day sulking over the flashbacks that keep haunting him. Blood and gore is all he can think of. He only killed Amp, but the way he did it was so grotesque that the images have clouded his thinking, and he can't seem to clear his mind of them long enough to enjoy pleasant thoughts of his lovely Jessie. Even when visions of Asa pop into his head, the child burst into tears, so he tries not to think of him. The only person he can think of with a measure of inner peace is Nakeisha, his daughter. He tries to keep her in his mind, but the sight of Amp's armless, blood-gushing body falling to the floor quickly intrudes.

The only thing he's been waiting for is nightfall, so he can go by his home in Annapolis to try to find some serenity from being close to his family. He knows that Jessie and the baby were discharged from the hospital early this morning because he was at the hospital when they were leaving with an older woman who looked a lot like Jessie. Benji had never seen her mother in person, but was sure that the woman was the same woman that he had seen in several pictures in Jessie's picture albums. He followed them until he saw them driving toward the vicinity of his neighborhood. He vowed that he would be home tonight.

He's approaching his turn and looks at the gas gauge because he knows he needs some gas. There's a Wawa gas station at the light, but he really doesn't want to stop there because they don't have full service, and there surely aren't any crackheads or bums around that can pump his gas. Getting out of the truck to pay for gas is an ill-advised thought, and he has no intentions on doing that.

As he pulls into the turning lane to make a left turn at the light, a car in the gas station causes him to double take. It's a white Lexus. Just like the one he had. It has tinted windows like his and the same chrome rims. He can't be sure if it's his car because the trunk is up preventing him from seeing the tag. The person standing at the rear of the car is wearing a hooded sweatshirt and gloves, so Benji can't make out who it could be. He's not even sure if it's his car, but it commands his attention more than the green arrow and clearing lane in front of him.

Bomp! The horn of the car behind him shouts.

Benji stomps on the gas pedal, glancing back and forth at the car as the hooded person scampers around the car to get in, appearing to be trying to get out of the cold as quickly as possible. Benji quickly makes the turn in order to pull into the gas station to get a closer look at the car and the driver.

The Lexus is on the move toward the exit out of the station parking lot, and Benji turns into the same driveway that the Lexus is exiting.

"That *is* my car!" he grumbles. "Who the . . ."

The driver can't be seen behind the tint, but this doesn't seem right to Benji.

What is my car doing down here? Did Jessie and Salina become friends?

"No way."

Well . . . Benji is dumbfounded. He shakes his head, totally unable to fathom what on earth his car is doing down here and who that could be.

Who was that?

Benji tries to make a quick circle around the gas pump, but another car pulling into the gas station from another entrance, muscling Benji for position and blocking his way.

"Damn fool. Shh . . ."

Benji puts the truck in reverse and swerves out of the parking lot in pursuit of his Lexus. It's gone, but he's one hundred percent sure that when he gets to his house, the car will be there. He drives like a bat out of hell until he pulls within a block of his street. When he turns down his street, he sees the break light of his car. The driver gets out, then walks around to the trunk, and lugs something that appears too heavy for the person. Benji stops at a good distance and watches as the person disappears into his yard.

In the yard, Salina manages to carry a five-gallon gas tank up to the front door of the house. She freezes when the sensor light comes on but proceeds when no one gives any indication of being aware that she is intruding. She opens the storm door and pours nearly a half a gallon of gasoline under the door so that it runs into the house, then she streams the gas along the wall under the window sill and around the house repeating the same process at every window and door opening on the first floor.

After she has finished dousing the perimeter of the house, she makes a trail of gas that follows her out the yard. In front of the house, there is a four-foot-tall fence of manicured hedges. Salina stops behind the hedges and sets the gas tank down in the grass, then reaches into her pocket on the front of her hoody, and pulls out a box of stick matches. She pulls off her left glove with her teeth, but before she can get a match out of the box, someone grabs her from behind.

Benji holds her firmly by her mouth and stomach. She tries to scream but is unable to mutter a sound loud enough for anybody more than six feet away to hear.

Although Benji hasn't been able to see the face of his hostage, he already knows who it is. Salina is wearing sweats that conceal her figure, but the Reebok Classics she has on is a dead giveaway.

"Lina, what are you doing?"

Here again, Benji has used a name that enables the person he's speaking to, to recognize that it is him.

Iblis is present, and he hopes that Salina doesn't faint before he can enter into her and try to lead her interaction with Benji before Benji foils a perfect opportunity for Iblis to rid himself of two likely threats.

Salina can hear herself think, unaware that the inner voice isn't her conscience speaking at all. *Stay calm, Salina. You just trippin. That can't be Benji, and if it is, then that must have been somebody else that got killed, and they buried the wrong person. Here's my chance to get my man back. Just light this match. Get rid of that . . .*

Benji can smell the gas but has no idea that Salina has poured gas all around his house. He would never guess that Salina would do something so fiendish. Whatever she was doing isn't that much of a concern to him at this point because now she'll never get a chance to pull it off.

"So what are you doin' harassing my family? That was you that drove my wife off the road. Wasn't it? Huh? Wasn't it?" Benji growls in her ear squeezing her tight.

Salina tries to mumble, but Benji can't make out what she's trying to say.

"If you scream, I swear I'll snap your neck."

He slowly moves his hand away from Salina's mouth.

"Benji, I wouldn't do anything to your family. I was just going to burn a big "X" in her yard to scare her." Salina tells him that to put him at ease so she can try to talk to him to divert his attention somehow while she lights the match to start the fire.

"I thought you were dead. Could you please let me go so I can see you? Please. I can't believe you're still alive."

Benji is shocked at how calm Salina is acting. He expected her to be hysterical and resistant, but she's not. He doesn't want her to see him, though, because that would certainly all change in an instant, once she sees his face. She'll know that he's been dead or *something,* and he won't be able to keep her calm enough to ask about the welfare of his two children. Besides, it feels good to hold her again even though he doesn't love her much. After all, he's been dead, so to hold a woman after going through something like that would cause any man to think twice before ruining such a moment.

"No, I'd rather hold you just like this. Just for a while."

When Iblis hears this, it spurs his assault on Salina's independent thinking. He knows how strongly she feels for him, and he also knows that Salina has used sex as a weapon to keep Benji from leaving her for years. Now would be the perfect time to prey on his masculinity. Iblis knows that in the back of Benji's mind that he knows his time is short, and it could end with the next sunrise, especially considering the incinerating wake he had this morning.

When the first rays of the rising sun filled the truck this morning, it felt like his blood was boiling, and his heart was about to burst. This morning's break of dawn was three times more excruciating than yesterday morning, and Benji couldn't move for two full hours after the tempestuously agonizing internal conflagration subsided.

He knows he won't make it through another morning, and Iblis is banking on him having that very outlook for the future. If that is the case, virtually any man in Benji's situation would fall snare to the advances of a seductive woman. Especially of one he's already been involved with before.

"Yeah, I don't mind you holding me. Just hold me a little closer. It's kind of cold," Salina says as she presses her butt against his groin area and mashes it from side to side in search of any type of hardness.

Benji is instantly aroused, and an irresistibly passionate urge rushes through his body. A feeling he hasn't felt so strongly since he last came home from prison and embraced Jessie for the first time in years. Benji's mind is telling him "no" but his body is not listening. He presses hard against Salina, fitting his third leg between the two humps of her behind. His breathing becomes heavy.

"Yeah, baby. I miss you too." Salina begins to talk to him in order to distort the sound of the match being lit. "Come on, boo. Let's get in the car, I want you."

She throws the match behind them, hoping it reaches the spot where she poured the gas; when nothing happens, she continues to talk dirty to him all the while lighting matches. Benji is so enthralled by his fervent quest of lust that he is past all moral and natural senses. He's like an unreasoning bull being led to the slaughter.

The gasoline catches fire, and it blazes a trail set straight for the house. When Salina sees the fire spread, she collapses her legs and pulls Benji down on top of her, with Benji hunched over her from behind and the two of them out of any possible view of any onlooker because of the shroud of darkness that covers them created by the bush and the Lexus parked at the curb, Salina begs for Benji to take her. She even pushes her sweat pants and underwear off her buttock exposing it to the crisp winter night air. Benji is blinded by passion not even noticing the light coming from the flames only a foot behind him. He fumbles with his pants in a frantic attempt to drive himself into Salina.

Just then a voice in Benji's head says, *No, your family.*

Benji's expedient movement gradually slows like a timepiece needing to be wound. There's light. He looks to his right and sees an inferno blazing beyond the hedges. He looks back at Salina, and everything that has happened to him flashes before his eyes; the one who caused it all he's sure is in his clutches, and now he intends on making her pay.

At first; it was passion that clouded his better judgment; now it's vengeance, and he has forgotten all about what's most important *right now.* He grips Salina tight around her neck with both hands.

"So you're the one that sent those niggas to my house? You're the reason why my wife was raped! You put 'em up to it! Now you gonna see what it feels like to be tortured!"

He pounds her and pounds her from behind and the more he pounds the more she grunts in agony. Each thrust is like a javelin being poked against her internal organs. He squeezes her neck tighter, and now she can't breathe.

"You killin' me," Salina whimpers. She can feel herself going out and with her last breath she tries to let him know that he's killing her, but her words are gibberish. Besides, even if Benji did understand what she was trying to say it would have made no difference to him. He is intent on bringing her own deeds upon her head.

Iblis withdraws from the body of Salina and watches in relishing delight as everything goes forward as he intended. Benji, the only possible savior of the innocent people inside the burning house, has been subverted by Iblis' oldest trick in the book—a man's attraction to the opposite sex.

Iblis could care less that Benji is killing the person he has used to launch fatal attacks against the child in the house. He's finished with her. The house is engulfed in flames, and soon he will rid himself of a human target that has caused him the most anxiety he's felt in nearly two thousand years. Asa will soon be out of the way.

Benji is practically out of his mind, but just before Salina's body goes limp in death, he retrieves his senses. He snaps out of the spell that his own vengeful rage had put him under. He shakes his head and blinks his only eye.

What are you doing, Benji, why are you doing this? Don't kill her. She's the mother of your children. What's that light? Aw!! The house!

Benji can see the fire that's raging through the bush.

"Oh no! Jessie . . . My boy."

Chapter 59

The Discovery Channel was once about the only thing that would captivate young Asa as he sat propped up in the bed next to his mother. The animals always seemed to be frolicking around like children in a field, but ever since he dreamt about the wolves mauling his mother, anything with big teeth that comes on the television causes him to break into a rabid tantrum of tears.

Jessie hasn't figured out what rattles her son so suddenly from time to time. She assumes it has to do with the traumatizing sight that he witnessed when his father was murdered. It has never dawned on her that long sharp teeth trigger the agitation because he'll watch the animals quietly for an extended period of time before he becomes annoyed.

He is looking at an animal kingdom segment right now, and he's completely engrossed in the fishes and dolphins that are being showcased in the program. His mother is lying down next to him propped up against a pile of pillows with a Walter Mosley novel spread cross her breast. Her eyes are closed, but she's not asleep. She will be soon.

Her mother is also in the bed with them. She's on the opposite side of Asa doing a crossword puzzle in the *Washington Times* newspaper. She looks just like Jessie except her hair has long streaks of gray mixed in with her black hair. She's wearing a pair of gold-rimmed reading glasses connected to a chain that drapes around her neck. She doesn't wear makeup, not even eyeliner. The wrinkles around her eyes and mouth shows a hint of her age and that she smiles a lot. She smiles even when she's not really smiling. She's not *really* smiling now.

The room is quiet and lit by the light of the television and the illumination of a lamp sitting on the rather tall nightstand next to the bed. It's quiet, that's until a great white shark flashes up on the screen, with its mouth wide open.

This is the moment Asa was anticipating the whole time. In his heart he was hoping that he could make it to the words that run up the screen, indicating that the show is over before the teeth came, but not today. One fleeting glance at those teeth sends Asa's morale into a tailspin, and his wailing kicks off instantaneously.

Jessie opens her eyes immediately and looks over at Asa. She follows his eyes back to the television where she sees a shark sinking his teeth into the side of a swordfish. The water is bloody and the shark is in a tearing frenzy, trying to rip a huge chunk of flesh from its prey.

"Mama, quick, turn the TV"

Loretta, her mother, scrambles for the remote control. She moves around the thesaurus, dictionary, and world almanac that she has scattered around her legs before finally placing the remote. She fidgets with it for a second and then finds a button that changes the channel. Asa is relieved that the vicious images are gone, but he can't stop crying. Jessie sits up and picks him up. She bounces him a few times as she sniffs the air before she looks at her mother, who is also sniffing around.

"Jessica? Is something burning?"

"Yeah Mama, it sure smells like it."

Loretta climbs down out of the bed and as she slips her slippers on, her eye catches sight of the flames that are growing up the side of the house just outside the window.

"Agh! My god! The house is on fire!" She throws both her hands in the air and does something that looks like a rain dance. "Lord, Lord, Lord! Help us, please!"

Jessie panics but is in too much pain to react physically to her emotions. She cries, saying to herself, *Why me? What did I do to deserve all this?* She slowly climbs out the bed still holding onto her crying baby. *God, why me?*

"Why meee?" she cries.

Jessie can now see the furious flames through the window on her side of the bed. By the looks of them, the other parts of the house outside the room are burning too. Smoke is seeping into the room. A sure indication that fire is inside the house as well. Her mother runs over to the door.

"Mama! Don't' open it!"

Jessie remembers learning in school that you should always touch the door before opening it in a fire. She also remembers watching the movie *Back Draft*. She doesn't want any flames blasting into the room.

"We gotta get outta here!" her mother frantically shouts.

"I know, Mama, but . . ." Jessie walks over to the door and touches it. It's not hot. Jessie reluctantly opens it and smoke plumes enter into the room. There are flames outside the room, but she can't distinguish exactly where they are through the smoke before she slams the door back shut.

"*Cough, cough.*" Jessie and her mother began to cough. Asa's face is buried in his mother's bosom, so he hasn't yet been affected by the smoke.

Jessie scoots over to the window and sees flames raging on both sides. The situation is hopeless and her mother appears gimpy, almost retarded. She's walking in circles, frazzled by the bleak outlook of survival through this perilous dilemma that she's found herself in. Jessie backs away from the window, looking out at the growing flames wondering how she's going to save her baby, who has just started coughing. She looks down at him then drops down to her knees.

"My baby, Mama . . ." Jessie cries desperately. "My baby . . . Why God? . . . Why?"

A loud ascension can be heard coming up the stairs in the hallway. Jessie hears it but is too astounded by the thought of her baby being burned alive to even speculate on who or what, if anything is coming up the steps. Loretta stops her bewildered parading in anticipating of her savior coming through the door.

"Thank you, Lord, Lord, Lord," she exclaims as the steps coming from outside the room approaches the door, and the door flings open.

Jessie and her mother can see the image of a man coming through the doorway with flames not far in the race behind him. The carpet that runs up the center of the steps and through the hallway is catching fire quite quickly, and it is evident that this man has had to move rather speedily through the flames to avoid catching on fire. The smoke that billows into the room with the man has masked over his face shielding the horrid appearance of their unexpected deliverer.

"Jess!" Benji shouts, "Where's the baby!"

He grabs Jessie's mother thinking that she's Jessie but soon realizes that he's grabbed the wrong person. Loretta's eyes lock on Benji's face, and she screams as loud as she can. Almost like a woman in an Alfred Hitchcock film. She coughs then screams again.

"Aggh!"

Jessie is still crouched on the floor holding her baby and can't believe what she's seeing. She wonders if she's hallucinating or is the devil trying to kill her or something. Her life reminds her of the life of the woman that Charlize Theron played in the *Devil's Advocate*. A mesmerizing feeling rushes through her body. Her breathing shortens. She's on the verge of fainting again, but she thinks of Asa and her cognizance revives.

You gotta stay strong. Gotta get my baby out of her. Please get me through this. I'm putting it in your hands. Please let my baby survive this.

Jessie says a short prayer. Never taking her eyes off the creature who called out her name in the same way Benji used to. There's no doubt that it is a demon playing tricks on her mind, but she is comforted by her prayer.

Benji looks the room over until his single eye finds his wife; she's looking up at him. He pauses, but realizes that there's no time to waste. The fire is spreading fast and smoke is filling the room. Jessie's mom is screaming and crying. She's virtually out of her mind.

"Jessie, Baby . . ." Benji mutters in his deep distorted voice. "We gotta go. The whole house is on fire."

He lets Loretta go to snatch the sheets off the bed. He moves quickly to the bathroom and drenches them in water. He returns and tells Jessie to wrap herself in the sheet. She takes the sheet from him still trying to hold Asa in her arms. Benji reaches for the baby.

"No! Not my baby!" Jessie becomes defensive and snatches back from the monster. She doesn't believe it's Benji and has tried not to think of what it could be. She's just trying to concentrate on how she's going to walk through the fire in her impaired condition. She staggers painfully to maintain her balance, realizing at this very moment that she and her baby are as good as dead if it depends upon her to run through the house before she catches fire or dies from smoke inhalation.

"Jess . . . *Cough*, it's me. I know you are afraid and confused right now, but look at you. You'll never get out of here. Look!"

Jessie looks out the door. The fire is encroaching on the threshold of the bedroom door.

"Let me take you, I can take you both. Just close your eyes and trust me. Here wrap yourself."

Jessie reluctantly takes the dripping sheet from Benji. He helps her wrap herself and the baby in the sheet. Jessie looks over at her mother who has dropped below the thick smoke.

"Mama, wrap yourself in the sheet. We gotta leave now."

Her mother crawls over and wraps herself in the sheet, but she isn't confident that she'll make it out alive.

"Jessica. I can't run through no fire," her mother cries.

"Mama, you have to. How else you gonna get out? He can't carry us all."

"Jessie, we don't have time," Benji interrupts. "Miss, just wrap up and run as fast as you can. The wet sheet won't burn. Just don't stop."

Benji grabs Jessie.

"Ouch, easy, easy."

Benji gingerly cradles Jessie and Asa in his arms. The abnormal strength that empowers his body couldn't have come at a better time. Jessie is almost featherweight to him. He steps to the door but stops to make sure her mother is ready to follow behind him. She's standing at the foot of the bed but doesn't look like she's preparing for any departure. She's just standing there coughing and crying.

"Ma'am, you have to come now," Benji grunts.

"OK, I'm coming."

"Mama, come on. Please," Jessie pleads.

"OK, I'm ready."

She gets behind Benji and as soon as he takes off through the flames, she follows. Benji makes a sharp turn at the stairs, but Loretta misses the turn and keeps straight ahead. She can hear the rumble of Benji's feet thunder down the steps, and instantly she realizes that she's passed the steps and has no idea how far she's gone past them.

The heat from the fire on the carpet is searing her feet and ankles and panic has taken hold of her.

"Jessie!"

Loretta is desperately trying to find the opening of the stairwell as she backtracks down the hallways.

"Mama!" cries Jessie. "Benji. My mother. She's back there." Loretta can faintly hear the voice of her daughter appealing to the man carrying her through the fire and calling through the flames and smoke. "Mama!"

"Jessie . . . I'm on fire . . . God, no! I'm on fire."

Loretta can feel herself burning under her night gown. It has caught fire, and the intense heat has caused Loretta to lose all control. When she finally reaches the steps, she doesn't have the presence of mind to run down them. She just leans forward and tumbles to the bottom. The wet sheet is hindering the flames from igniting the top part of her gown, but it's also hindering her ability to get up off the floor. She struggles for a moment and then finally breaks free of the entangled cloth that is her only protection from the surrounding flames.

Still disoriented, Loretta franticly calls to her daughter in order to prompt a response that will act as a homing device, leading her to an exit.

"Mama! This way."

Jessie's voice came from out of the kitchen. They've exited out of the side door in the kitchen that leads to refuge beyond the wooden deck adjacent to the house outside the door.

Loretta follows the guiding calls. She doesn't realize that her foot is snared by the wet sheet that she has left behind, and just as she reaches the blazing comforter that once covered the entrance to the family room where Benji was murdered, her feet get entangled sending her falling toward the inflamed opening. The corridor that she is treading is not completely ablaze because the floor is hardwood, but this is not the case with the room her body is toppling into. The room is an inferno. Loretta is able to grab hold of the wall but is unable to stop herself from plunging into the sea of fire that is raging in the sublevel family room that sits two stair steps below the level she falls from. The room is also carpeted from wall to wall; so it's like King Nebuchadnezzar's furnace. Every inch of the floor is amassed in flames.

"Agh!"

"Mama . . ."

Chapter 60

Benji storms back into the burning house, leaving his wife and child in the yard at a safe distance from any possible falling debris. Jessie is screaming her head off knowing that her mother is parched by now, near death if not already dead.

Returning into the door he came out of, Benji skips through the kitchen. "Ms. Jessie, Ms. Jessie," he calls.

There's no response as Benji rushes past the family room. His attention is caught by the sheet in the hallway. He stops, looks around, and then concludes from the way the sheet is headed toward the doorway of the family room that Loretta has taken a wrong turn and is probably, more than likely, dead as a doornail by now. He takes a hasty step toward the fiery opening before shrewdness overpowers his thoughts of invincibility.

Damn! That's a lot of fire. Man, I ain't goin in there. "Ms. Glockner."

A nearly inaudible whine that a normal human would never hear catches Benji's attention and moves him to action. It's all the confirmation he needs to know that Jessie's mother is still alive. Saving her would mean getting Jessie to trust him. He senses the detachment and wants nothing more than to be able to connect with her emotionally one more time. Risking his own consciousness to save somebody who was already dead didn't register well, but now that he knows she's still alive, the benefit of returning to Jessie with her mother in his arms outweighs the risk.

He snatches the sheet off the floor and leaps into the flames. Scampering around the room, he kicks his feet from left to right with hopes of stumbling over her body.

"Ah, what was that?" He kicks again. It's her.

Benji bends over and snatches the log out of the fire and breaks for the door. She's totally covered in flames, and now not only is Benji's pants on fire, so is his coat. He emerges out the house appearing to Jessie to be a great ball of fire.

"Jessie, bring your sheet!"

The sheet is the only shelter that Jessie and Asa have from the cool night air. Jessie looks at her baby, then realizes that he'll survive the cold, but her mother and her rescuer are on fire. They need the sheet more. She stands up and unwraps herself and then approaches the man carrying her mother.

Benji indiscriminately drops Loretta to the ground, then drops himself down, and rolls around trying to put out the flames. Meanwhile, Jessie lays the sheet on her mother and attempts, with one hand, to smother the flames, while she holds tight to her son with her other hand.

Disheartened by the sight of her mother's charred body, Jessie shows no urgency in putting out the flames. The efforts appear useless. She may as well be beating a dead horse, and that's exactly how she feels as she watches the skin literally melting off her mother's lifeless body.

Jessie isn't the only one awestruck by the grisly sight. Salina is sneaking up quietly behind Jessie; she would have probably shot her by now, as she's pointing a gun in Jessie's direction if she hadn't taken notice of the roasted carcass.

Iblis has once again entered into Salina and is desperately trying to drive her to do away with Jessie, and even Asa, but Salina is ignoring her inner voice unable to pull her attention away from the burning heap of flesh. She steps on a fallen twig and breaks it drawing Jessie's attention. When Jessie turns and sees the hooded Salina standing behind her wielding a handgun, she is at a loss for words. Her eyes bulge, and her mouth sags open.

Salina has now focused her attention on Jessie and her baby. The sight of Jessie's baby sparks intense jealousy in Salina.

"Because of you . . . My life is ruined. I hate you! You and that stupid baby!"

Salina aims the gun to shoot.

"Benji!" Jessie shouts out.

Salina applies pressure to the trigger.

Whoof. The sound of swooping bird passes over Jessie's head.

Jessie doesn't see what it is until whatever it was finds its target. The crunching sound of breaking bone is accompanied by the sight of a rather large knife penetrating Salina's neck around her collar bone area. The jolt from the velocity of the knife pushes Salina back a few steps. She fires the gun, but doesn't hit anyone. The sight of the large knife handle gives

Salina a hint of how big the blade must be. She drops to her knees after dropping the gun at her feet.

"I loved you, Benji. Why'd you do to me like that?" Salina gargles her words. "I loved you . . ."

Her eyes are full of tears, but she's not crying because she's about to die. Dying is actually something she's wanted to do for sometime now. She is crying because her life is flashing before her, and she feels sorry for herself as she thinks of what could have been if it weren't for Benji loving Jessie more than he loved her, and if only she'd have been a lot sweeter to the man she wanted to be with for the rest of her life. The misery is too great to bear. Death is her only escape. Still Iblis won't give up. It could be years before he finds another soul on earth to hate Jessie or her baby to death.

Don't let her live either. I gotta kill her. The voice in Salina's mind makes one last ditch effort to spur her on.

In the distance, fire engines can be heard blasting their horns through the streets of this wealthy suburbia. No doubt the police will converge as well, considering that a gunshot would be altogether alien to the ears of the locals that live in the neighboring homes around this ruinous scene.

"Jessie, come with me. I've got to go. The police will be here soon. I don't have time to explain, and I beg for just a moment with you . . . Please."

Jessie turns from the slumping Salina to look at the man she supposes was once her handsome husband. She's reluctant to leave her mother but looking at her, it's obvious that remaining would be useless. After all, if this is her husband, how could she pass up the opportunity to share another conversation with him?

"Please . . ." Benji whispers once more.

Jessie slowly stands up, and Benji moves toward her. She looks at him, and he stops. Jessie looks him in his eye, and she can see her husband behind the deathly mask. She blinks and relaxes. Benji watches as the tension drains out of Jessie's body.

"Let's get the baby out of the cold," Jessie says. "What are you driving?"

"My truck is up the street."

They pick up their pace as they leave the yard unaware that the hunched over Salina has reclaimed her gun and is about to shoot one of them in the back. Like Lot's wife, Jessie turns to take one last look at her burning house before she turns to go up the street.

"Benji, watch out!"

Jessie ducks to avoid being shot.

Pow! Pow! Pow, Pow, Pow! Click.

Benji falls forward.

"Benji, no!" cries Jessie. Just when the feeling of gratitude had filled her heart due to the fact that she had somehow been granted to see her beloved husband again, she is demoralized as she watches a bad dream turn into a nightmare.

"Go, Jess. Get in the car." Benji points to his white Lexus. Jessie hobbles over and gets into the backseat of the car, still clutching her baby. Benji turns his attention to Salina. He feels his time here on earth is short, and there's no way he'll be able to protect his wife and son from this woman's relentless attacks against their life, so he knows what he must do.

He stands to his feet and walks toward Salina, who is lying flat on her back. He is intent on finishing her off, but by the time he reaches her, her body lies impotent in death. Her eyes are still open, but it's obvious that there's no life in them. Benji looks her over for a moment.

She's dead. Good because I need to get out of here.

The sound of the fire engines are bending the corner and will have the road completely blocked off in the next thirty seconds making it impossible for Benji to leave the vicinity in a vehicle before the police arrive. He looks up the street toward the approaching emergency vehicles as he runs for the car. He hops in and then bounces the front end of the Lexus upon the curb as he U-turns in the street. The white Lexus zooms past the approaching fire truck and is out of sight in a matter of seconds.

"Call the police, Lacy. Hurry, call the cops," says a middle-aged white man who lives across the street from the Powell's residence. He's been watching since Salina shot the first gunshot and then fell to the ground grabbing her neck.

"Did you get the tag number?" calls a voice from inside the house.

"No! Just tell them it's a big white Benz or something of the sort. They've gotta get them before they get too far."

Chapter 61

"Damn it!" shouts the flabbergasted Lindsey Miles as he receives the news that the Annapolis Police Department didn't send a unit to the Powell's residence in time enough to place surveillance on the house in wait to nab Benji. Miles knew he would eventually make his way home, and that's why he insisted that Anne Arundel County get there as soon as possible.

"I called you almost an hour ago. Did you send anybody then?"

The response from the person on the other end of the phone prompts Miles to slap the dash board of his car as he always does when he becomes agitated by job-related miscues. He undoes his tie and the top button of his white shirt and grimaces as he lets the steam out his collar.

"You guys are frickin' idiots! If this guy gets away, somebody over there is going into an early retirement. I mean heads are gonna roll, trust me. Christ!"

Miles hangs up his phone, and then direct connects with Faraday.

"Jeff, ETA at the Powells'?"

The voice of Faraday returns through Miles' Sprint. "I'm on Route 50 passing Riva Road. I guess ten minutes or less."

"Well, our guy has struck there already and gone."

"Gone?"

"Yeah. Gone. He wreaked havoc, left a couple of dead bodies on the lawn, and there is no telling' how many inside the house, which is on fire, and left in a white car with dark windows. Oh, did I mention he left with his wife."

"How do you know?"

"Well, according to one of the neighbors, the woman who got into the car with him was carrying a baby in her arms, so I assume that the woman was Jessica Powell."

Faraday doesn't come back, and there's a long silence in Miles' car.

"Why do I feel like I'm in the twilight zone?" Faraday returns through the phone.

Miles doesn't respond; he just lays his phone down on the passenger seat and then runs his fingers through his hair. He starts biting his thumb again. Something he hardly ever does except when he's afraid that whatever mission he's on will have detrimental effects on his well-being. He's having that feeling now.

We're chasing a gotdamn dead man. And he's leaving a trail of dead bodies all over town. This is nuts Linz—a name he calls himself. *You need to let this one go. He got shot with a shotgun, and mud came out. I didn't believe in God till now. Maybe he did resurrect Jesus. Maybe the Bible wasn't lying.*

He takes a deep breath, looks over at his phone, and then back to the road.

Miles picks the phone up again and makes another call. He calls his field office, hoping to catch Janet there. She's an agent too, but she spends a lot of time at the office, listening to wire taps and reading intercepted e-mails of various suspects that the bureau is building cases on.

"Janet. Good, I'm glad I caught you. This is Linz. I need you to do me a favor."

Janet has the hots for Miles, and he knows if he asks her to put an all-point bulletin out for the Lexus that Benji is driving, she will have no problem with stopping what she was doing to do his bidding. She is a bit confused as to why he didn't call the police to do it, though.

"Sure, Linz," she says almost seductively, "anything for you, but why me? You just wanted to hear my voice, didn't you?"

"Ah, well . . . Sure. I always enjoy the sound of your lovely voice, but really I need you. I can't depend on the county to get anything done immediately. I need this done now. Right this minute," Miles says anxiously. "Please, Janet, could you get on top of that for me?"

Janet senses the urgency in Miles' tone, and she immediately gets serious. "You got it. I'll call you just as soon as I confirm that it's in. Anything else I can help you with?"

"Naw. Not now, hun. But I'll let you know."

"OK, you let me know." She wants to ask him what's got him so uptight, but she recognizes that Miles doesn't have any patience for the slightest hint of delay on carrying out his request, so she ends the conversation with a brief request to be kept posted.

"Sure thing," replies Miles then he hangs up the phone without another word.

In a daze he continues down the road en route to the fiery murder scene, wondering if any of this is real. Nothing seems real to any of the people involved in connection with Benji. They all know he had died, yet it's been eerily brought to their attention that he's not dead. In fact, he's going around killing people in the most atrocious way.

Who's gonna be next? Miles thinks to himself. *Is he some kind of ghost that knows all? I wonder if he knows about me . . . Naw.*

Miles is nervous and sweating in his palms—not knowing how his night will end or his life for that matter. Nevertheless, he presses forward. Nothing will keep him from this manhunt. There's somebody or something out there killing at will and no telling who he is about to kill next.

Chapter 62

Unknowing to Benji, he has just driven past Lindsey Miles, who is hunting for him, as they drive in opposite directions on Route 50. Miles hadn't noticed the white Lexus, so Benji need not worry about being pulled over any time soon, but he desires greatly to pull over so he can focus his attention on his wife and child quietly riding along in the backseat.

Neither Benji nor Jessie has muttered as much as a word since they left their house. The relief that she feels from having gotten her precious baby out of the fire won't allow her to feel neither grief nor apprehension over where Benji has come from or where he might be taking them. He's won enough confidence from her not to evoke any doubt about his intentions.

The only utterances to be heard are those coming from Asa. He seems to be reaching out toward the man driving the car as if he's trying to say something to him. Benji glances back from time to time to acknowledge his son's cooing. Benji feels the warmth of love in his soul for the first time since being back from six in green. He only hopes that Jessie will experience the same rush of emotional adrenaline inside her body that he's enjoying now as he engages with a silent conversation with his boy.

As they approach an exit, Benji dashes across three lanes in order to get off the highway so he can pull over and try to comfort his wife, whom he assumes is distraught over the events that have just transpired over the past thirty minutes or so.

Immediately off the exit is a large school to the right. Benji surveys the front of the school and then pulls down into its parking lot. He finds a fairly dark area to park at the side of the school in the parking lot.

The school is Benjamin Tasker located in the greater part of Bowie, Maryland. It made national headlines when a young middle-school student was gunned down by the infamous DC sniper, who terrorized the entire region in the fall of 2002. Benji doesn't realize that this is that school, but even if he did, after several years since the incident, what difference would it make? This is a quiet community where, besides shoplifters at the local shopping centers, speeders, and red-light runners, there's not much reason for the police to be on high alert.

Benji leans back in his seat and rests sideways on his elbow so he can feel closer to his wife without making her feel uncomfortable by him hopping in the backseat. Jessie looks at him not knowing what to say. Really, how do you start a conversation with your dead spouse? What do you say? Jessie has no idea, but she's very interested in hearing what he has to say. Like everybody else who became aware of Benji's reappearance on the world scene, she wonders if she is dreaming or not, and she has basically decided that if it's meant for something bad to happen, then, after all that has already happened, there is nothing she can do to prevent it from happening, so why worry about circumstances beyond her control?

"Are you afraid?" Benji asks.

Shouldn't I be, Jessie thinks to herself, looking at him with a blank expression, and then shaking her head no.

"Well, good. I'm not a monster. I know this seems crazy. I'm kinda confused about what . . . well, not what, but why I'm back here. I know I died. When Amp shot me, I . . ."

"Amp?" Jessie has to make sure she heard what she thought she heard. "Did you say Amp?"

"Yeah, why?" Benji knows Jessie doesn't know Amp, so he's curious as to why she's acting shocked at hearing his name in connection with his death. He doesn't breathe while he waits for her answer.

"I met a guy named Amp at the repast after we left the grave site. He said he was your friend. He said that he would personally get the people who did this to you . . ." She paused from sorrow. She can't imagine a person could have such a seared conscience.

He was so sincere. So nice.

"Are you sure, Benji? What makes you say that? They had on mask . . . Don't you remember? How do you know?"

Jessie doesn't want to believe that the young man that consoled her with kindness and promises of revenge was responsible for the worst day in her life. She doesn't want to believe that people are so conniving. Only a demon could commit such a heinous act and then display such a benign demeanor toward the victim.

"I heard his voice before he shot me. It's starting to come back to me. I didn't remember that until earlier today, but when I woke up . . . or . . . came back to life, I knew who killed me. I wasn't sure how I knew, but I just knew."

"Do you remember being dead? I mean, you *are* Benji? You *are* my husband, aren't you?"

"Yes, bae. It's me. It's me," he says as tenderly as his bestial voice will allow him.

Jessie's eyes well up. She feels the pain of that day all over again—the rape—the murder—the baby crying after the gun shot—the gore—her world spinning. Then tears start to roll down her face, and she reaches her hand toward Benji. He touches her knee, while she rests her hand on his extended arm.

My god! He's as cold as ice. She nearly recoils when she feels how cold Benji's hand is through her gown. They've been in the warmth of the car's heat for more than forty minutes, but it's as if Benji's been riding with his hand hanging out the window. Her thoughts swirl; then discernment tells her that this man must be her dead husband back from the dead because if he were a normal person, the blood in his body wouldn't allow him to be so cold.

The sensation Jessie feels from realizing that this really is the man she's been in love with all her adult life makes her heart flutter. It's not just his body but his mind. His memory. His love.

He called me bae. It's him. It really is Benji.

She starts to cry.

"Benji," she says through the tears, "I've missed you so much."

The tears stream down her face, and they share the silence in the car as their souls reconnect, and they revisit in their minds all the joy they once shared before they were torn apart.

Chapter 63

They've been sitting in the car with it running for some time now. Jessie and Asa are sound asleep in the backseat of the car, and Benji has dozed off while he was watching his wife and child. He wakes up to see the two of them just as they were before he dozed off.

Suddenly, a ray of light cuts through the darkness of the car. The light produces a red dot on the backseat that moves across the seat to his wife's shoulder. Benji immediately throws his arm up to block the beam from his wife. He looks over his shoulder and sees the source of the red laser beam about thirty yards across the lot.

Flood lights blind Benji, and a man's voice comes out of a loud speaker and wakes both Jessie and Asa.

"Get out the car with your hands up. You are surrounded."

Benji looks to the side, but the light is coming from that direction too. He can't see a thing.

"Damn it!" Benji shouts.

"Benji, what are you gonna do?" Jessie whispers.

"I gotta get out of here."

Benji can't afford to be locked up. He knows that could mean unbearable pain if he happens to be anywhere the sunlight might reach. After the episode he had at the last dawn, he knows that next one might be his last one, and he's not ready to depart from his family again, nor will he ever be.

Although he can't see much of anything, he can almost guess where his possible escape route is. There's a gap of darkness between the bright lights off to his left, and Benji is intent on making a charge for it. He wastes no time sitting up and putting the car in drive. He whips the car toward the opening and the loud voice makes one last command.

"Stop or we'll shoot!"

When the engine of the Lexus roars despite the warning, the police officers open fire on the car. Bullets rip through the windshield, doors, and side windows as Benji streaks through the partial barricade. He continues out the parking lot onto Route 197. The exit ramp to Route 50 is just beyond the intersection, and in no time Benji has the Lexus pushing 130 mph down the highway.

Jessie and Asa have been quiet since he left the parking spot they were snoozing in.

"Are you all right?" Benji finally takes the time to think of something else besides getting away.

There is no answer. Benji looks back only to find that they're not all right.

"God, No! No! No. No. No!"

The police are in his rearview mirror, and so is the horizon. The sun is rising to his rear as he travels westbound toward DC, and the dawn is about to break. Benji is out running the police behind him, but there is no way he can outrun the rising sun.

As the sun climbs from behind the horizon, the rays feed into the rearview mirror. Benji turns to look in the mirror; the sun's rays stun him, and the flesh around his eyes conflagrates like a burning book of matches.

He hollers and slams his hand down on the gear shifter.

"Aghhhhhhhhh*!"*

Chapter 64

Benji wakes up from his terrible nightmare. He looks to the place where his wife and son were nestled in the backseat before he fell asleep. They're still there. Sound asleep. He exhales a big sigh of relief, leans his head back, closes his eyes, and then reopens them. When he focuses, his eyes catch a glimpse of red and blue lights through the trees set off at a distance across the school grounds. His full attention turns in that direction.

Benji can see that it's a police car once it gets to an opening, and he notices also that it has turned off its lights. He never heard a siren, so he instantly gets on high alert yanking his head this way and that way looking to see if he's surrounded. He's not surrounded, but there are at least two other police cars sitting in fairly inconspicuous spots in his vicinity. They're not on the school grounds, but they appear to be poised for some sort of convergence once enough backup gets to the location.

Benji and Jessie have been knocked out for hours and were comfortable as they could be just being close to each other for what may be the last time in their lives.

"I love you so much, Jess," Benji told her before she fell asleep while he rested his hand on her knee. "I don't know what is going on, but damn, I'm happy to be with you. I would have come to you two days ago, but I was afraid that I'd give you a heart attack if I just popped up at the house."

"Yeah, you're right. I don't think I would have been able to handle that. I would have just died. But when I saw you burst through that door, I knew God was answering my prayer to save my baby. I wouldn't have cared if you were Freddy Krueger. As you were talking about getting me and Asa out of the house, I was glad to see you."

Benji kinda laughed.

"Yeah, I know that's right."

"But, Benji . . . What was it like?"

"Shut, I didn't think nothing of it. I knew y'all was in there so I just did what I knew I had to do to get y'all out. I wasn't about to . . ."

"No," Jessie interrupted, "I mean . . . how should I say it . . . ah . . . ?"

"Oh, you mean death?"

"Yeah." She didn't want to use that word because she thought it would be like jinxing him.

"I don't' know. I don't remember a thing."

"Huh?"

"Yeah. The first thing that came to mind when I took time to actually reflect on how I got into the hole I dug myself out of . . ."

"Wait, you climbed out of your own grave?"

"Yeah, I dreamt about you. It was a wild dream, I'll tell you about that later. But ahh . . . I woke up and pushed the coffin door open. It was pitch-black all around me, and when I felt around, I could tell I was surrounded by dirt. That's when I remembered I was shot. I thought to myself, 'They must have buried me, but I ain't dead,' so I started diggin'. And before long, I saw the sky."

Jessie sat there in amazement, intrigued by what she was hearing and just short of aghast at the fact that she's in the presence of someone who's actually been buried six feet deep. Anyone would shudder to know that they're talking to a dead man.

"But you know, there was something strange about the dream I had."

"What?"

"Well, in the dream, you had a heart attack or something, and that's what gave me the idea not to come to the house, but that's not what was strange . . . After you had fallen out, I had looked out the window and saw three suns in the sky. They blinded me."

"Three suns?" Jessie wonders what that could mean. "Maybe they mean something."

"Yeah, I think so too. I wonder if it has anything to do with why my body feels like it's about to burst into flames every morning the sun rises."

"What do you mean?"

"It's like . . . you know, Count Dracula can't take the sun's rays? It burns him."

"Yeah."

"That's what it's like for me. And it gets worse and worse every time I see the morning sun. I dread to be out of my coffin for another daybreak."

"So what are you gonna do?"

"I don't know, but whatever I do, I gotta get somewhere out the sight of the sunlight."

They talked on for about another hour before Jessie fell asleep, listening to Benji's talk. He dozed off afterward, then dreamt of what would befall him if he stayed parked in the spot where he is now. It really wasn't a dream; it's another vision given to him, this time, by Apollyon to warn him of imminent danger.

He sits up.

"Jessie," he whispers, "Jess . . ."

She wakes up.

"Put your seat belt on, quick."

She looks around for the police but doesn't see any.

"Why, what's wrong, Benji?"

"The police. They're everywhere. We gotta get out of here."

"Are you sure? I don't see . . ." Just then she sees one under the dimly lit morning sky. The sun will be clearing the horizon in about fifteen minutes, and already it's starting to remove the veil of the night darkness.

"Oh, I see one. No two!"

"There're actually three and more coming," Benji assures her.

"But what makes you think they know you're here? Maybe they're not even thinking about us!"

Benji pulls off and darts for an exit. One of the cruisers near the exit moves toward the driveway to block the Lexus from getting out of the parking lot, so Benji detours up on the curb and cuts across the lawn. At the corner, he reaches the intersection at London Lane and 197, dashes across it, and then onto Route 50, followed by two of the three white PG County police cars that were waiting for the SWAT team to arrive.

Benji is considered armed and extremely dangerous. Instructions have been given to contain but not to attempt to apprehend. A couple more minutes, and they would have had him pinned down, but now the chase is on.

Chapter 65

Miles and Faraday make a mad dash for their car that is double parked in front of the office building that the FBI has here at Landover. They've just been notified that the white Lexus has been located and the driver has managed to escape the perimeter that was being formed around him.

Imbeciles, Miles thinks. The county police in both Anne Arundel and Prince George's have bungled every facet of this manhunt, and the only thing left for them to do now is allow Benji to elude them yet again. Miles knows they'll never get another chance at catching him. It's now or never.

They reach the car with Miles making it a point to go straight for the driver side. Faraday has to wait for Miles to unlock the door. Once inside, Miles takes off before Faraday gets his foot in the door.

"Hey!" Faraday shouts.

Miles switches to the PG Police Channel on his CB.

"He's getting off. He's getting off," declares an officer in hot pursuit of the white Lexus. "He is taking the Landover Road Exit. Not sure of his direction yet."

There's a split at the end of the exit ramp off Route 50 onto Landover Road. One takes you toward the DC line, and the other into Landover toward the stadium.

"South. He's headed southbound," assures the officer.

"Alright . . . he must be planning to go to his sister's or his parents' house," Faraday says out loud.

He calls to one of his sources at the PG Police Department on the phone and instructs him to get a car at the address of Benji's mother and father's house and another at his sister's.

"How do you figure he's going to one of these places?" asks the man on the other end of the phone.

"One's his sister's, one's his mother's. Where else would he go?"

"Well, maybe he has some friends in the area."

"Yeah, I'm sure, but we don't have their addresses now, do we?"

A silence.

"Look, man, just do it. We don't wanna miss this guy."

It isn't long before the officer in pursuit announces that the chase has taken them into Kentland, the community that both Benji's parents and sister lives in.

"This is where he loses them," Miles speculates, assuming that Benji plans on finding refuge at one of those houses.

Both Miles and Faraday listen intently as they frantically make their way down Martin Luther King Highway, just minutes away from the vicinity of the chase.

✧   ✧   ✧

Benji is driving the 450 LX like Richter drives his corvette. The growing numbers of police cars in pursuit are really the least of Benji's worries. He's racing the increasing light of the morning sky. The sun is only a few minutes from shedding its glorious light on the surface of the metropolitan area where Benji is located.

Asa is crying his head off. Jessie is screaming at the top of her lungs begging Benji to just ease up before he crashes the car. Every turn through the streets of Kentland leaves the trailing police cars further behind until they can only be heard but not seen.

Benji doesn't relax, however, because he is very aware that he's in a red zone district, not very far from the PG County Police headquarters.

Gotta get to Harmony, Benji thinks. He's already starting to feel the effects of the curse placed upon him by the Omega. If he doesn't make it to his grave before the rays of the sun shines upon him, he'll be completely annihilated as a punishment for the dreadful deeds he performed since he's been resurrected. The only hope he has of ever being brought back to life on the Day of Judgment is to make it back to his resting place where he'll be reserved until Apollyon will be authorized to raise whomever he wishes.

"Benji! They're gone! Slow down!"

"Jessie, I told you. I gotta get back. These dreams. They mean something. They warn me of things that are gonna happen. I dreamt the police were trying to trap me."

He doesn't want to tell her that she and Asa were killed in his dream. He hopes he's past that danger. There's no sign of any police, but the shrill of the sirens can be heard echoing off the houses. He turns right onto East Marlboro Road and then left onto Columbia Park Road. He sights police cars headed in his direction to his rear.

"Shucks!"

He floors the pedal and dodges the cars sitting at a red light at Martin Luther King Highway. He cuts through the lot of an Exxon gas station to get back into free flowing traffic. As he drives down the road, he can see the police cars on the other side of the median strip traveling in the opposite direction. Each officer goose-necking in his direction as he burns up the road going the other way. All of them radioing his whereabouts over the air waves.

"It's hot—so hot," Benji whispers. He looks up at the brightening sky. "I ain't gonna make it."

"Baby. You almost there," Jessie says consolingly.

She's no longer panicking, considering how effortlessly Benji has been able to wheel this large sedan around, never seeming to once lose control of its handling. She also imagines that maybe God has his hand in all of this. The mere fact that Benji is alive is one clue, and then he's the one who saved her and the baby. Not to mention the dreams.

Benji is leaning forward, gripping the steering wheel like an adolescent joyrider being tailed by the police. He keeps glancing up at the sky, then to his rearview mirror, and then back to the road again. He's approaching his last turn before he reaches Harmony Cemetery. He catches a break at Sherriff Road. The left turn arrow is green, allowing him to make an unimpeded turn toward his refuge.

No doubt, the police cars a quarter mile back can see that he's making the turn and are calling it in.

As Benji makes his way around the bend just before the entrance to the cemetery, he notices the taillights of a car that has just entered into the gate of Harmony. He also sees the lights of police cars coming over the hill, headed in his direction. The intense heat he's feeling is burning him inside out. A rancid smell compels Jessie to let the window down.

"Ugh. What's that smell?"

Benji turns into the gate of Harmony and to his dismay, the car he had seen entering into the gate has stopped just inside, blocking the road leading to the area of his grave site.

"Hold the boy and get down!"

Benji has no intention of stopping, nor does he want the bullets of the two detectives pointing their guns at his windshield to find Asa or Jessie.

The Lexus smashes into the back corner of the Crown Victoria that Miles and Faraday are driving as Benji powers his way through a small opening they left between their car and the brick post of the gate. Miles fires several shots into the windshield aiming for the driver, but Faraday elects not to shoot keeping in mind that the woman and child are probably still in the car.

Benji makes it through but can feel his car is not driving as free-wheeling as it was. The back tire has been shot out. When Benji looks over his shoulder to check to see how his wife and child are doing, he sees white police cars bottlenecked at the gate behind the detectives' car he just smashed into.

"Jessie!"

"Huh, I'm okay."

Benji can hear his son's continued crying, and it's music to his ears. Now that Jessie has responded favorably, his only focus is getting to his grave and somehow digging his way into it before he's smoldered by the sun.

He's panting like a dog. The Lexus is hardly able to move forward. Benji looks over his shoulder again, and now he can see the cars that are trapped at the gate, flooding the grounds of the cemetery. He looks to the top of the hill and can see the place where he was buried. To his relief, it's already dug out. The police had it excavated in order to investigate whether or not his body was still in the coffin.

"Agh." Benji can feel his partially decayed body starting to have a reaction to the increasing heat that he's feeling. He isn't sure if he's melting or about to explode, but he knows he only has a matter of seconds before the sun becomes unveiled by the trees, houses, schools, and the stadium that covers the horizon to his left.

He's only fifty yards from mounds of dirt and shovels that mark the location of his grave. There are two analim, angels of Apollyon, standing there as well, but there is nothing they can do to intervene in the situation unfolding. Benji can't see them either. What he can see is the swarm of police quickly approaching.

"Run, Benji, run!" shouts Jessie.

Benji too realizes that running is his only hope of reaching the top of the hill where his grave is located, now about thirty-five yards away. He stumbles getting out of the car, catches his balance, and then makes a mad dash for the site. Jessie gets out of the car with the crying baby Asa in her arms urging her husband on.

"Run, Benji! Here they come!"

The police cars are on the grass now driving insolently over other peoples' graves. Since there are virtually no tombstones, one of the cars quickly blocks Benji's path. Benji is relentless. He jumps up onto the hood and runs clean across it.

"Freeze!"

Benji ignores the command. Now, only twenty yards from his grave, he presses on, but he is absolutely exhausted. His feet are getting heavier and heavier with every step. The light of the sun can be seen shedding its light on the top of half of a tree near the grave. Benji will soon be exposed to the rays of the sun if he doesn't get behind the walls of his six foot resting place.

The analim helplessly watch as another car, the car Miles and Faraday are in, hits Benji. Benji flips up into the air.

"No!" Jessie screams as she watches from afar as her husband is tossed in the air only a few more strides from the security of his grave.

Benji is languishing in pain. Not from the hit he absorbed from the car but from the intense heat that is already consuming his flesh and will soon overwhelm completely. Benji's soul is knocking at oblivion's door, but his power hasn't given up yet!

The police officers along with Miles and Faraday are all pointing their guns at the crawling Benjamin Powell and yelling "freeze" as he nears his grave. The light of the sun is just above his head, and he can see the shadows of the men standing behind him.

"Give it up, Benji," says Miles, "It is all over now."

Benji has reached his grave but hasn't got the strength to stand up in order to jump down into it. Besides that, Benji realizes that the police are on top of him, and so he'll likely be handcuffed any second now. There's no use.

Suddenly, a brilliant flash of light appears. Then it's gone. Benji looks back and sees all of the police down on their knees covering their eyes. Whatever the light was, it has temporarily blinded his captors. The suffering Benji looks to the rising sun; then with a renewed determination to beat the sun, he grabs hold of the top of his grave and with all his might pulls himself until he is able to fall over the edge.

His body drops down into the propped-open coffin. He looks one last time at the sky. The sunlight shines onto the top wall of his grave, and Benji kicks the wooden stick that was holding his door open. Blackness once again consumes his world, and the sound of falling dirt and rock pound on the door of his coffin until he can no longer hear anything.

Benji lies there with his eyes closed, thinking about his wife and child, content that he was privileged to see them once again. Not only that, but to know that his killers won't get away with what they did, and that Salina, the only person that Jessie and Asa had to worry about bringing them harm, is out the way too, gives Benji a sublime feeling that tells him he will truly be able to rest in peace.

To Be Continued . . .

Edwards Brothers,Inc!
Thorofare, NJ 08086
04 March, 2011
BA2011063